THE IMMORTAL IRON FIST

THE LAST IRON FIST STORY

THE IMMORTAL IRON FIST

THE LAST IRON FIST STORY

Writers: Ed Brubaker & Matt Fraction
Artists: David Aja with
Travel Foreman & Derek Fridolfs (Issues #1-5)
Russ Heath (Issues #3 & 6)
John Severin (Issue #2)
Sal Buscema & Tom Palmer (Issue #4)
Colorists: Matt Hollingsworth with Dean White (Issue #2) & Laura Martin (Issue #6)
Special thanks to Raul Allen
Letterer: Dave Lanphear
Cover Artist: David Aja
Assistant Editor: Alejandro Arbona
Editor: Warren Simons

Collection Editor: Jennifer Grünwald
Assistant Editors: Cory Levine & John Denning
Associate Editor: Mark D. Beazley
Senior Editor, Special Projects: Jeff Youngquist
Senior Vice President of Sales: David Gabriel
Vice President of Creative: Tom Marvelli

Editor in Chief: Joe Quesada
Publisher: Dan Buckley

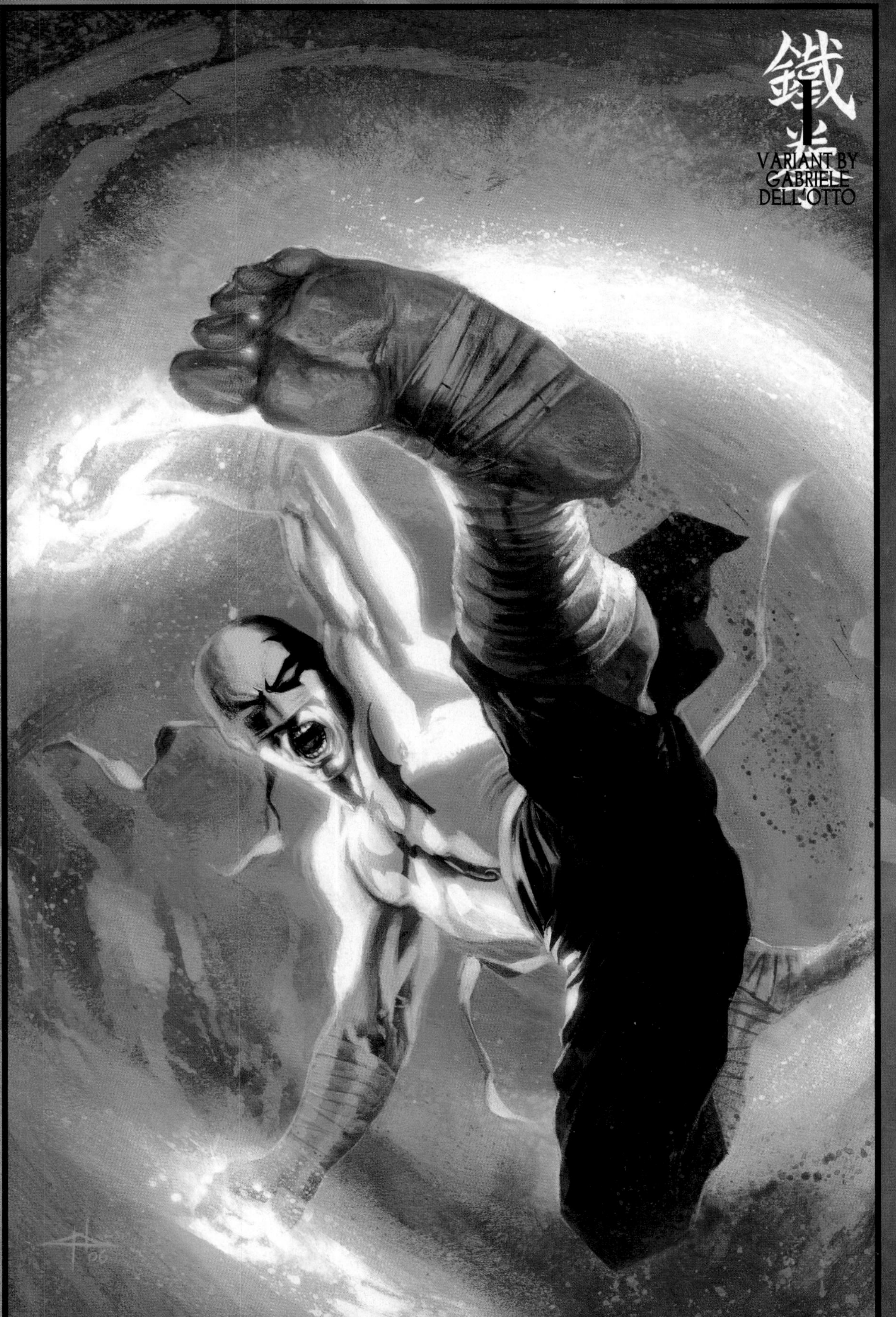
鐵拳
VARIANT BY
GABRIELE
DELL'OTTO

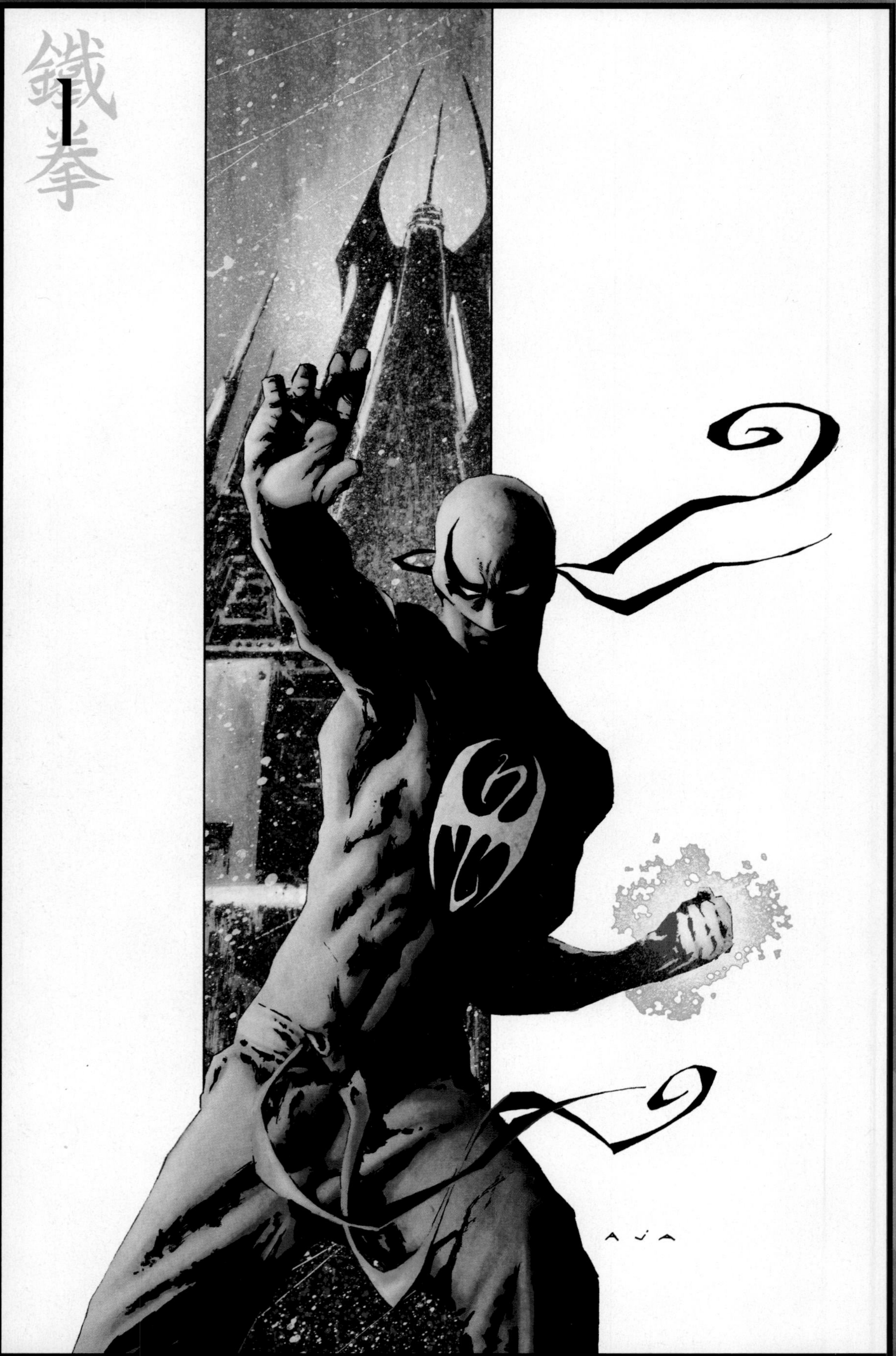
1
鐵拳
AJA

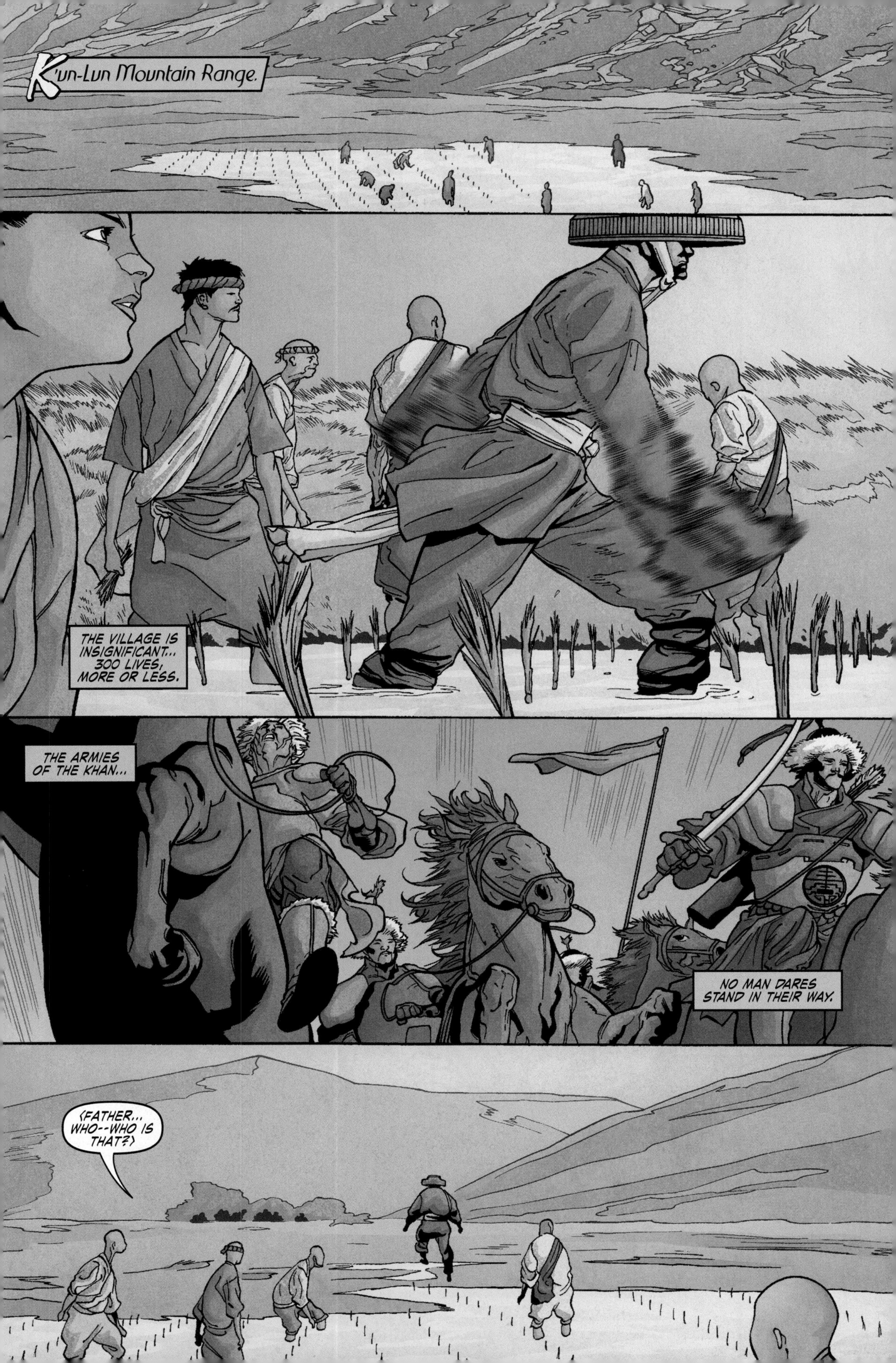
K'un-Lun Mountain Range.
THE VILLAGE IS INSIGNIFICANT... 300 LIVES, MORE OR LESS.
THE ARMIES OF THE KHAN...
NO MAN DARES STAND IN THEIR WAY.
<FATHER... WHO--WHO IS THAT?>

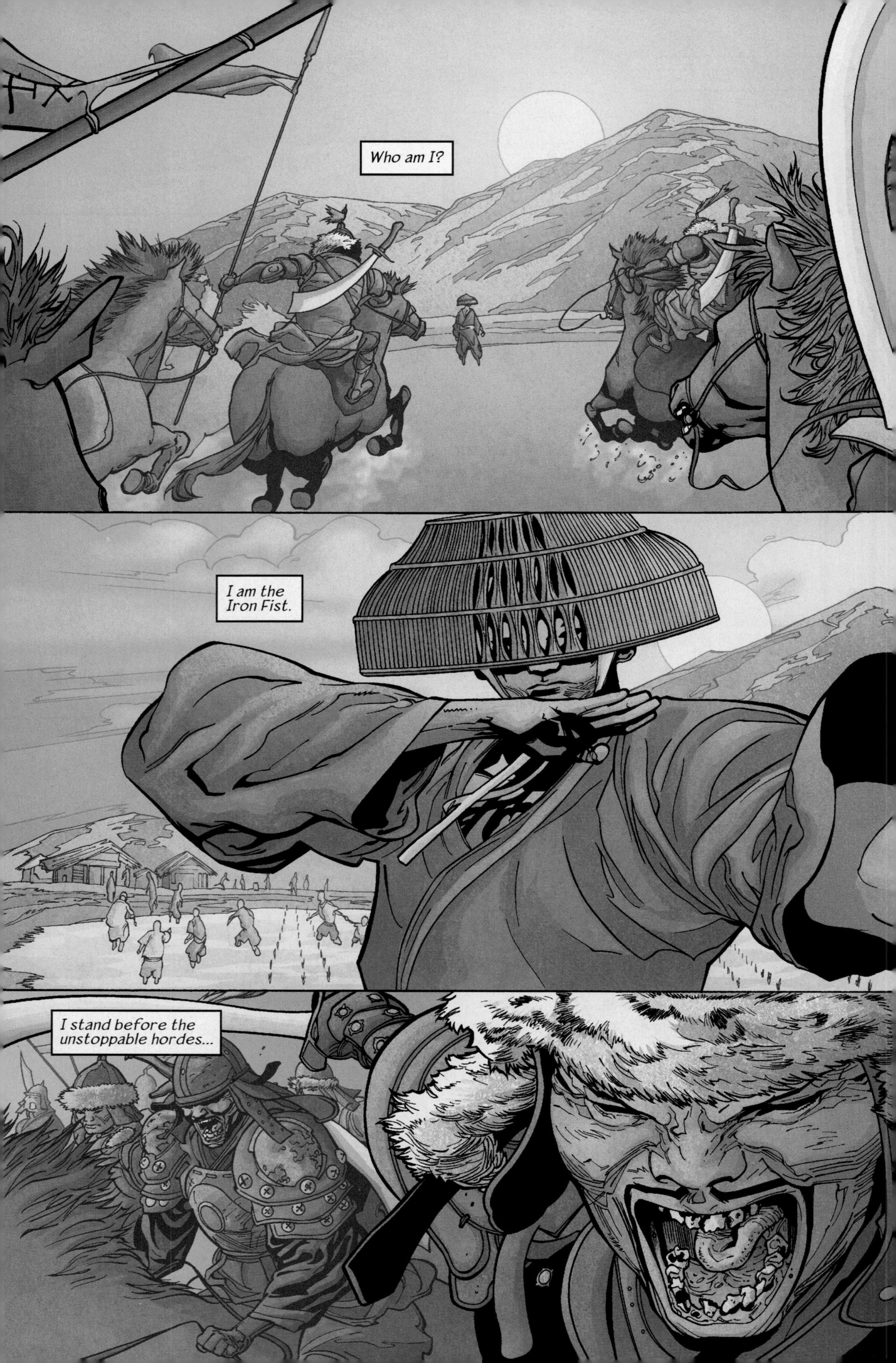
Who am I?
I am the Iron Fist.
I stand before the unstoppable hordes...

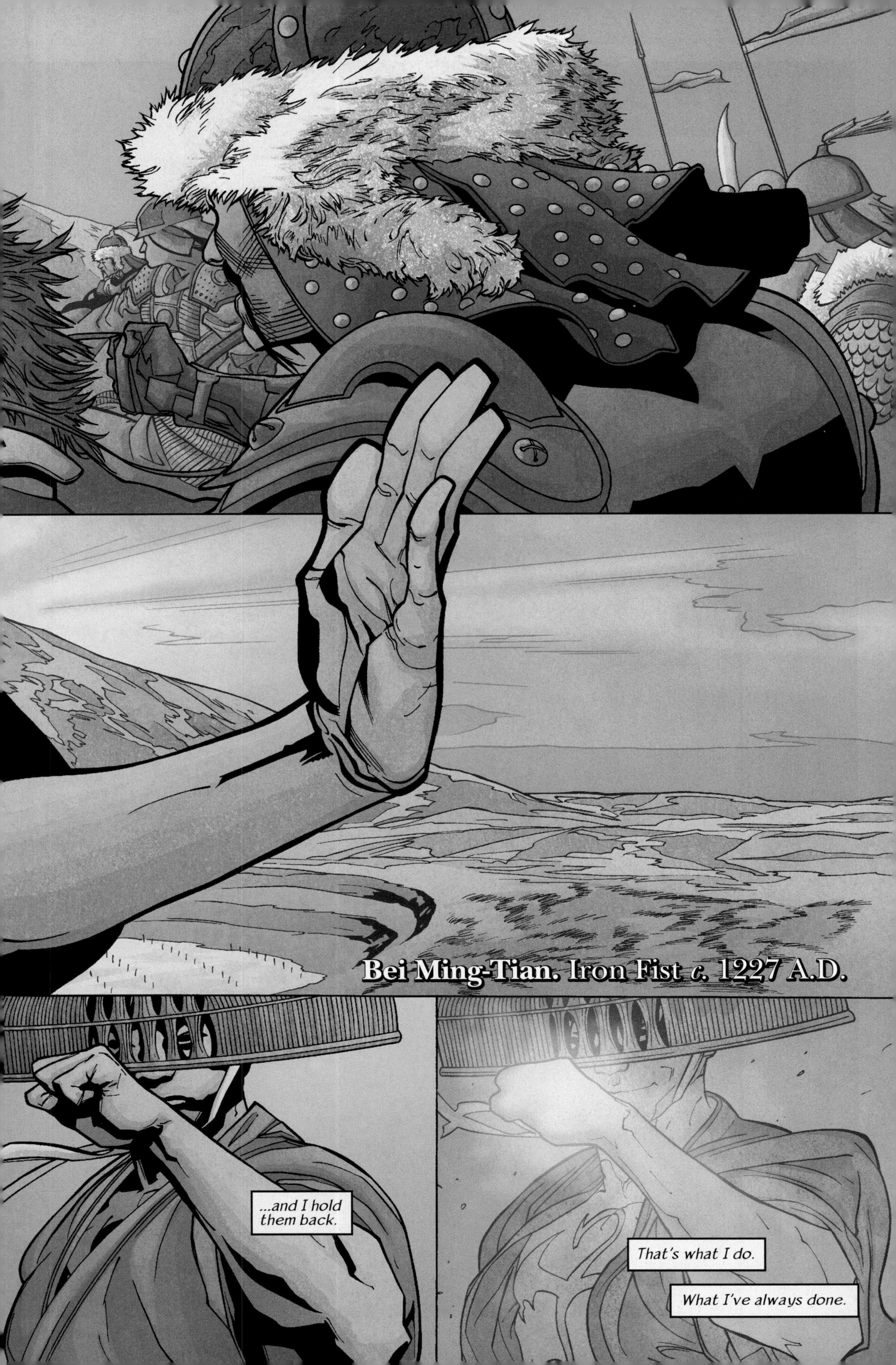
Bei Ming-Tian. Iron Fist c. 1227 A.D.
...and I hold them back.
That's what I do.
What I've always done.

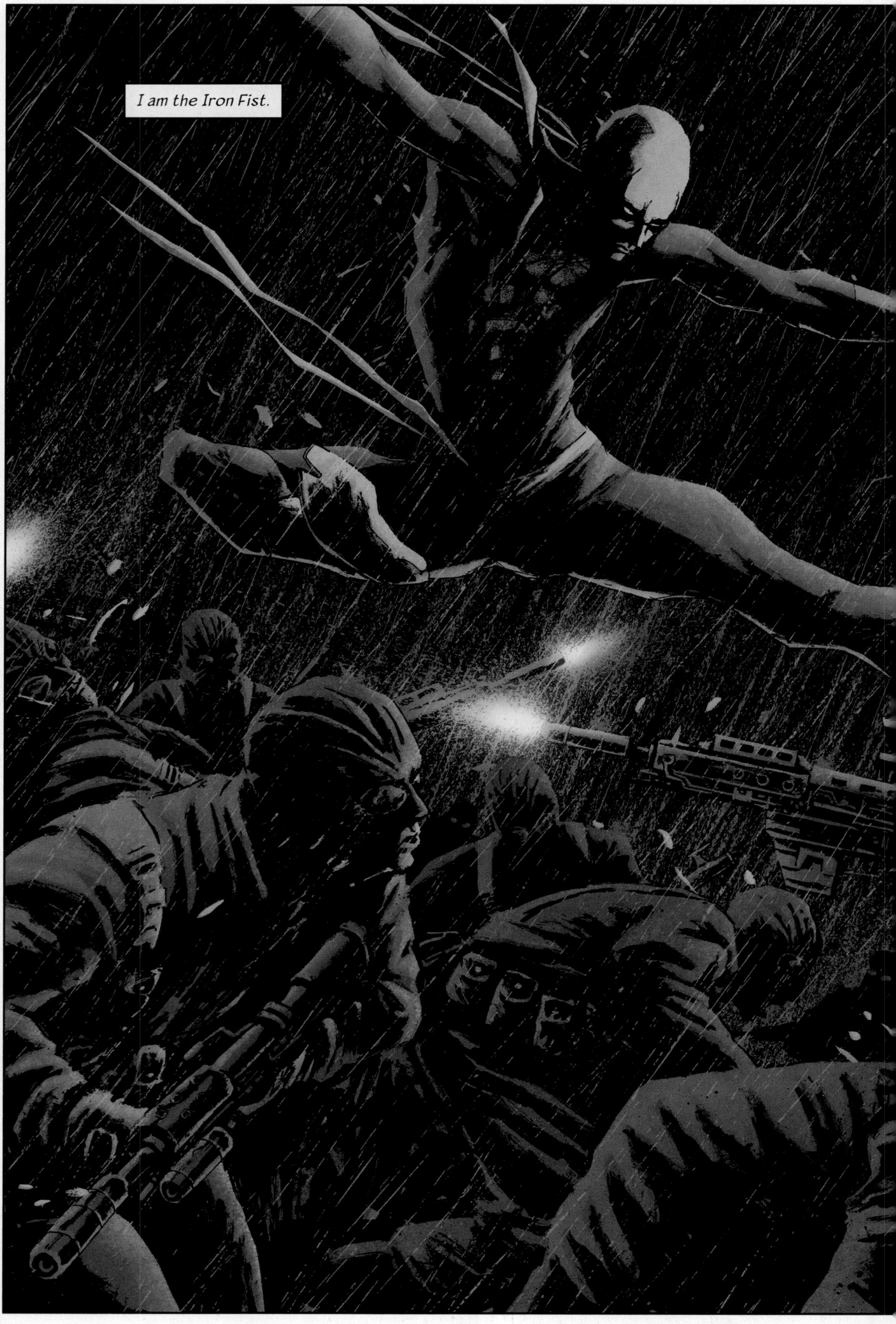
I am the Iron Fist.

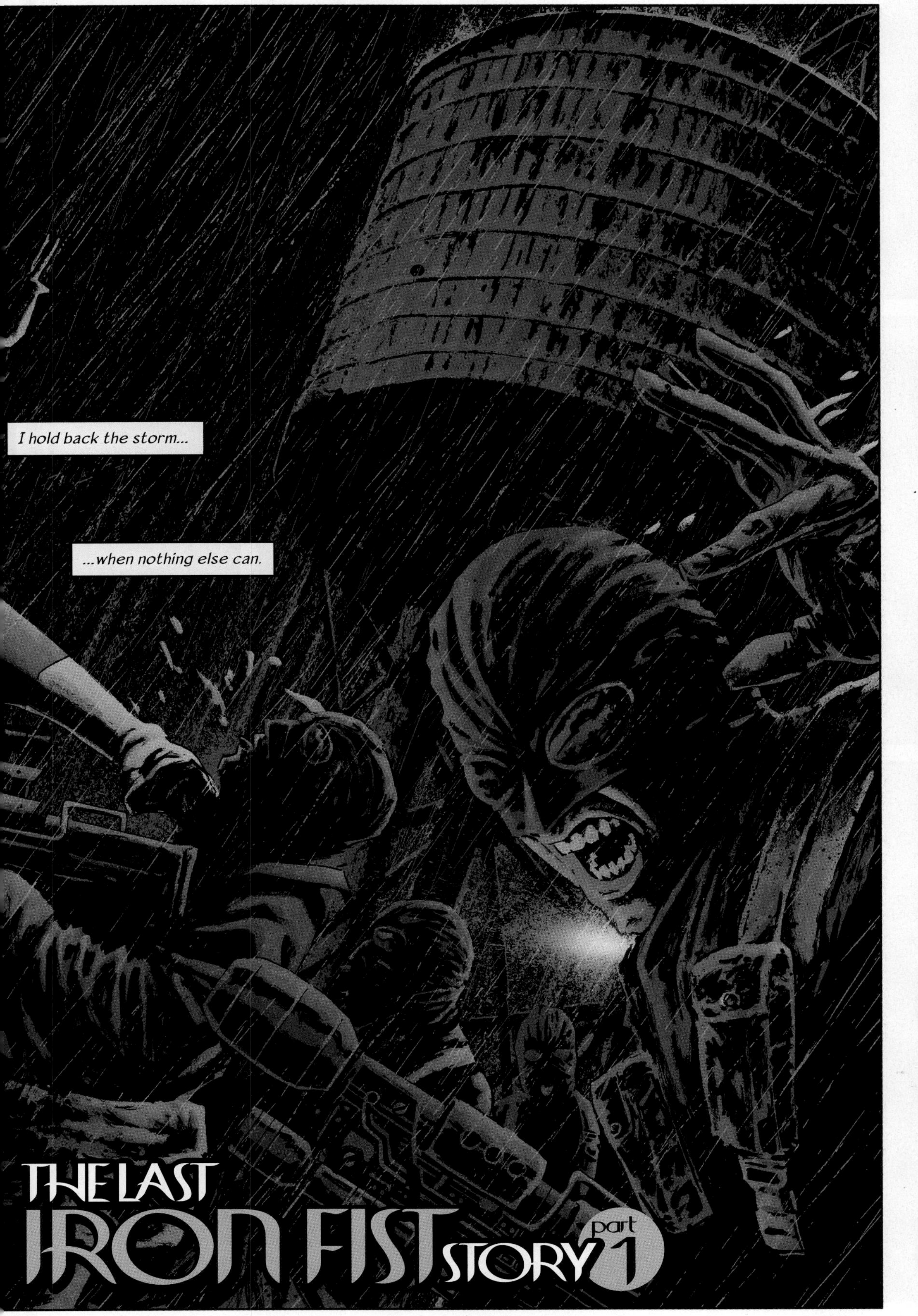
I hold back the storm...
...when nothing else can.
THE LAST IRON FIST STORY part 1

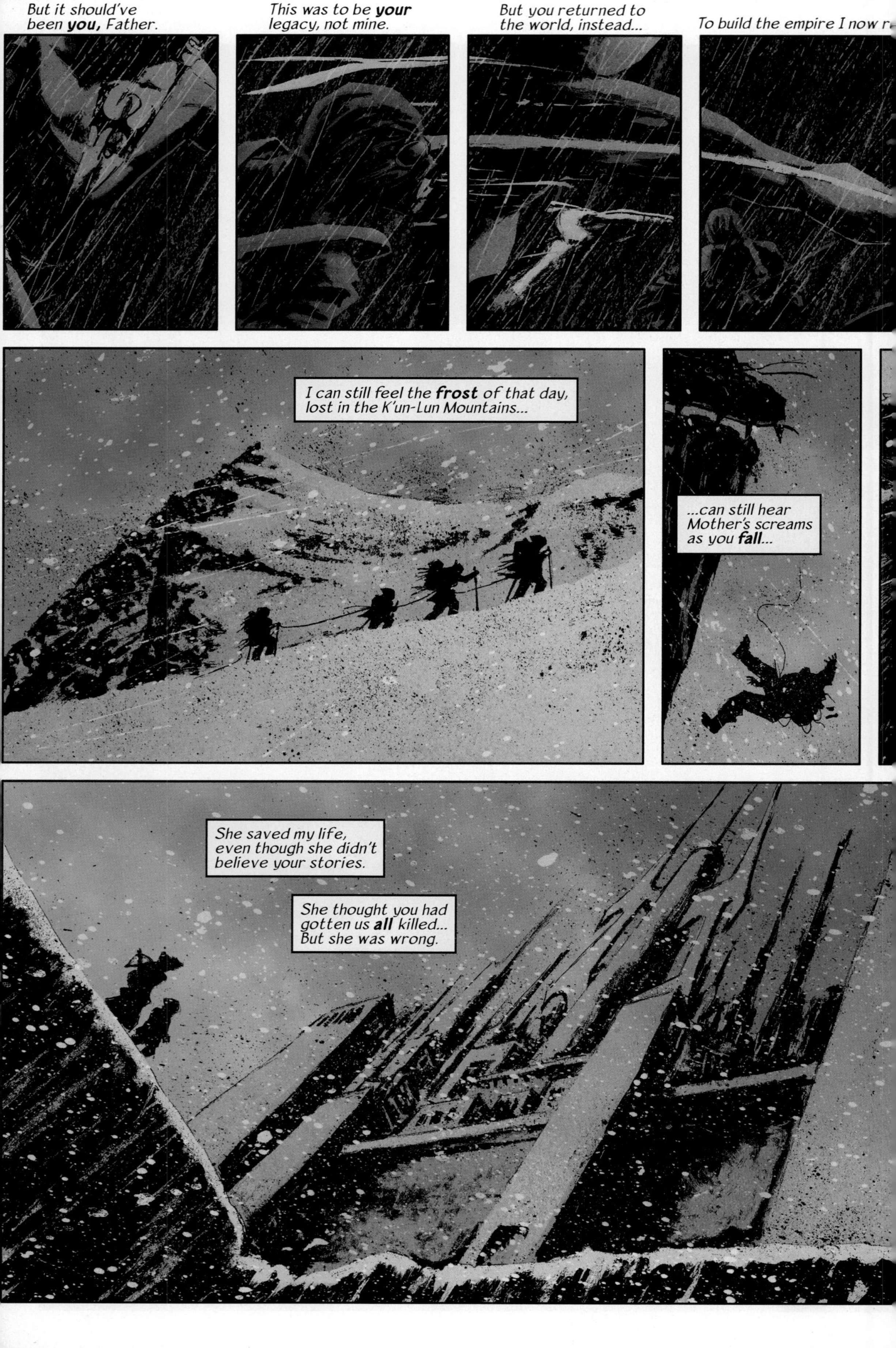
But it should've been **you,** Father.
This was to be **your** legacy, not mine.
But you returned to the world, instead...
To build the empire I now
I can still feel the **frost** of that day, lost in the K'un-Lun Mountains...
...can still hear Mother's screams as you **fall**...
She saved my life, even though she didn't believe your stories.
She thought you had gotten us **all** killed... But she was wrong.

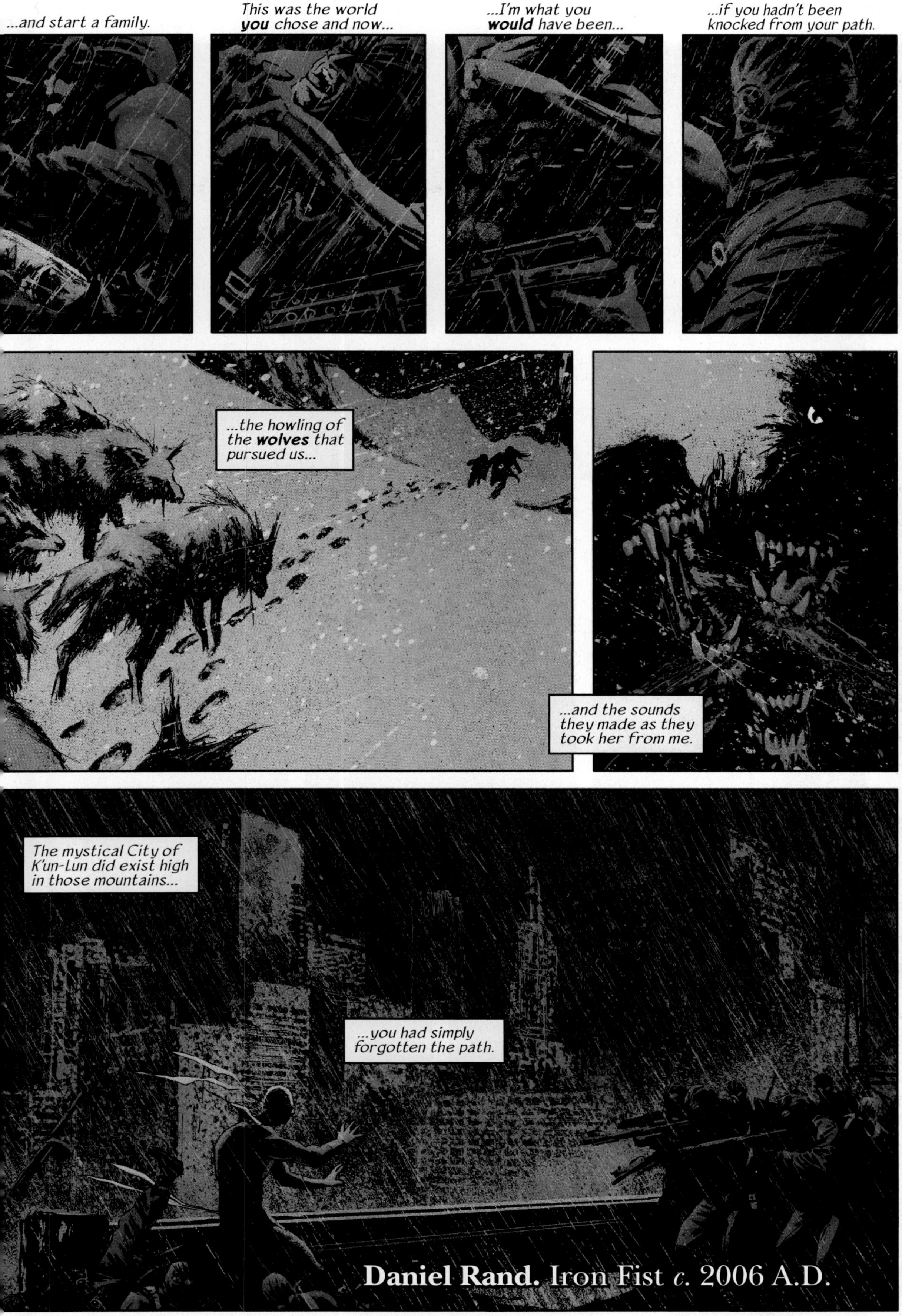
...and start a family.
This was the world **you** chose and now...
...I'm what you **would** have been...
...if you hadn't been knocked from your path.
...the howling of the **wolves** that pursued us...
...and the sounds they made as they took her from me.
The mystical City of K'un-Lun did exist high in those mountains...
...you had simply forgotten the path.
Daniel Rand. Iron Fist c. 2006 A.D.

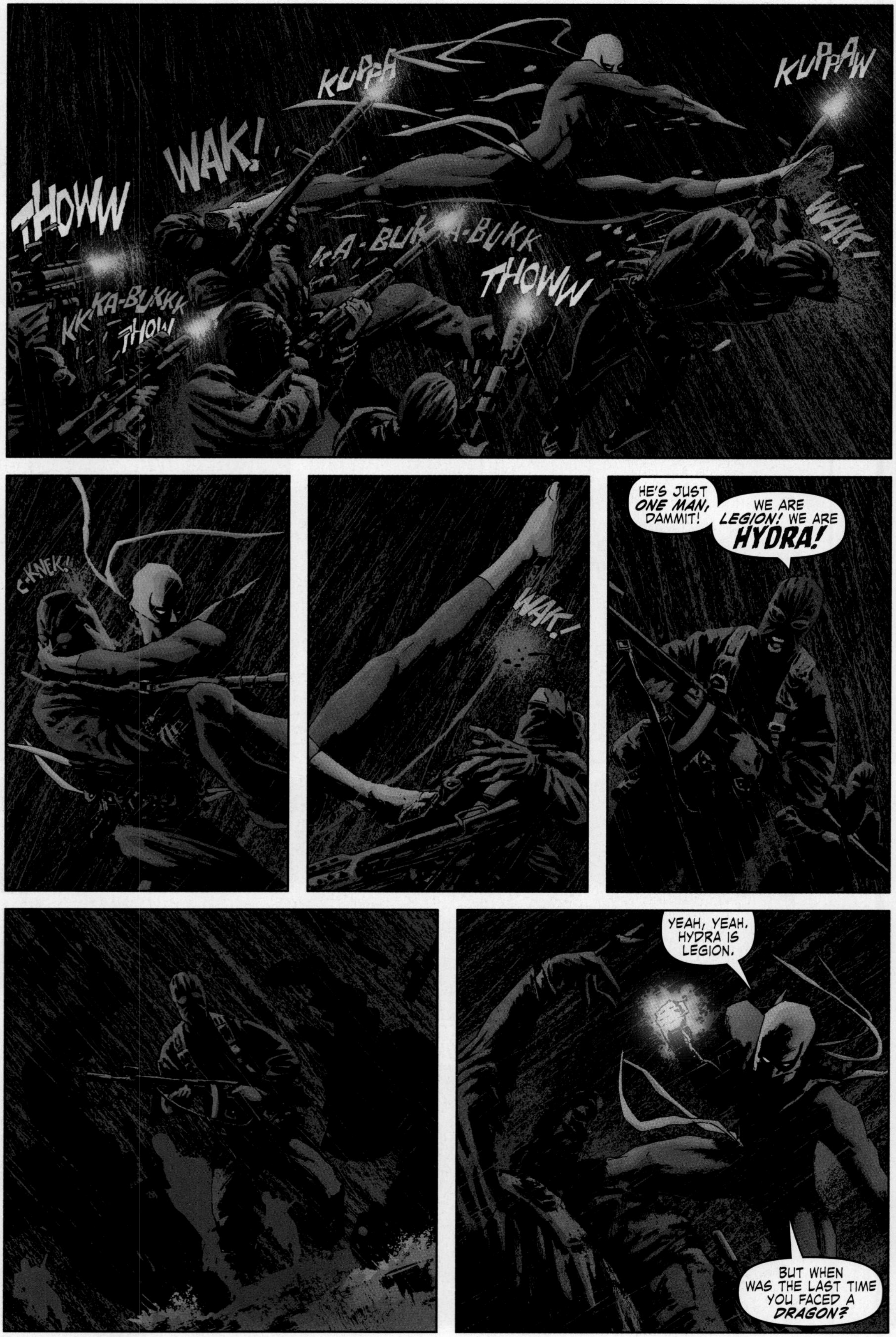
KUPPA
WAK!
THOWW
KUPPAW
KA-BUKKA-BUKK
WAK!
THOWW
KK-KA-BUKKK
THOW
C-KNEK!!
WAK!
HE'S JUST ONE MAN, DAMMIT!
WE ARE LEGION! WE ARE HYDRA!
YEAH, YEAH. HYDRA IS LEGION.
BUT WHEN WAS THE LAST TIME YOU FACED A DRAGON?

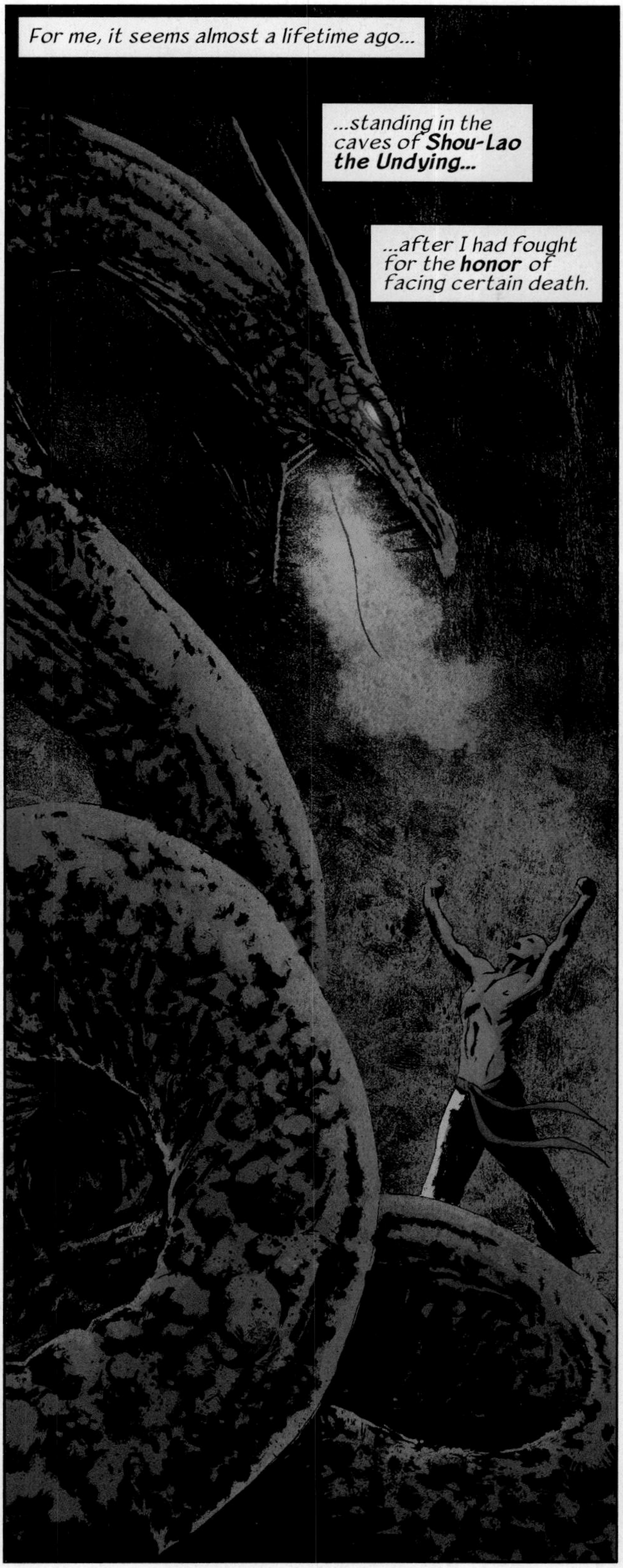
For me, it seems almost a lifetime ago...
...standing in the caves of **Shou-Lao the Undying...**
...after I had fought for the **honor** of facing certain death.

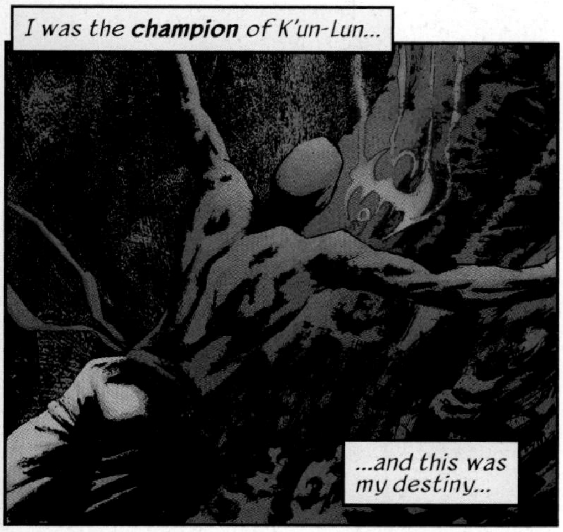
I was the **champion** of K'un-Lun...
...and this was my destiny...

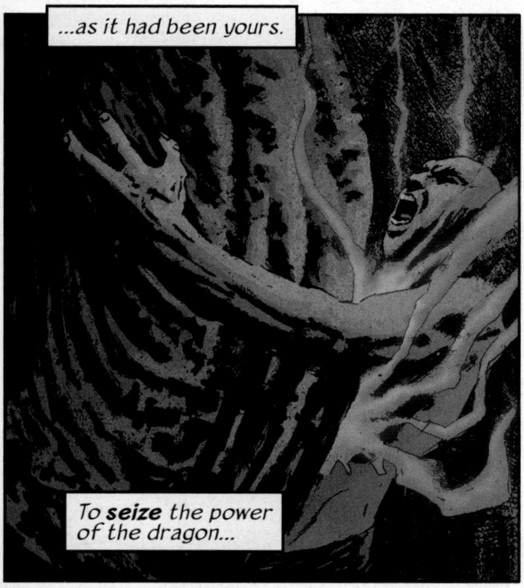
...as it had been yours.
To **seize** the power of the dragon...

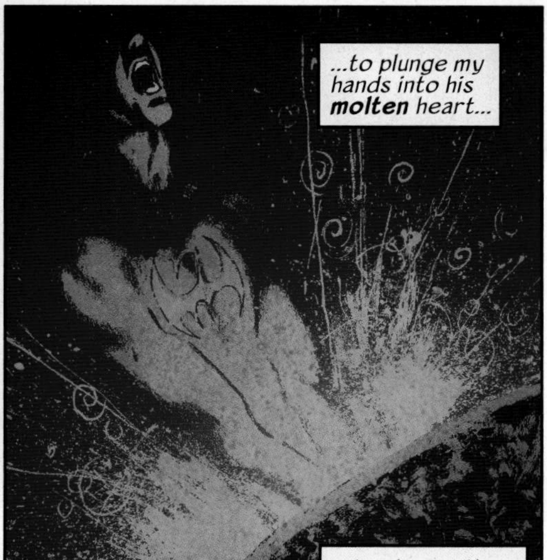
...to plunge my hands into his **molten** heart...
...to change them into things ...

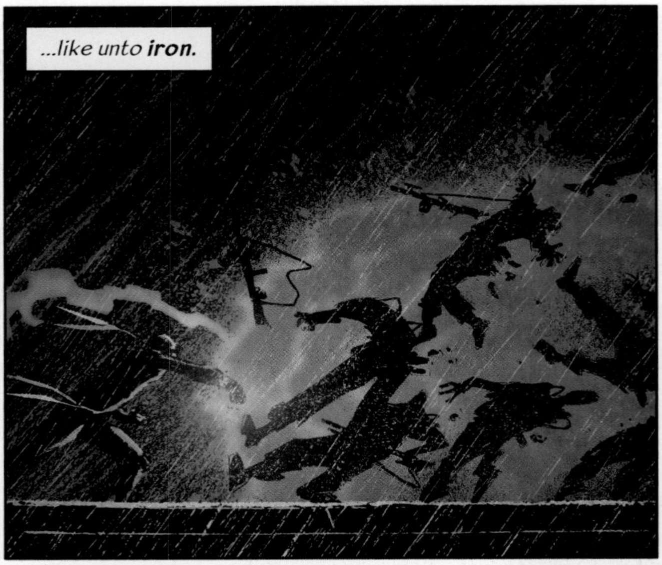
...like unto iron.

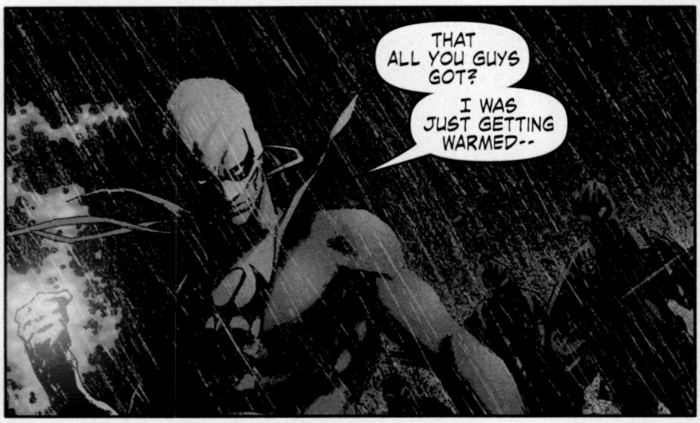
THAT ALL YOU GUYS GOT?
I WAS JUST GETTING WARMED--

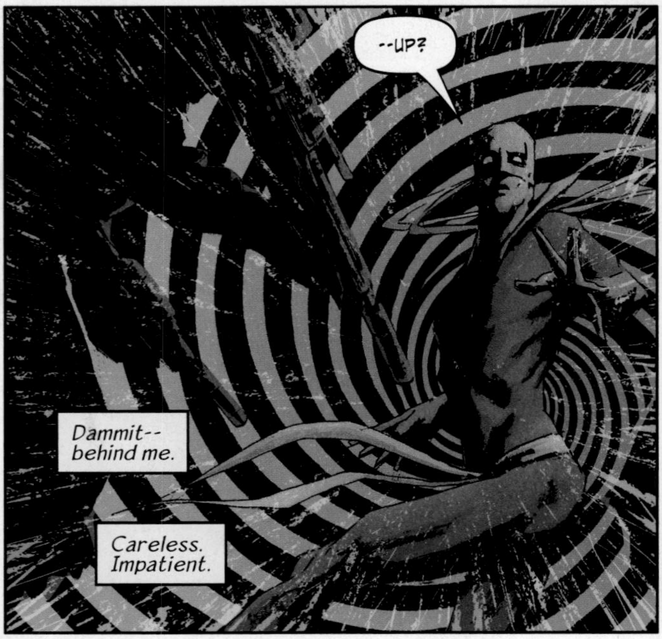
--UP?
Dammit-- behind me.
Careless. Impatient.

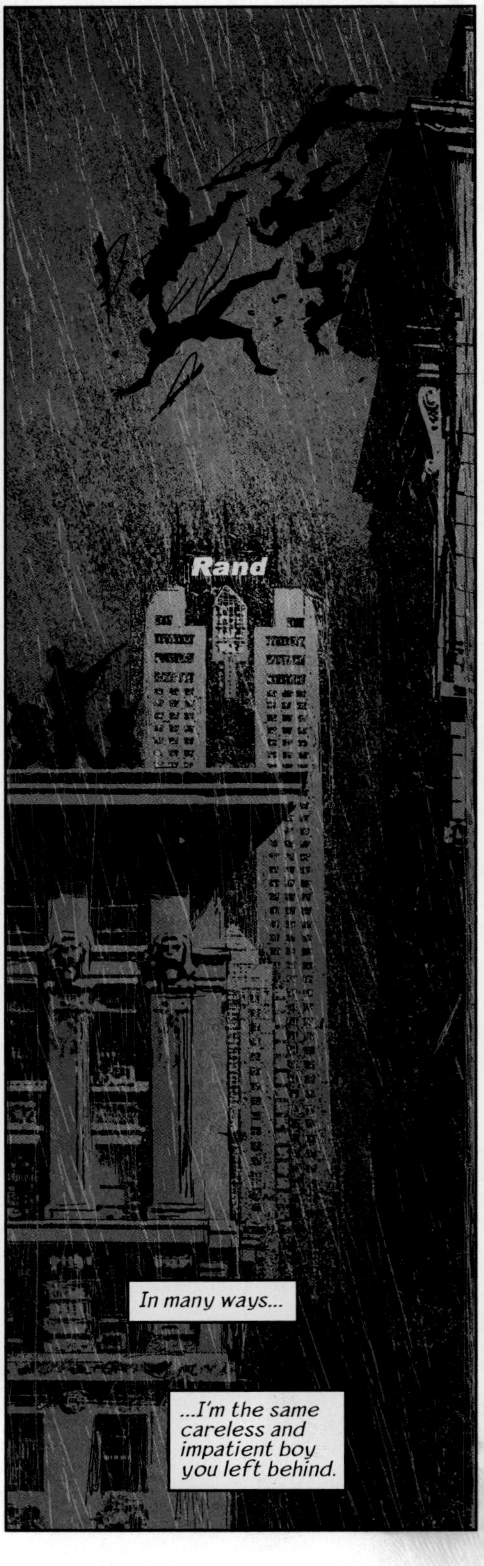
Rand
In many ways...
...I'm the same careless and impatient boy you left behind.

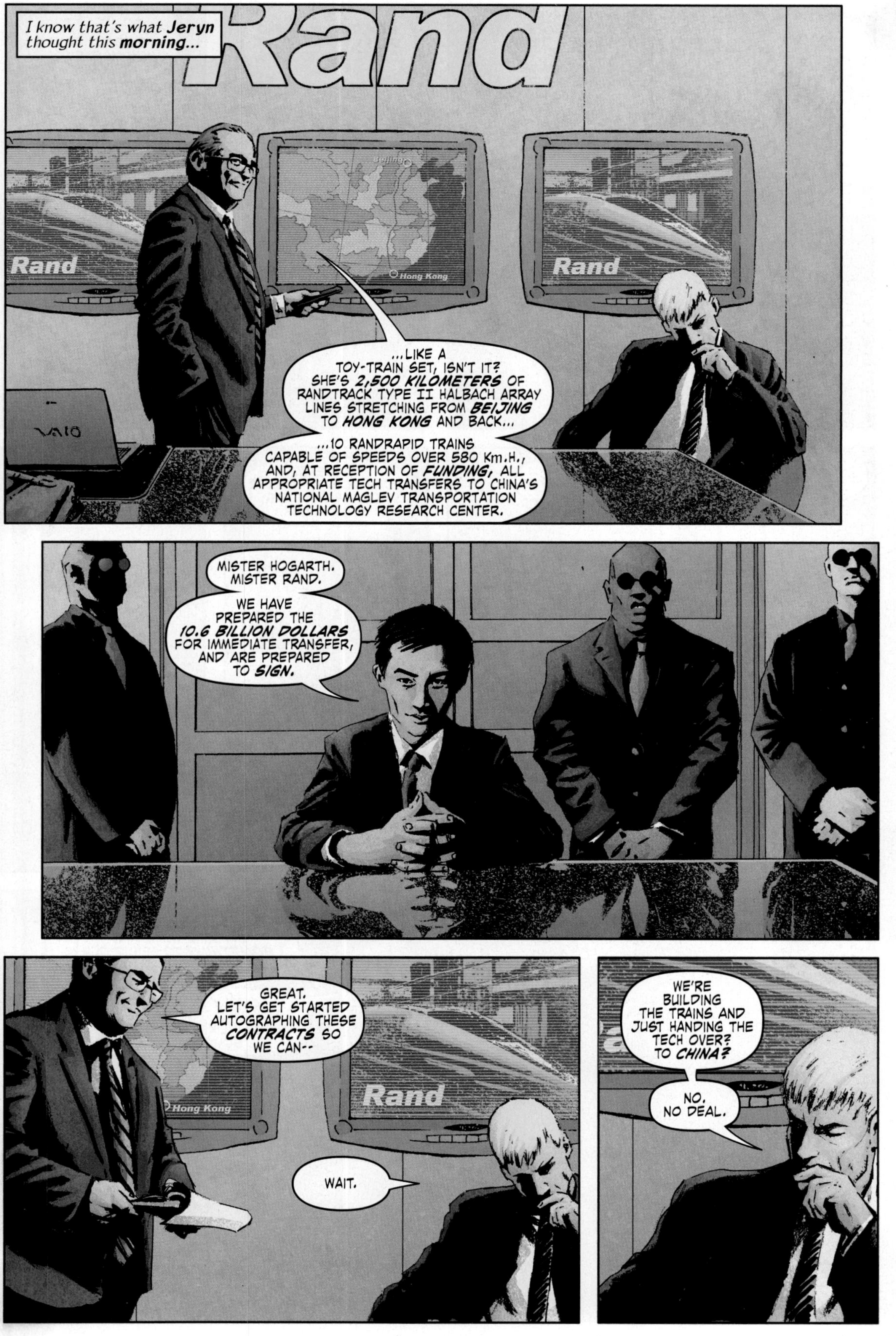
I know that's what **Jeryn** thought this **morning...**
Rand
Beijing
Hong Kong
Rand
Rand
VAIO
...LIKE A TOY-TRAIN SET, ISN'T IT? SHE'S **2,500 KILOMETERS** OF RANDTRACK TYPE II HALBACH ARRAY LINES STRETCHING FROM **BEIJING** TO **HONG KONG** AND BACK...
...10 RANDRAPID TRAINS CAPABLE OF SPEEDS OVER 580 Km.H., AND, AT RECEPTION OF **FUNDING,** ALL APPROPRIATE TECH TRANSFERS TO CHINA'S NATIONAL MAGLEV TRANSPORTATION TECHNOLOGY RESEARCH CENTER.
MISTER HOGARTH. MISTER RAND.
WE HAVE PREPARED THE **10.6 BILLION DOLLARS** FOR IMMEDIATE TRANSFER, AND ARE PREPARED TO **SIGN.**
GREAT. LET'S GET STARTED AUTOGRAPHING THESE **CONTRACTS** SO WE CAN--
Hong Kong
Rand
WAIT.
WE'RE BUILDING THE TRAINS AND JUST HANDING THE TECH OVER? TO **CHINA?**
NO. NO DEAL.

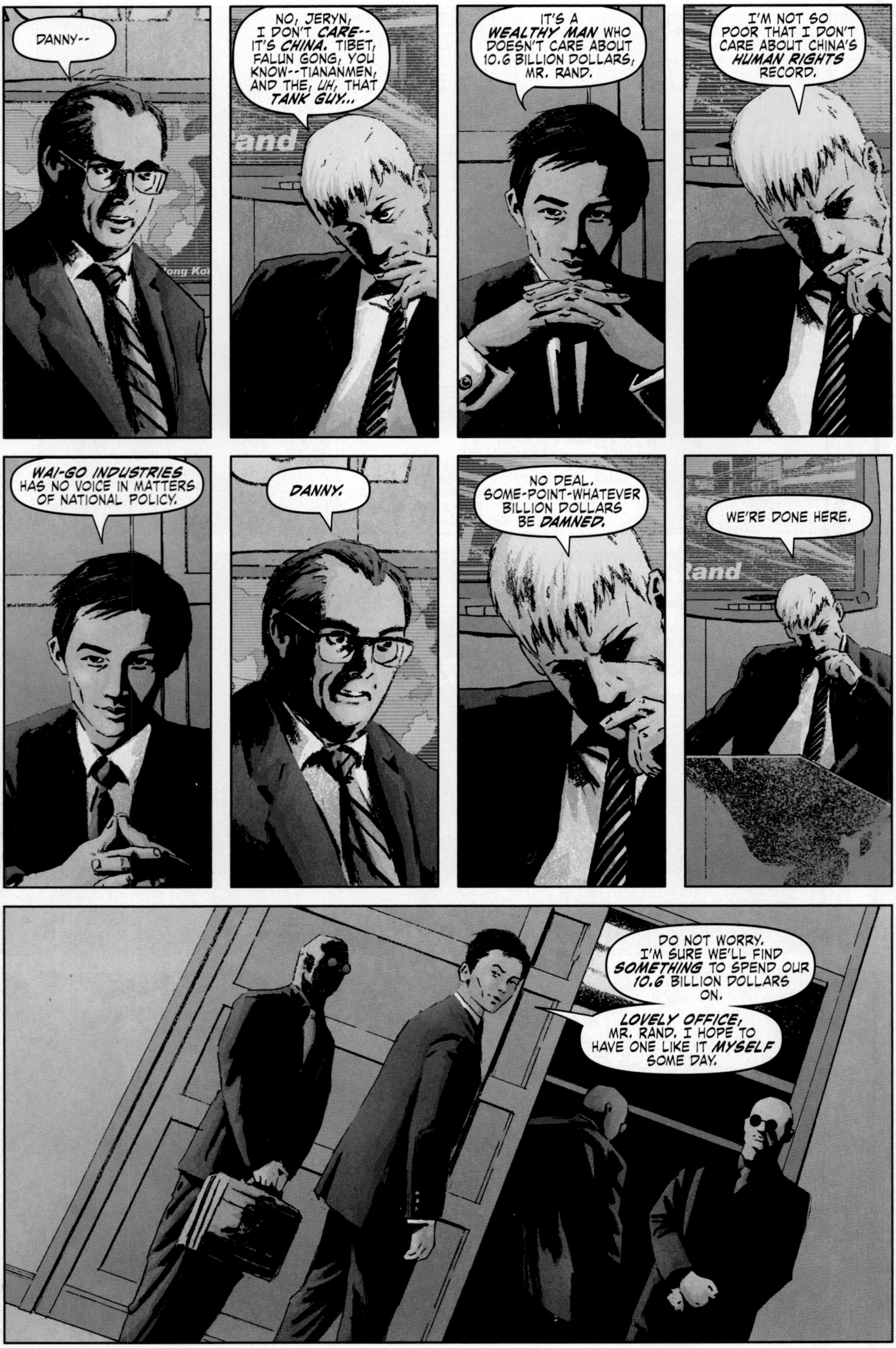
DANNY--
NO, JERYN, I DON'T CARE-- IT'S CHINA. TIBET, FALUN GONG, YOU KNOW--TIANANMEN, AND THE, UH, THAT TANK GUY...
IT'S A WEALTHY MAN WHO DOESN'T CARE ABOUT 10.6 BILLION DOLLARS, MR. RAND.
I'M NOT SO POOR THAT I DON'T CARE ABOUT CHINA'S HUMAN RIGHTS RECORD.
WAI-GO INDUSTRIES HAS NO VOICE IN MATTERS OF NATIONAL POLICY.
DANNY.
NO DEAL. SOME-POINT-WHATEVER BILLION DOLLARS BE DAMNED.
WE'RE DONE HERE.
DO NOT WORRY. I'M SURE WE'LL FIND SOMETHING TO SPEND OUR 10.6 BILLION DOLLARS ON.
LOVELY OFFICE, MR. RAND. I HOPE TO HAVE ONE LIKE IT MYSELF SOME DAY.

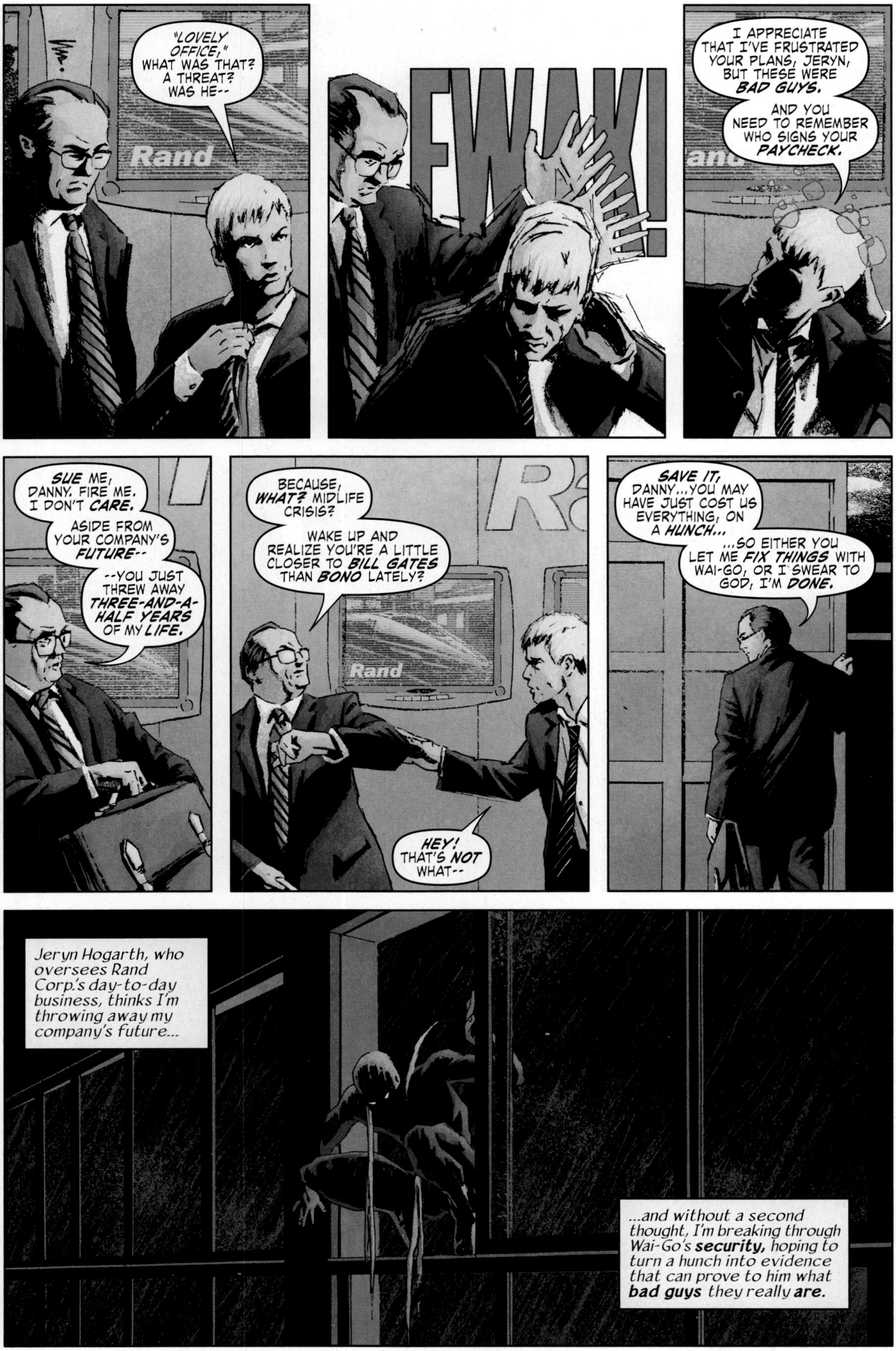
"LOVELY OFFICE," WHAT WAS THAT? A THREAT? WAS HE--
Rand
FWAK!
I APPRECIATE THAT I'VE FRUSTRATED YOUR PLANS, JERYN, BUT THESE WERE BAD GUYS.
AND YOU NEED TO REMEMBER WHO SIGNS YOUR PAYCHECK.
SUE ME, DANNY. FIRE ME. I DON'T CARE.
ASIDE FROM YOUR COMPANY'S FUTURE--
--YOU JUST THREW AWAY THREE-AND-A-HALF YEARS OF MY LIFE.
BECAUSE, WHAT? MIDLIFE CRISIS?
WAKE UP AND REALIZE YOU'RE A LITTLE CLOSER TO BILL GATES THAN BONO LATELY?
Rand
HEY! THAT'S NOT WHAT--
SAVE IT, DANNY...YOU MAY HAVE JUST COST US EVERYTHING, ON A HUNCH...
...SO EITHER YOU LET ME FIX THINGS WITH WAI-GO, OR I SWEAR TO GOD, I'M DONE.
Jeryn Hogarth, who oversees Rand Corp.'s day-to-day business, thinks I'm throwing away my company's future...
...and without a second thought, I'm breaking through Wai-Go's security, hoping to turn a hunch into evidence that can prove to him what bad guys they really are.

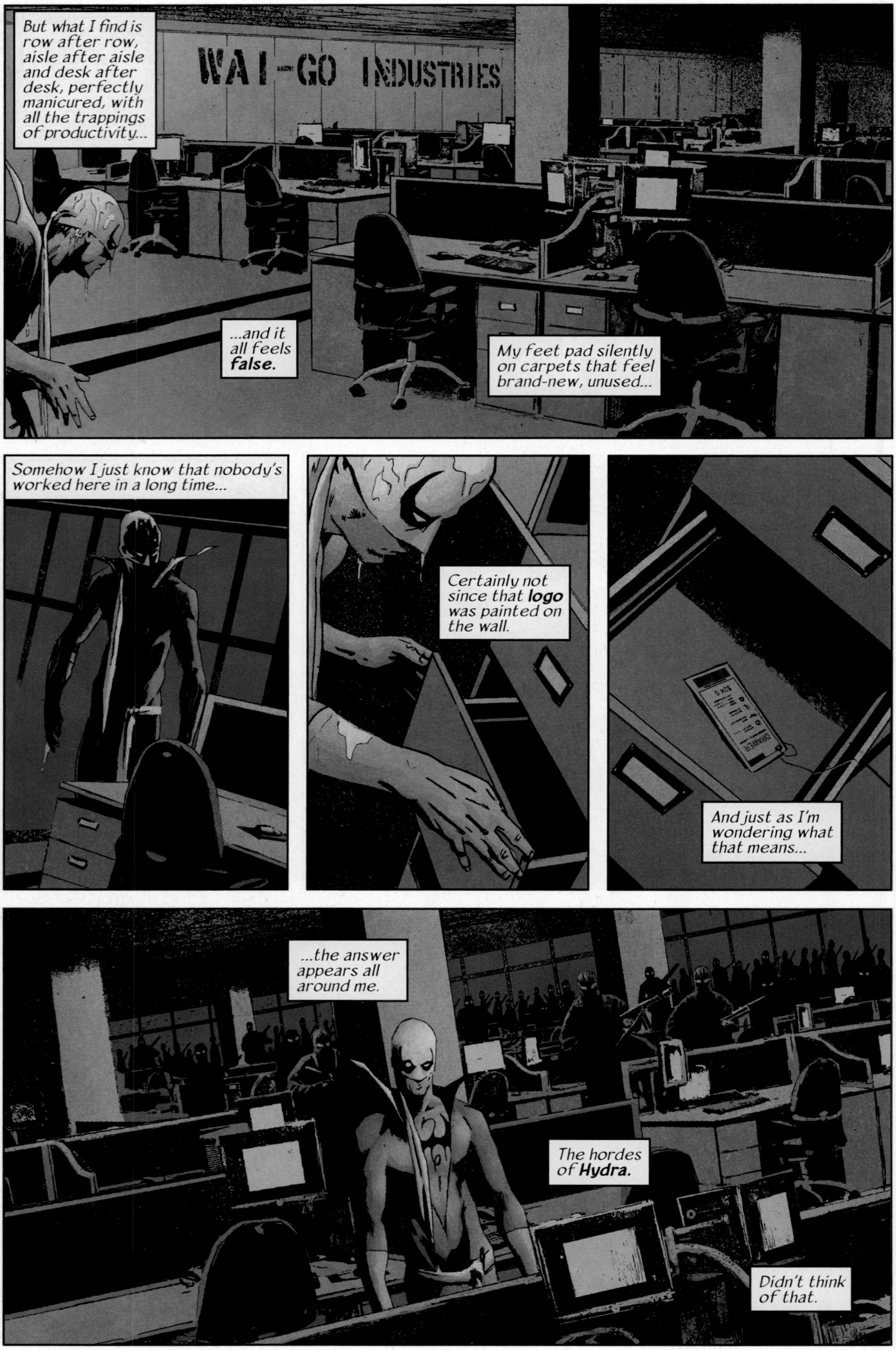
But what I find is row after row, aisle after aisle and desk after desk, perfectly manicured, with all the trappings of productivity...
WAI-GO INDUSTRIES
...and it all feels **false.**
My feet pad silently on carpets that feel brand-new, unused...
Somehow I just know that nobody's worked here in a long time...
Certainly not since that **logo** was painted on the wall.
And just as I'm wondering what that means...
...the answer appears all around me.
The hordes of **Hydra.**
Didn't think of that.

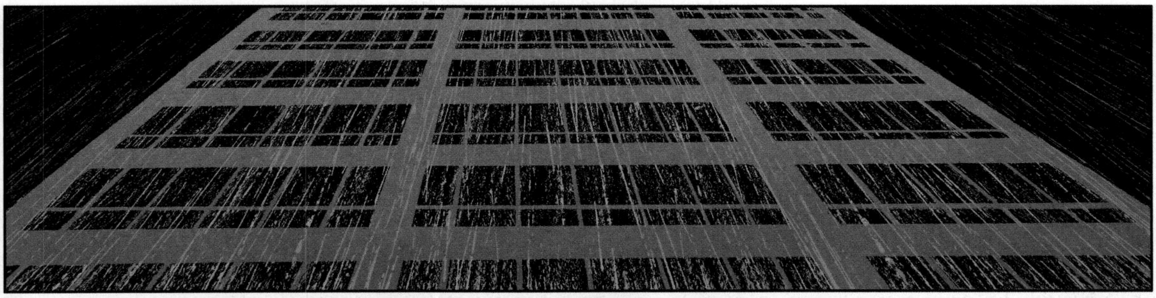

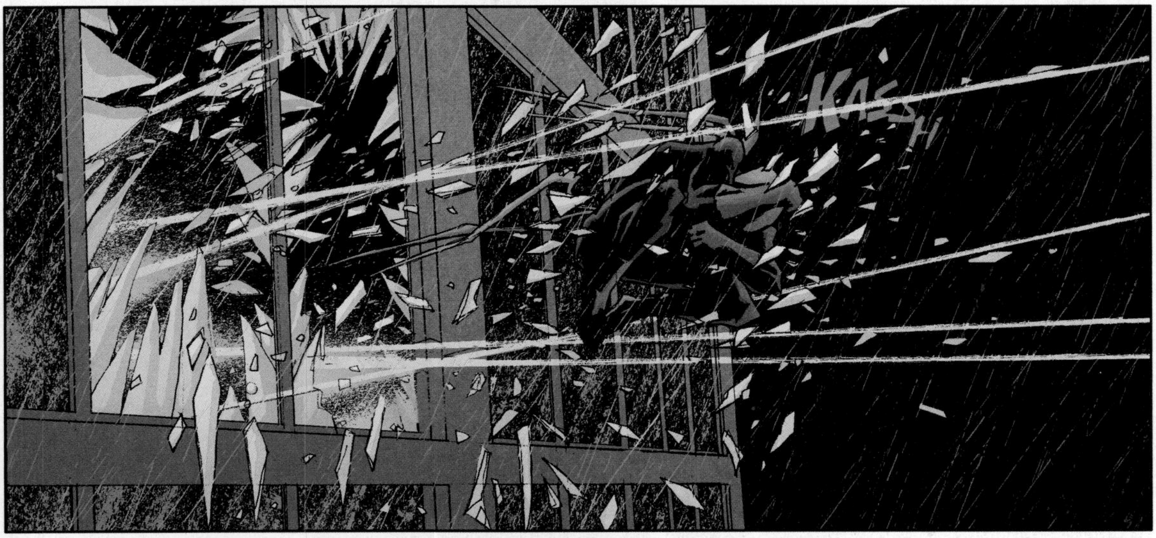
KASSH

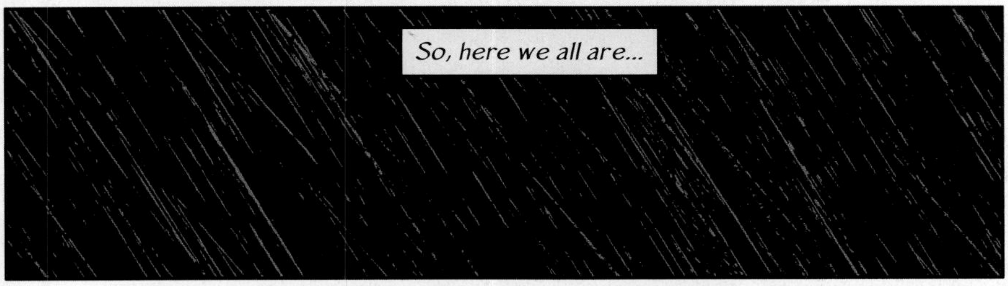
So, here we all are...
...a **Hydra legion** chasing me across the rooftops of Manhattan...
...while a Hydra **front** corporation is making moves against Rand Corp.

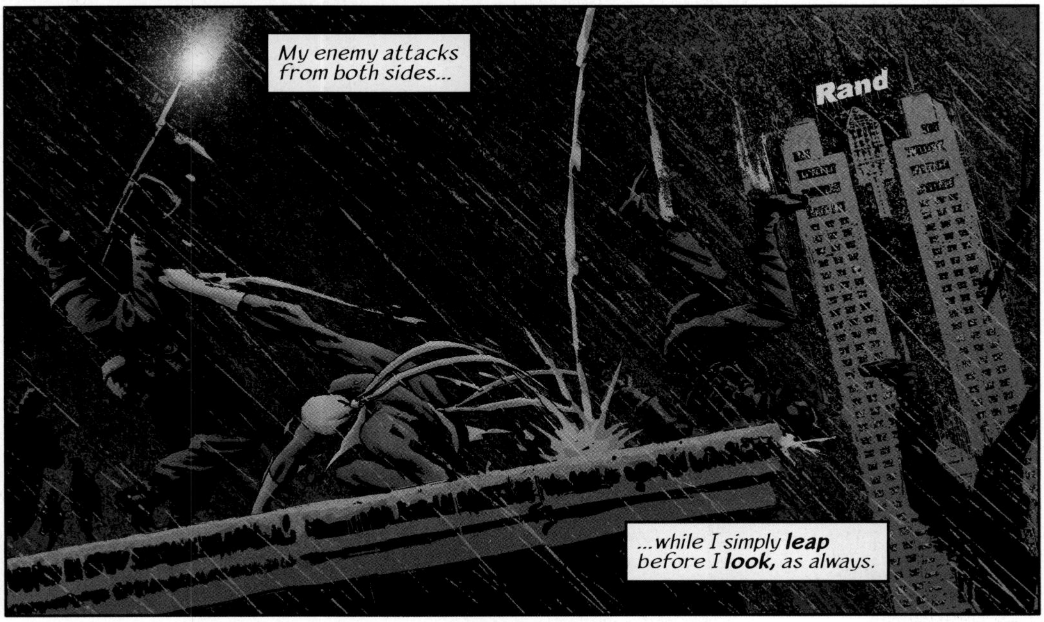
My enemy attacks from both sides...
Rand
...while I simply **leap** before I **look,** as always.

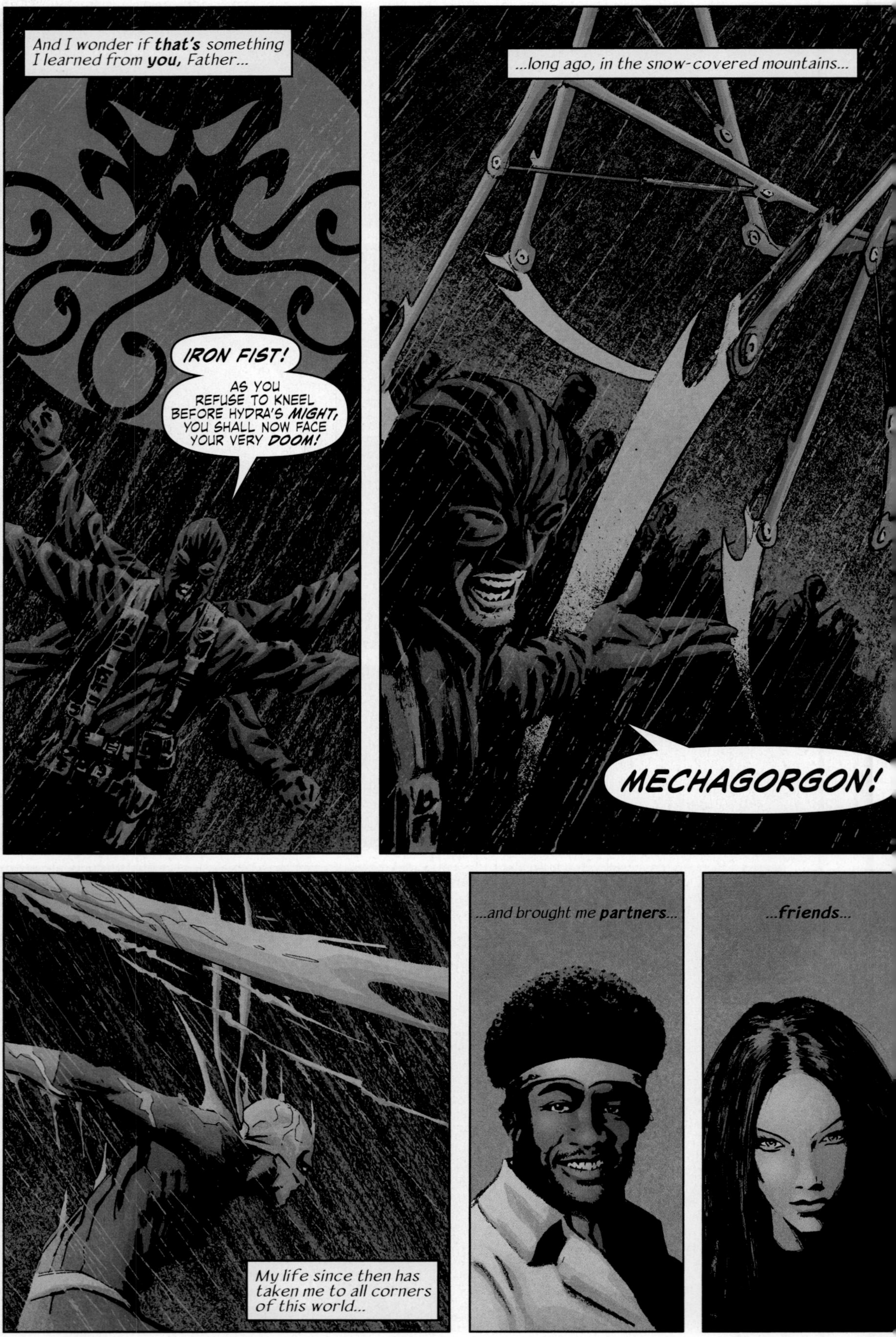
And I wonder if **that's** something I learned from **you,** Father...
IRON FIST!
AS YOU REFUSE TO KNEEL BEFORE HYDRA'S MIGHT, YOU SHALL NOW FACE YOUR VERY DOOM!
...long ago, in the snow-covered mountains...
MECHAGORGON!
My life since then has taken me to all corners of this world...
...and brought me **partners**...
...**friends**...

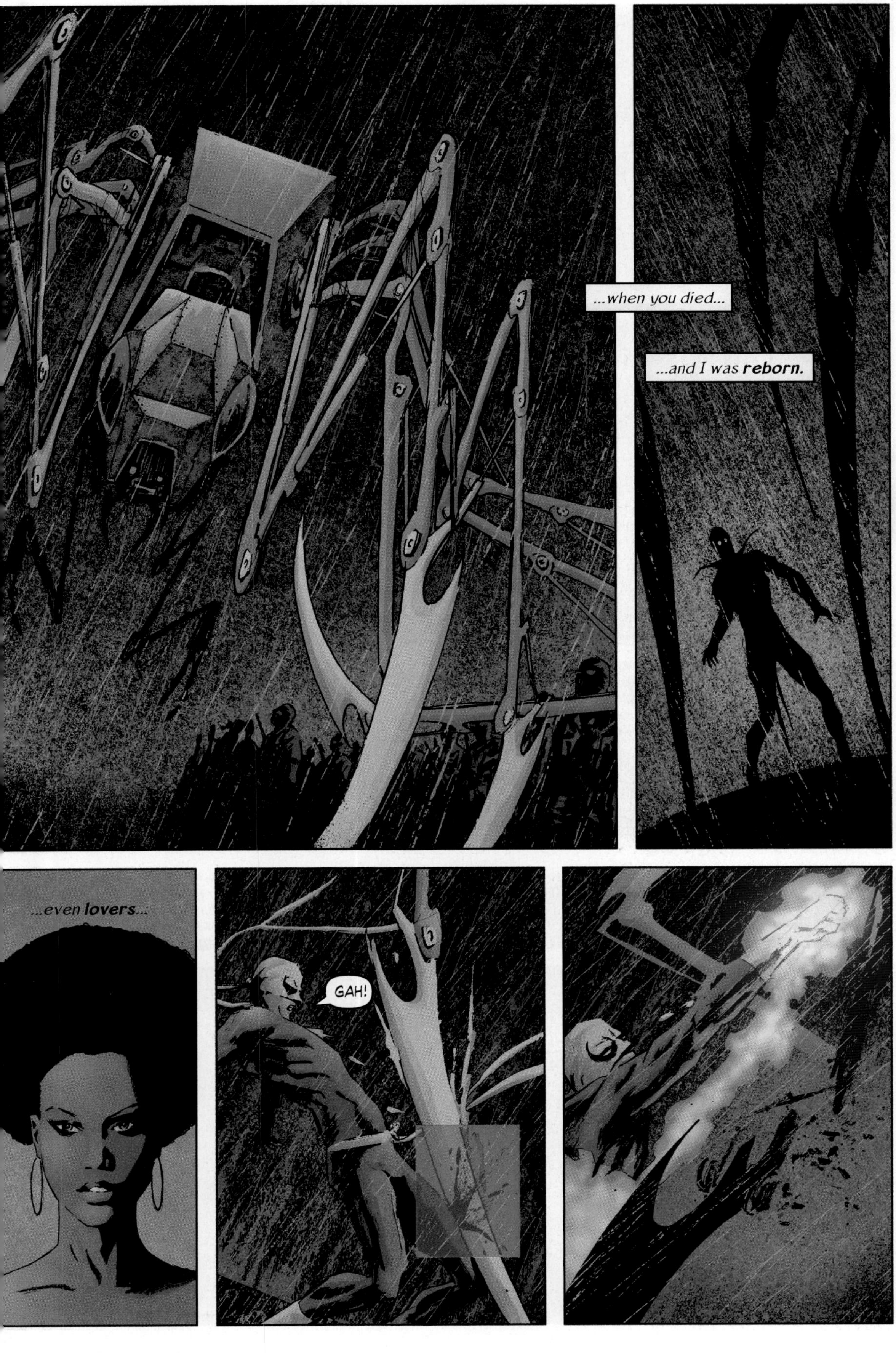
...when you died...
...and I was reborn.
...even lovers...
GAH!

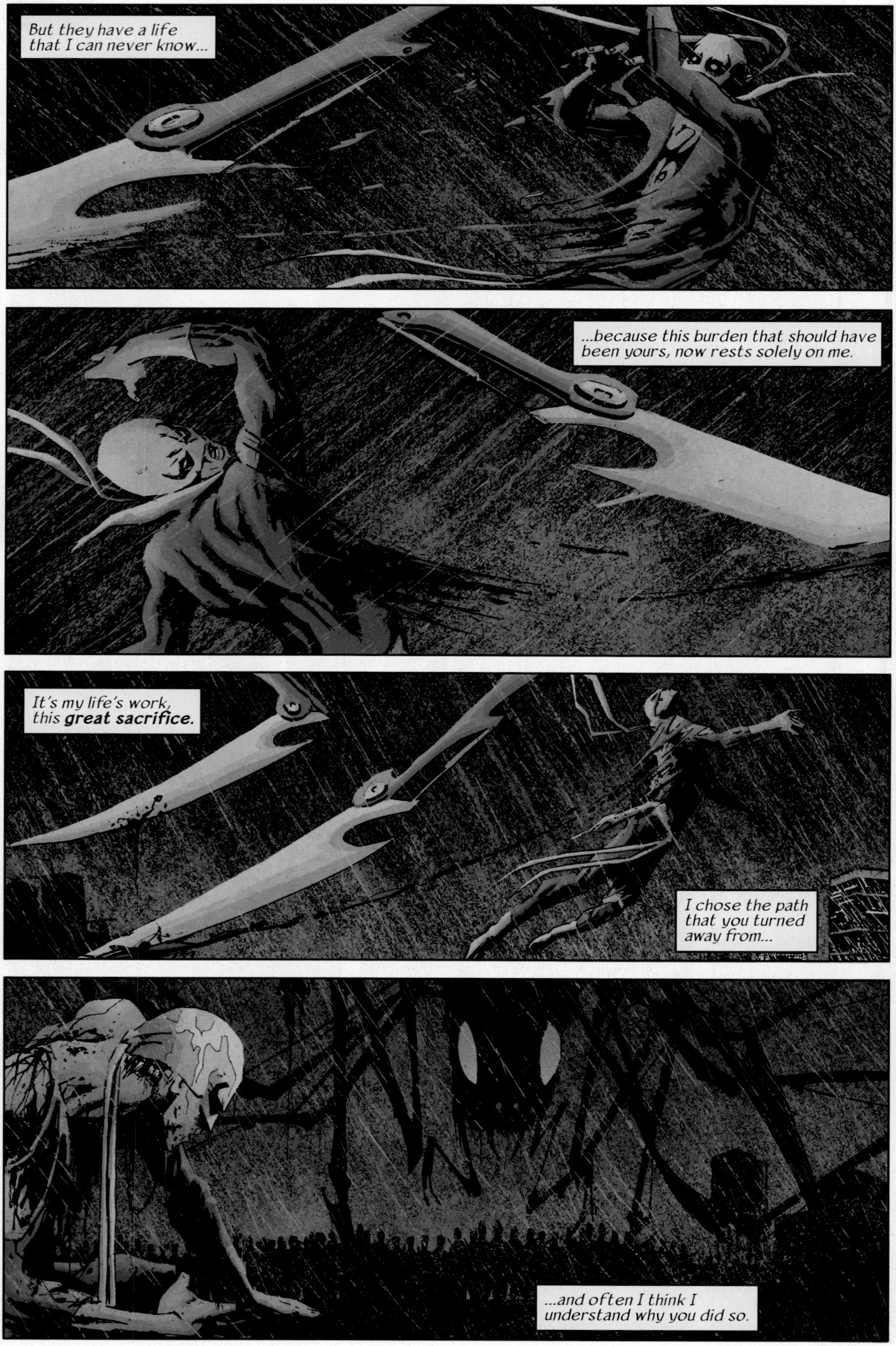
But they have a life that I can never know...
...because this burden that should have been yours, now rests solely on me.
It's my life's work, this **great sacrifice.**
I chose the path that you turned away from...
...and often I think I understand why you did so.

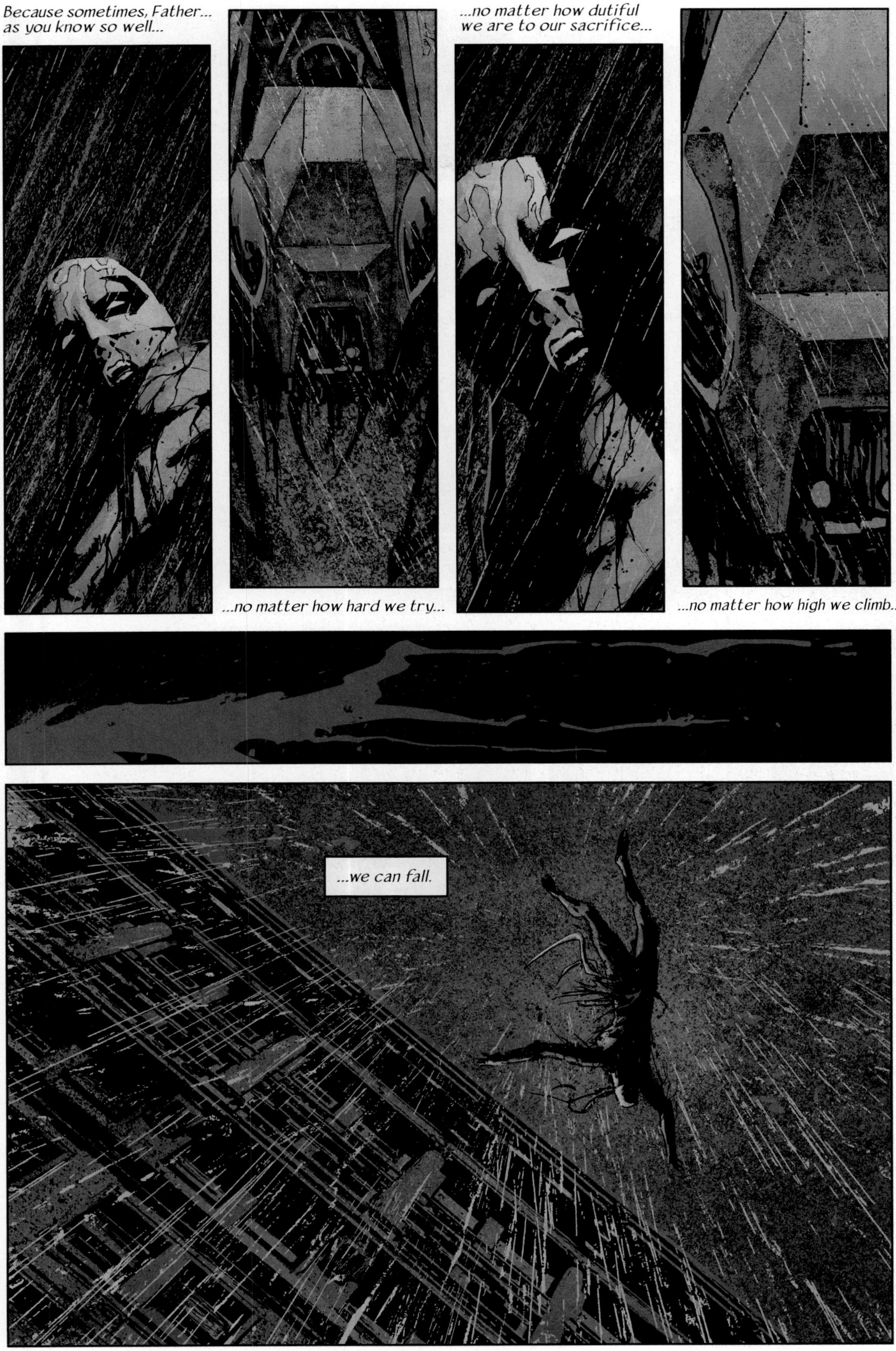
Because sometimes, Father... as you know so well...
...no matter how hard we try...
...no matter how dutiful we are to our sacrifice...
...no matter how high we climb...
...we can fall.

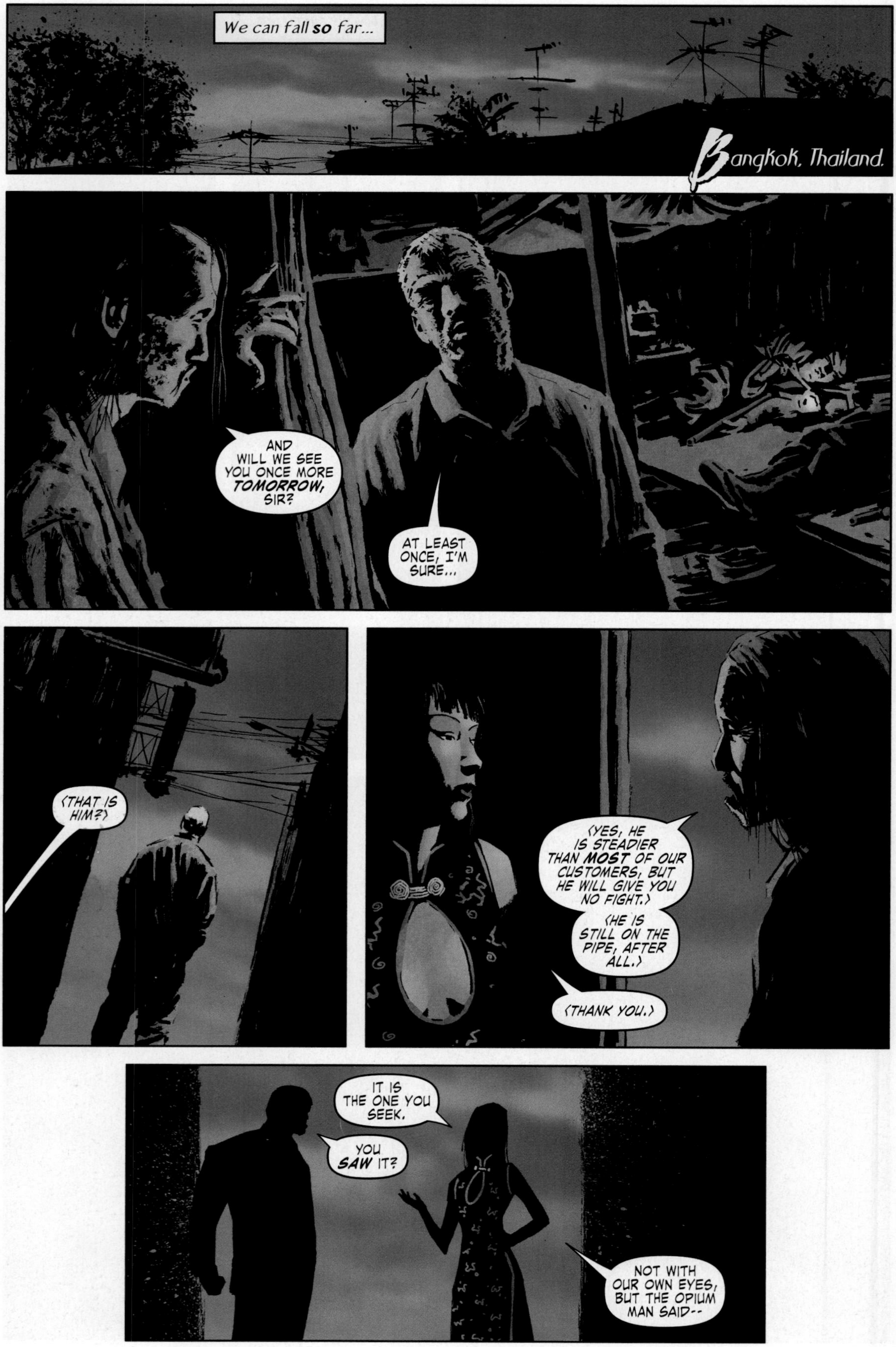
We can fall so far...
Bangkok, Thailand.
AND WILL WE SEE YOU ONCE MORE TOMORROW, SIR?
AT LEAST ONCE, I'M SURE...
‹THAT IS HIM?›
‹YES, HE IS STEADIER THAN MOST OF OUR CUSTOMERS, BUT HE WILL GIVE YOU NO FIGHT.›
‹HE IS STILL ON THE PIPE, AFTER ALL.›
‹THANK YOU.›
IT IS THE ONE YOU SEEK.
YOU SAW IT?
NOT WITH OUR OWN EYES, BUT THE OPIUM MAN SAID--

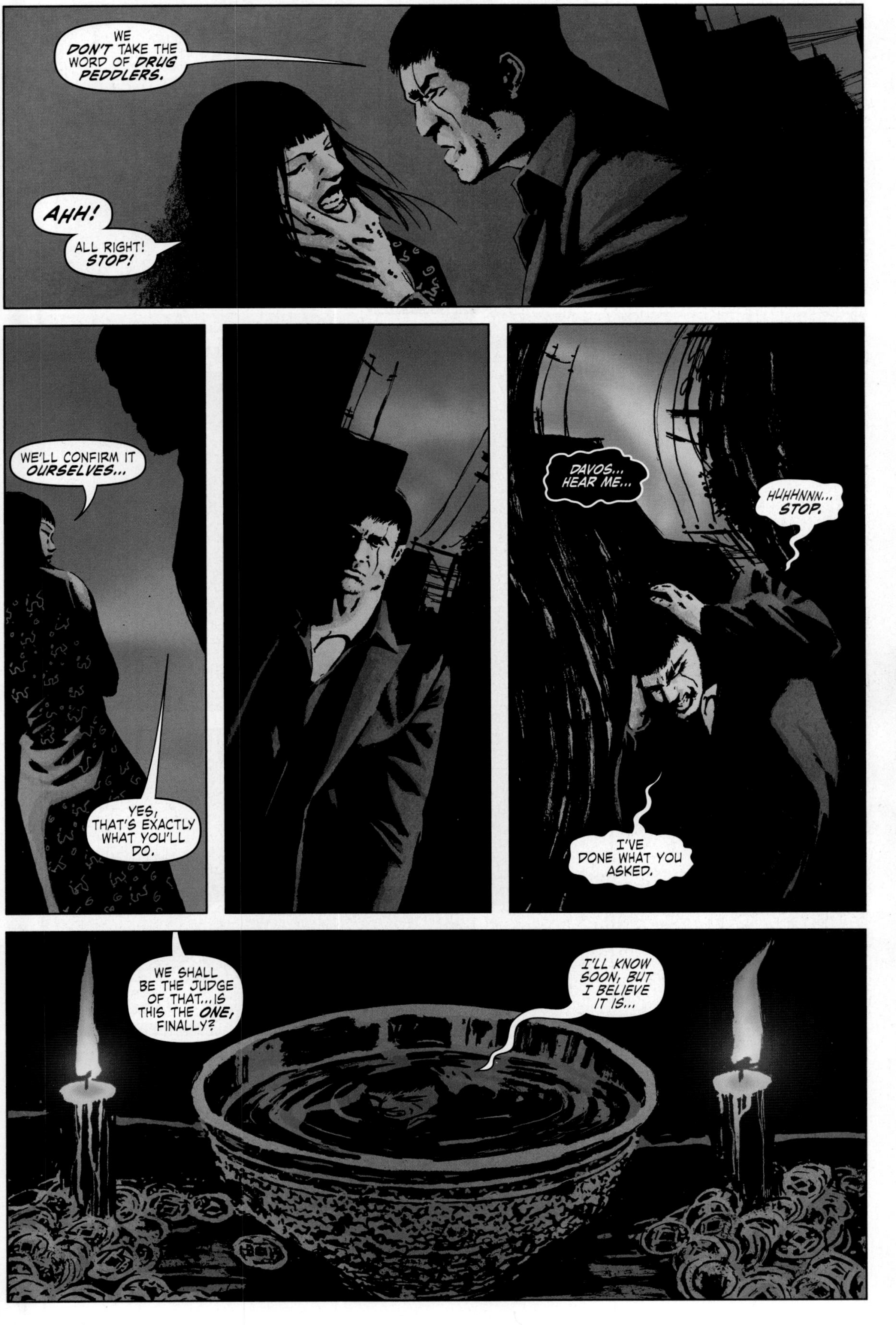
WE DON'T TAKE THE WORD OF DRUG PEDDLERS.
AHH!
ALL RIGHT! STOP!
WE'LL CONFIRM IT OURSELVES...
YES, THAT'S EXACTLY WHAT YOU'LL DO.
DAVOS... HEAR ME...
HUHHNNN... STOP.
I'VE DONE WHAT YOU ASKED.
WE SHALL BE THE JUDGE OF THAT...IS THIS THE ONE, FINALLY?
I'LL KNOW SOON, BUT I BELIEVE IT IS...

...MY FATHER'S *JOURNAL* DIDN'T LIE.

YOU SHOULD PRAY IT DID NOT.

WE BROUGHT YOU BACK FOR A REASON, DAVOS...

...BUT WE WILL BE MORE THAN HAPPY TO TAKE YOU AWAY AGAIN.

JUST GIVE ME A LITTLE MORE TIME, DAMN YOU...

"...HE IS NEARLY IN MY GRASP."

MISTER?

MY SISTER AND I HAVE COME, AS *DESIRED*...

KNOCK KNOCK

KNOCK KNOCK

HELLO? THEY TOLD US ROOM 12...

WHAT THE HELL...?

I'M SORRY, GIRLS, YOU'VE *REALLY* GOT THE WRONG--

AH!

SHHHIRT

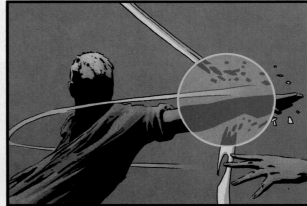

IT IS HE.

IT IS HE.

WHO *SENT* YOU?

ONE WHO WILL HAVE YOUR HEART.

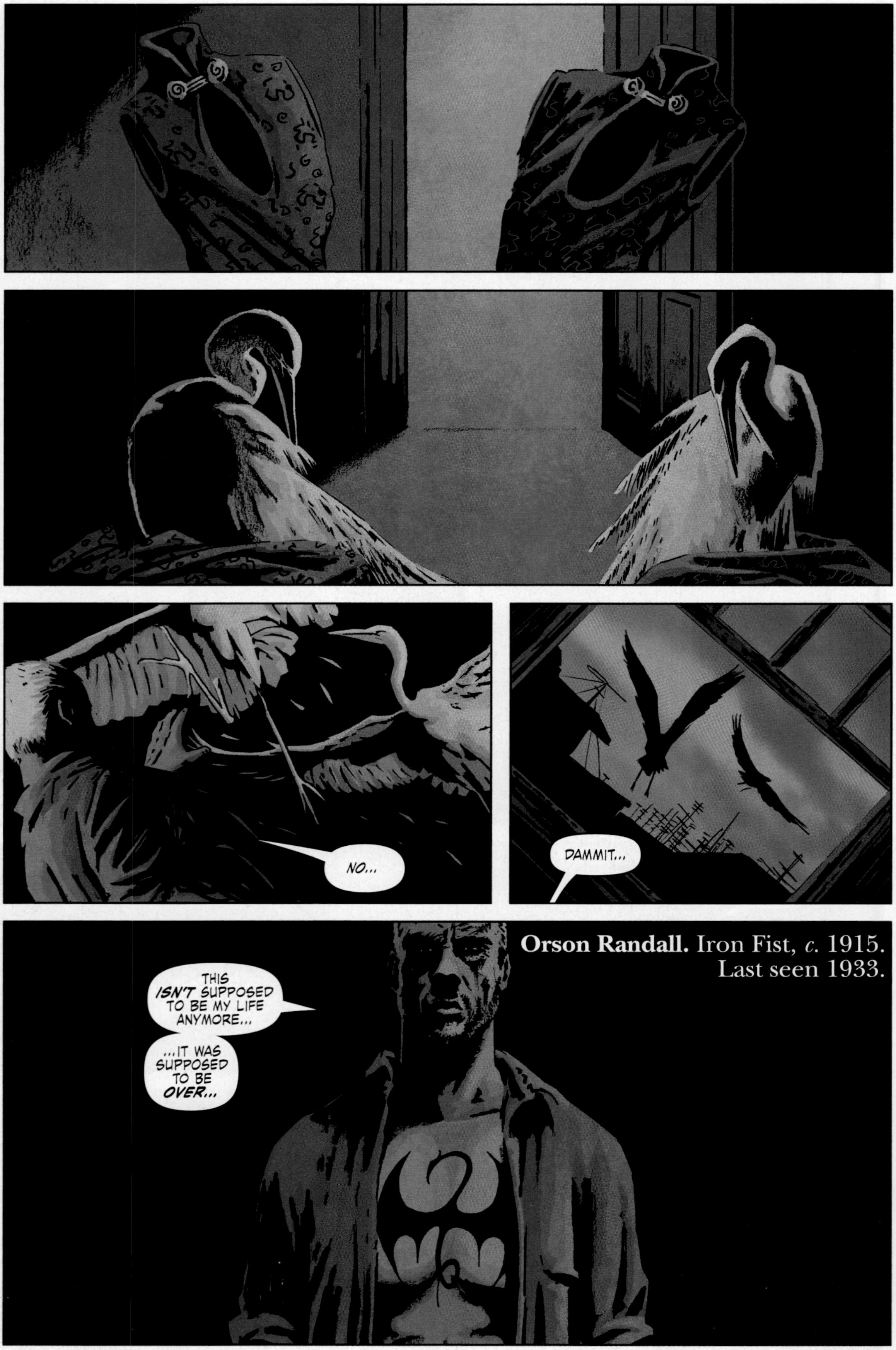
NO...
DAMMIT...
Orson Randall. Iron Fist, c. 1915. Last seen 1933.
THIS ISN'T SUPPOSED TO BE MY LIFE ANYMORE...
...IT WAS SUPPOSED TO BE OVER...

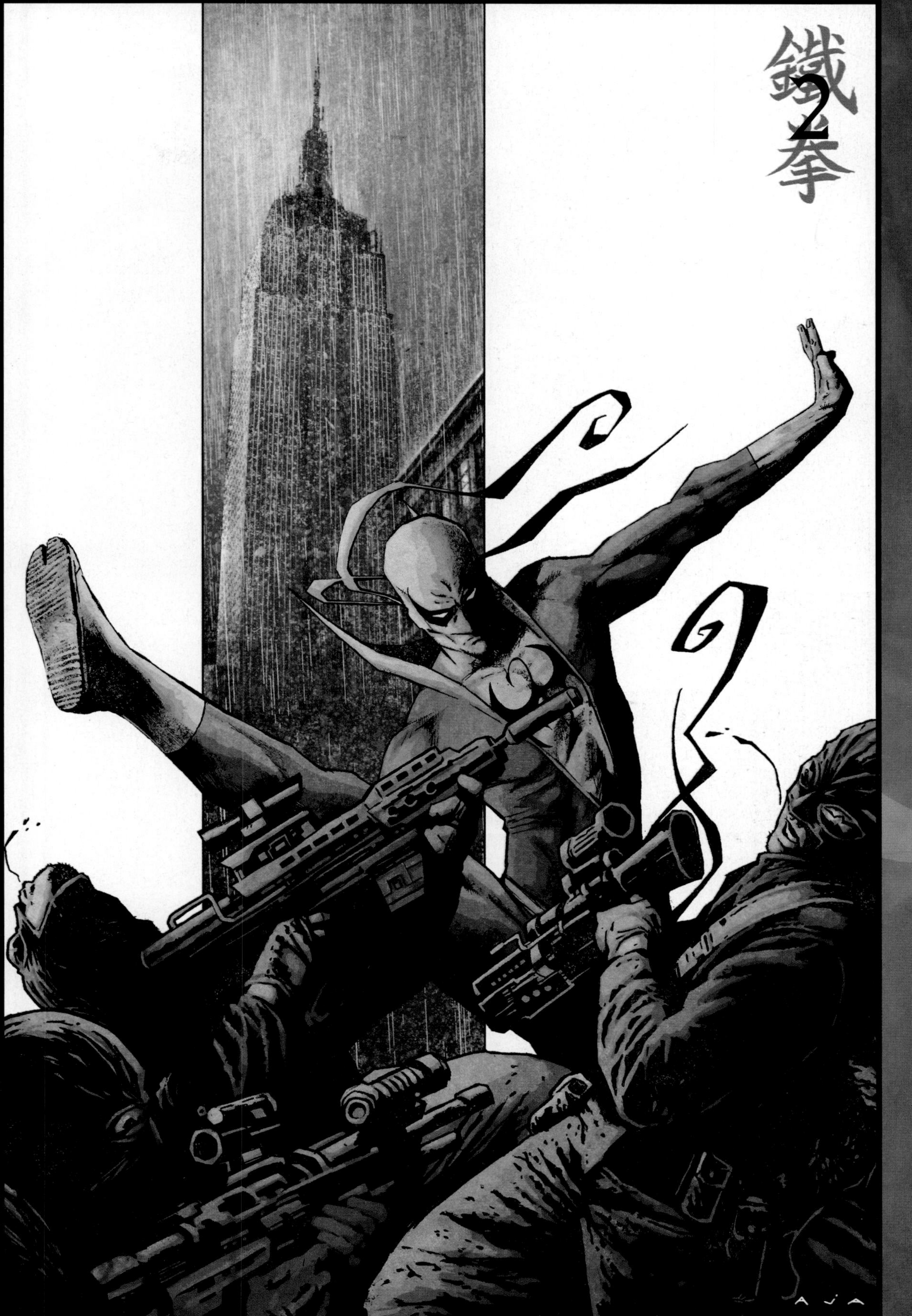
鐵拳
2
AJA

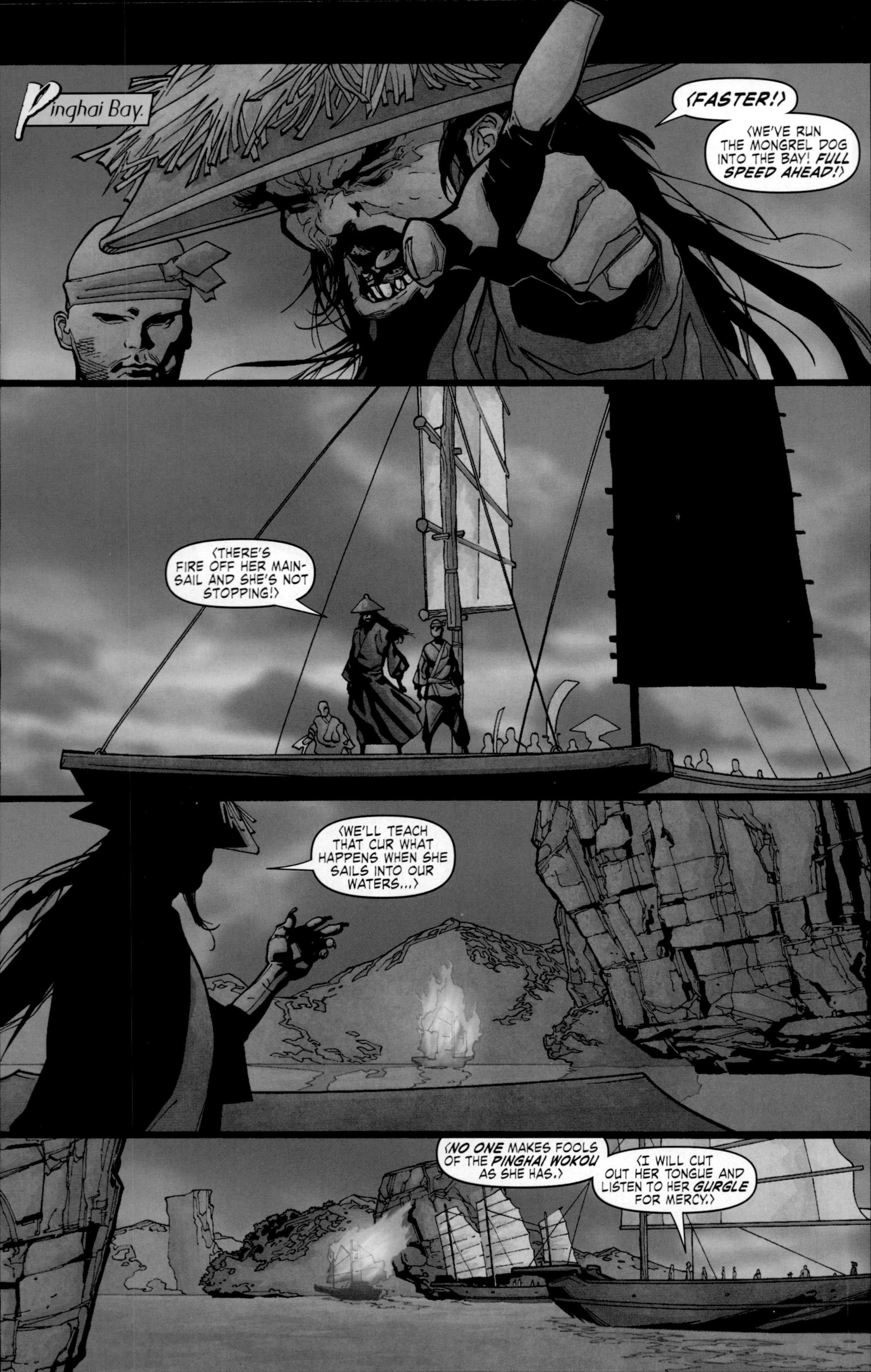
Pinghai Bay.
⟨FASTER!⟩
⟨WE'VE RUN THE MONGREL DOG INTO THE BAY! FULL SPEED AHEAD!⟩
⟨THERE'S FIRE OFF HER MAIN-SAIL AND SHE'S NOT STOPPING!⟩
⟨WE'LL TEACH THAT CUR WHAT HAPPENS WHEN SHE SAILS INTO OUR WATERS...⟩
⟨NO ONE MAKES FOOLS OF THE PINGHAI WOKOU AS SHE HAS.⟩
⟨I WILL CUT OUT HER TONGUE AND LISTEN TO HER GURGLE FOR MERCY.⟩

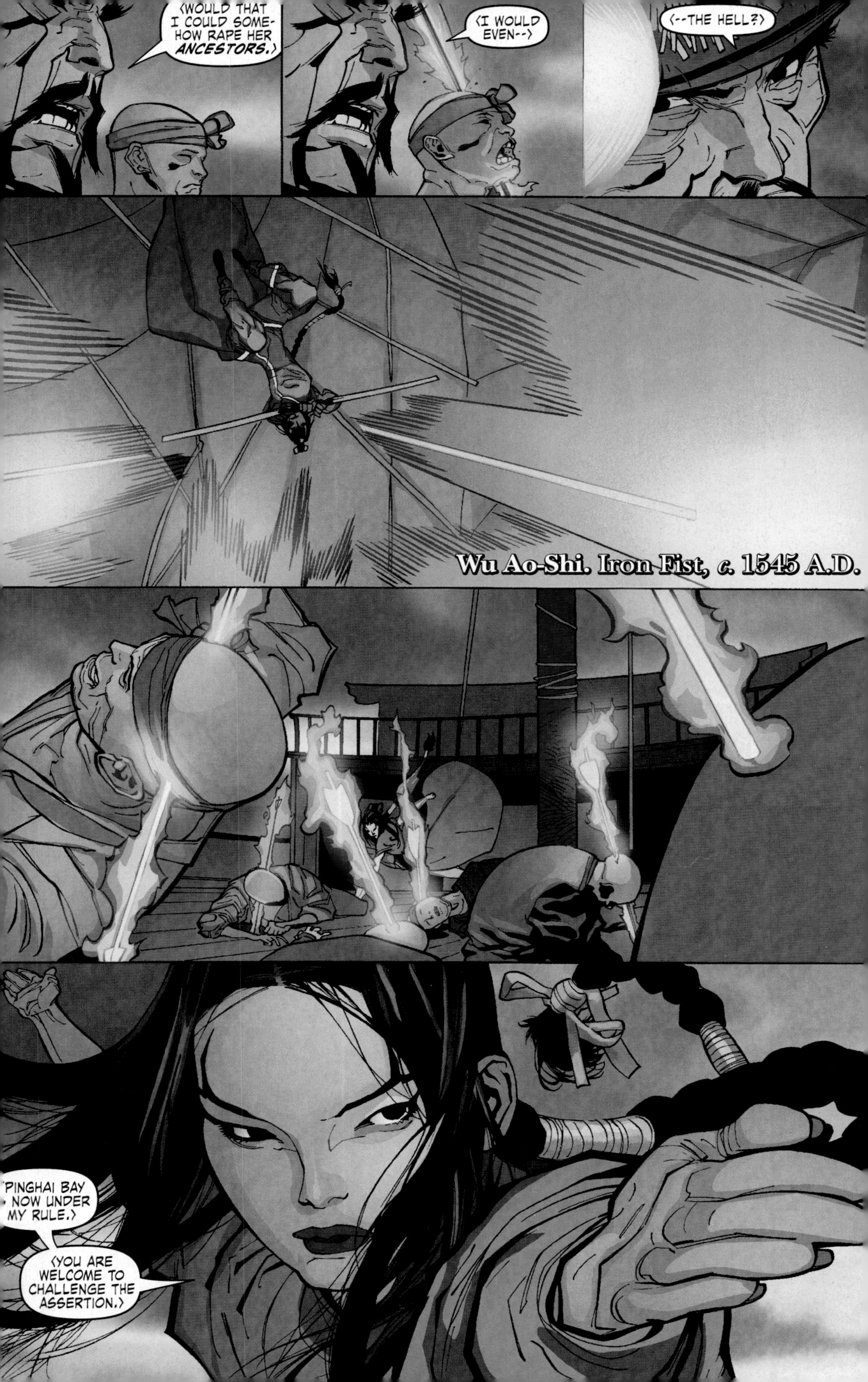

<WOULD THAT I COULD SOMEHOW RAPE HER ANCESTORS.>
<I WOULD EVEN-->
<--THE HELL?>
Wu Ao-Shi. Iron Fist, c. 1545 A.D.
PINGHAI BAY NOW UNDER MY RULE.>
<YOU ARE WELCOME TO CHALLENGE THE ASSERTION.>

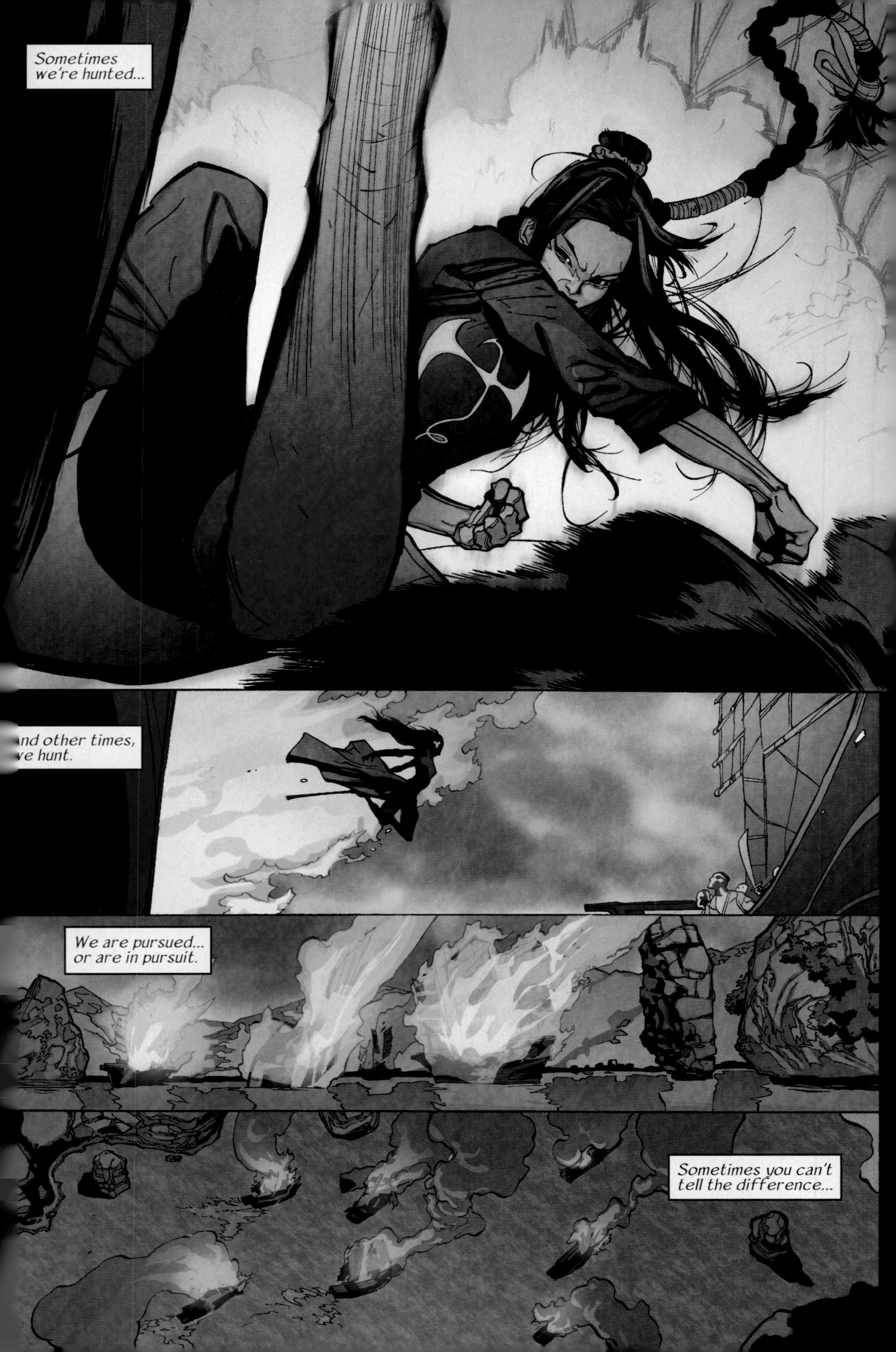
Sometimes we're hunted...
nd other times, ve hunt.
We are pursued... or are in pursuit.
Sometimes you can't tell the difference...

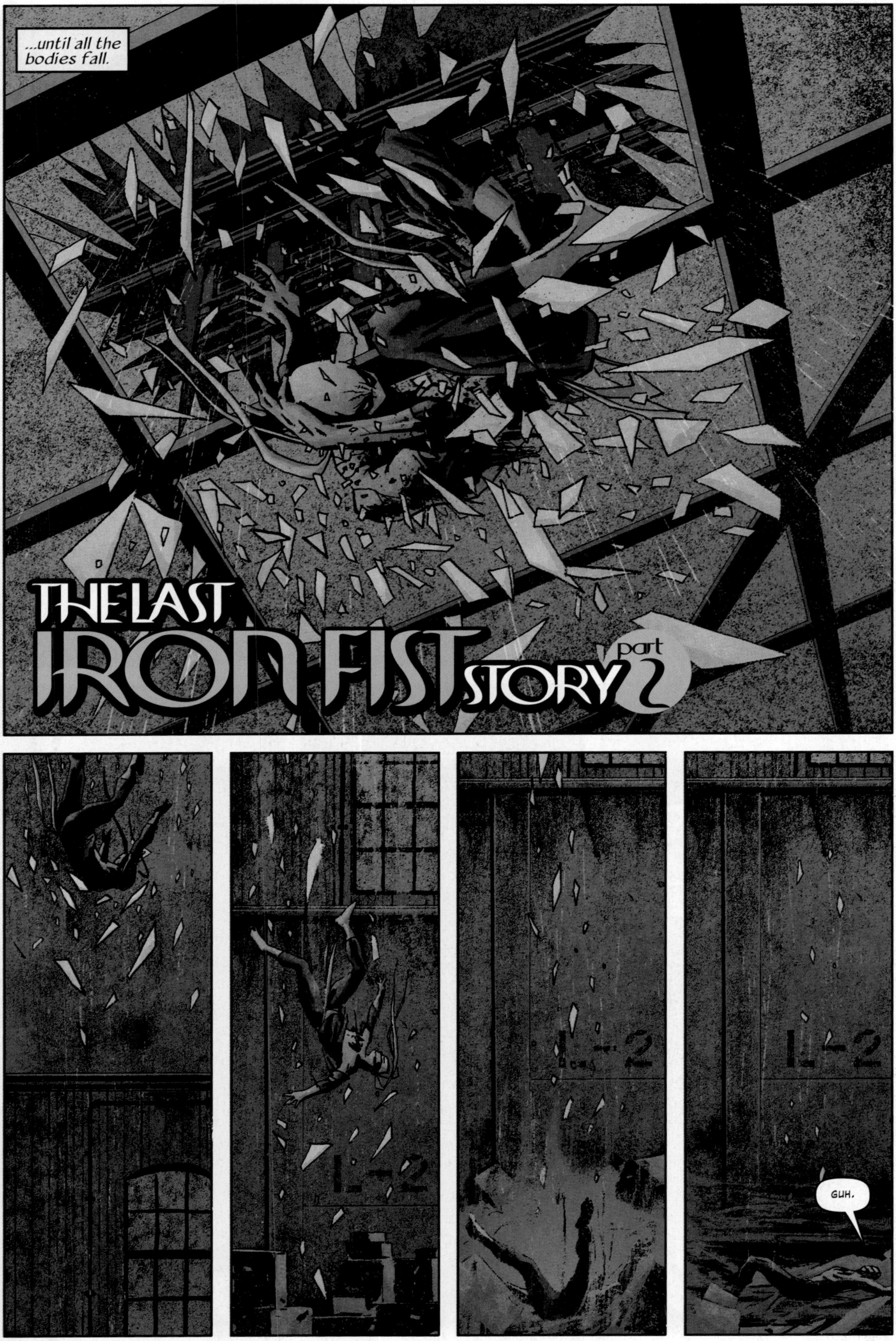
...until all the bodies fall.
THE LAST IRON FIST STORY part 2
GUH.

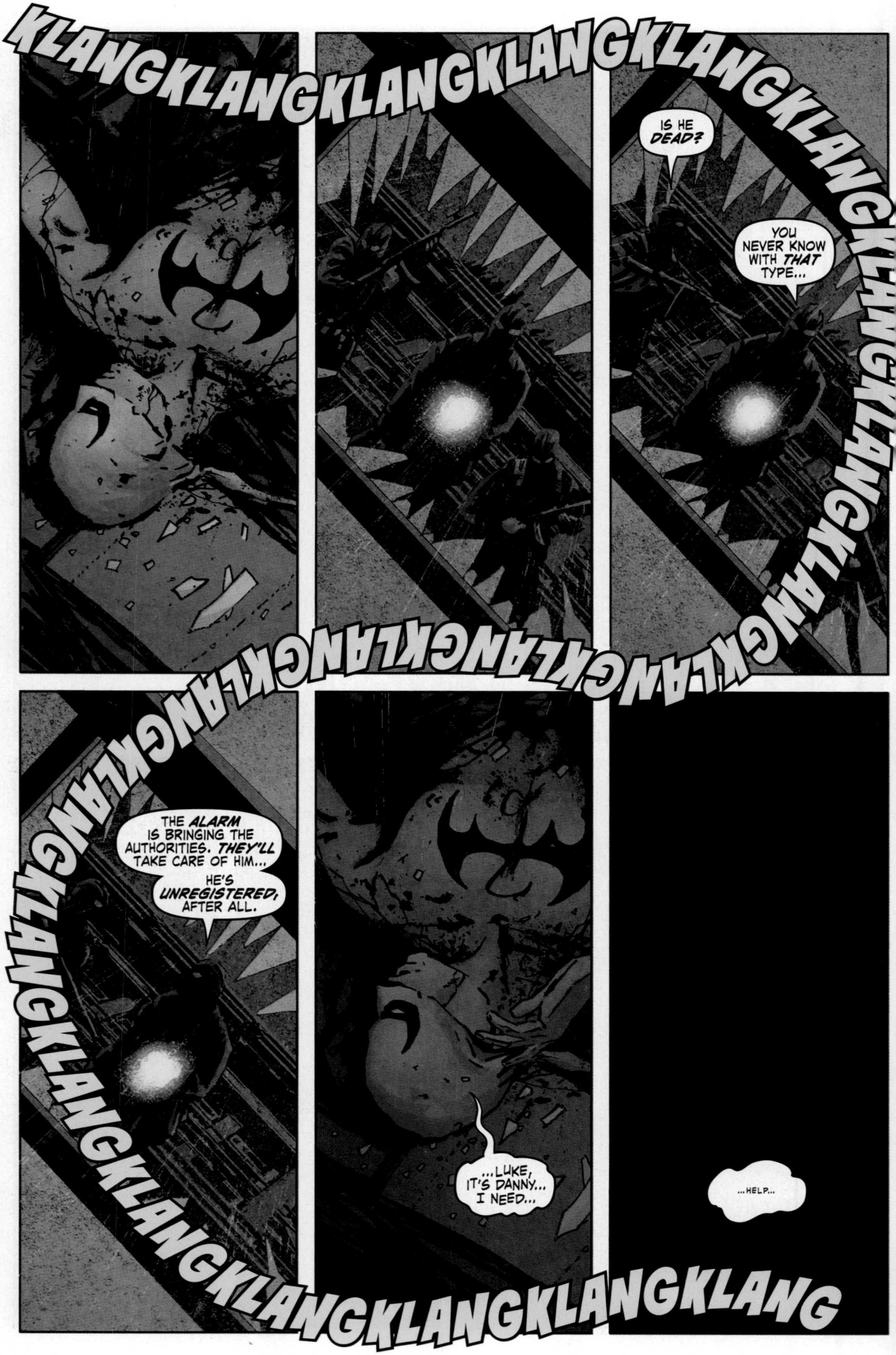
KLANGKLANGKLANGKLANG
IS HE DEAD?
YOU NEVER KNOW WITH THAT TYPE...
THE ALARM IS BRINGING THE AUTHORITIES. THEY'LL TAKE CARE OF HIM...
HE'S UNREGISTERED, AFTER ALL.
...LUKE, IT'S DANNY... I NEED...
...HELP...
KLANGKLANGKLANGKLANG

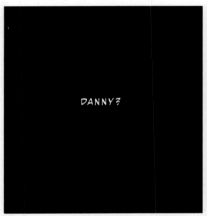

DANNY?

DO YOU KNOW WHERE YOU ARE, DANNY?

CAN YOU TELL ME YOUR NAME?

WHAT? I... WHAT?

HELLLLLO, NURSE.

I THINK HE'S COMING OUT OF IT.

SHE WANTS TO KNOW YOUR *NAME*, DANNY.

OH! MY NAME IS *DANIEL RAND*. I AM *IRON FIST* AND I KNOW KUNG FU.

HI-YAHH.

SORRY. HE ALWAYS ACTS STUPID WHEN HE HAS A HEAD INJURY.

THANKS FOR LOOKING AFTER HIM THIS TIME OF NIGHT.

OH, *LUKE*, PLEASE...

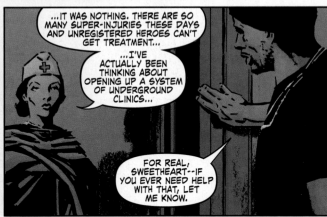

...IT WAS NOTHING. THERE ARE SO MANY SUPER-INJURIES THESE DAYS AND UNREGISTERED HEROES CAN'T GET TREATMENT...

...I'VE ACTUALLY BEEN THINKING ABOUT OPENING UP A SYSTEM OF UNDERGROUND CLINICS...

FOR REAL, SWEETHEART--IF YOU EVER NEED HELP WITH THAT, LET ME KNOW.

SHE'S HOT.

SHUT UP.

WHOOP

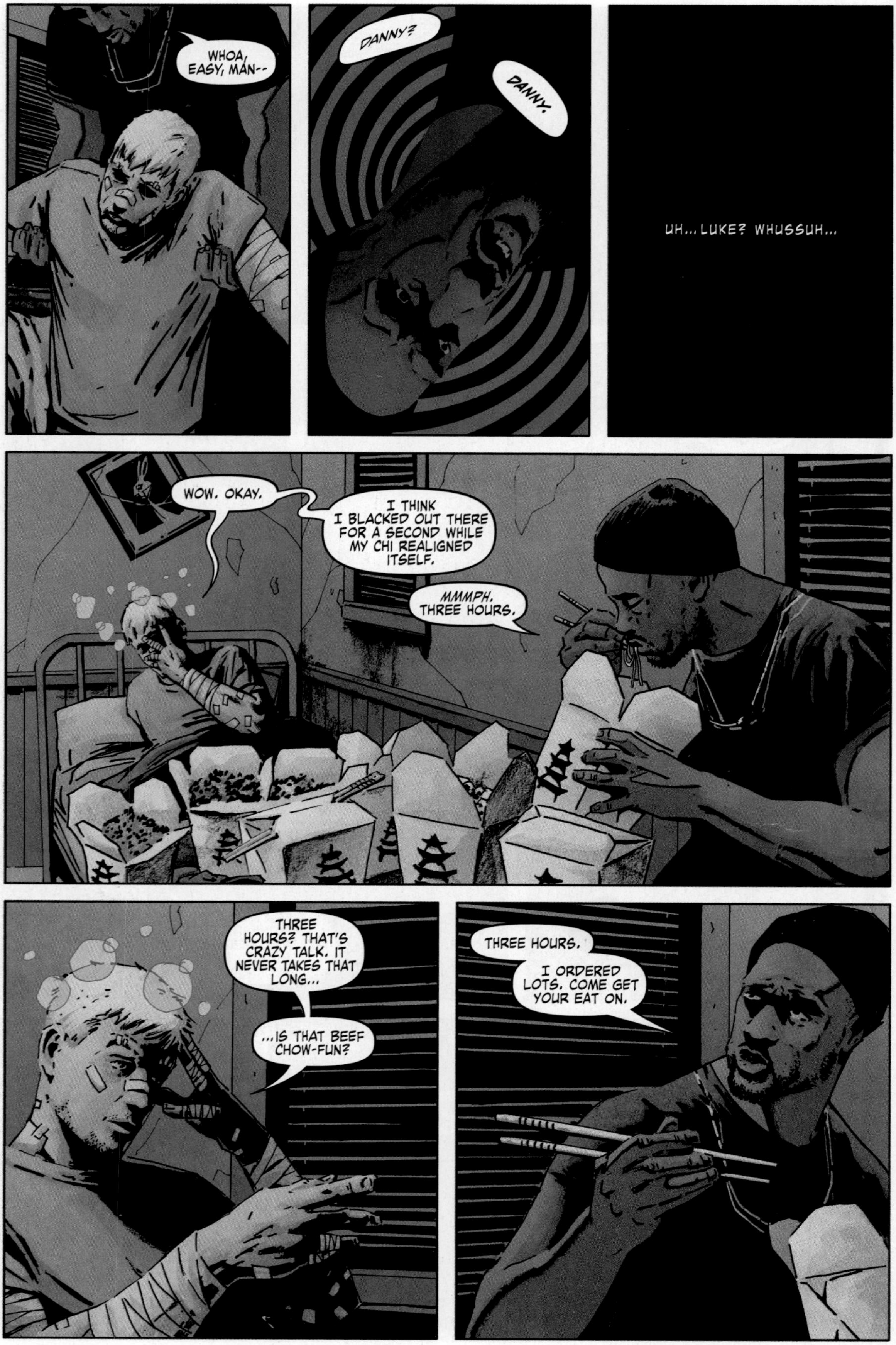
WHOA, EASY, MAN--
DANNY?
DANNY.
UH... LUKE? WHUSSUH...
WOW. OKAY.
I THINK I BLACKED OUT THERE FOR A SECOND WHILE MY CHI REALIGNED ITSELF.
MMMPH. THREE HOURS.
THREE HOURS? THAT'S CRAZY TALK. IT NEVER TAKES THAT LONG...
...IS THAT BEEF CHOW-FUN?
THREE HOURS.
I ORDERED LOTS. COME GET YOUR EAT ON.

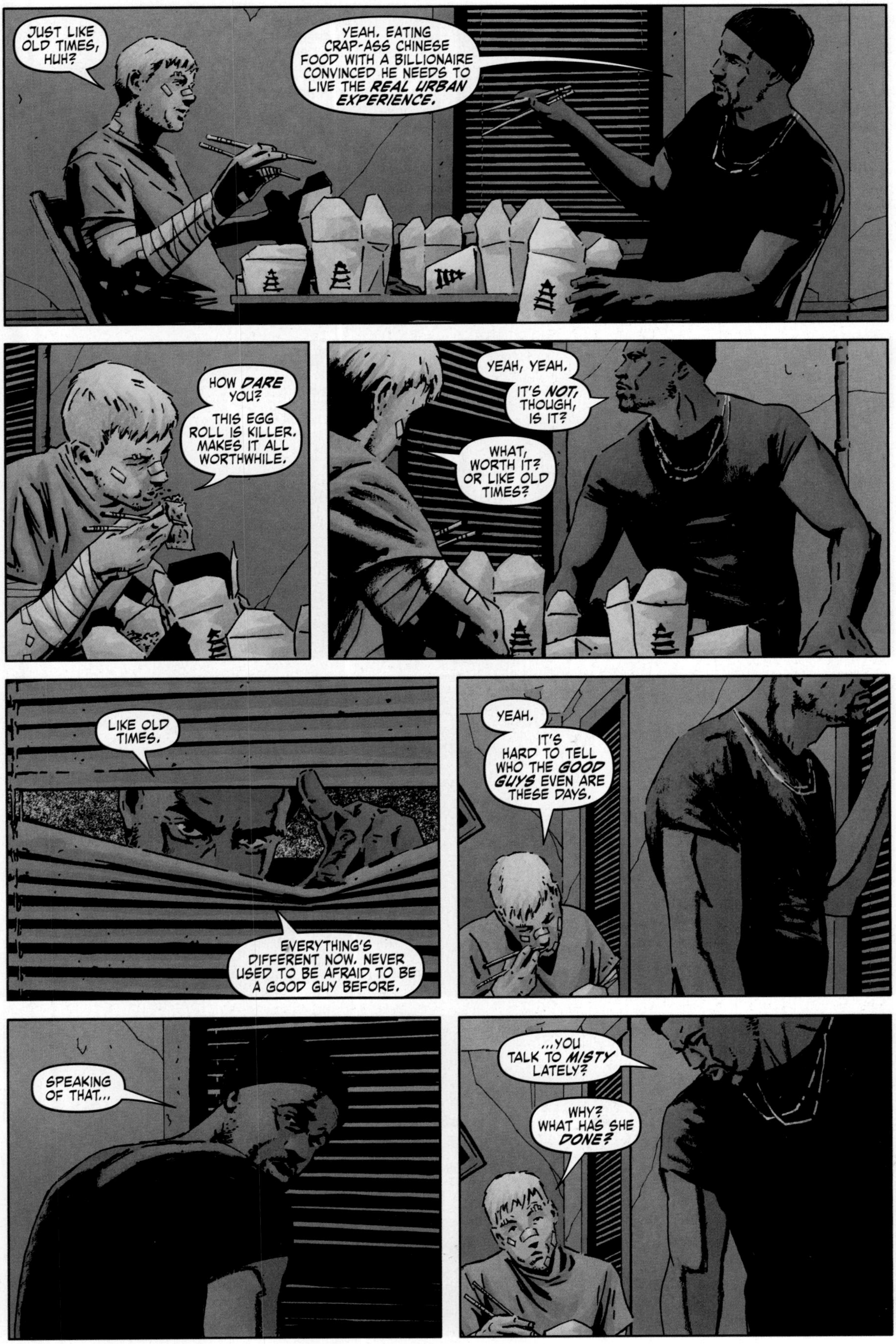
JUST LIKE OLD TIMES, HUH?
YEAH. EATING CRAP-ASS CHINESE FOOD WITH A BILLIONAIRE CONVINCED HE NEEDS TO LIVE THE REAL URBAN EXPERIENCE.
HOW DARE YOU?
THIS EGG ROLL IS KILLER. MAKES IT ALL WORTHWHILE.
YEAH, YEAH.
IT'S NOT, THOUGH, IS IT?
WHAT, WORTH IT? OR LIKE OLD TIMES?
LIKE OLD TIMES.
EVERYTHING'S DIFFERENT NOW. NEVER USED TO BE AFRAID TO BE A GOOD GUY BEFORE.
YEAH.
IT'S HARD TO TELL WHO THE GOOD GUYS EVEN ARE THESE DAYS.
SPEAKING OF THAT...
...YOU TALK TO MISTY LATELY?
WHY? WHAT HAS SHE DONE?

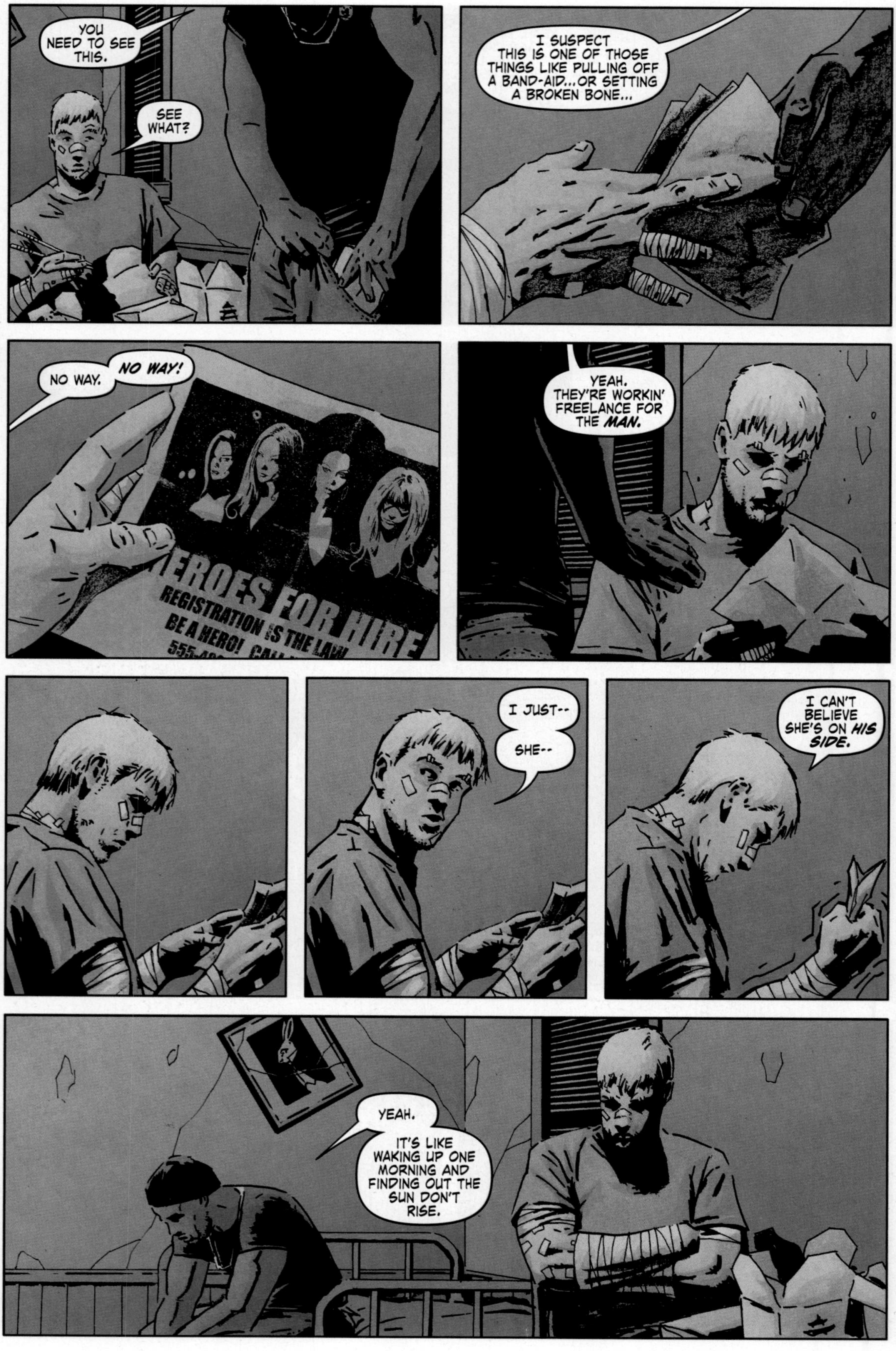
YOU NEED TO SEE THIS.
SEE WHAT?
I SUSPECT THIS IS ONE OF THOSE THINGS LIKE PULLING OFF A BAND-AID...OR SETTING A BROKEN BONE...
NO WAY.
NO WAY!
EROES FOR HIRE
REGISTRATION IS THE LAW
BE A HERO!
YEAH. THEY'RE WORKIN' FREELANCE FOR THE *MAN.*
I JUST--
SHE--
I CAN'T BELIEVE SHE'S ON *HIS SIDE.*
YEAH.
IT'S LIKE WAKING UP ONE MORNING AND FINDING OUT THE SUN DON'T RISE.

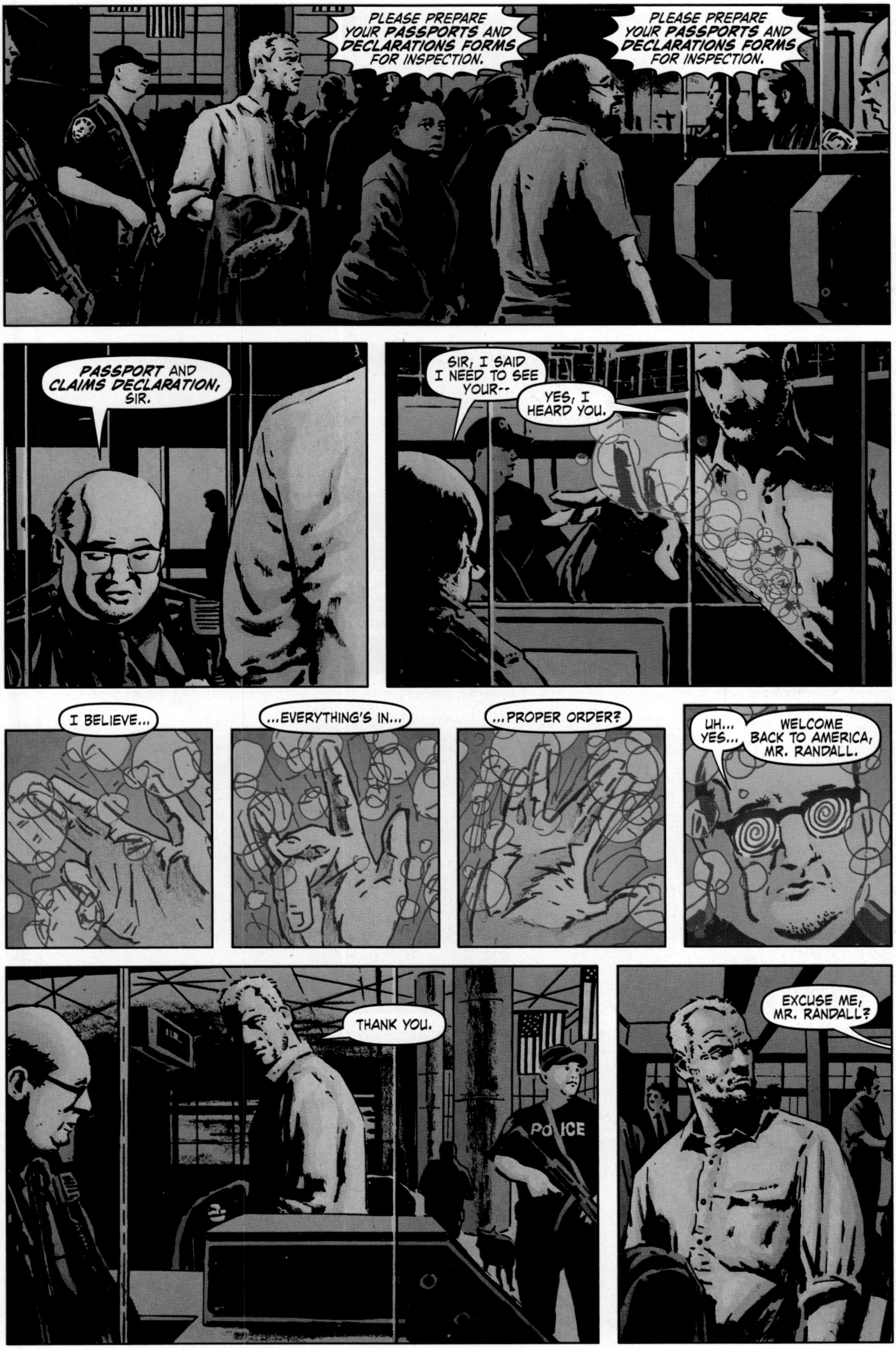
PLEASE PREPARE YOUR **PASSPORTS** AND **DECLARATIONS FORMS** FOR INSPECTION.
PLEASE PREPARE YOUR **PASSPORTS** AND **DECLARATIONS FORMS** FOR INSPECTION.
PASSPORT AND **CLAIMS DECLARATION,** SIR.
SIR, I SAID I NEED TO SEE YOUR--
YES, I HEARD YOU.
I BELIEVE...
...EVERYTHING'S IN...
...PROPER ORDER?
UH... YES...
WELCOME BACK TO AMERICA, MR. RANDALL.
THANK YOU.
POLICE
EXCUSE ME, MR. RANDALL?

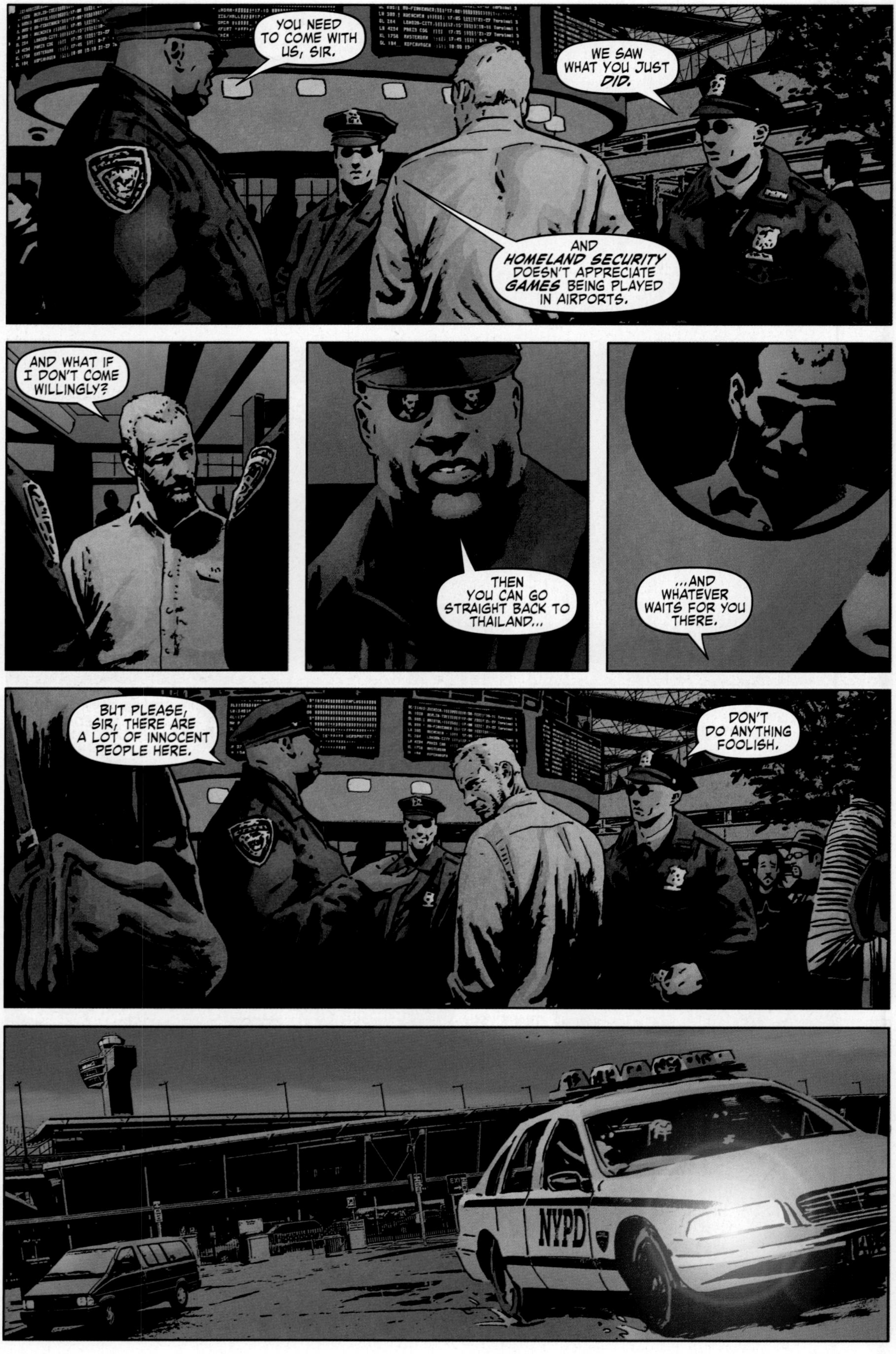
YOU NEED TO COME WITH US, SIR.
WE SAW WHAT YOU JUST *DID.*
AND *HOMELAND SECURITY* DOESN'T APPRECIATE *GAMES* BEING PLAYED IN AIRPORTS.
AND WHAT IF I DON'T COME WILLINGLY?
THEN YOU CAN GO STRAIGHT BACK TO THAILAND...
...AND WHATEVER WAITS FOR YOU THERE.
BUT PLEASE, SIR, THERE ARE A LOT OF INNOCENT PEOPLE HERE.
DON'T DO ANYTHING FOOLISH.
NYPD

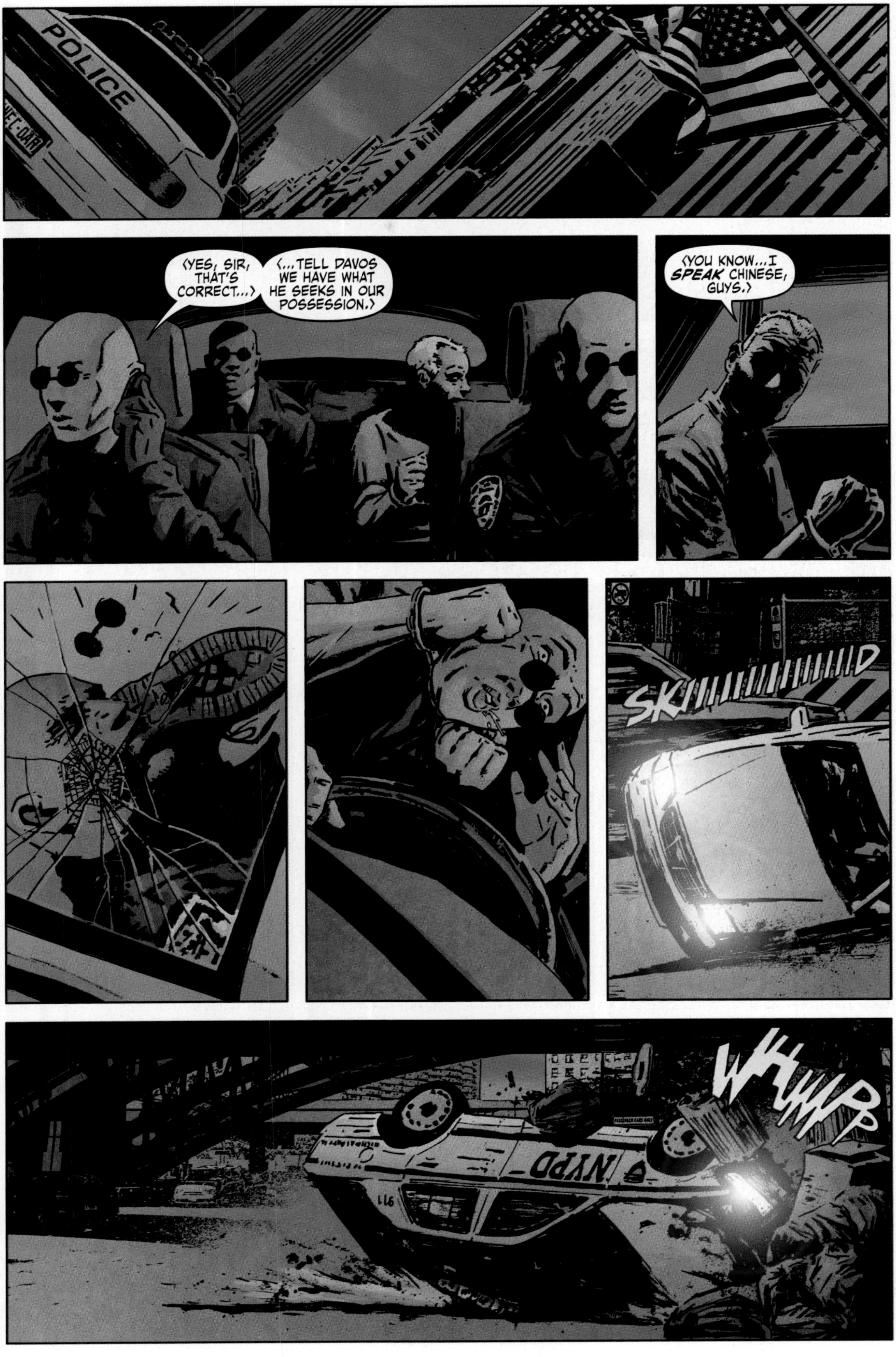

POLICE
‹YES, SIR, THAT'S CORRECT...›
‹...TELL DAVOS WE HAVE WHAT HE SEEKS IN OUR POSSESSION.›
‹YOU KNOW...I SPEAK CHINESE, GUYS.›
SKIIIIIIIIIIIIID
NYPD
WHUMP

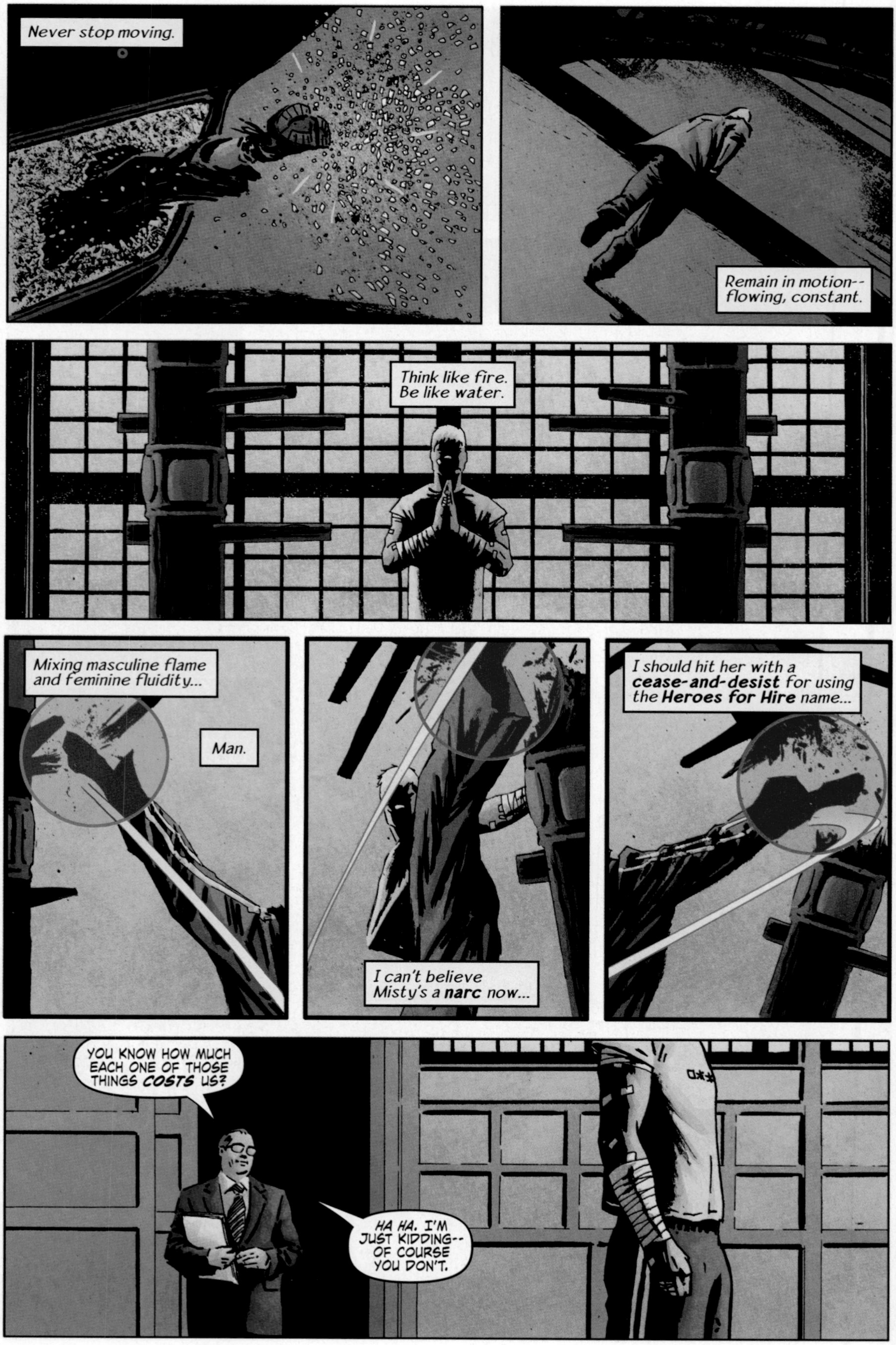
Never stop moving.
Remain in motion--
flowing, constant.
Think like fire.
Be like water.
Mixing masculine flame
and feminine fluidity...
Man.
I can't believe
Misty's a **narc** now...
I should hit her with a
cease-and-desist for using
the **Heroes for Hire** name...
YOU KNOW HOW MUCH
EACH ONE OF THOSE
THINGS ***COSTS*** US?
HA HA. I'M
JUST KIDDING--
OF COURSE
YOU DON'T.

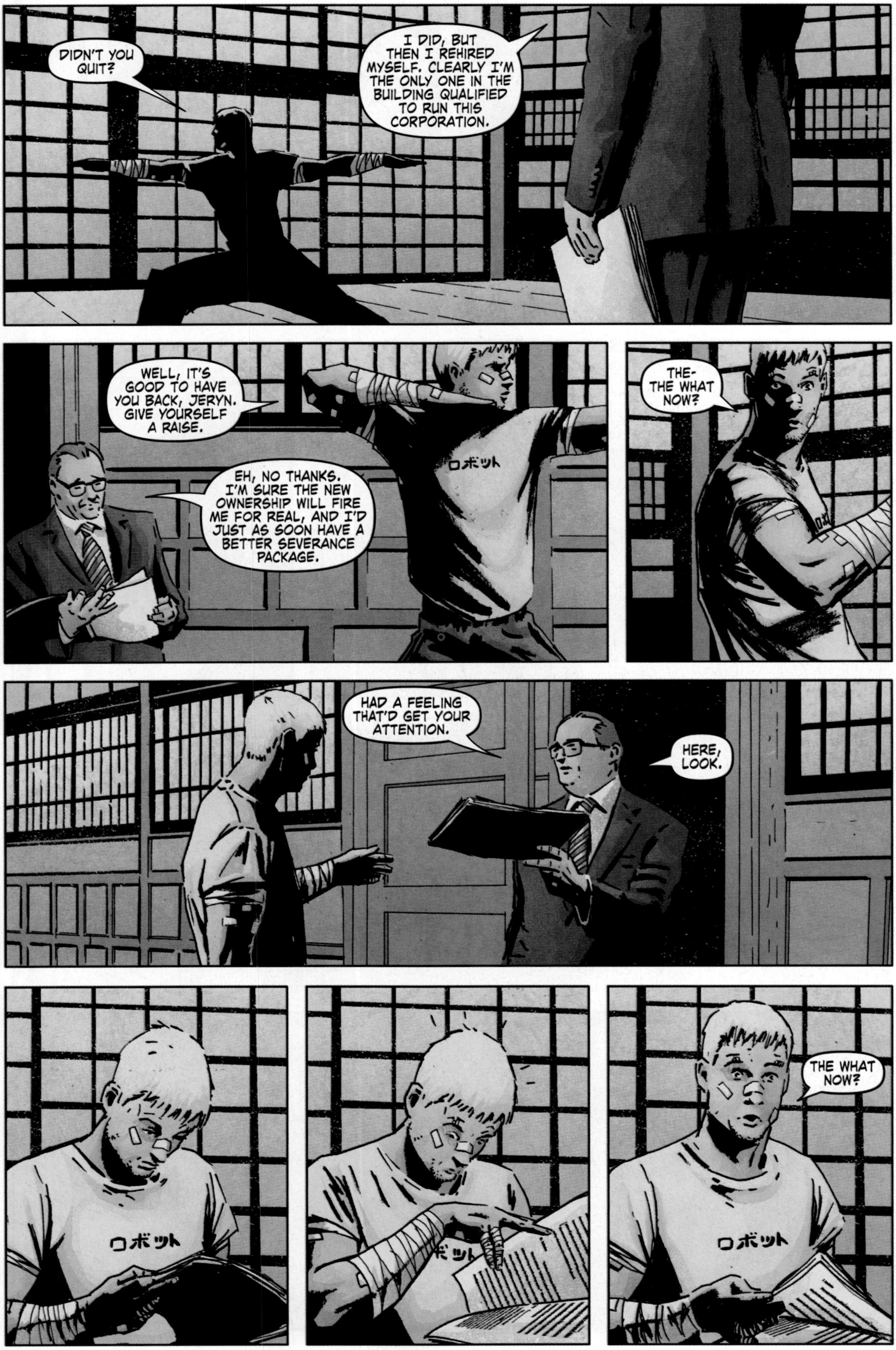
DIDN'T YOU QUIT?
I DID, BUT THEN I REHIRED MYSELF. CLEARLY I'M THE ONLY ONE IN THE BUILDING QUALIFIED TO RUN THIS CORPORATION.
WELL, IT'S GOOD TO HAVE YOU BACK, JERYN. GIVE YOURSELF A RAISE.
ロボット
EH, NO THANKS. I'M SURE THE NEW OWNERSHIP WILL FIRE ME FOR REAL, AND I'D JUST AS SOON HAVE A BETTER SEVERANCE PACKAGE.
THE- THE WHAT NOW?
HAD A FEELING THAT'D GET YOUR ATTENTION.
HERE, LOOK.
ロボット
ロボット
THE WHAT NOW?

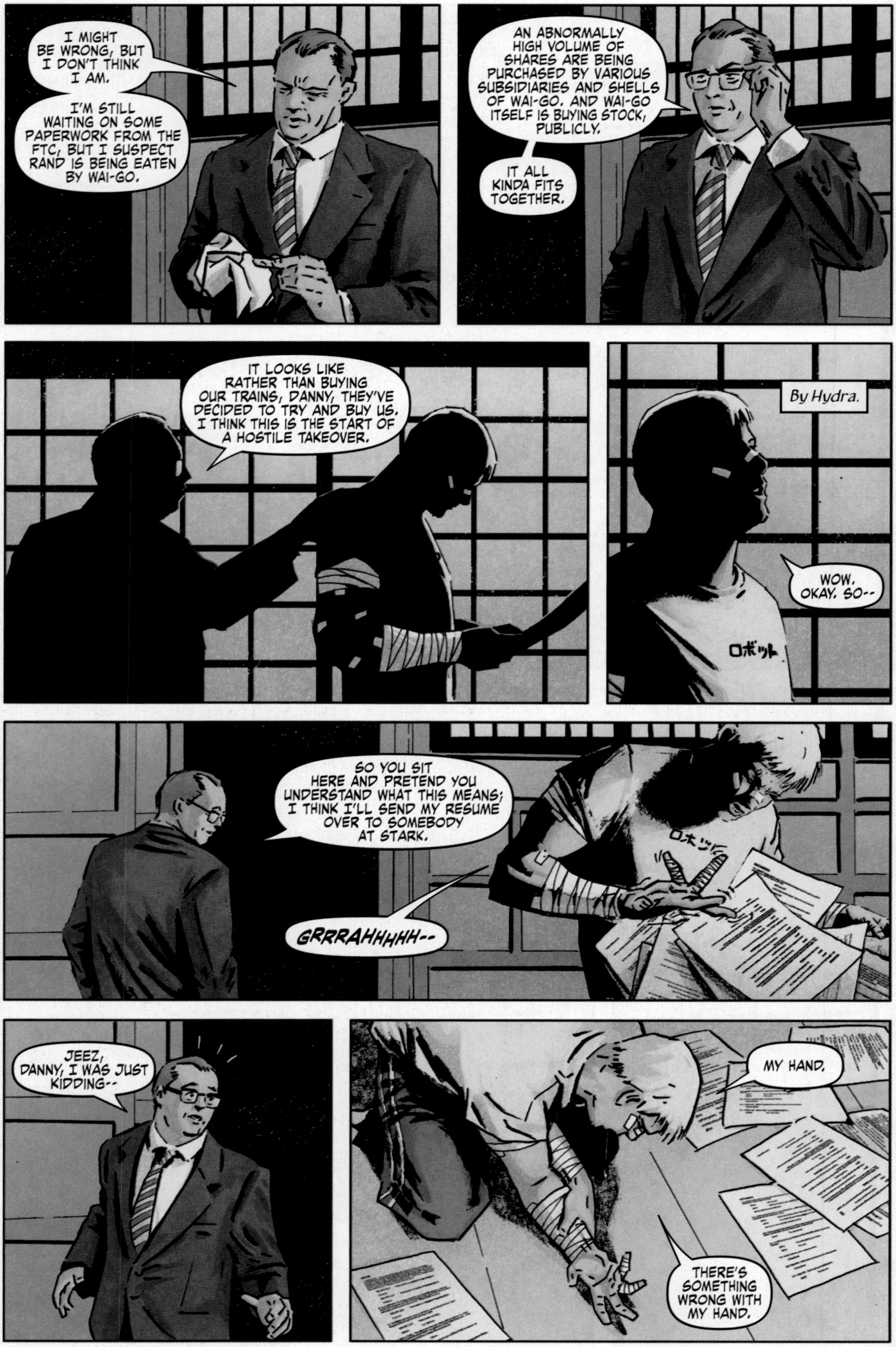
I MIGHT BE WRONG, BUT I DON'T THINK I AM.
I'M STILL WAITING ON SOME PAPERWORK FROM THE FTC, BUT I SUSPECT RAND IS BEING EATEN BY WAI-GO.
AN ABNORMALLY HIGH VOLUME OF SHARES ARE BEING PURCHASED BY VARIOUS SUBSIDIARIES AND SHELLS OF WAI-GO. AND WAI-GO ITSELF IS BUYING STOCK, PUBLICLY.
IT ALL KINDA FITS TOGETHER.
IT LOOKS LIKE RATHER THAN BUYING OUR TRAINS, DANNY, THEY'VE DECIDED TO TRY AND BUY US. I THINK THIS IS THE START OF A HOSTILE TAKEOVER.
By Hydra.
WOW. OKAY. SO--
ロボット
SO YOU SIT HERE AND PRETEND YOU UNDERSTAND WHAT THIS MEANS; I THINK I'LL SEND MY RESUME OVER TO SOMEBODY AT STARK.
GRRRAHHHHH--
JEEZ, DANNY, I WAS JUST KIDDING--
MY HAND.
THERE'S SOMETHING WRONG WITH MY HAND.

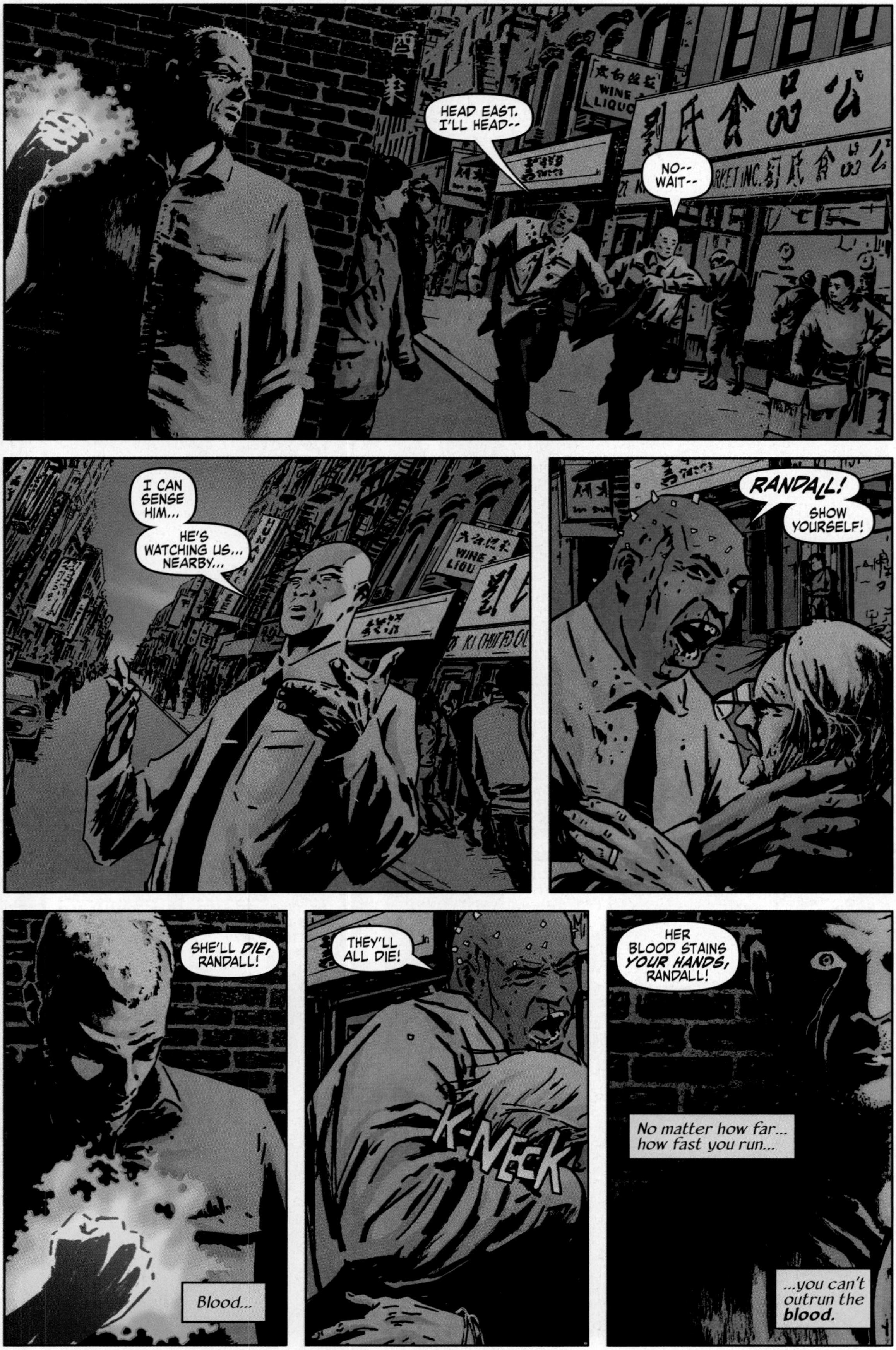
HEAD EAST. I'LL HEAD--
NO-- WAIT--
I CAN SENSE HIM...
HE'S WATCHING US... NEARBY...
RANDALL!
SHOW YOURSELF!
SHE'LL DIE, RANDALL!
Blood...
THEY'LL ALL DIE!
K-NECK
HER BLOOD STAINS YOUR HANDS, RANDALL!
No matter how far... how fast you run...
...you can't outrun the blood.

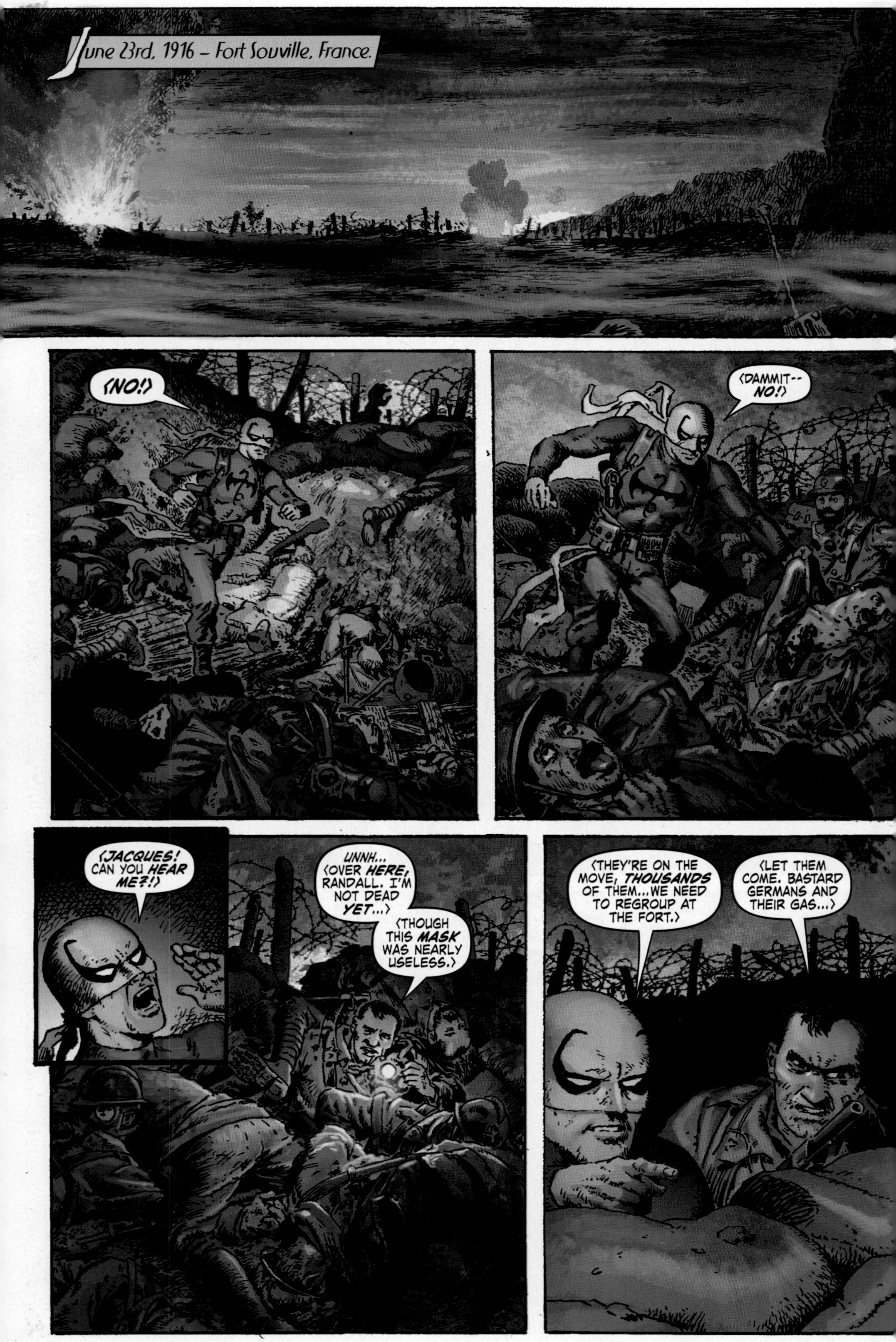
June 23rd, 1916 – Fort Souville, France.
‹NO!›
‹DAMMIT-- NO!›
‹JACQUES! CAN YOU HEAR ME?!›
UNNH... ‹OVER HERE, RANDALL. I'M NOT DEAD YET...›
‹THOUGH THIS MASK WAS NEARLY USELESS.›
‹THEY'RE ON THE MOVE, THOUSANDS OF THEM...WE NEED TO REGROUP AT THE FORT.›
‹LET THEM COME. BASTARD GERMANS AND THEIR GAS...›

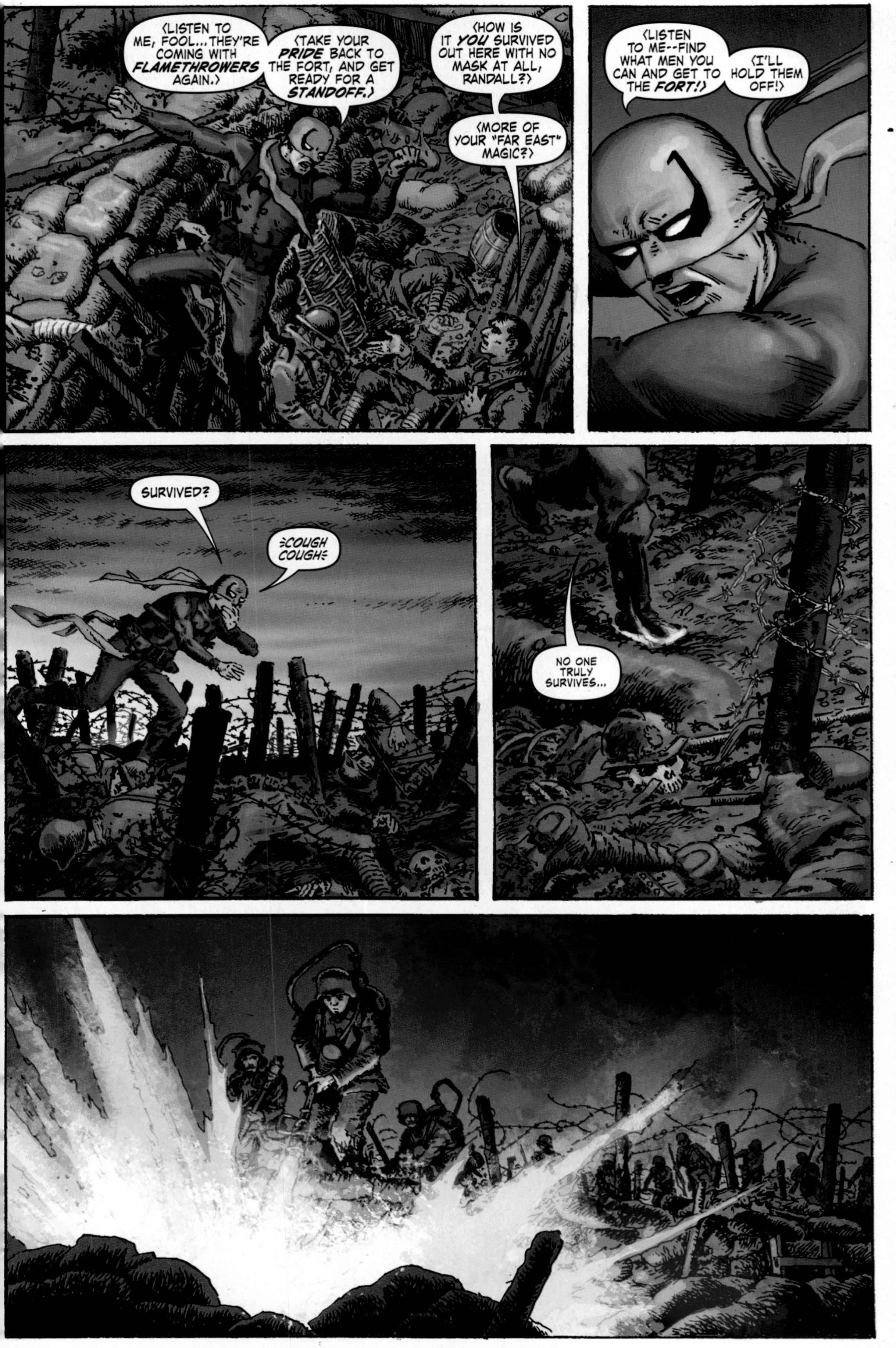
<LISTEN TO ME, FOOL... THEY'RE COMING WITH FLAMETHROWERS AGAIN.>
<TAKE YOUR PRIDE BACK TO THE FORT, AND GET READY FOR A STANDOFF.>
<HOW IS IT YOU SURVIVED OUT HERE WITH NO MASK AT ALL, RANDALL?>
<MORE OF YOUR "FAR EAST" MAGIC?>
<LISTEN TO ME--FIND WHAT MEN YOU CAN AND GET TO THE FORT!>
<I'LL HOLD THEM OFF!>
SURVIVED?
=COUGH COUGH=
NO ONE TRULY SURVIVES...

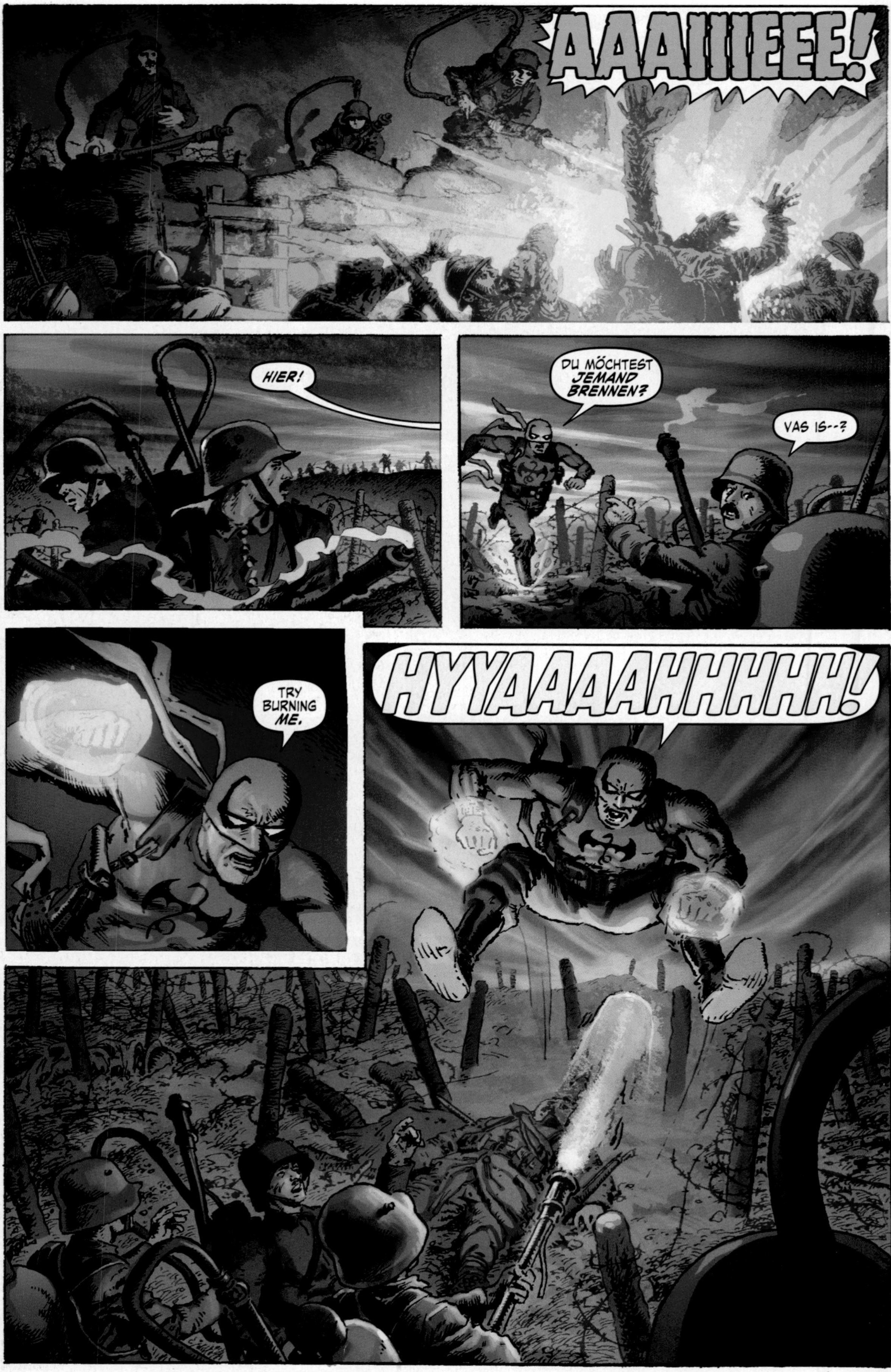
AAAIIIEEE!
HIER!
DU MÖCHTEST *JEMAND BRENNEN?*
VAS IS--?
TRY BURNING *ME.*
HYYAAAAAHHHHH!

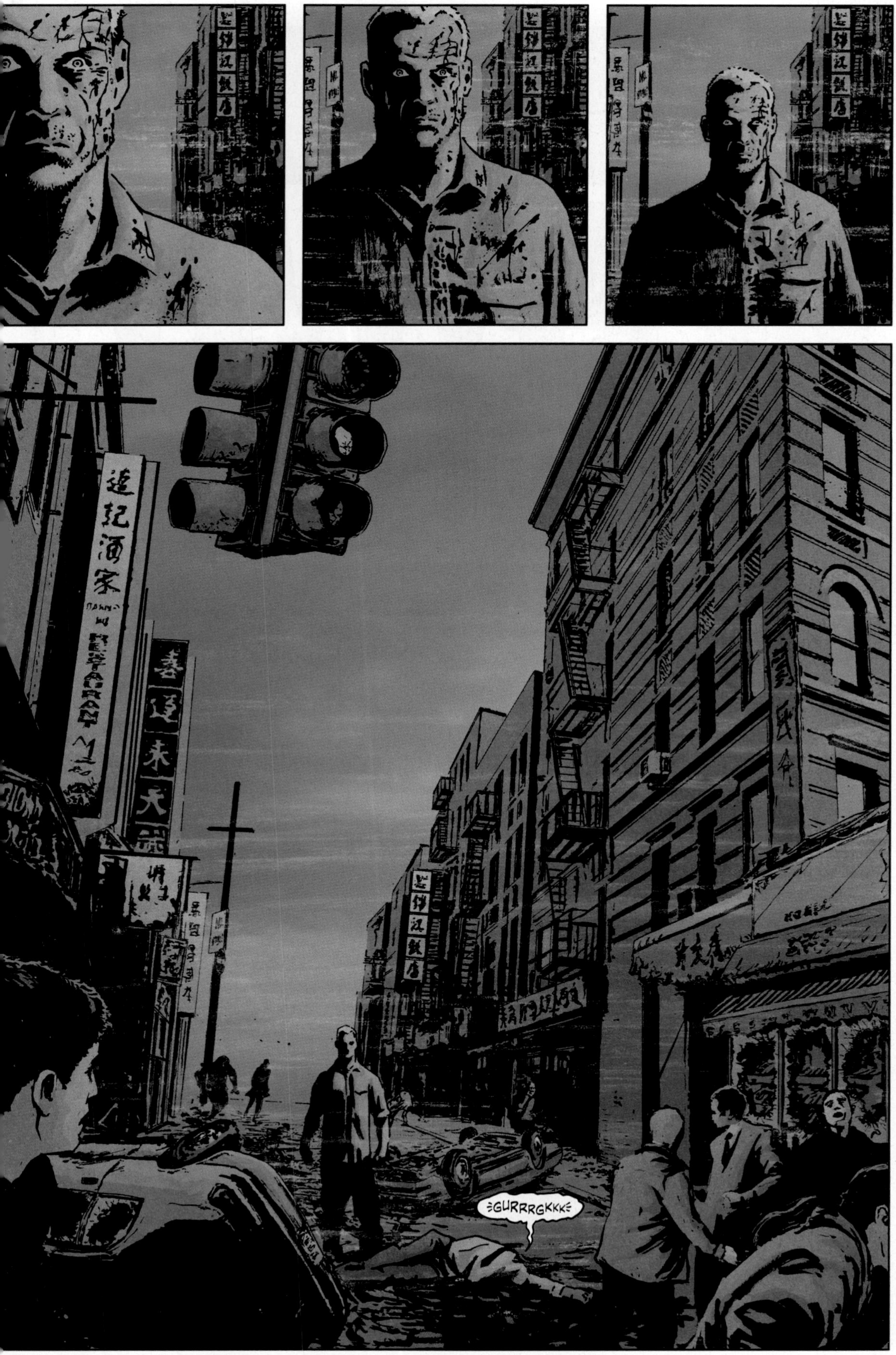
GURRRGKKK

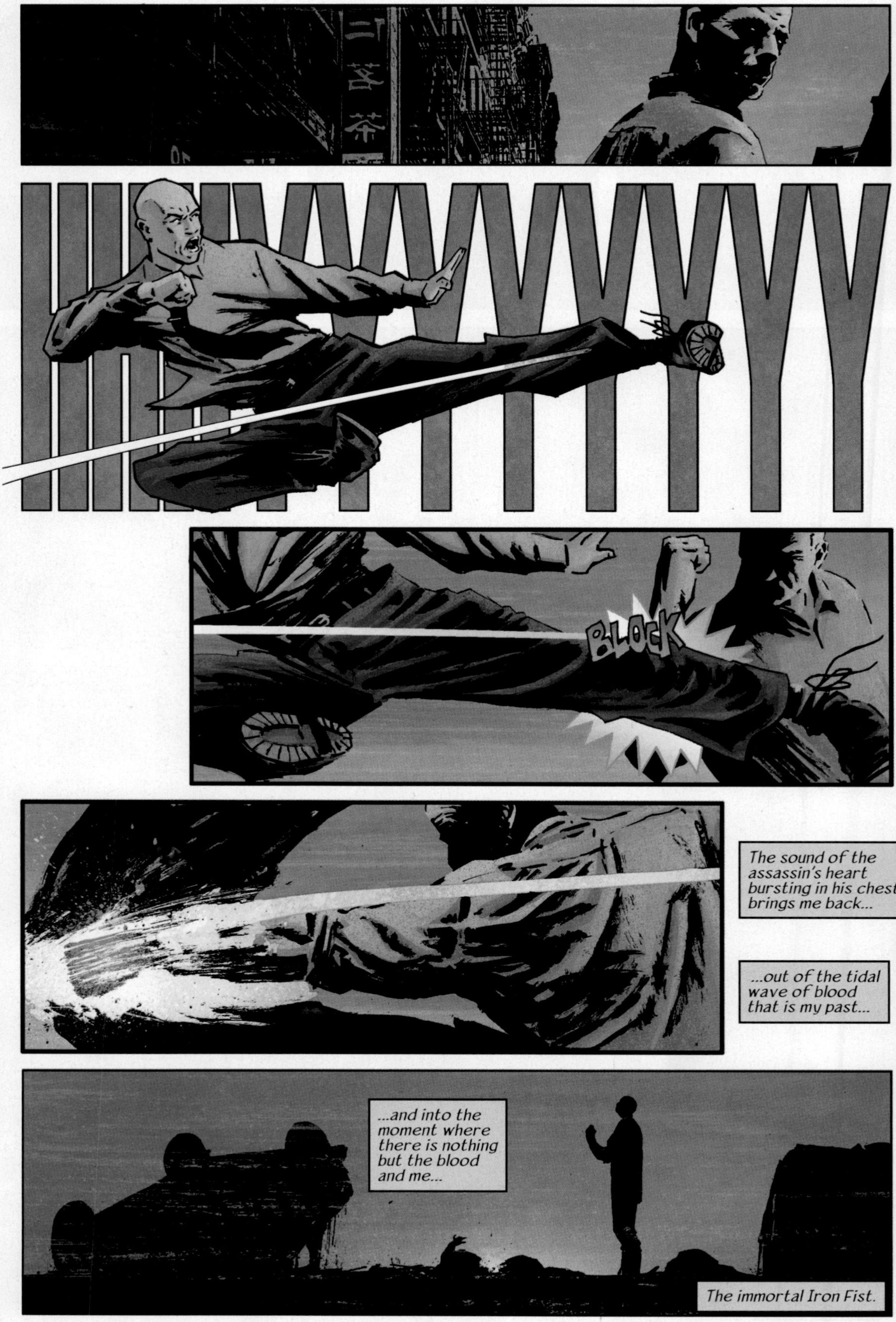
BLOCK
The sound of the assassin's heart bursting in his chest brings me back...
...out of the tidal wave of blood that is my past...
...and into the moment where there is nothing but the blood and me...
The immortal Iron Fist.

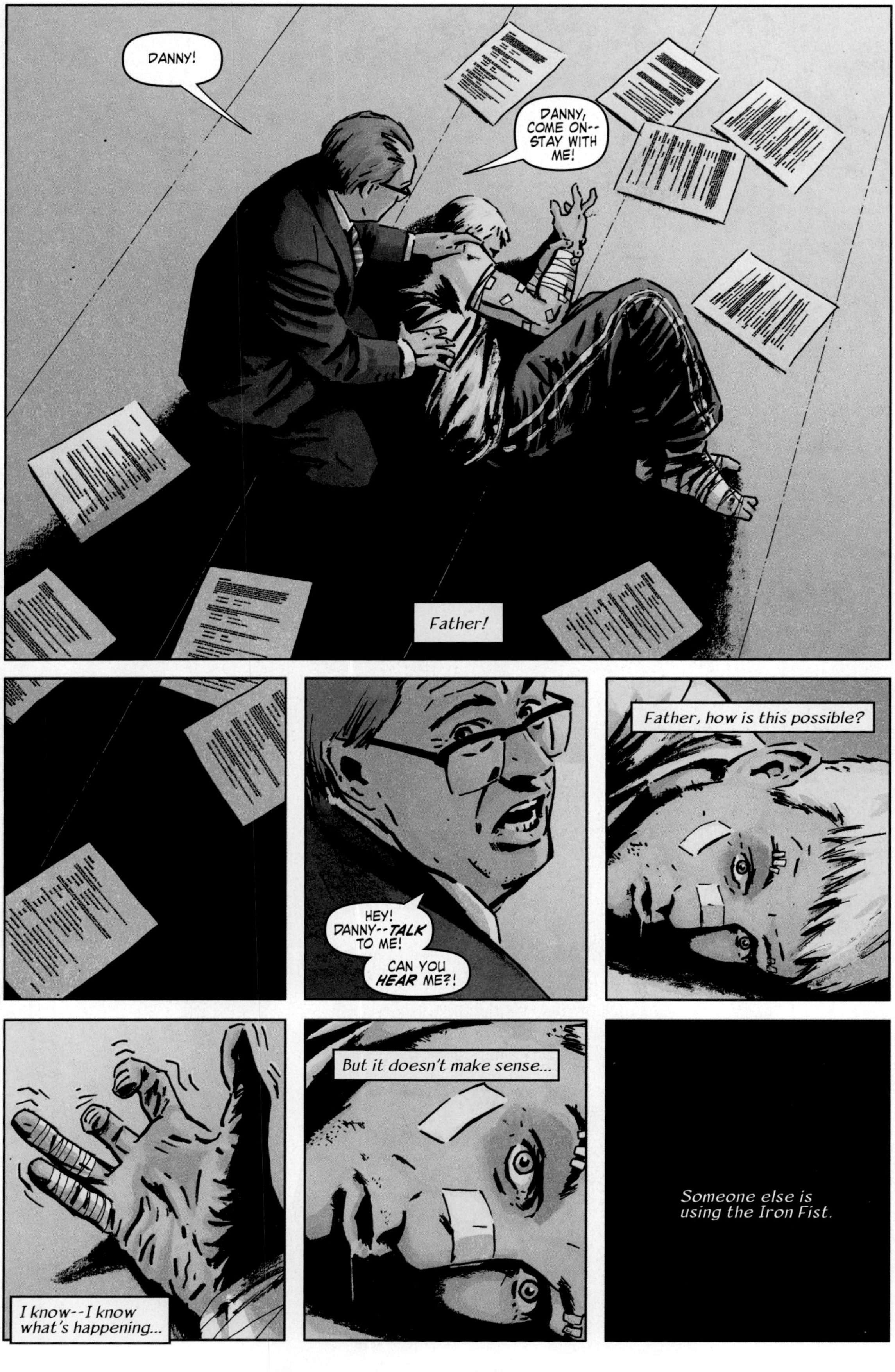
DANNY!
DANNY, COME ON-- STAY WITH ME!
Father!
HEY! DANNY--TALK TO ME!
CAN YOU HEAR ME?!
Father, how is this possible?
I know--I know what's happening...
But it doesn't make sense...
Someone else is using the Iron Fist.

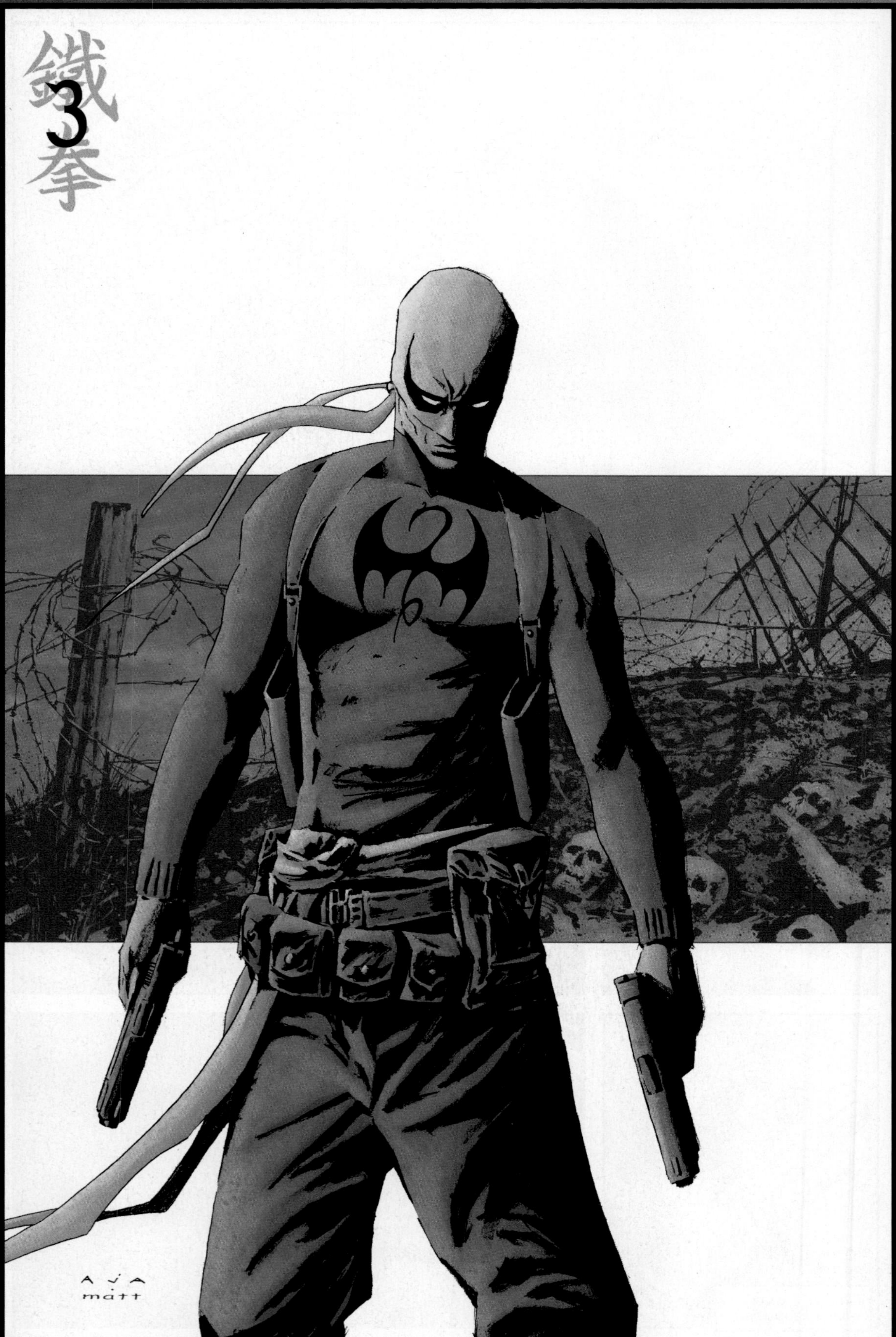
鐵拳
3
AJA
matt

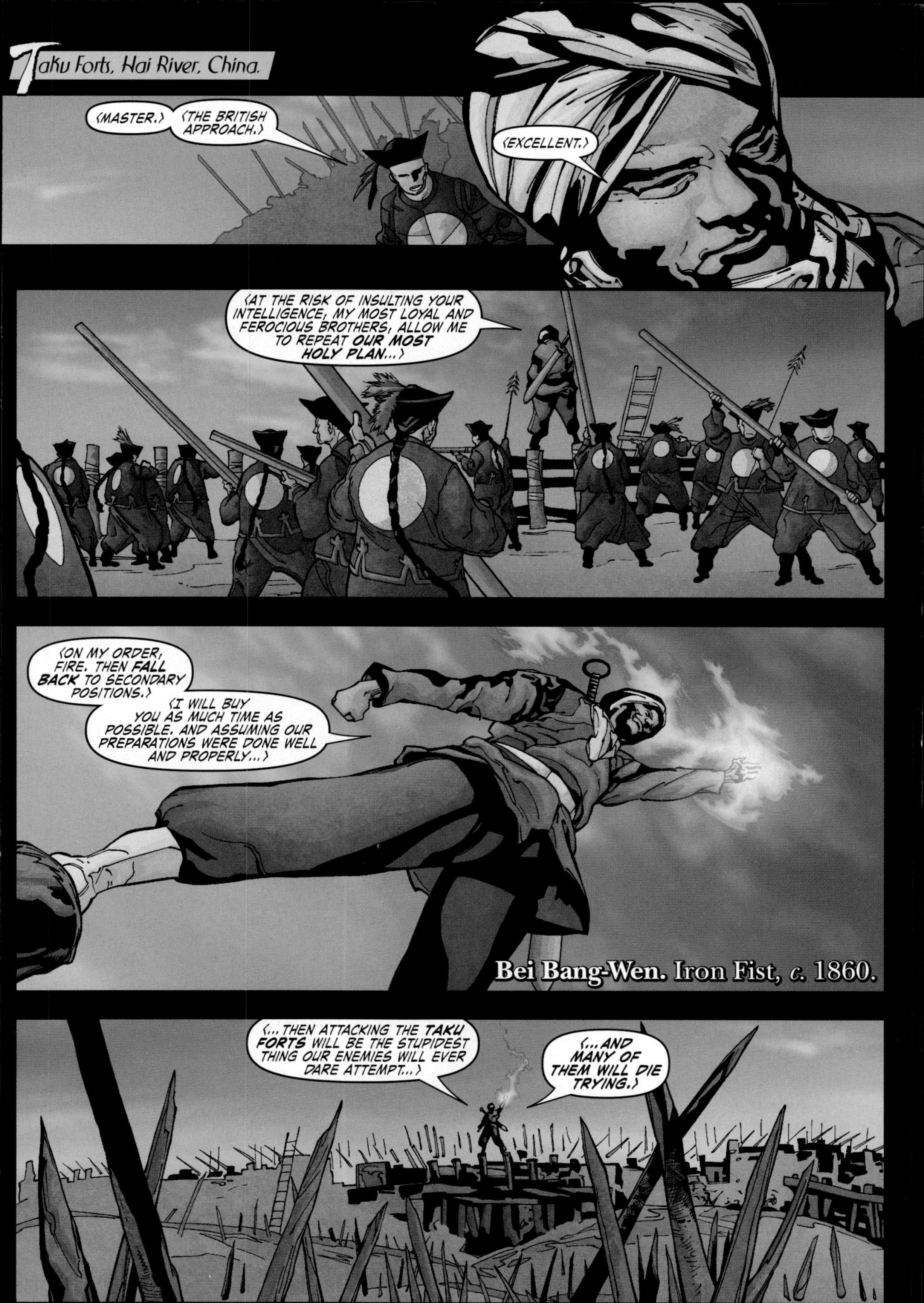
Taku Forts, Hai River, China.
‹MASTER.›
‹THE BRITISH APPROACH.›
‹EXCELLENT.›
‹AT THE RISK OF INSULTING YOUR INTELLIGENCE, MY MOST LOYAL AND FEROCIOUS BROTHERS, ALLOW ME TO REPEAT OUR MOST HOLY PLAN...›
‹ON MY ORDER, FIRE. THEN FALL BACK TO SECONDARY POSITIONS.›
‹I WILL BUY YOU AS MUCH TIME AS POSSIBLE. AND ASSUMING OUR PREPARATIONS WERE DONE WELL AND PROPERLY...›
Bei Bang-Wen. Iron Fist, c. 1860.
‹...THEN ATTACKING THE TAKU FORTS WILL BE THE STUPIDEST THING OUR ENEMIES WILL EVER DARE ATTEMPT...›
‹...AND MANY OF THEM WILL DIE TRYING.›

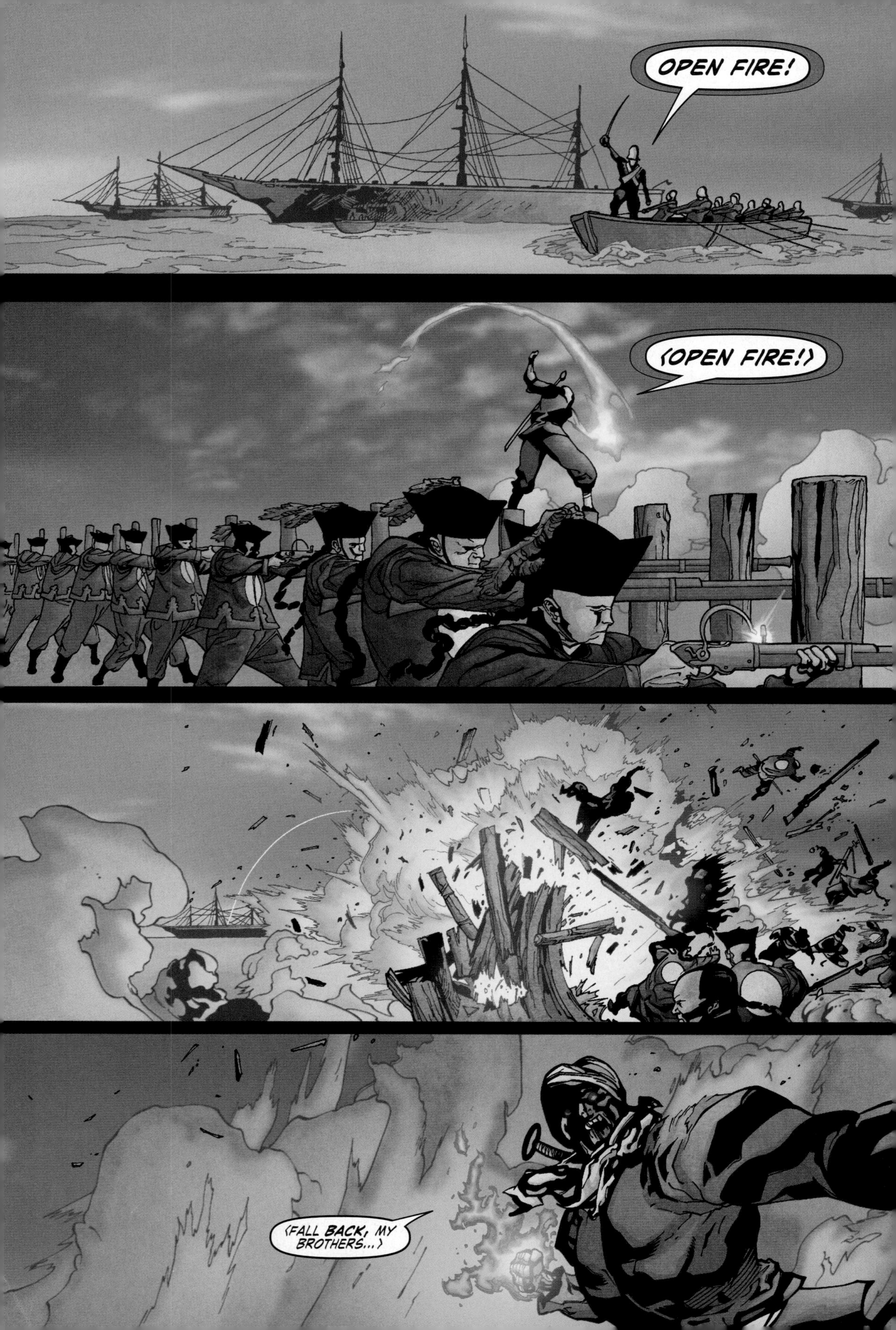
OPEN FIRE!
<OPEN FIRE!>
<FALL BACK, MY BROTHERS...>

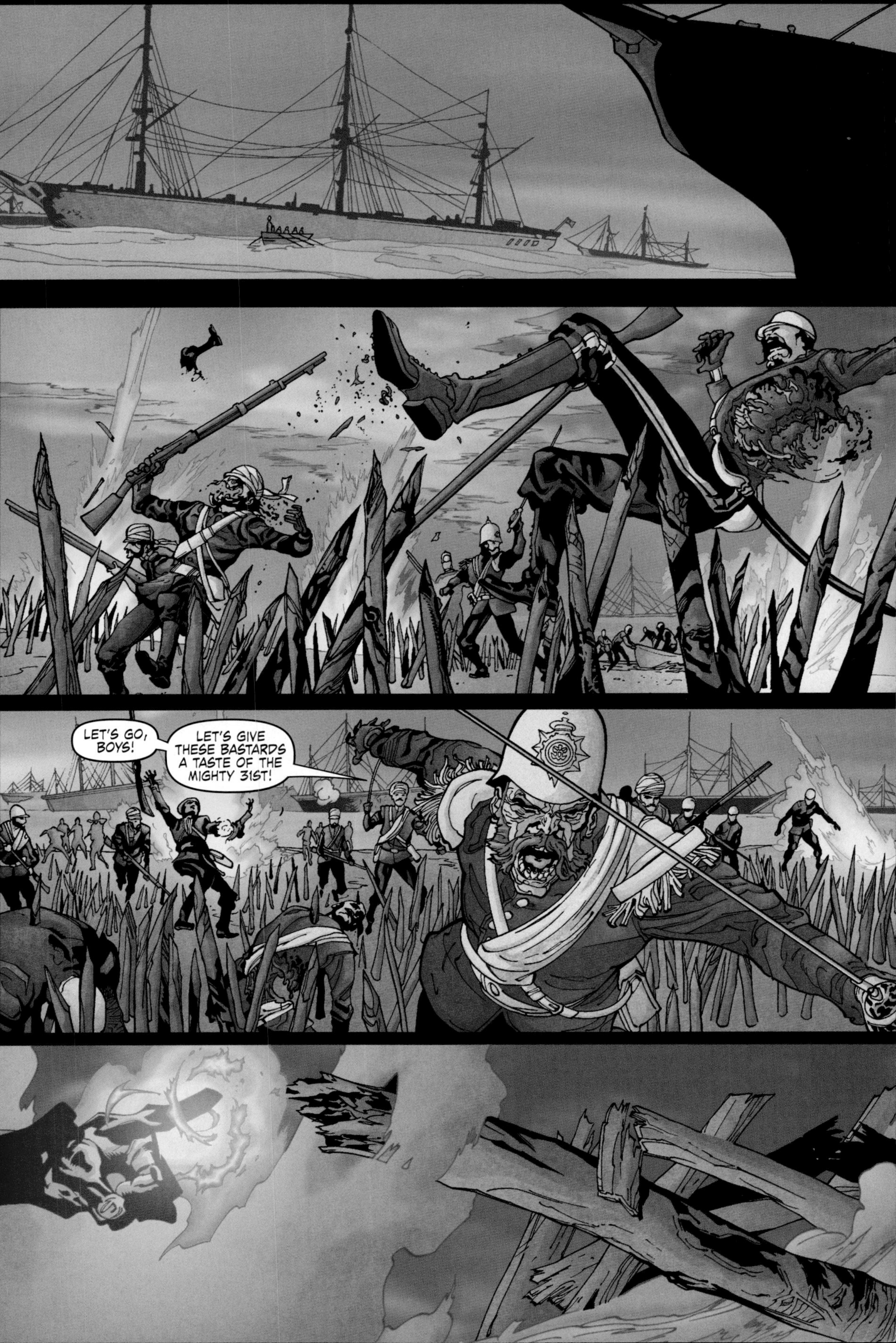
LET'S GO, BOYS!
LET'S GIVE THESE BASTARDS A TASTE OF THE MIGHTY 31ST!

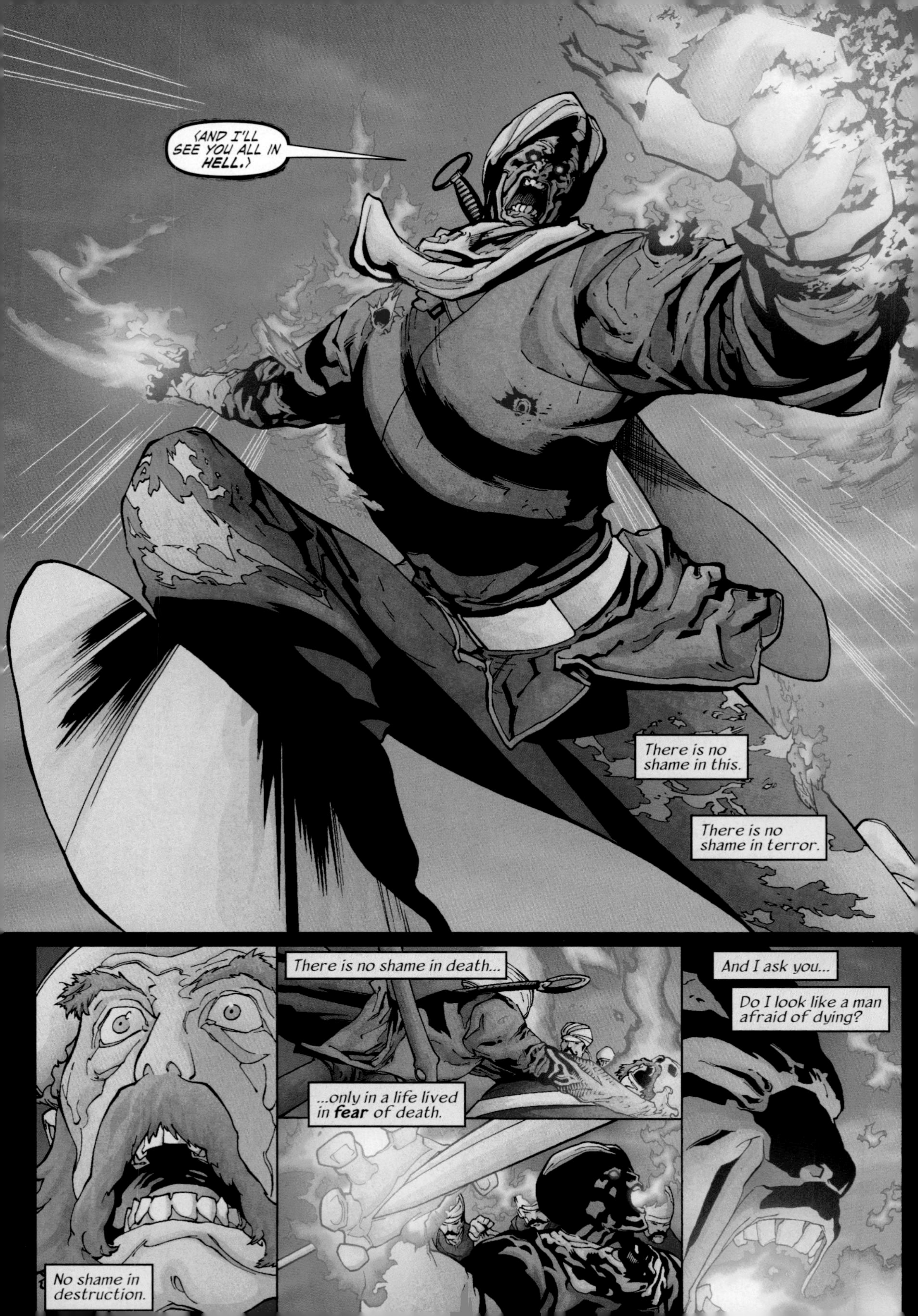

‹AND I'LL SEE YOU ALL IN HELL.›
There is no shame in this.
There is no shame in terror.
No shame in destruction.
There is no shame in death...
...only in a life lived in fear of death.
And I ask you...
Do I look like a man afraid of dying?

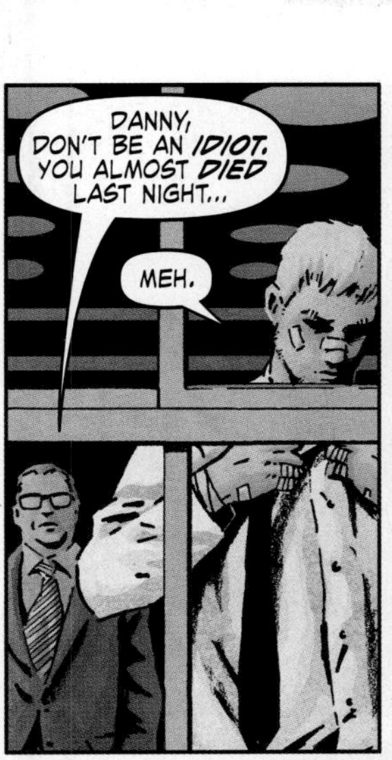
DANNY, DON'T BE AN *IDIOT*. YOU ALMOST *DIED* LAST NIGHT...
MEH.
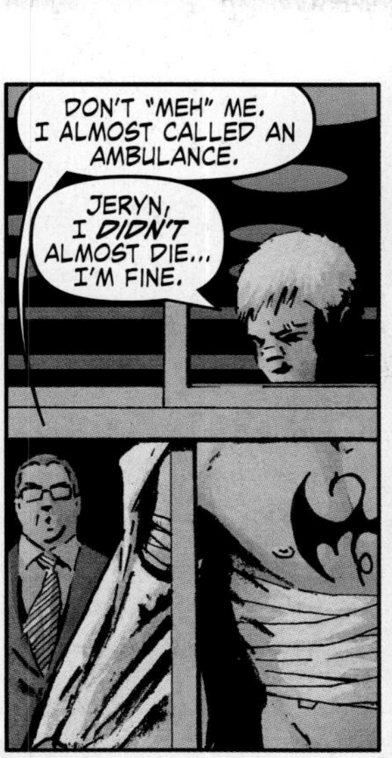
DON'T "MEH" ME. I ALMOST CALLED AN AMBULANCE.
JERYN, I *DIDN'T* ALMOST DIE... I'M FINE.
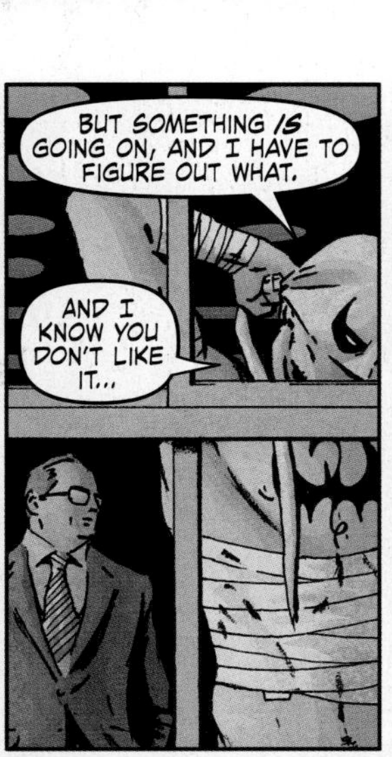
BUT SOMETHING *IS* GOING ON, AND I HAVE TO FIGURE OUT WHAT.
AND I KNOW YOU DON'T LIKE IT...
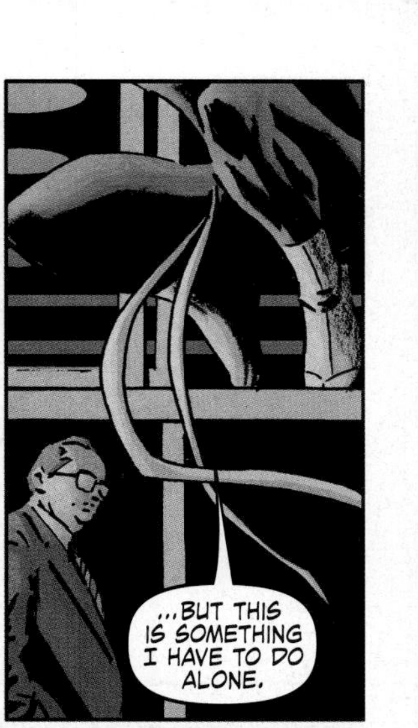
...BUT THIS IS SOMETHING I HAVE TO DO ALONE.
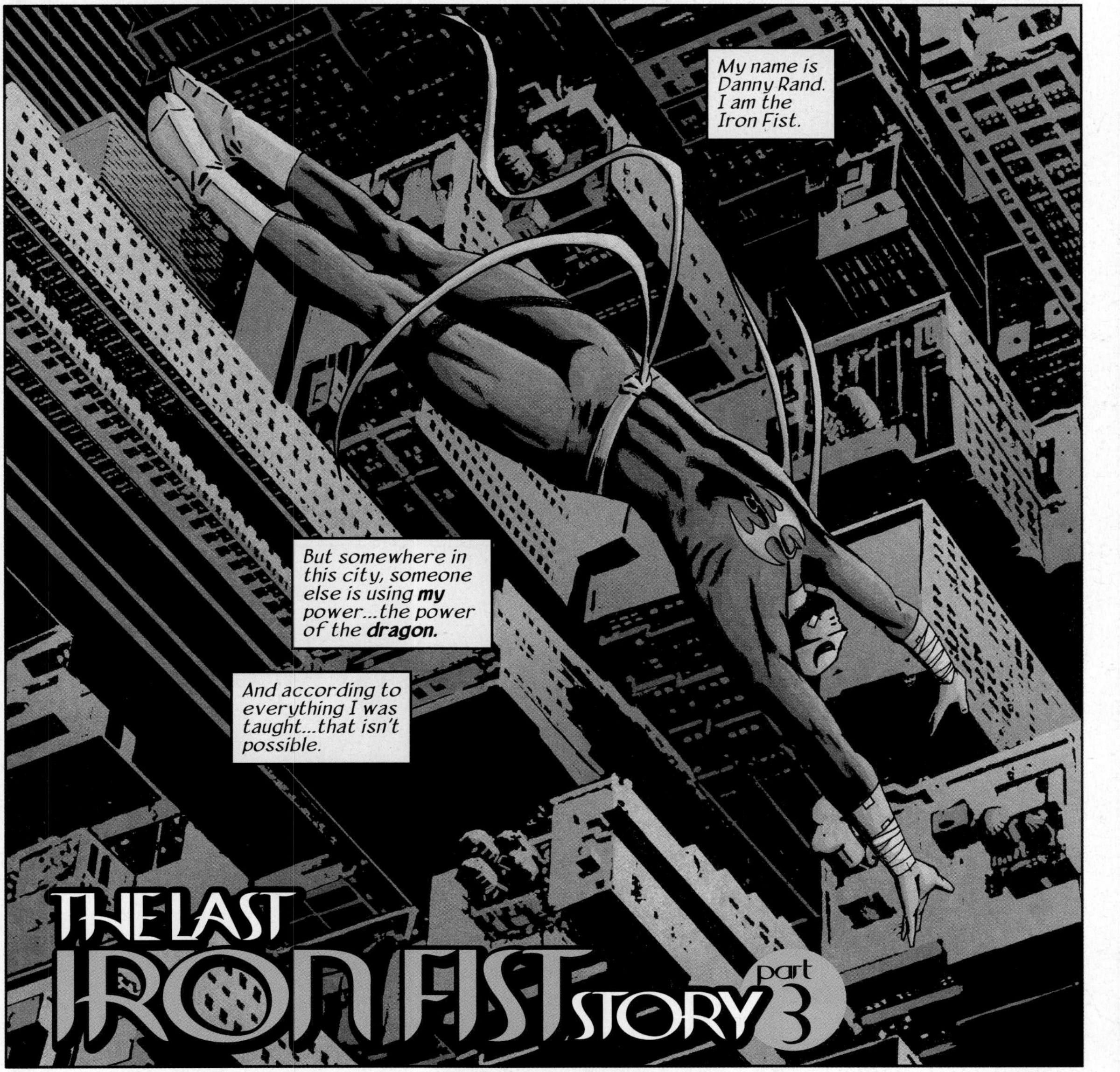
My name is Danny Rand. I am the Iron Fist.
But somewhere in this city, someone else is using **my** power...the power of the **dragon.**
And according to everything I was taught...that isn't possible.
THE LAST IRON FIST STORY part 3

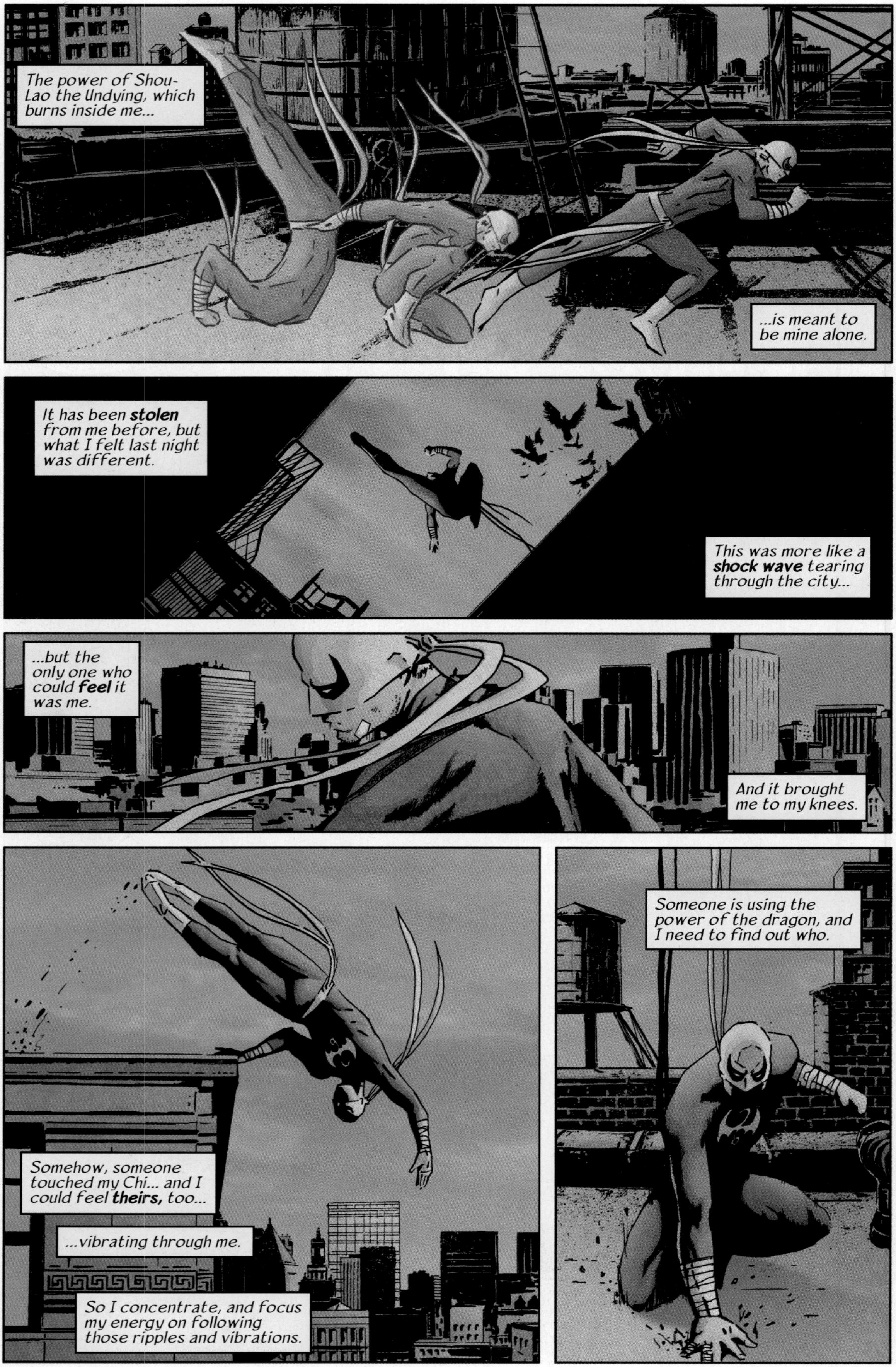
The power of Shou-Lao the Undying, which burns inside me...
...is meant to be mine alone.
It has been **stolen** from me before, but what I felt last night was different.
This was more like a **shock wave** tearing through the city...
...but the only one who could **feel** it was me.
And it brought me to my knees.
Somehow, someone touched my Chi... and I could feel **theirs,** too...
...vibrating through me.
So I concentrate, and focus my energy on following those ripples and vibrations.
Someone is using the power of the dragon, and I need to find out who.

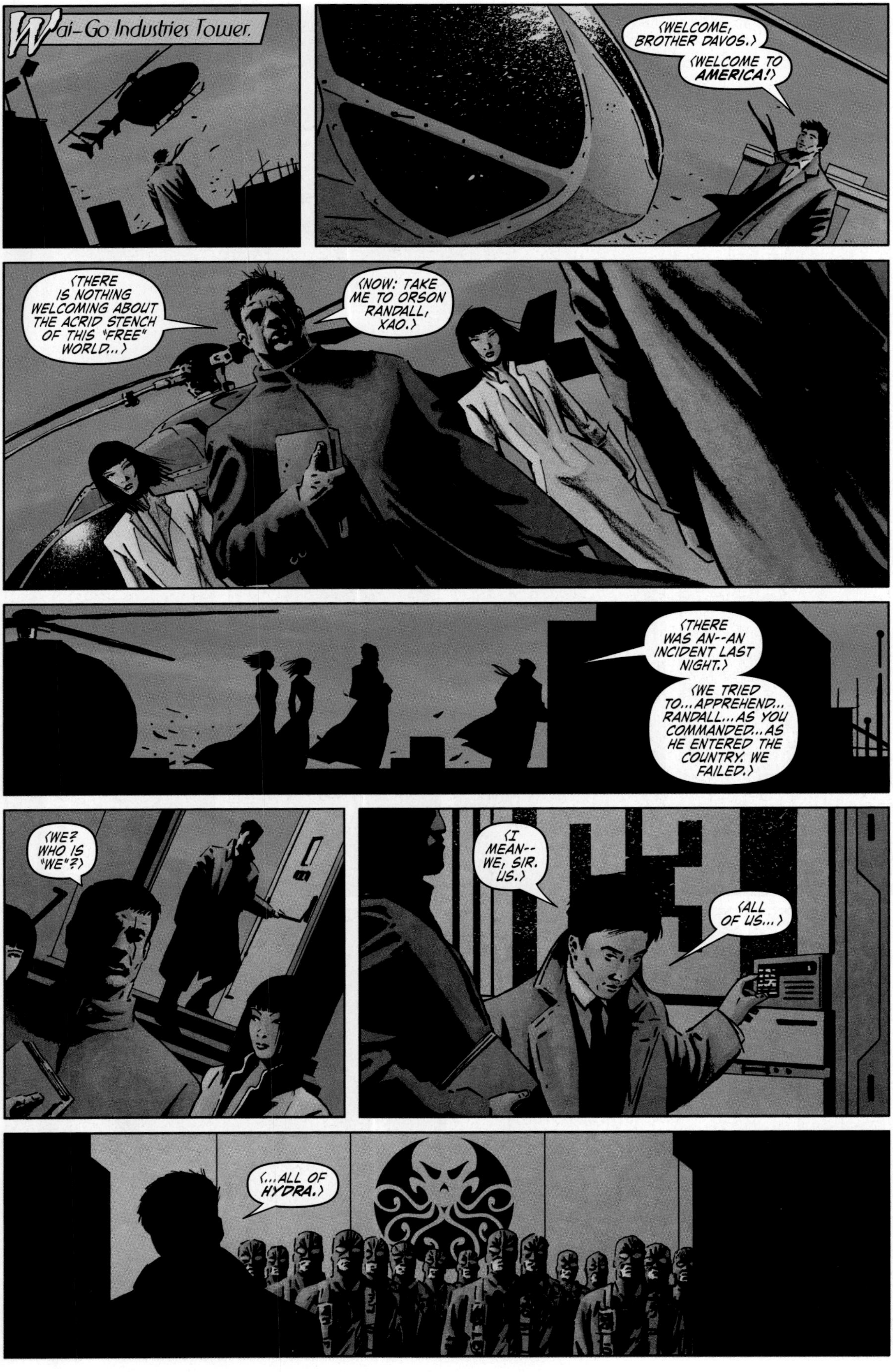

Wai-Go Industries Tower.
⟨WELCOME, BROTHER DAVOS.⟩
⟨WELCOME TO AMERICA!⟩
⟨THERE IS NOTHING WELCOMING ABOUT THE ACRID STENCH OF THIS "FREE" WORLD...⟩
⟨NOW: TAKE ME TO ORSON RANDALL, XAO.⟩
⟨THERE WAS AN--AN INCIDENT LAST NIGHT.⟩
⟨WE TRIED TO...APPREHEND... RANDALL...AS YOU COMMANDED...AS HE ENTERED THE COUNTRY. WE FAILED.⟩
⟨WE? WHO IS "WE"?⟩
⟨I MEAN-- WE, SIR. US.⟩
⟨ALL OF US...⟩
⟨...ALL OF HYDRA.⟩

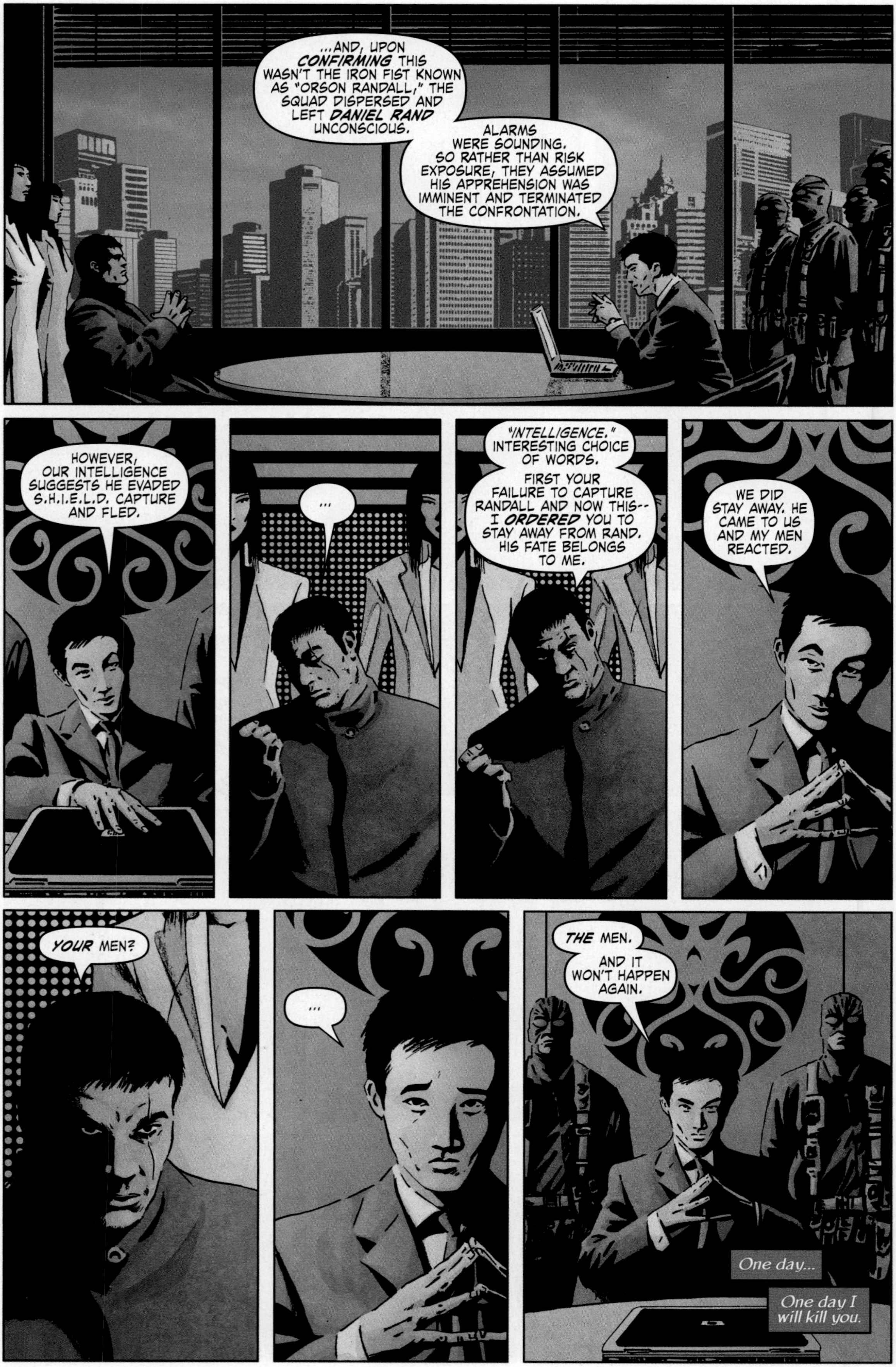
...AND, UPON CONFIRMING THIS WASN'T THE IRON FIST KNOWN AS "ORSON RANDALL," THE SQUAD DISPERSED AND LEFT DANIEL RAND UNCONSCIOUS.
ALARMS WERE SOUNDING. SO RATHER THAN RISK EXPOSURE, THEY ASSUMED HIS APPREHENSION WAS IMMINENT AND TERMINATED THE CONFRONTATION.
HOWEVER, OUR INTELLIGENCE SUGGESTS HE EVADED S.H.I.E.L.D. CAPTURE AND FLED.
...
"INTELLIGENCE." INTERESTING CHOICE OF WORDS.
FIRST YOUR FAILURE TO CAPTURE RANDALL AND NOW THIS-- I ORDERED YOU TO STAY AWAY FROM RAND. HIS FATE BELONGS TO ME.
WE DID STAY AWAY. HE CAME TO US AND MY MEN REACTED.
YOUR MEN?
...
THE MEN.
AND IT WON'T HAPPEN AGAIN.
One day...
One day I will kill you.

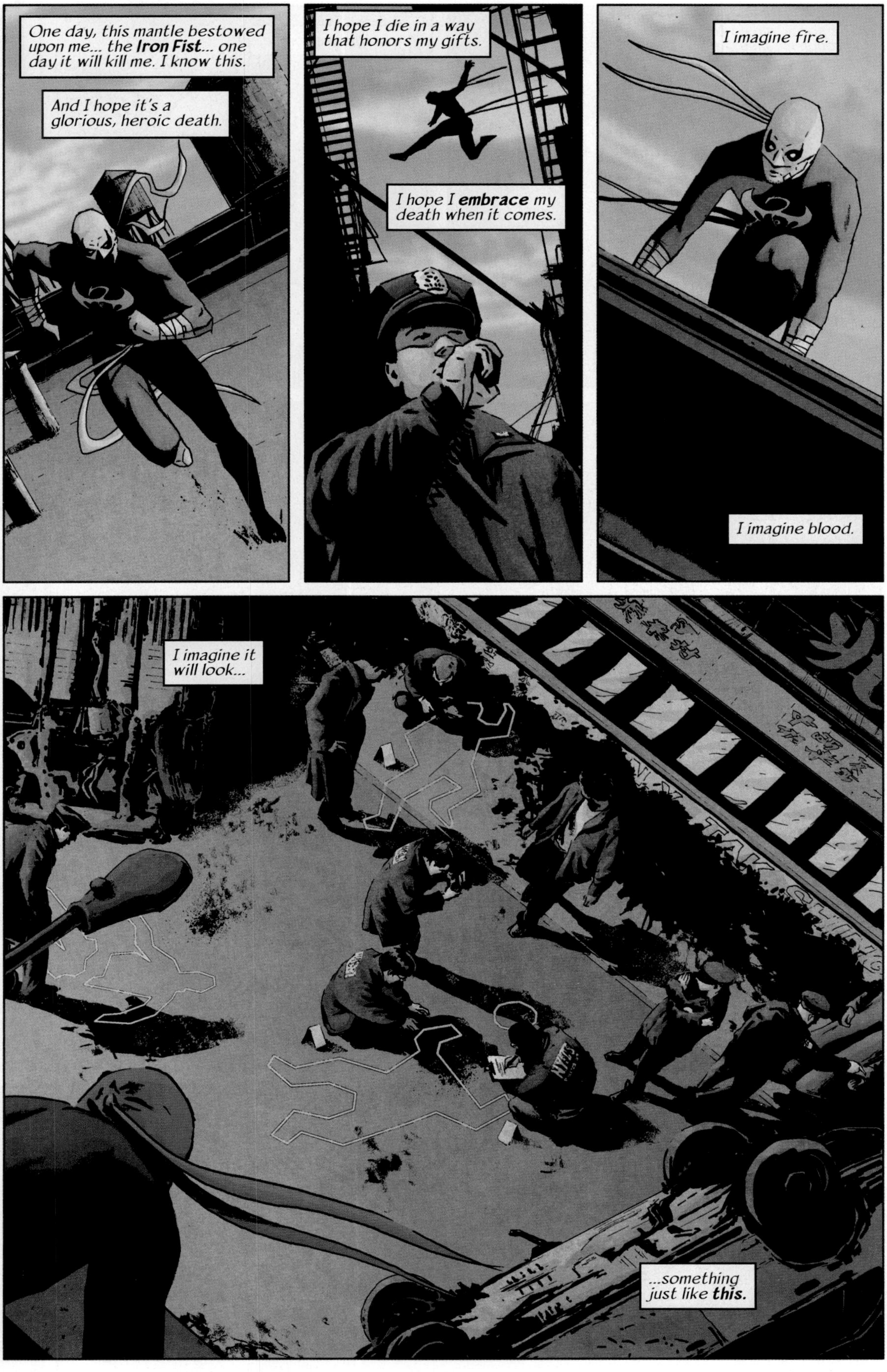
One day, this mantle bestowed upon me... the **Iron Fist**... one day it will kill me. I know this.
And I hope it's a glorious, heroic death.
I hope I die in a way that honors my gifts.
I hope I **embrace** my death when it comes.
I imagine fire.
I imagine blood.
I imagine it will look...
...something just like **this.**

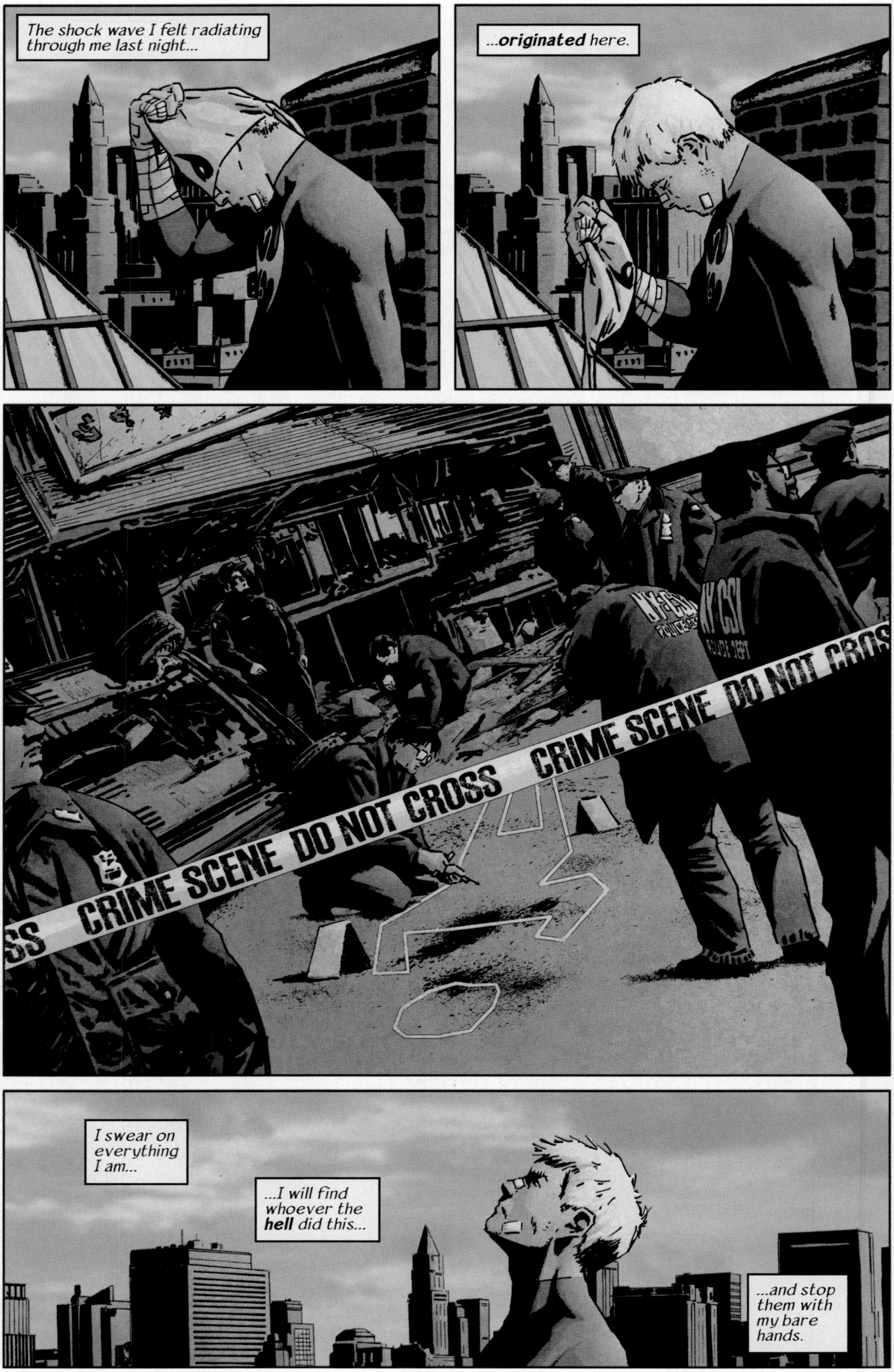

The shock wave I felt radiating through me last night...
...**originated** here.
CRIME SCENE DO NOT CROSS
NY CSI
CRIME SCENE DO NOT CROSS
I swear on everything I am...
...I will find whoever the **hell** did this...
...and stop them with my bare hands.

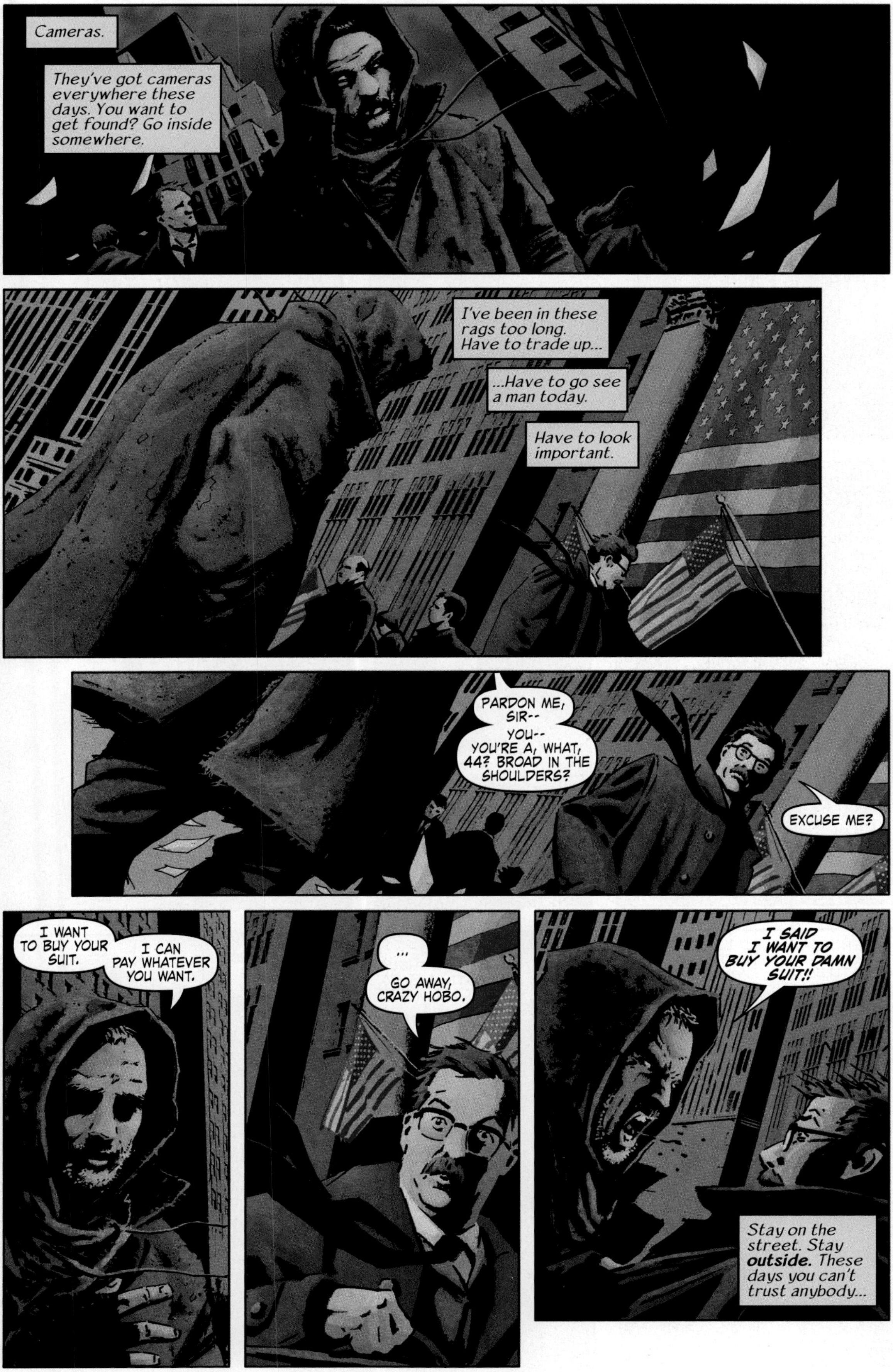
Cameras.
They've got cameras everywhere these days. You want to get found? Go inside somewhere.
I've been in these rags too long. Have to trade up...
...Have to go see a man today.
Have to look important.
PARDON ME, SIR-- YOU-- YOU'RE A, WHAT, 44? BROAD IN THE SHOULDERS?
EXCUSE ME?
I WANT TO BUY YOUR SUIT.
I CAN PAY WHATEVER YOU WANT.
...
GO AWAY, CRAZY HOBO.
I SAID I WANT TO BUY YOUR DAMN SUIT!!
Stay on the street. Stay **outside.** These days you can't trust anybody...

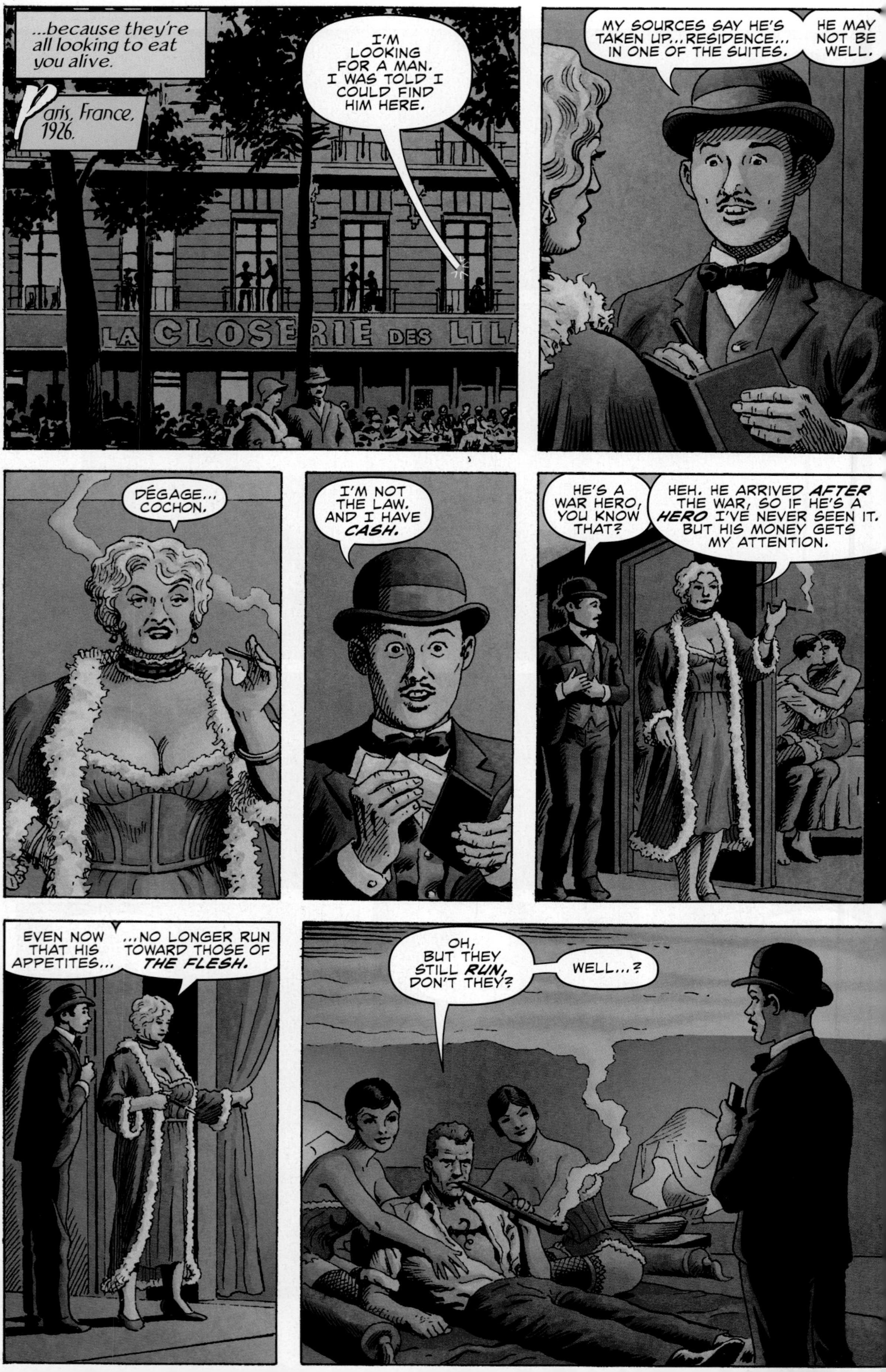
...because they're all looking to eat you alive.
Paris, France, 1926.
I'M LOOKING FOR A MAN. I WAS TOLD I COULD FIND HIM HERE.
LA CLOSERIE DES LIL
MY SOURCES SAY HE'S TAKEN UP... RESIDENCE... IN ONE OF THE SUITES.
HE MAY NOT BE WELL.
DÉGAGE... COCHON.
I'M NOT THE LAW. AND I HAVE **CASH.**
HE'S A WAR HERO, YOU KNOW THAT?
HEH. HE ARRIVED **AFTER** THE WAR, SO IF HE'S A **HERO** I'VE NEVER SEEN IT. BUT HIS MONEY GETS MY ATTENTION.
EVEN NOW THAT HIS APPETITES...
...NO LONGER RUN TOWARD THOSE OF **THE FLESH.**
OH, BUT THEY STILL **RUN,** DON'T THEY?
WELL...?

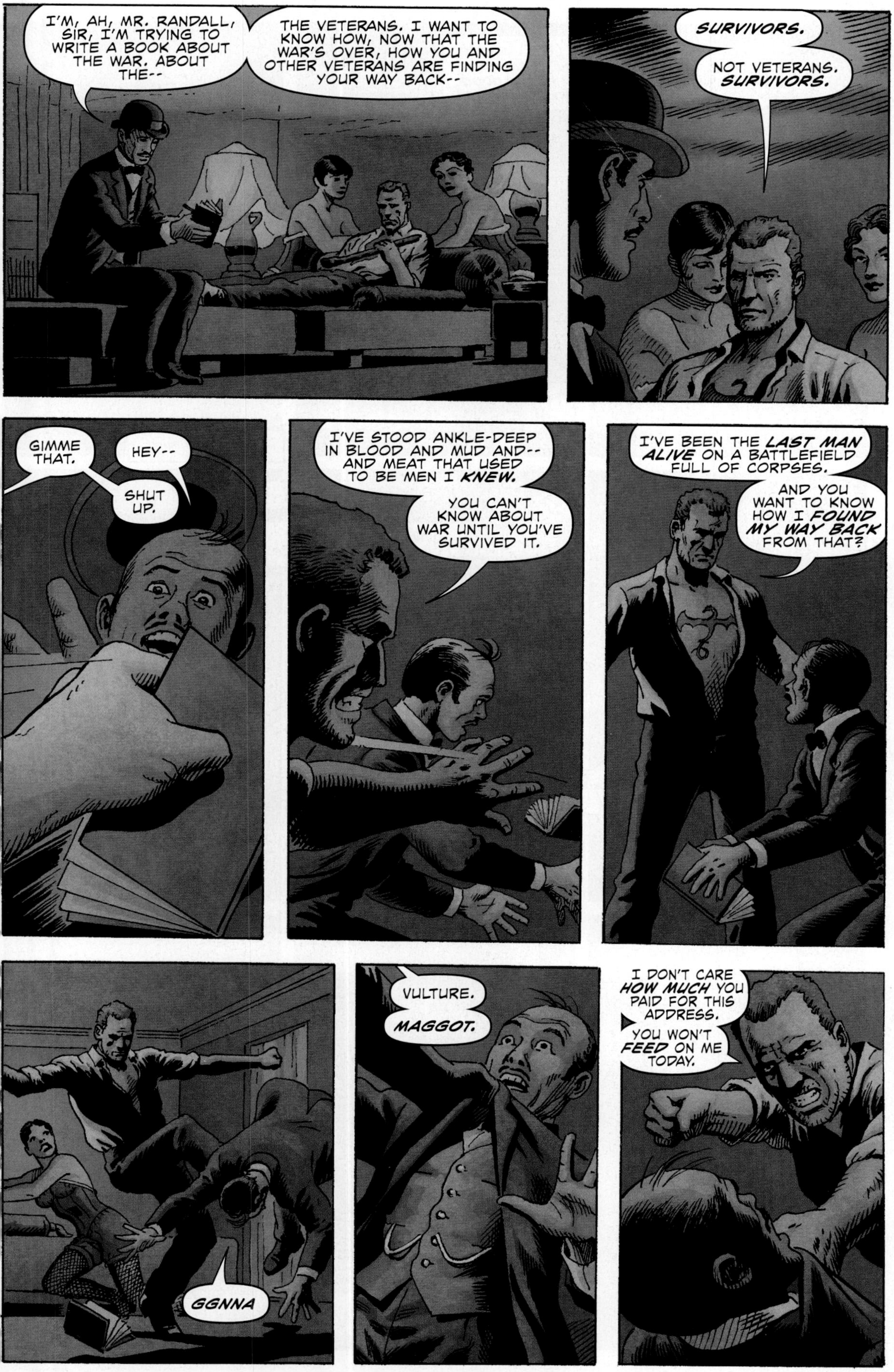
I'M, AH, MR. RANDALL, SIR, I'M TRYING TO WRITE A BOOK ABOUT THE WAR. ABOUT THE--
THE VETERANS. I WANT TO KNOW HOW, NOW THAT THE WAR'S OVER, HOW YOU AND OTHER VETERANS ARE FINDING YOUR WAY BACK--
SURVIVORS.
NOT VETERANS. SURVIVORS.
GIMME THAT.
HEY--
SHUT UP.
I'VE STOOD ANKLE-DEEP IN BLOOD AND MUD AND-- AND MEAT THAT USED TO BE MEN I KNEW.
YOU CAN'T KNOW ABOUT WAR UNTIL YOU'VE SURVIVED IT.
I'VE BEEN THE LAST MAN ALIVE ON A BATTLEFIELD FULL OF CORPSES.
AND YOU WANT TO KNOW HOW I FOUND MY WAY BACK FROM THAT?
GGNNA
VULTURE.
MAGGOT.
I DON'T CARE HOW MUCH YOU PAID FOR THIS ADDRESS.
YOU WON'T FEED ON ME TODAY.

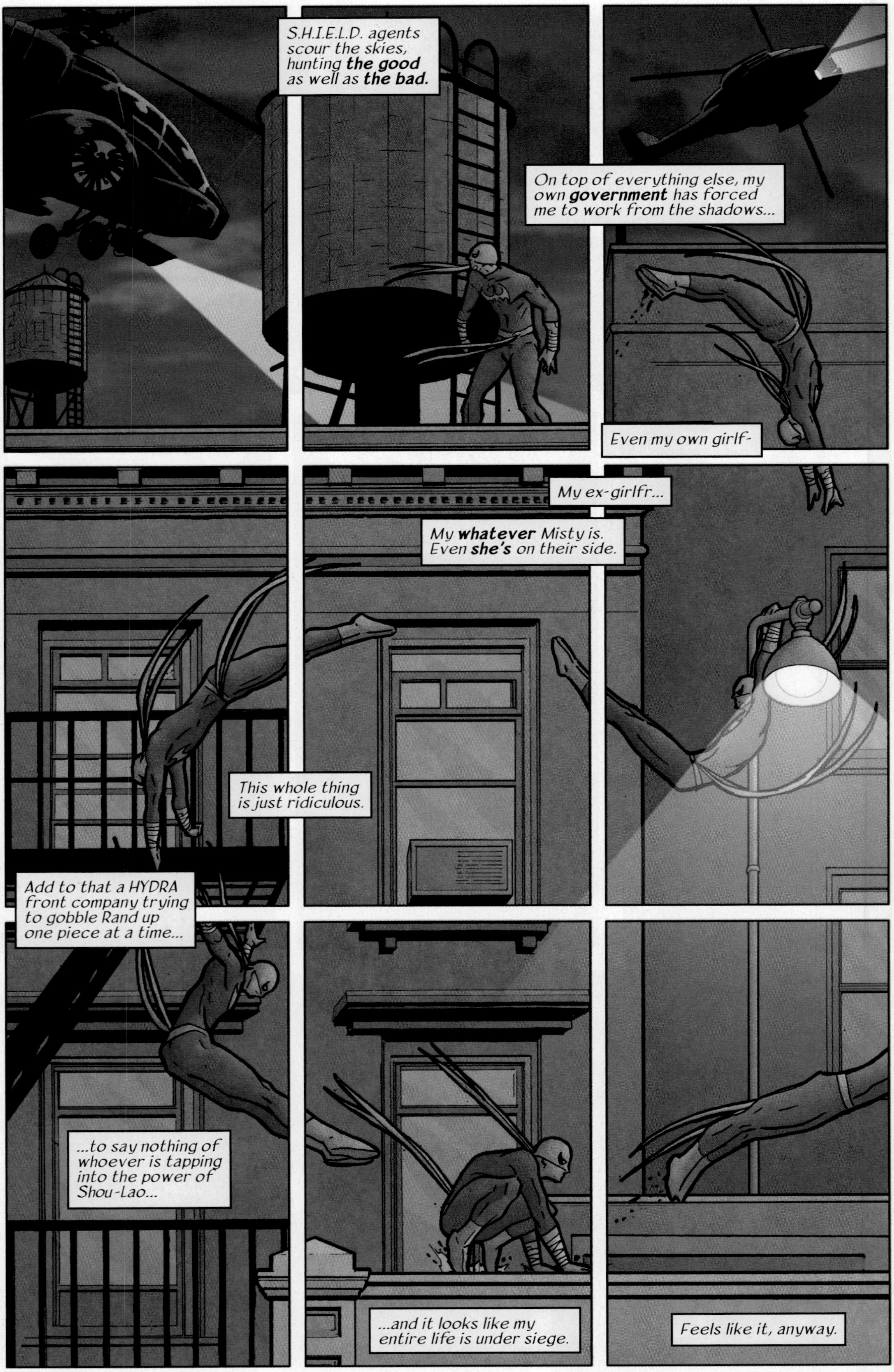
S.H.I.E.L.D. agents scour the skies, hunting **the good** as well as **the bad.**
On top of everything else, my own **government** has forced me to work from the shadows...
Even my own girlf-
My ex-girlfr...
My **whatever** Misty is. Even **she's** on their side.
This whole thing is just ridiculous.
Add to that a HYDRA front company trying to gobble Rand up one piece at a time...
...to say nothing of whoever is tapping into the power of Shou-Lao...
...and it looks like my entire life is under siege.
Feels like it, anyway.

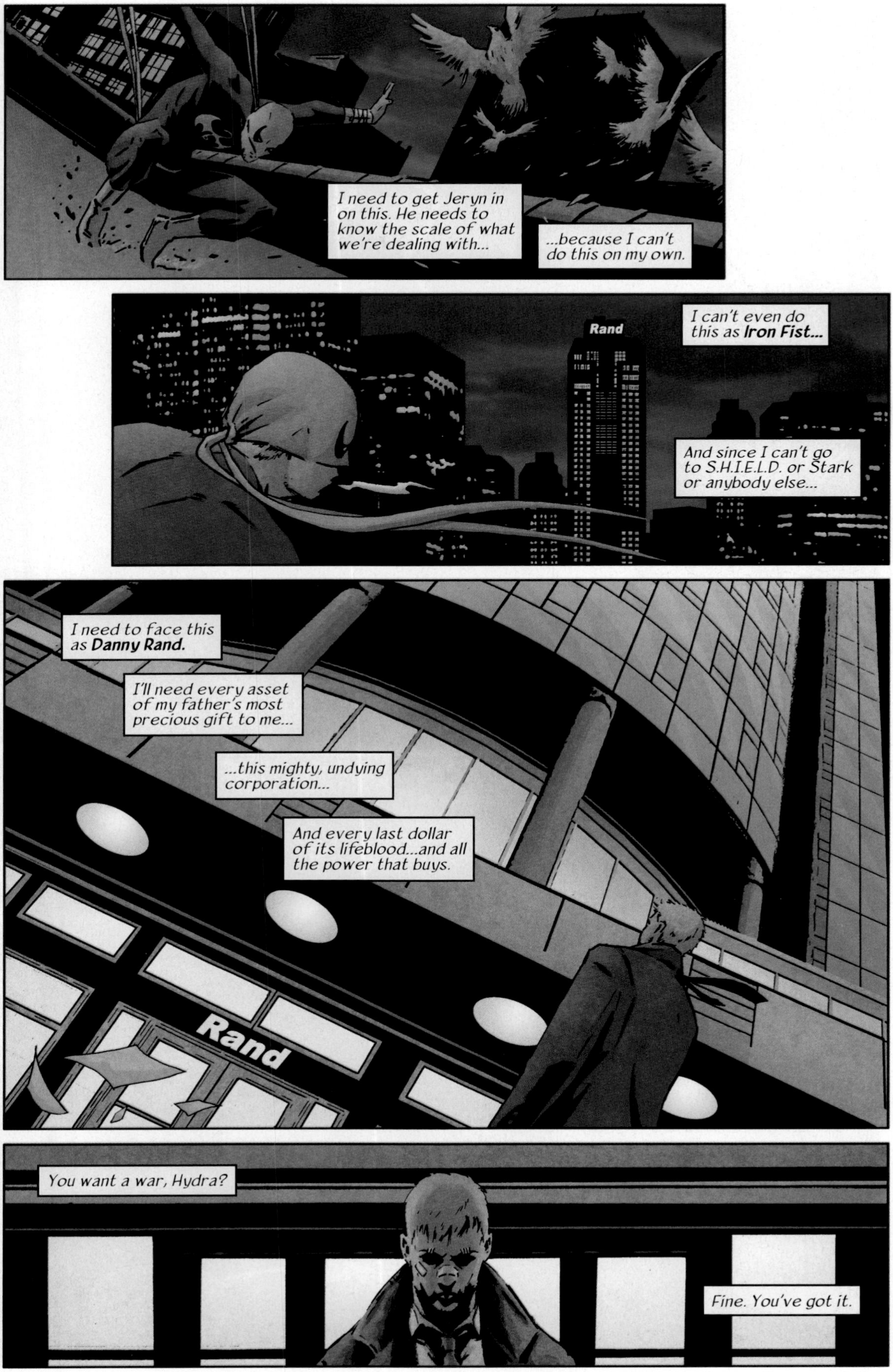
I need to get Jeryn in on this. He needs to know the scale of what we're dealing with...
...because I can't do this on my own.
I can't even do this as Iron Fist...
Rand
And since I can't go to S.H.I.E.L.D. or Stark or anybody else...
I need to face this as Danny Rand.
I'll need every asset of my father's most precious gift to me...
...this mighty, undying corporation...
And every last dollar of its lifeblood...and all the power that buys.
Rand
You want a war, Hydra?
Fine. You've got it.

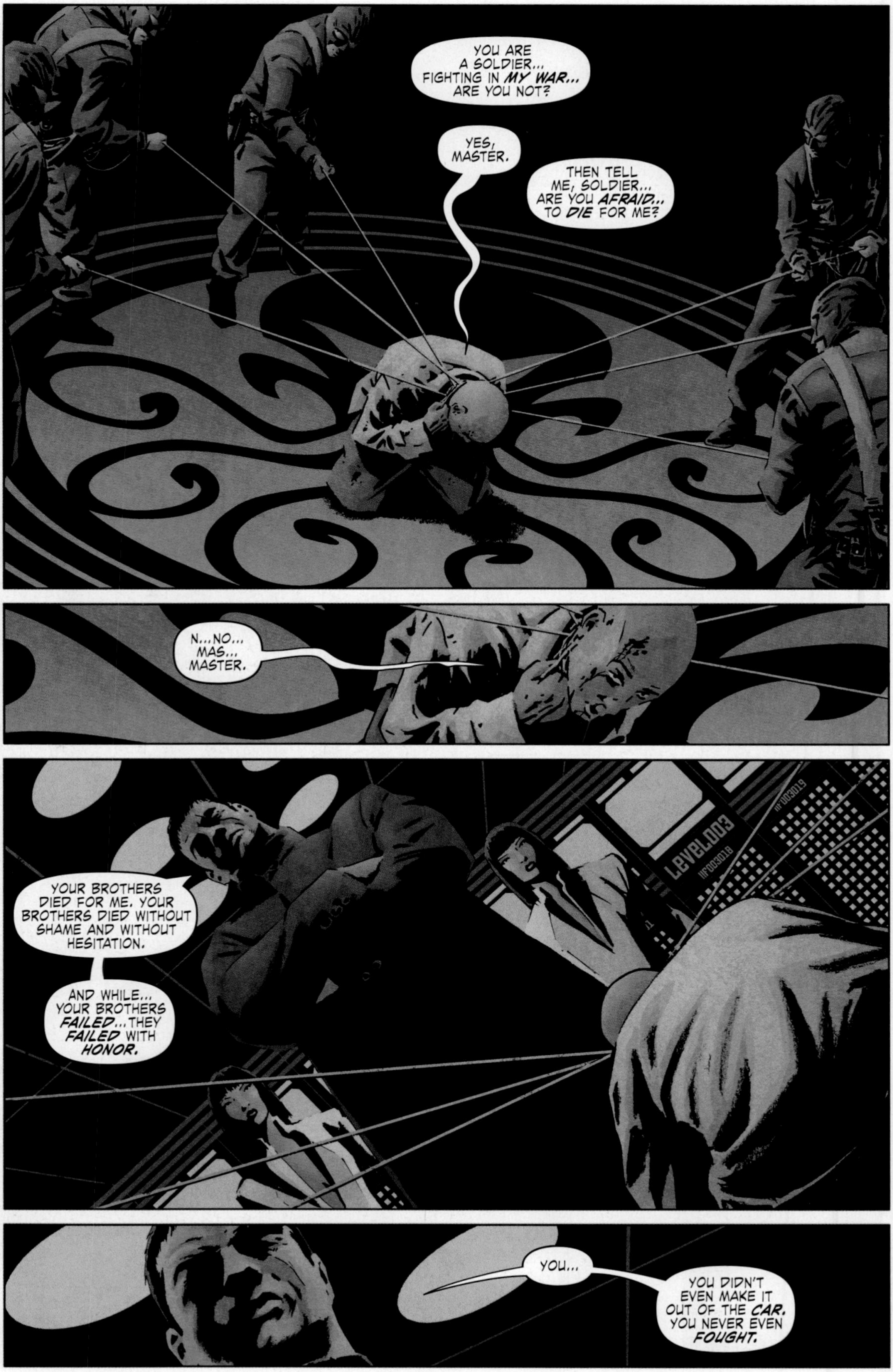
YOU ARE A SOLDIER... FIGHTING IN MY WAR... ARE YOU NOT?
YES, MASTER.
THEN TELL ME, SOLDIER... ARE YOU AFRAID... TO DIE FOR ME?
N...NO... MAS... MASTER.
YOUR BROTHERS DIED FOR ME. YOUR BROTHERS DIED WITHOUT SHAME AND WITHOUT HESITATION.
AND WHILE... YOUR BROTHERS FAILED...THEY FAILED WITH HONOR.
LEVEL003
IIF003018
IIF003019
YOU...
YOU DIDN'T EVEN MAKE IT OUT OF THE CAR. YOU NEVER EVEN FOUGHT.

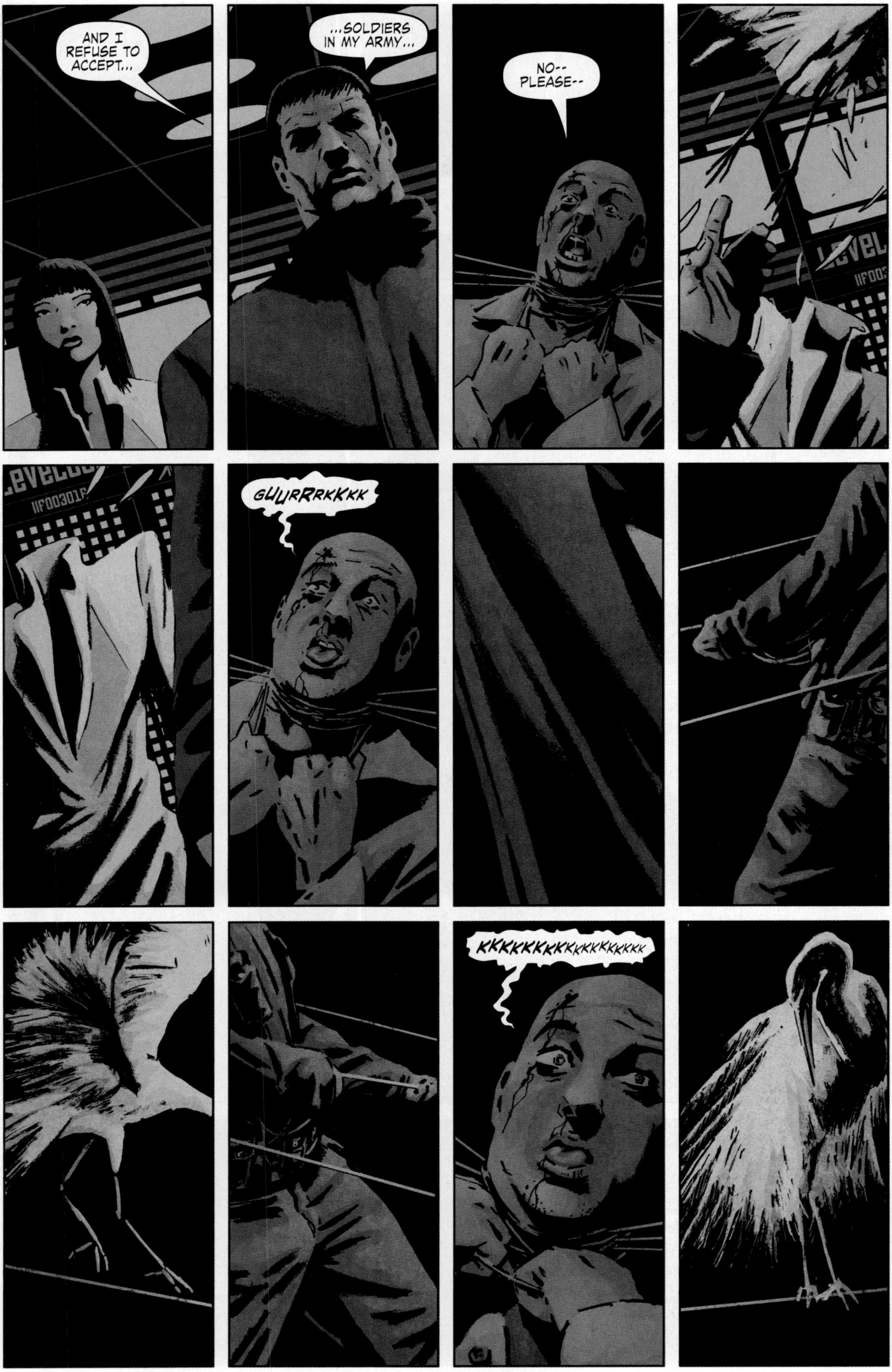
AND I REFUSE TO ACCEPT...
...SOLDIERS IN MY ARMY...
NO-- PLEASE--
GUURRRKKKK
KKKKKKKKKKKKKKKKKK

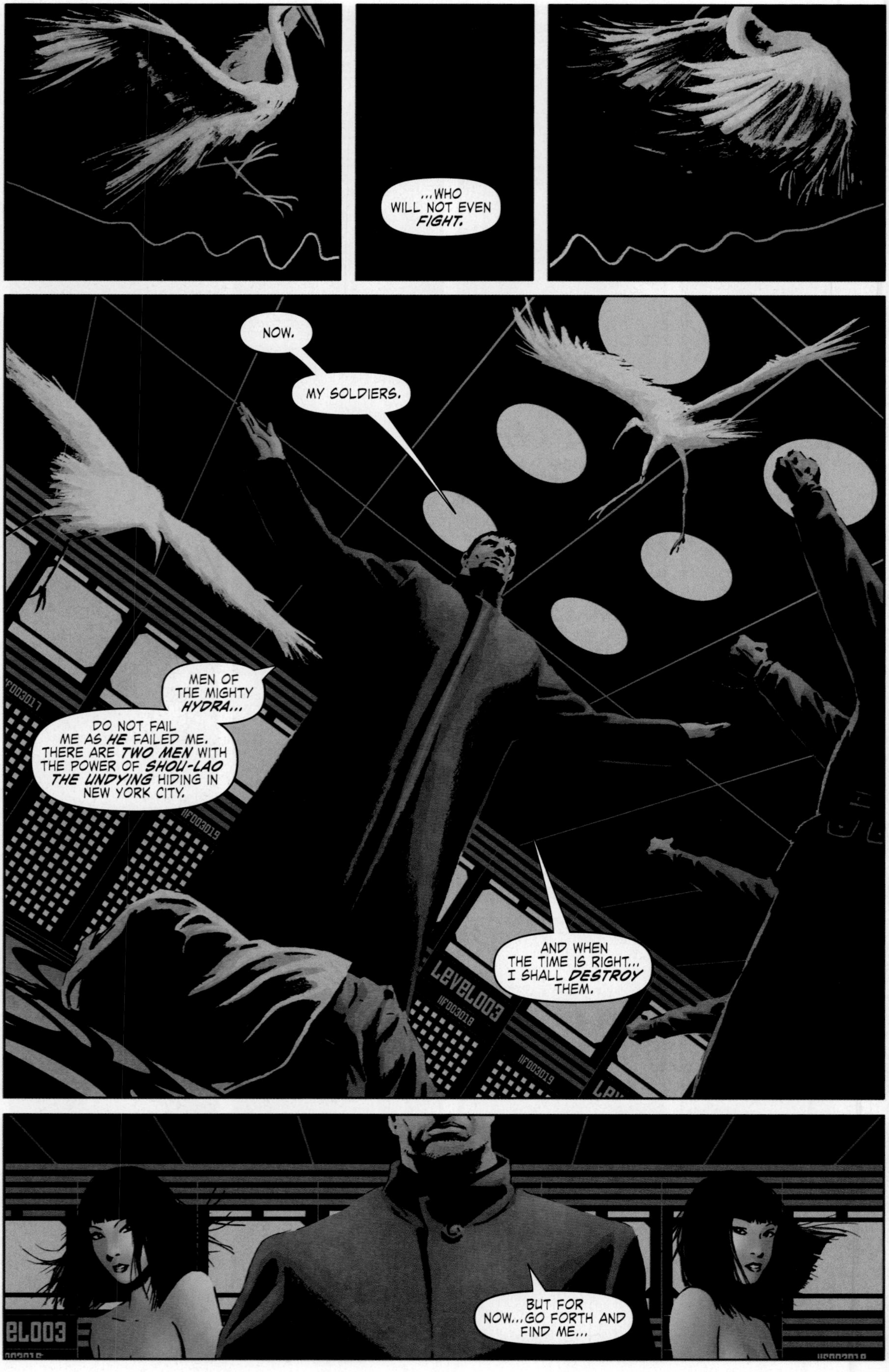
...WHO WILL NOT EVEN *FIGHT.*
NOW.
MY SOLDIERS.
MEN OF THE MIGHTY *HYDRA...*
DO NOT FAIL ME AS *HE* FAILED ME. THERE ARE *TWO MEN* WITH THE POWER OF *SHOU-LAO THE UNDYING* HIDING IN NEW YORK CITY.
AND WHEN THE TIME IS RIGHT... I SHALL *DESTROY* THEM.
BUT FOR NOW...GO FORTH AND FIND ME...

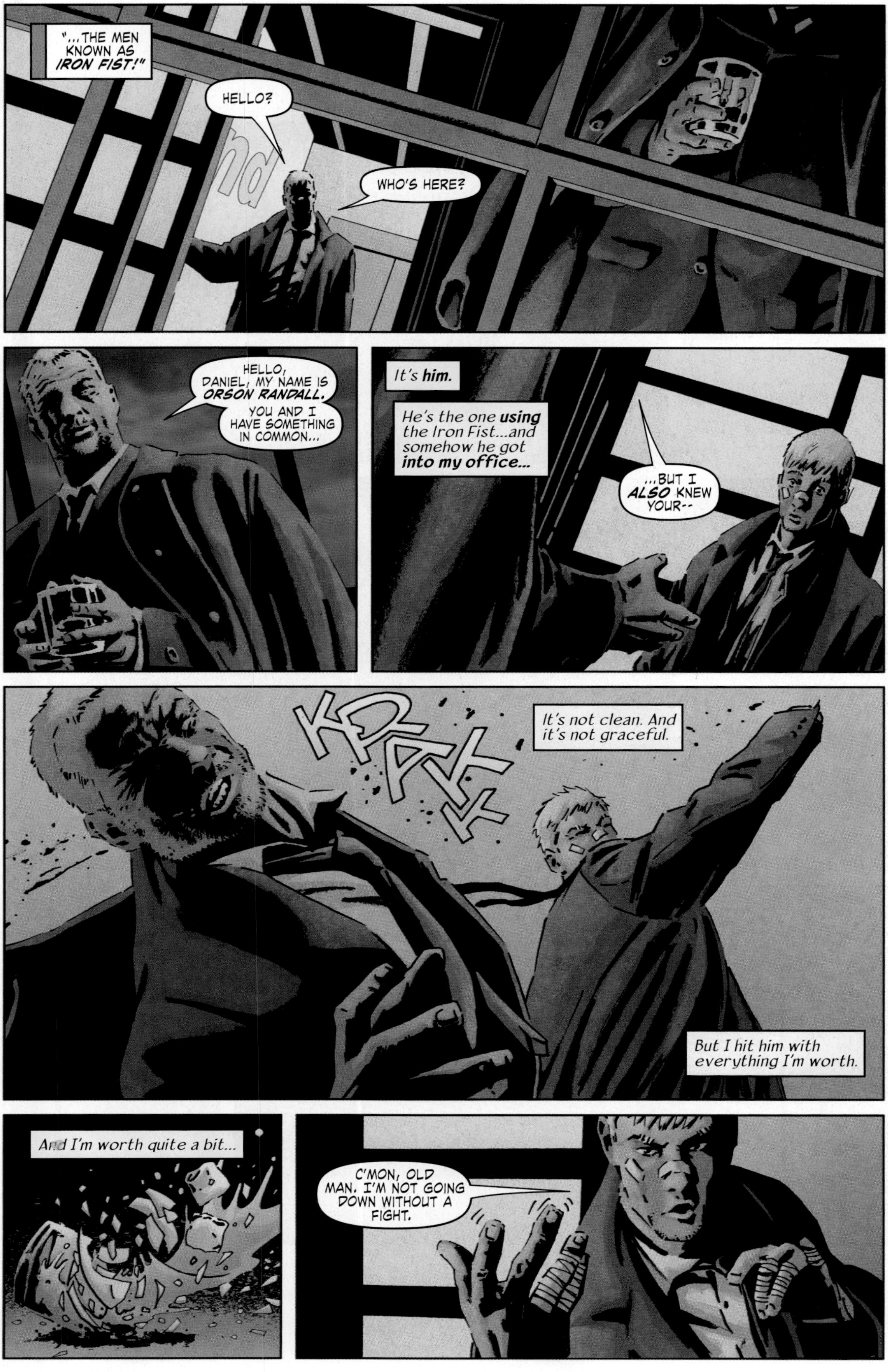
"...THE MEN KNOWN AS IRON FIST!"
HELLO?
WHO'S HERE?
HELLO, DANIEL, MY NAME IS ORSON RANDALL.
YOU AND I HAVE SOMETHING IN COMMON...
It's him.
He's the one using the Iron Fist...and somehow he got into my office...
...BUT I ALSO KNEW YOUR--
KRAKK
It's not clean. And it's not graceful.
But I hit him with everything I'm worth.
And I'm worth quite a bit...
C'MON, OLD MAN. I'M NOT GOING DOWN WITHOUT A FIGHT.

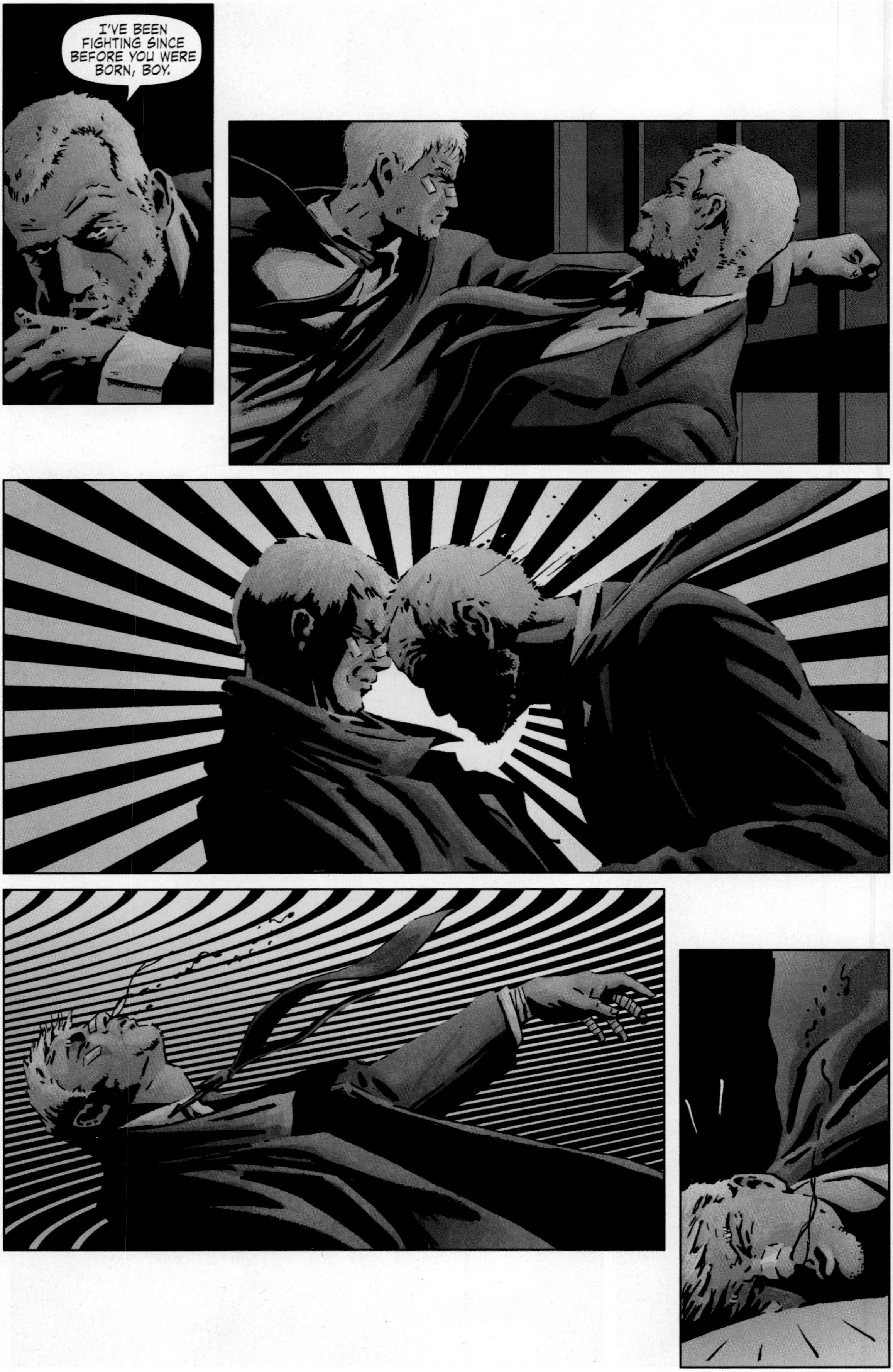
I'VE BEEN FIGHTING SINCE BEFORE YOU WERE BORN, BOY.

Focus on the pain.

COME ON, THEN, LET'S SEE IT.

Pain cuts through the fear...

...and with the fear gone...

...I find the clarity...

...and the focus...

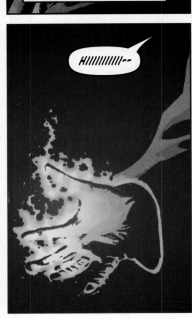

HIIIIIIIIII--

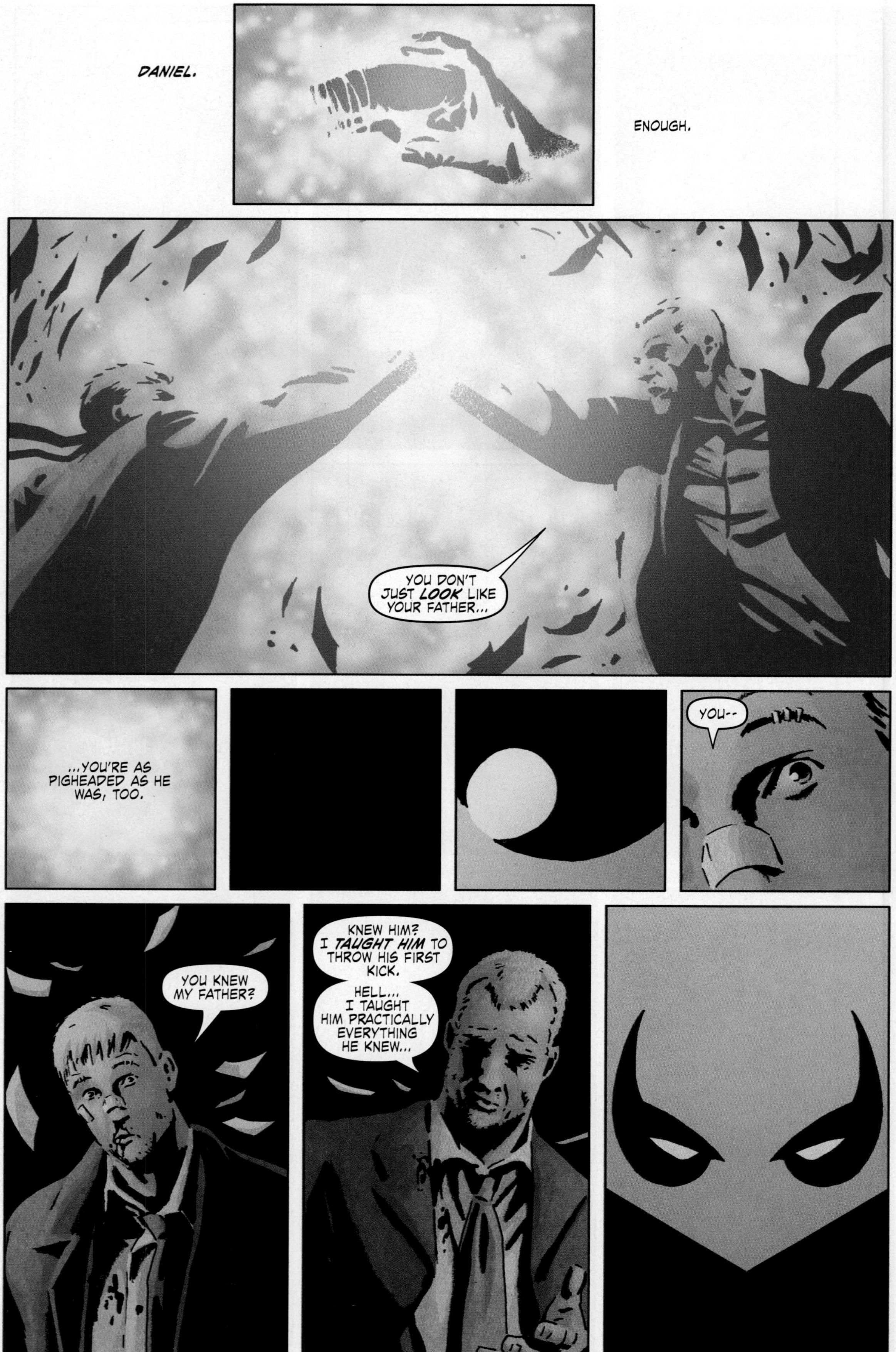
DANIEL.
ENOUGH.
YOU DON'T JUST LOOK LIKE YOUR FATHER...
...YOU'RE AS PIGHEADED AS HE WAS, TOO.
YOU--
YOU KNEW MY FATHER?
KNEW HIM? I TAUGHT HIM TO THROW HIS FIRST KICK.
HELL... I TAUGHT HIM PRACTICALLY EVERYTHING HE KNEW...

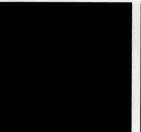

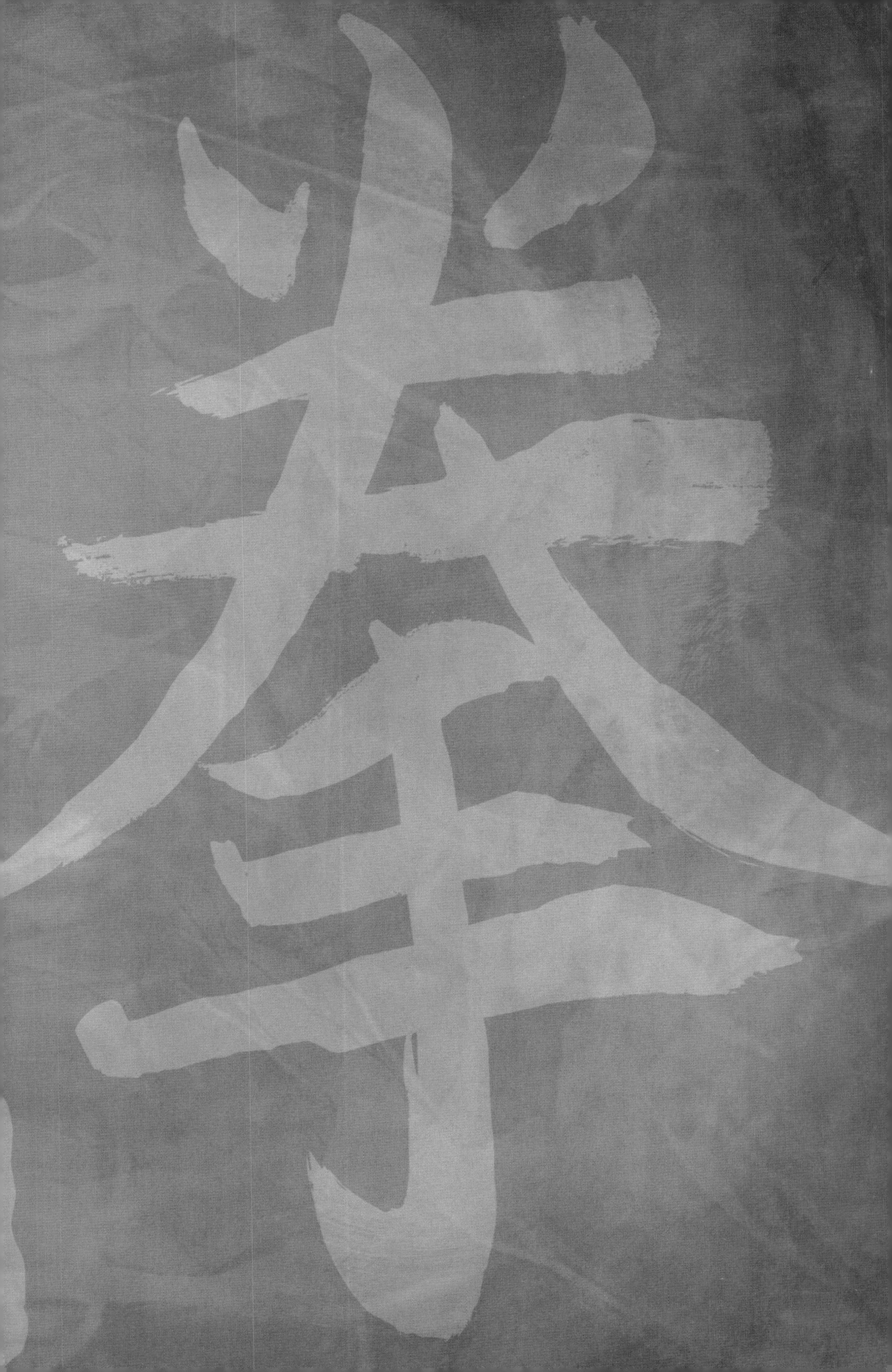
拳

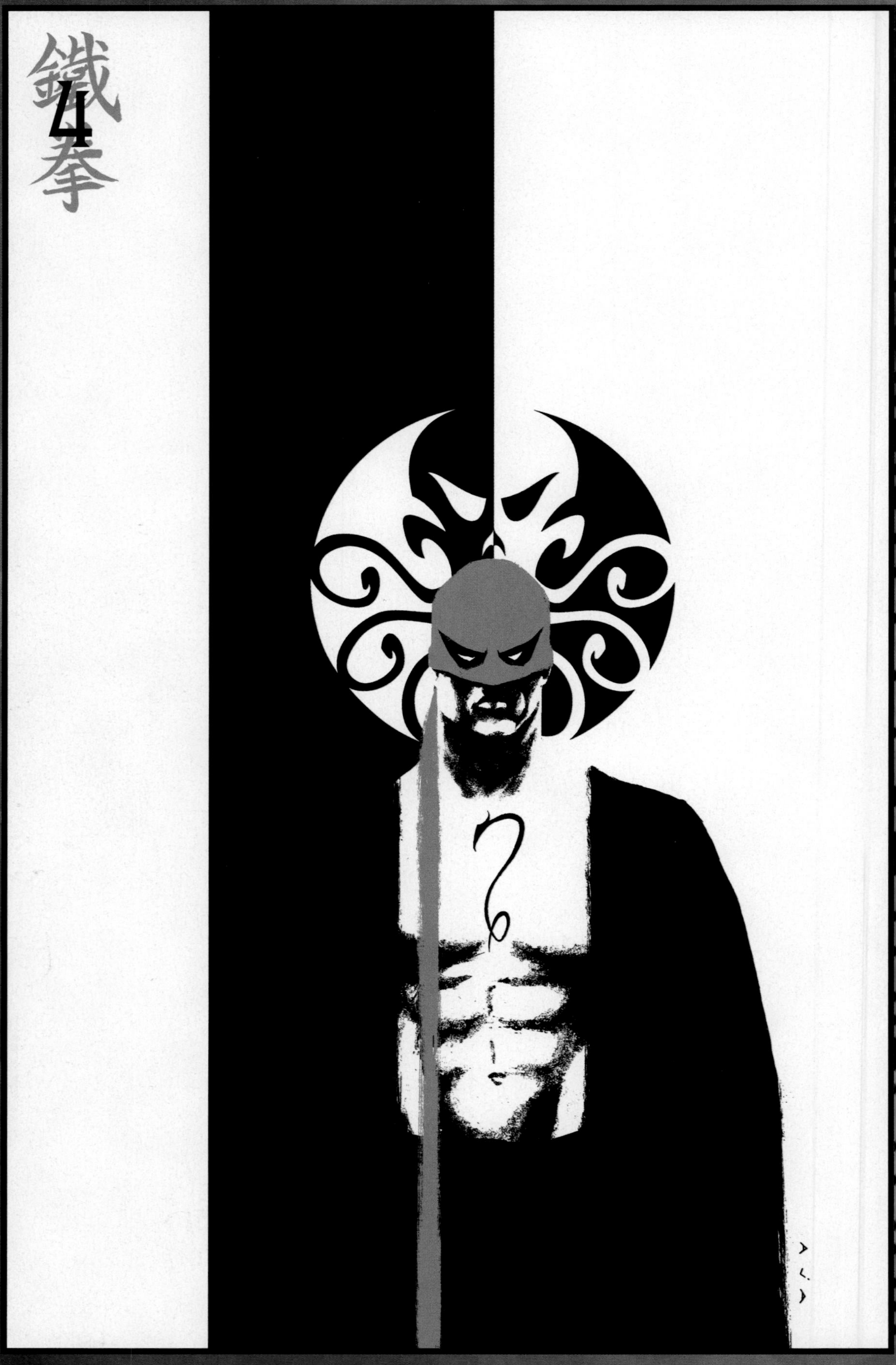
鐵拳
4

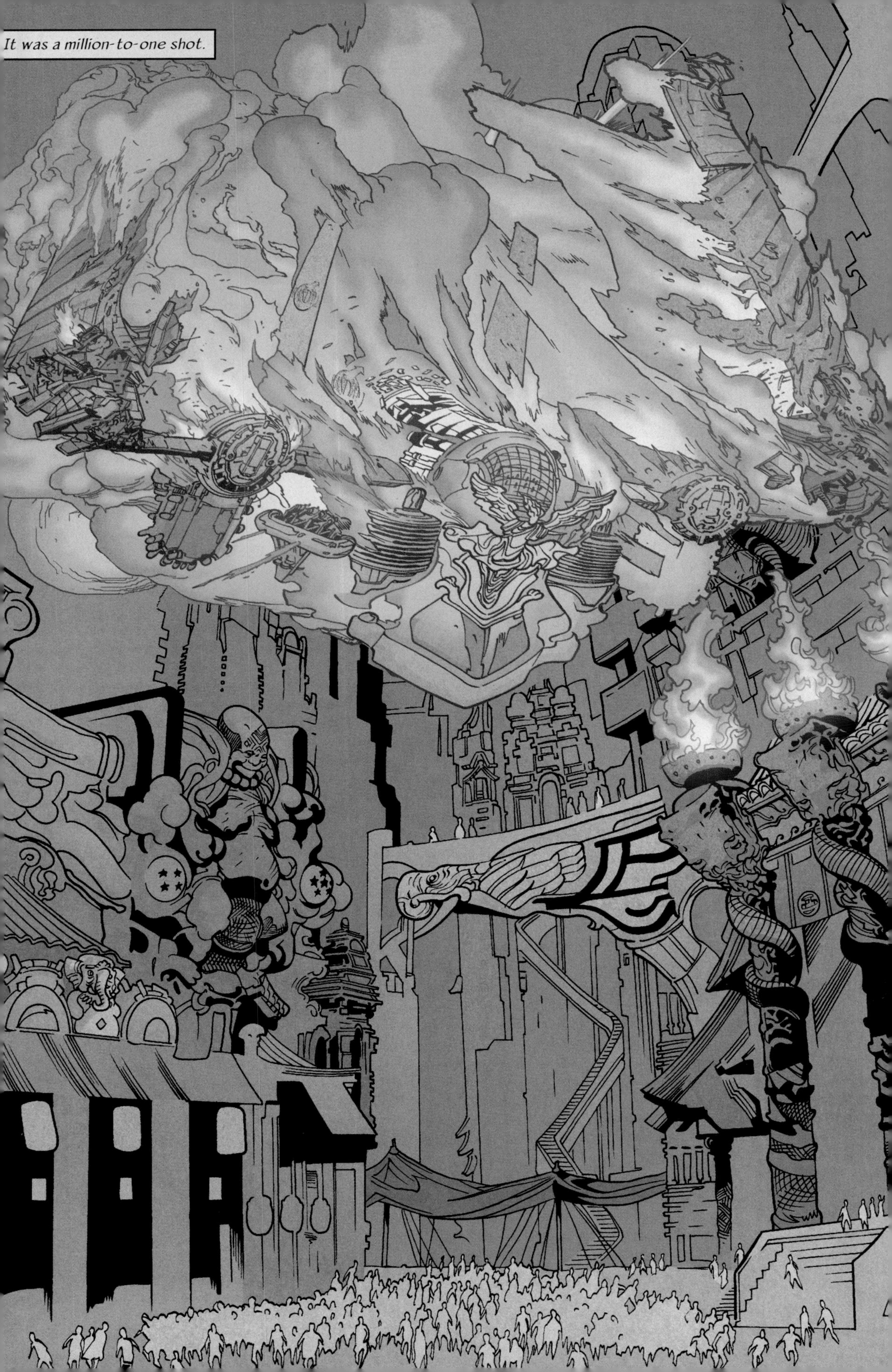
It was a million-to-one shot.

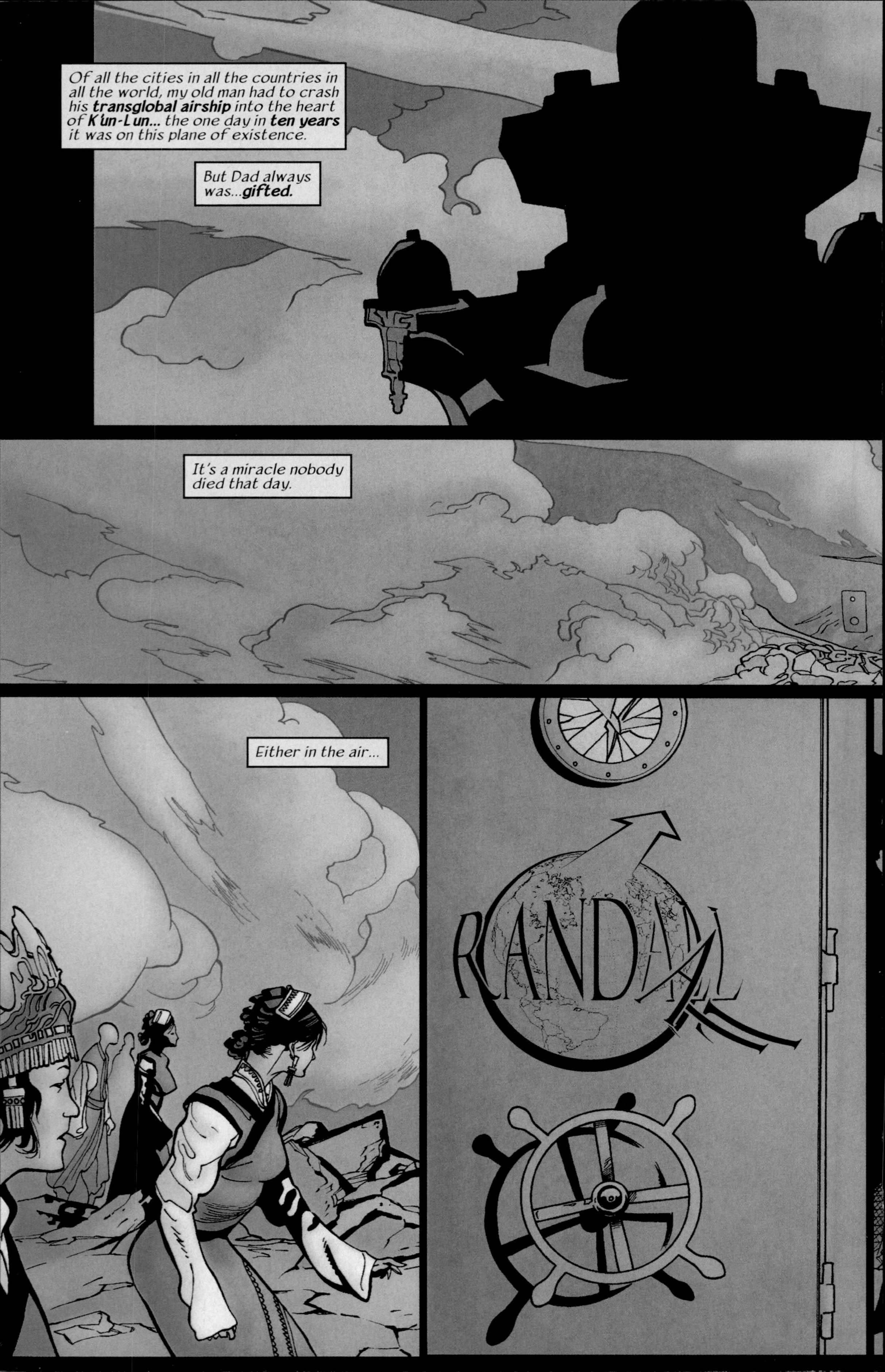

Of all the cities in all the countries in all the world, my old man had to crash his **transglobal airship** into the heart of **K'un-Lun...** the one day in **ten years** it was on this plane of existence.
But Dad always was...**gifted.**
It's a miracle nobody died that day.
Either in the air...
RANDALL

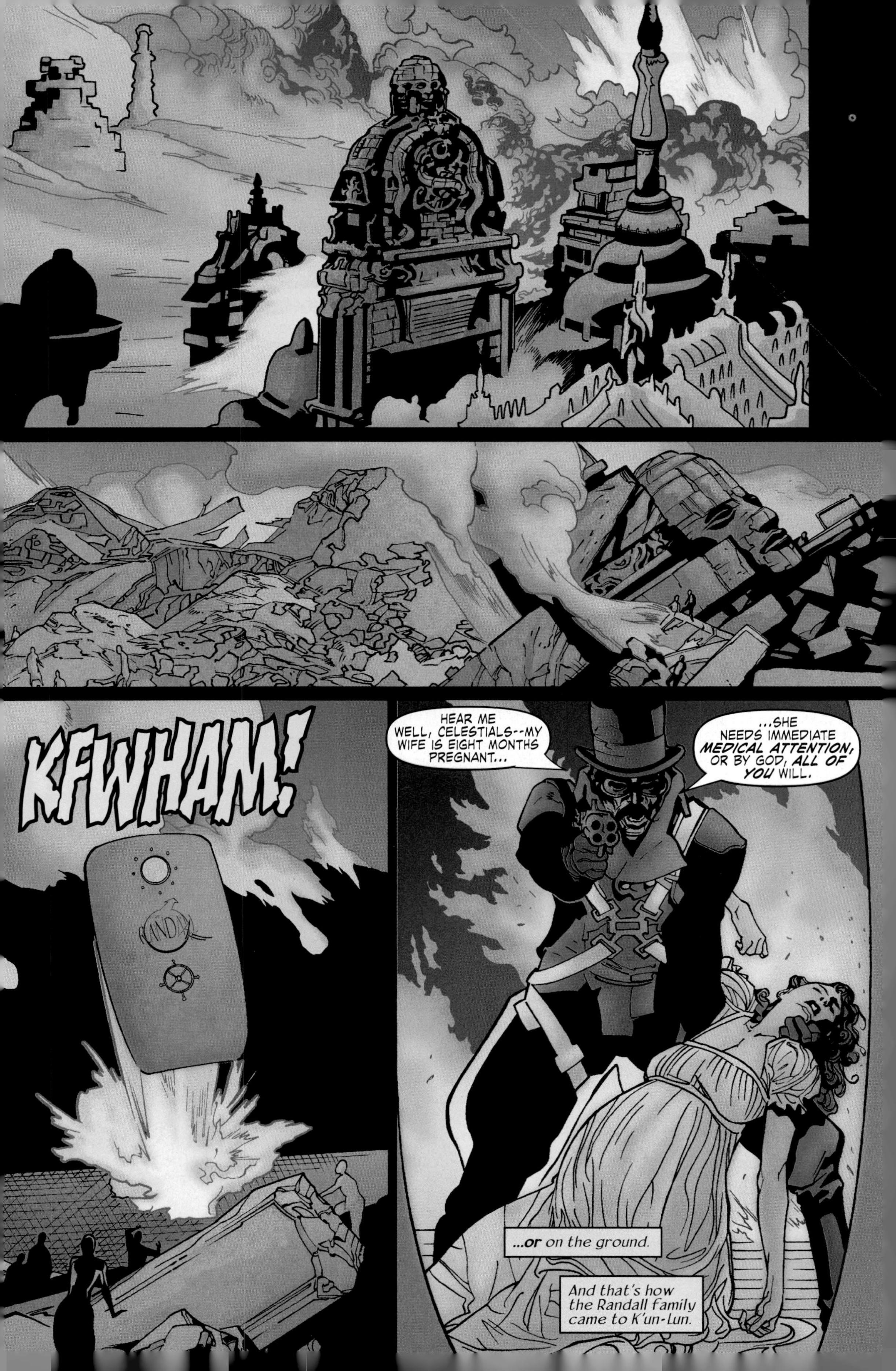
KFWHAM!
RANDALL
HEAR ME WELL, CELESTIALS--MY WIFE IS EIGHT MONTHS PREGNANT...
...SHE NEEDS IMMEDIATE *MEDICAL ATTENTION*, OR BY GOD, *ALL OF YOU* WILL.
...or *on the ground.*
And that's how the Randall family came to K'un-Lun.

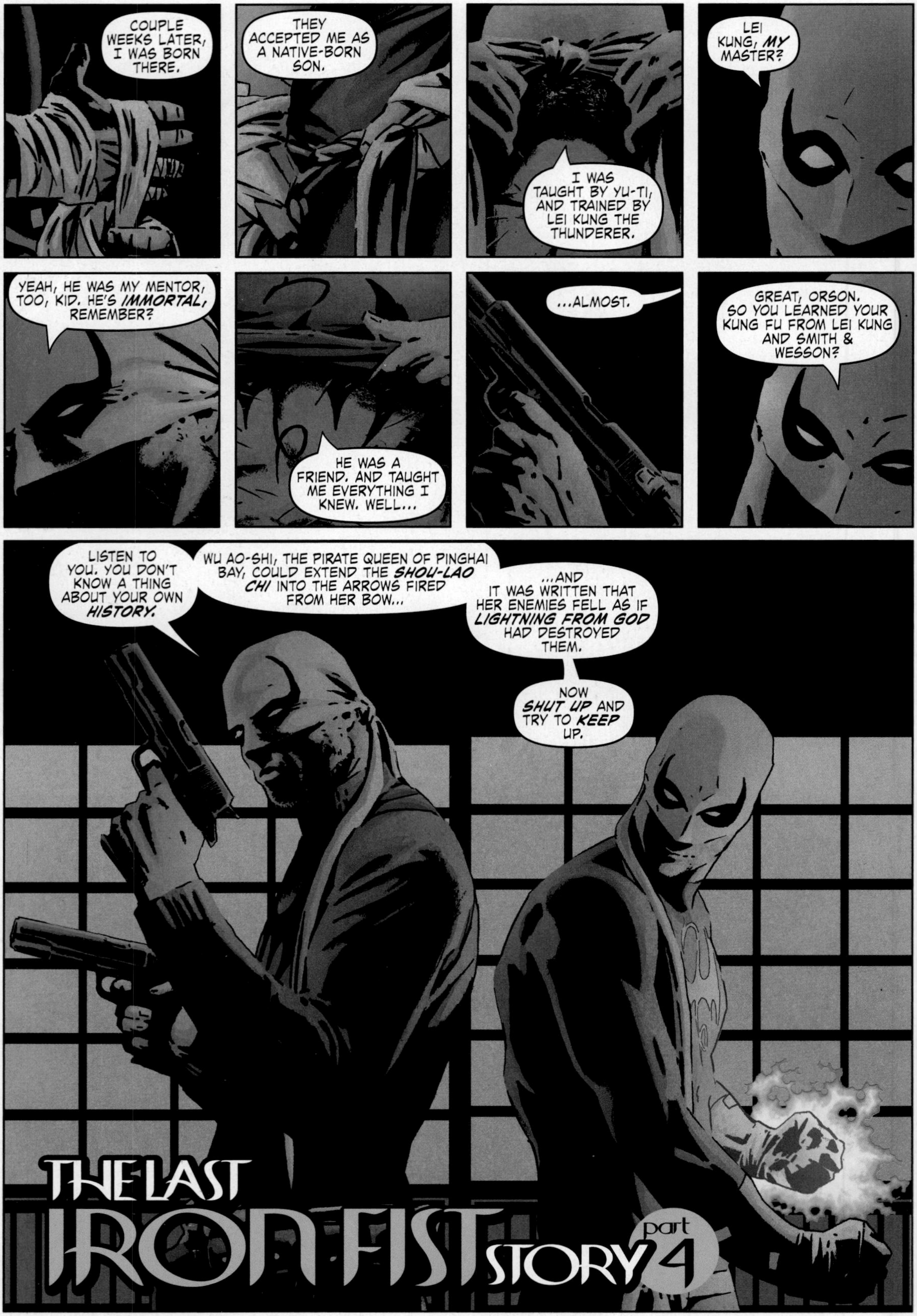
COUPLE WEEKS LATER, I WAS BORN THERE.
THEY ACCEPTED ME AS A NATIVE-BORN SON.
I WAS TAUGHT BY YU-TI, AND TRAINED BY LEI KUNG THE THUNDERER.
LEI KUNG, MY MASTER?
YEAH, HE WAS MY MENTOR, TOO, KID. HE'S IMMORTAL, REMEMBER?
HE WAS A FRIEND, AND TAUGHT ME EVERYTHING I KNEW. WELL...
...ALMOST.
GREAT, ORSON. SO YOU LEARNED YOUR KUNG FU FROM LEI KUNG AND SMITH & WESSON?
LISTEN TO YOU. YOU DON'T KNOW A THING ABOUT YOUR OWN HISTORY.
WU AO-SHI, THE PIRATE QUEEN OF PINGHAI BAY, COULD EXTEND THE SHOU-LAO CHI INTO THE ARROWS FIRED FROM HER BOW...
...AND IT WAS WRITTEN THAT HER ENEMIES FELL AS IF LIGHTNING FROM GOD HAD DESTROYED THEM.
NOW SHUT UP AND TRY TO KEEP UP.
THE LAST IRON FIST STORY part 4

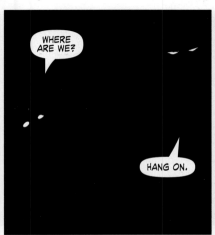

WHERE ARE WE?

HANG ON.

THERE.

I CAN *FEEL* THAT, WHEN YOU USE THE *POWER*. IT HURTS A LITTLE.

YOU NEED TO GET USED TO THAT. THE CHI OF SHOU-LAO ISN'T *A RIVER* THAT HAPPENS TO FLOW INTO YOU--YOU'RE A RIVER THAT FLOWS INTO *IT*.

AND IT...IS *AN OCEAN*.

DIVE IN, SON. YOU HAVE NO IDEA HOW DEEP YOU CAN GO.

AND SPEAKING OF DEEP: WE'RE IN *THE UNDERWORLD* NOW, SO KEEP MOVING.

WE GOT ANOTHER COUPLE *MILES* YET BEFORE WE REACH MY FATHER'S *PNEUMATIC SUBWAY STATION*.

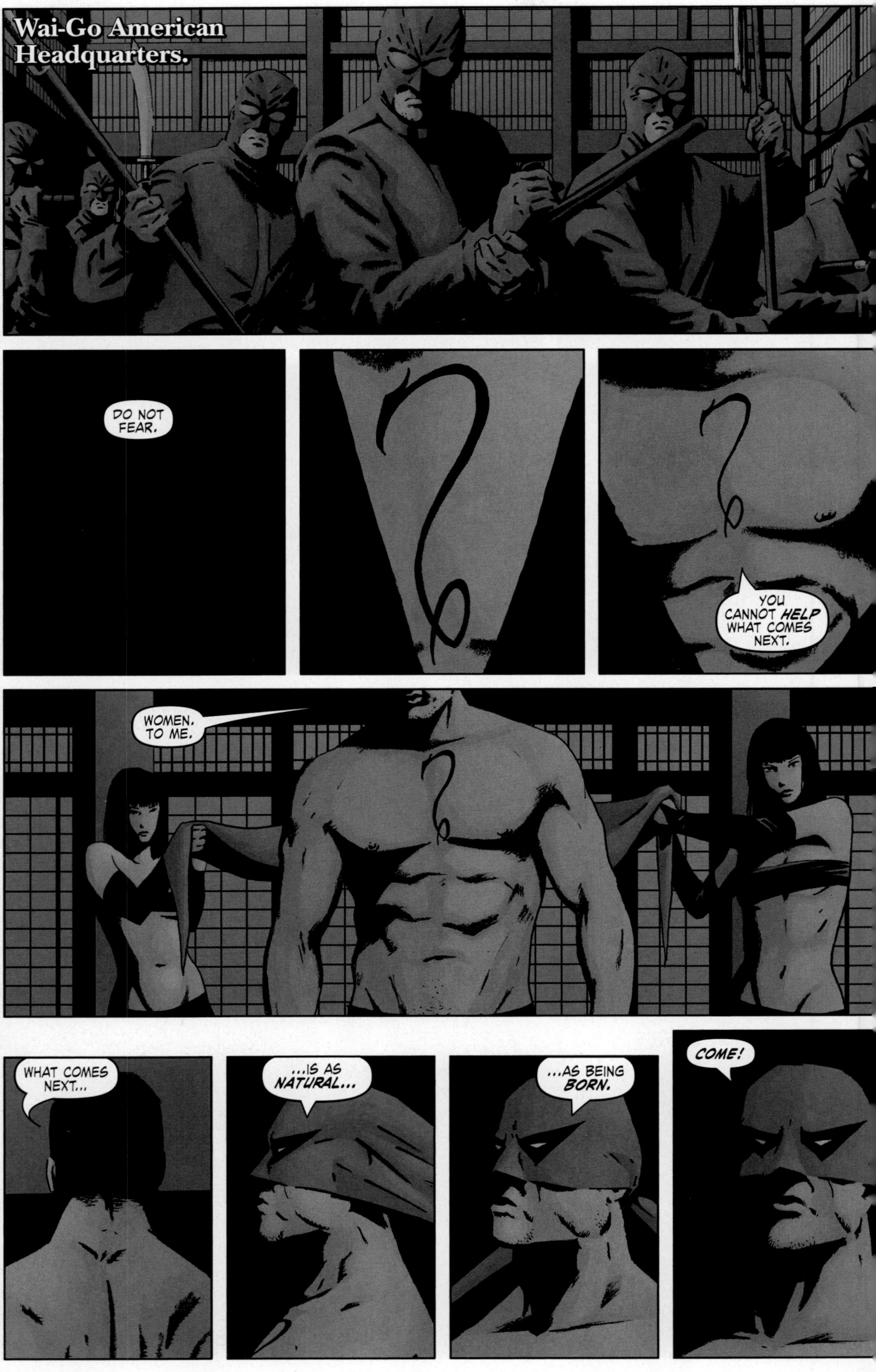
Wai-Go American Headquarters.
DO NOT FEAR.
YOU CANNOT *HELP* WHAT COMES NEXT.
WOMEN. TO ME.
WHAT COMES NEXT...
...IS AS *NATURAL...*
...AS BEING *BORN.*
COME!

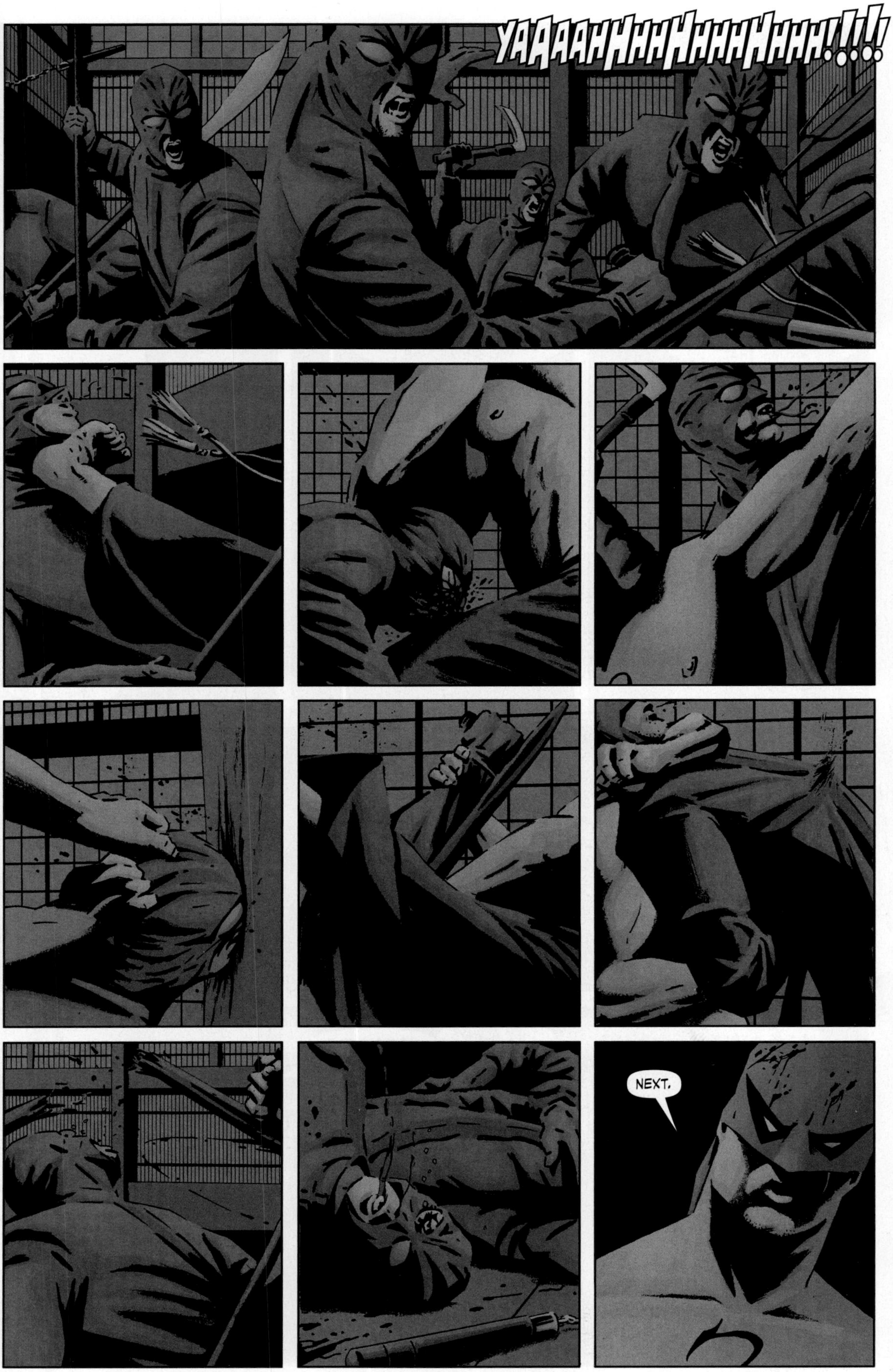
YAAAAHHHHHHHHHHHH!!!!
NEXT.

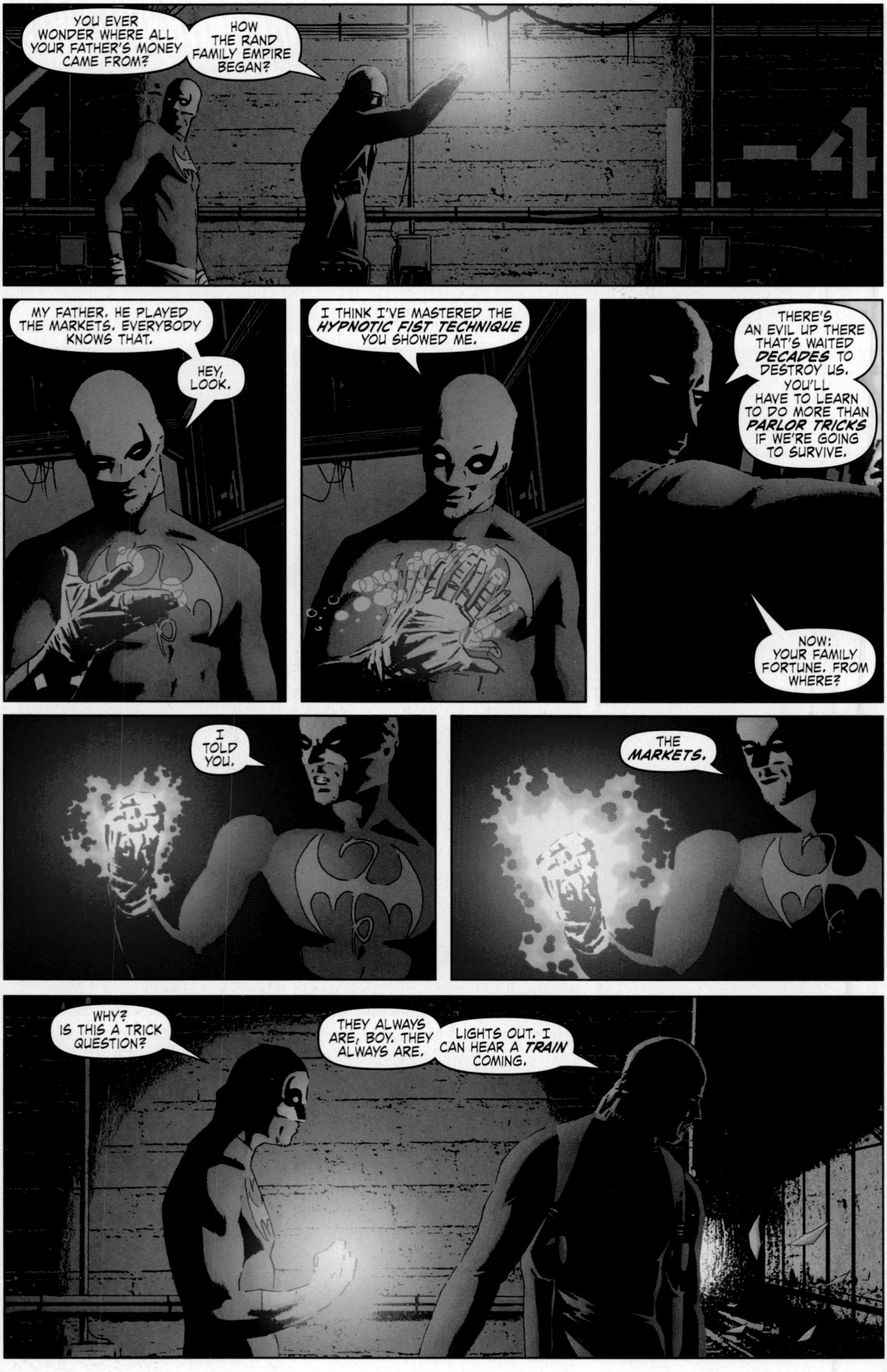
YOU EVER WONDER WHERE ALL YOUR FATHER'S MONEY CAME FROM?
HOW THE RAND FAMILY EMPIRE BEGAN?
MY FATHER. HE PLAYED THE MARKETS. EVERYBODY KNOWS THAT.
HEY, LOOK.
I THINK I'VE MASTERED THE HYPNOTIC FIST TECHNIQUE YOU SHOWED ME.
THERE'S AN EVIL UP THERE THAT'S WAITED DECADES TO DESTROY US.
YOU'LL HAVE TO LEARN TO DO MORE THAN PARLOR TRICKS IF WE'RE GOING TO SURVIVE.
NOW: YOUR FAMILY FORTUNE. FROM WHERE?
I TOLD YOU.
THE MARKETS.
WHY? IS THIS A TRICK QUESTION?
THEY ALWAYS ARE, BOY. THEY ALWAYS ARE.
LIGHTS OUT. I CAN HEAR A TRAIN COMING.

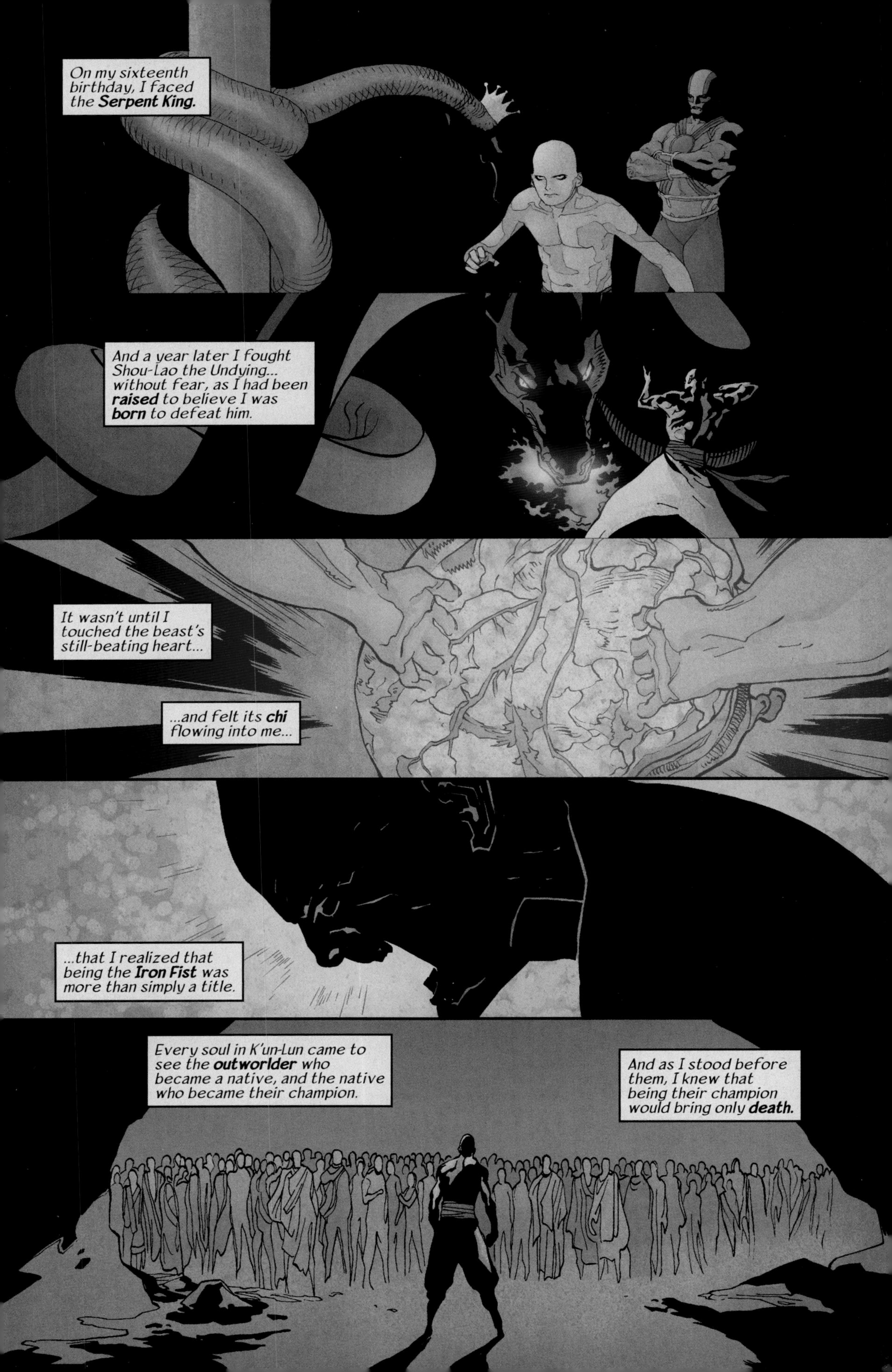
On my sixteenth birthday, I faced the **Serpent King.**
And a year later I fought Shou-Lao the Undying... without fear, as I had been **raised** to believe I was **born** to defeat him.
It wasn't until I touched the beast's still-beating heart...
...and felt its **chi** flowing into me...
...that I realized that being the **Iron Fist** was more than simply a title.
Every soul in K'un-Lun came to see the **outworlder** who became a native, and the native who became their champion.
And as I stood before them, I knew that being their champion would bring only **death.**

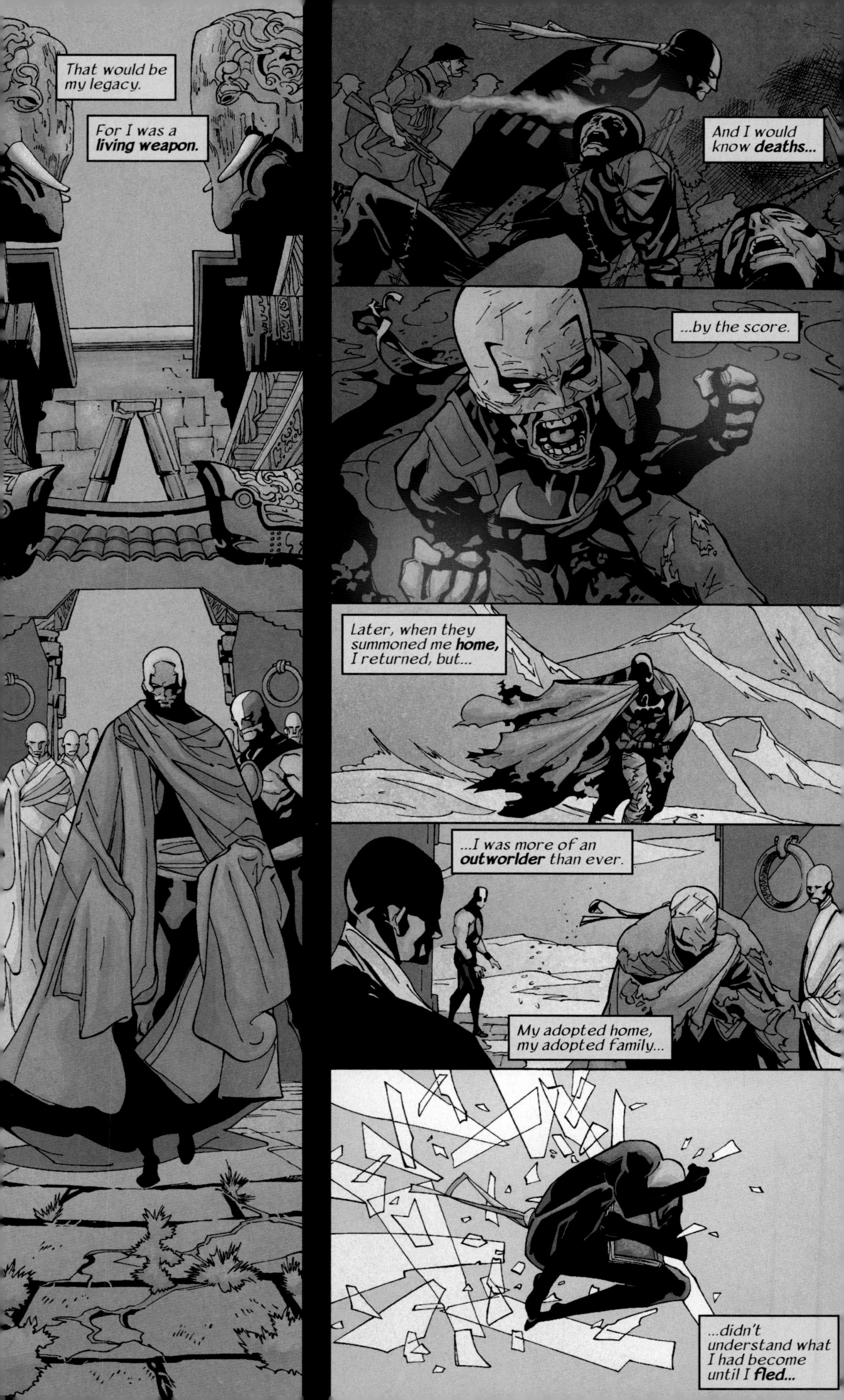
That would be my legacy.
For I was a **living weapon.**
And I would know **deaths...**
...by the score.
Later, when they summoned me **home,** I returned, but...
...I was more of an **outworlder** than ever.
My adopted home, my adopted family...
...didn't understand what I had become until I **fled...**

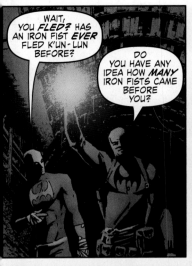

WAIT, YOU *FLED?* HAS AN IRON FIST *EVER* FLED K'UN-LUN BEFORE?

DO YOU HAVE ANY IDEA HOW *MANY* IRON FISTS CAME BEFORE YOU?

I HAD A *VISION* OF *MANY* ONCE. A FEW DOZEN, PERHAPS.

I HATE TO SAY I DON'T KNOW... BUT THE *LEGACY* ISN'T DISCUSSED MUCH.

THERE'S A REASON FOR *THAT,* TOO.

THERE HAVE BEEN SIXTY-SIX MEN AND WOMEN TO CARRY THE MANTLE OF THE *IRON FIST.*

EVER WONDER WHY YOUR *FATHER* WASN'T ONE OF THEM?

WE'RE *HERE,* BY THE WAY. RIGHT WHERE I LEFT IT.

NOW: STAND LIKE THIS. EXTEND YOUR HAND OUTWARD.

WHAT STANCE IS THAT? *SCORPION?*

JUST DO AS I DO.

EXTEND *YOUR POWER* OUTWARD... FROM YOUR CHEST THROUGH THE SHOULDER...THE SHOULDER DOWN TO THE HAND...

AND AWAY...FEEL THE SPACE BETWEEN *YOUR HAND* AND *THE WALL...*

...FEEL *THE ICON* OF *SHOU-LAO* BEFORE YOU...

NOW...

FEEL IT RISE IN YOUR CHEST AND...

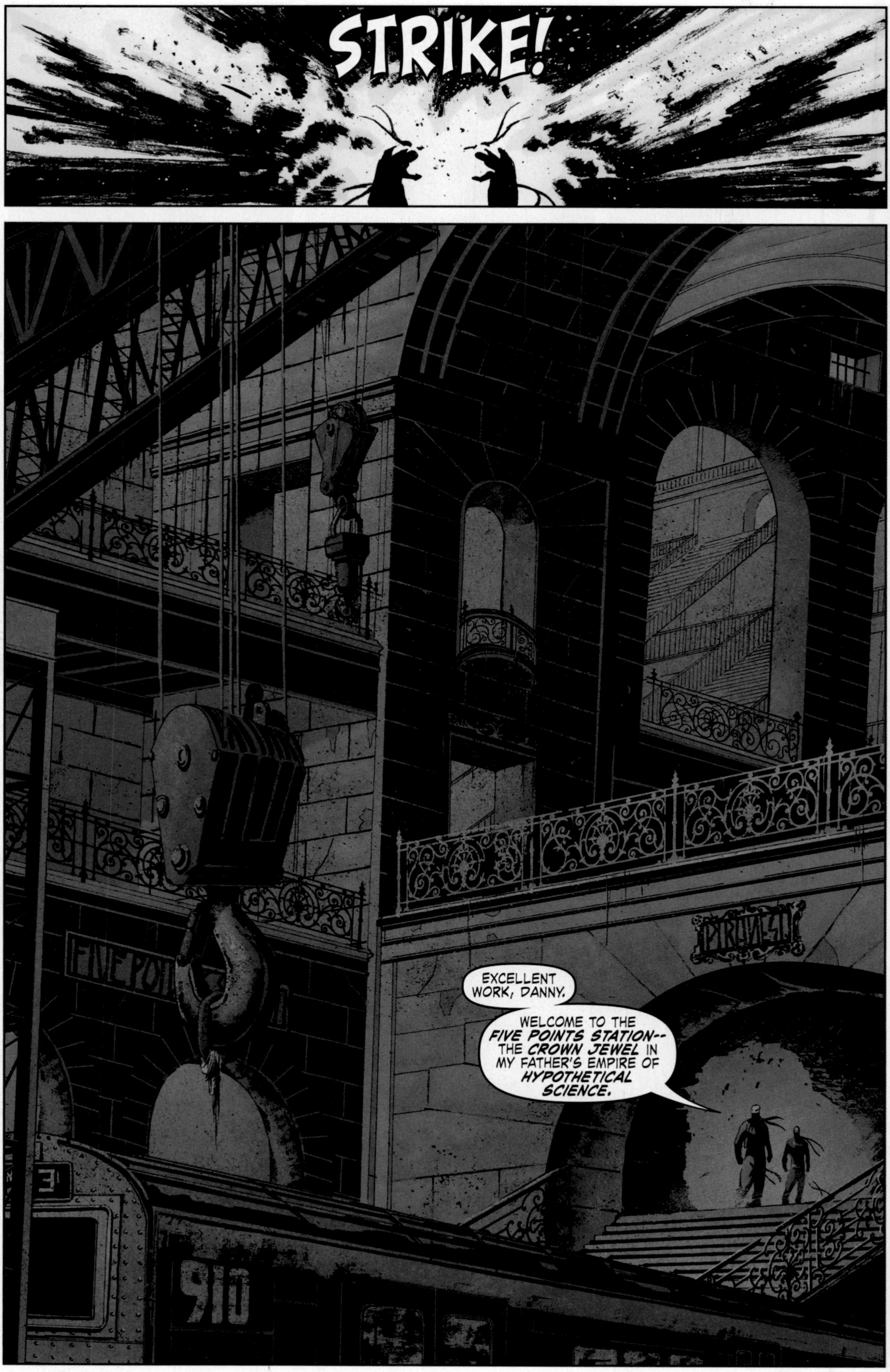
STRIKE!
EXCELLENT WORK, DANNY.
WELCOME TO THE *FIVE POINTS STATION*-- THE *CROWN JEWEL* IN MY FATHER'S EMPIRE OF *HYPOTHETICAL SCIENCE.*
910

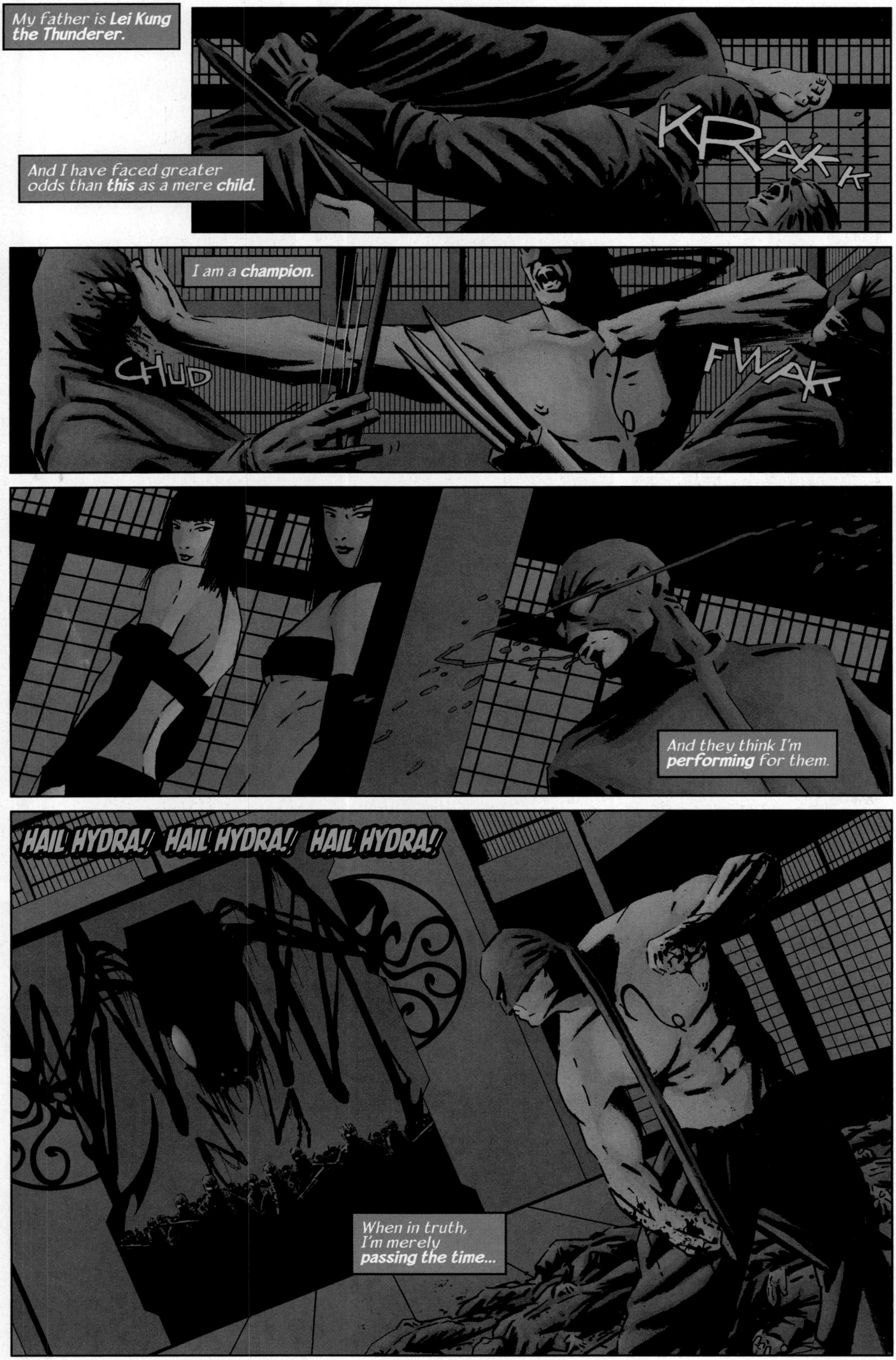

My father is Lei Kung the Thunderer.
And I have faced greater odds than this as a mere child.
KRAKK
I am a champion.
CHUD
FWAK
And they think I'm performing for them.
HAIL HYDRA! HAIL HYDRA! HAIL HYDRA!
When in truth, I'm merely passing the time...

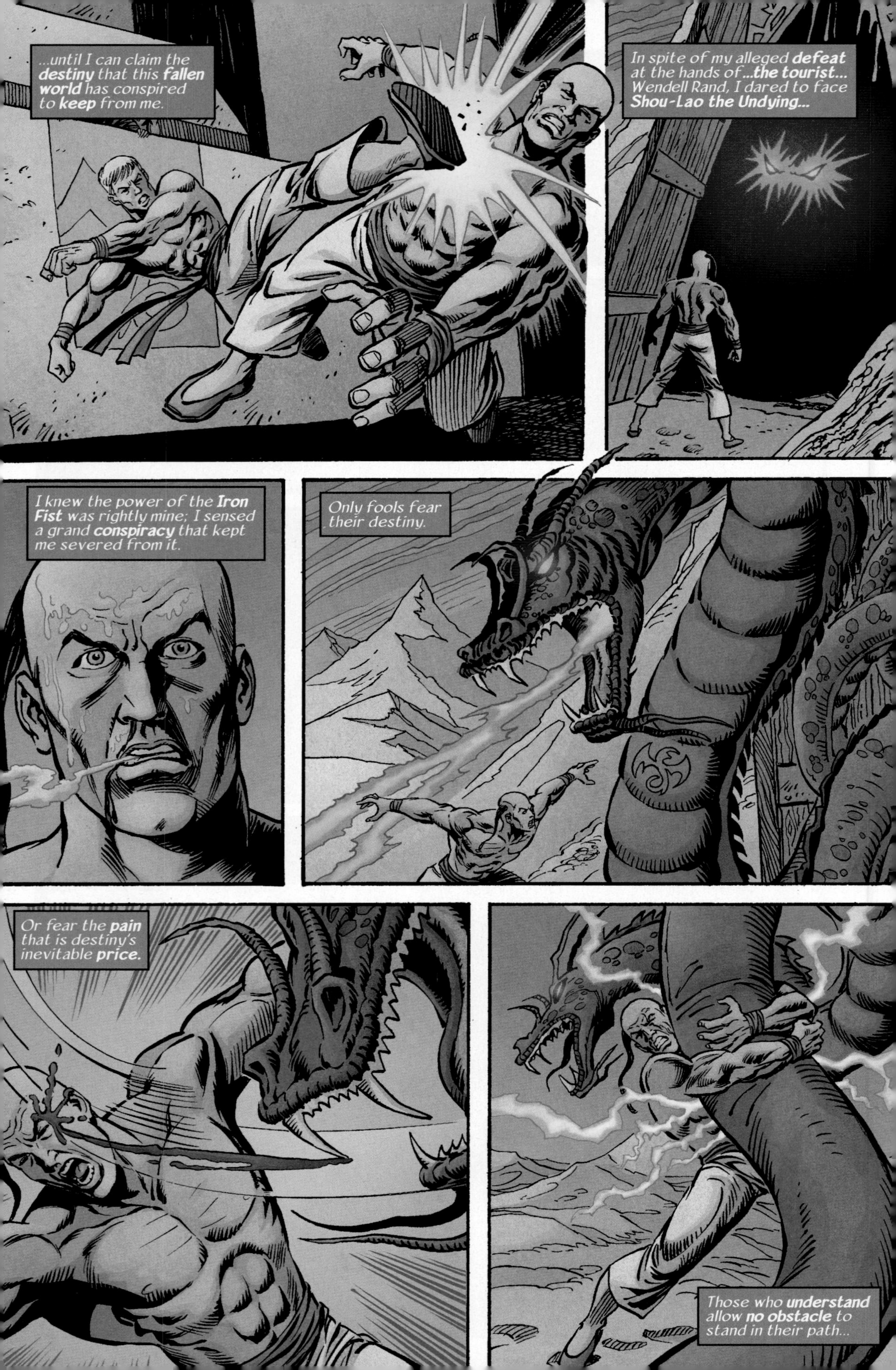
...until I can claim the destiny that this fallen world has conspired to keep from me.
In spite of my alleged defeat at the hands of ...the tourist... Wendell Rand, I dared to face Shou-Lao the Undying...
I knew the power of the Iron Fist was rightly mine; I sensed a grand conspiracy that kept me severed from it.
Only fools fear their destiny.
Or fear the pain that is destiny's inevitable price.
Those who understand allow no obstacle to stand in their path...

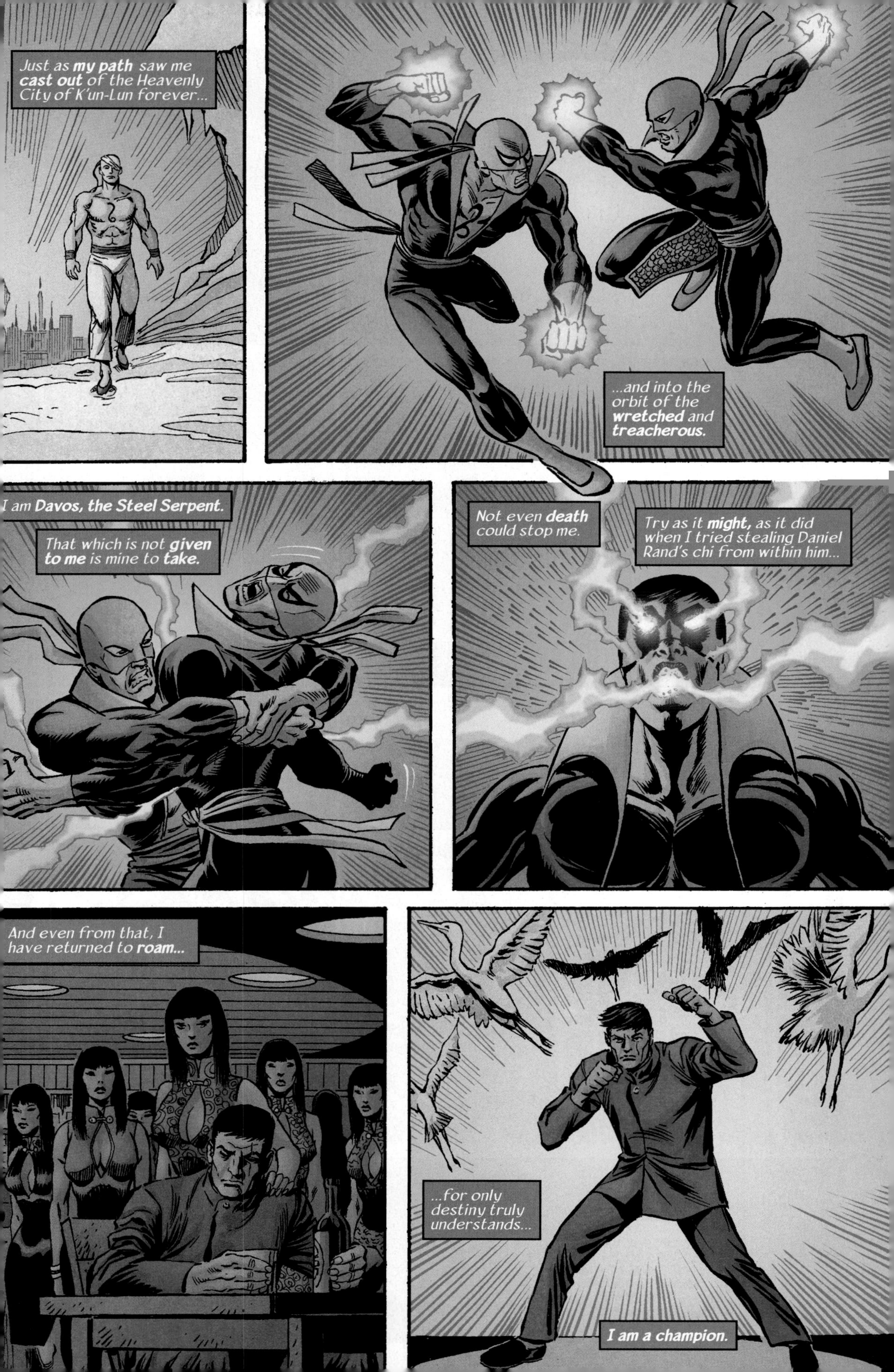
Just as my path saw me cast out of the Heavenly City of K'un-Lun forever...
...and into the orbit of the wretched and treacherous.
I am Davos, the Steel Serpent.
That which is not given to me is mine to take.
Not even death could stop me.
Try as it might, as it did when I tried stealing Daniel Rand's chi from within him...
And even from that, I have returned to roam...
...for only destiny truly understands...
I am a champion.

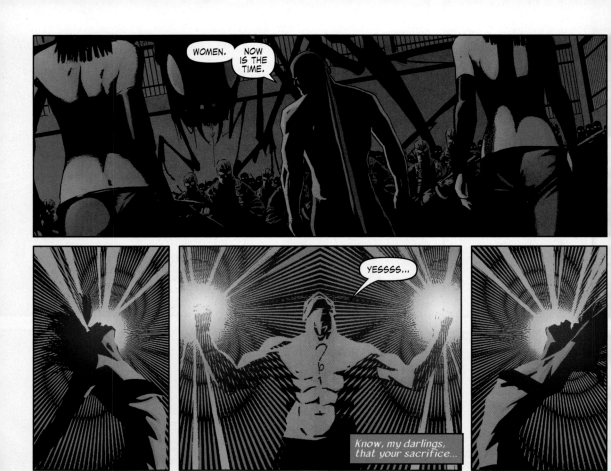

WOMEN. NOW IS THE TIME.

YESSSS...

Know, my darlings, that your sacrifice...

WHAT THE--

KKKRRRZZZZZZZZZZKKK

...was not in *vain*.

TWO HYDRA LEGIONS AND *MECHAGORGON.* NOT A SINGLE ONE OF THEM MANAGED TO EVEN *TOUCH* ME.

MOTHER. I'M *READY* AT LAST...

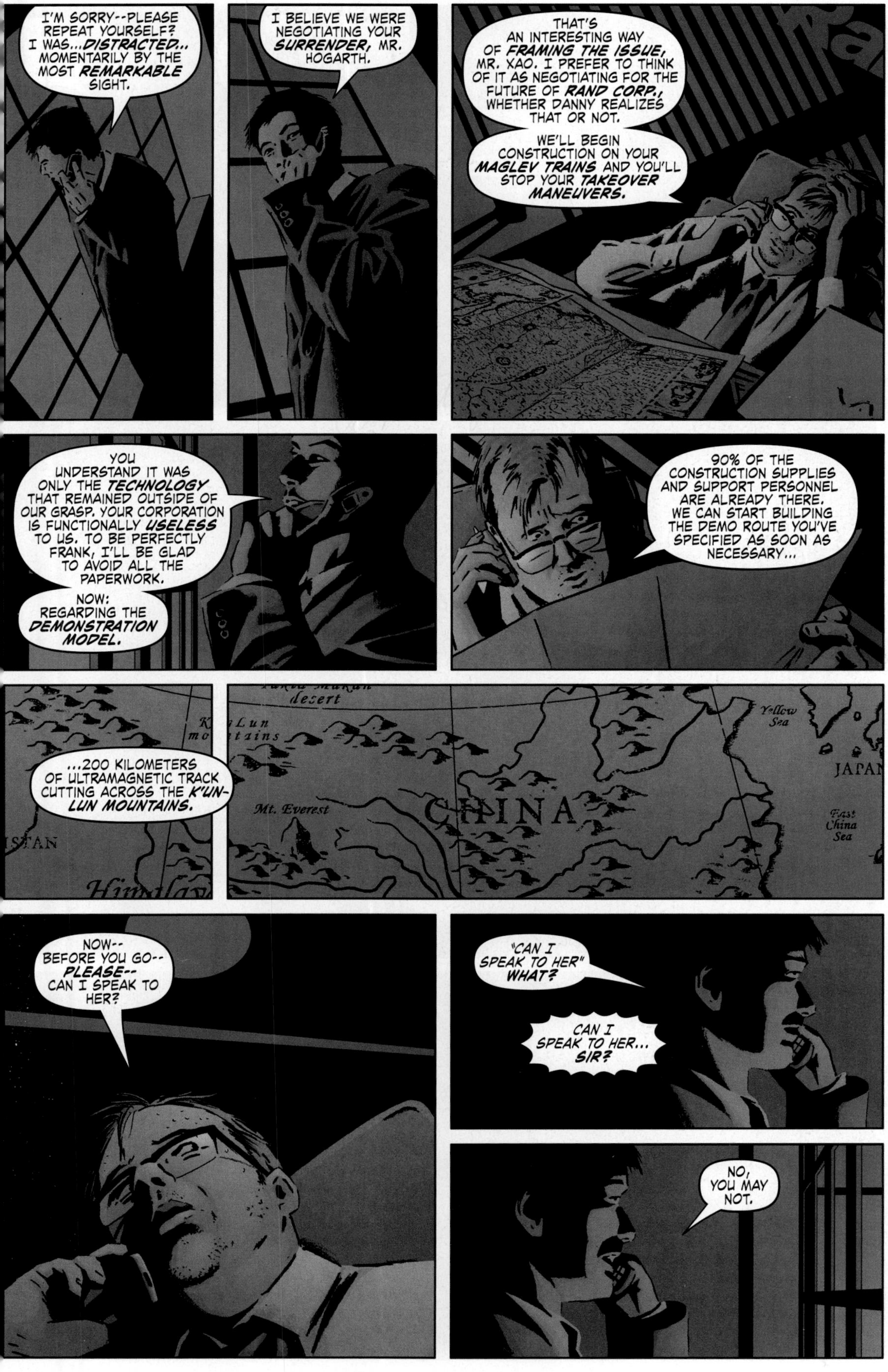

I'M SORRY--PLEASE REPEAT YOURSELF? I WAS...*DISTRACTED*... MOMENTARILY BY THE MOST *REMARKABLE* SIGHT.
I BELIEVE WE WERE NEGOTIATING YOUR *SURRENDER,* MR. HOGARTH.
THAT'S AN INTERESTING WAY OF *FRAMING THE ISSUE,* MR. XAO. I PREFER TO THINK OF IT AS NEGOTIATING FOR THE FUTURE OF *RAND CORP.,* WHETHER DANNY REALIZES THAT OR NOT.
WE'LL BEGIN CONSTRUCTION ON YOUR *MAGLEV TRAINS* AND YOU'LL STOP YOUR *TAKEOVER MANEUVERS.*
YOU UNDERSTAND IT WAS ONLY THE *TECHNOLOGY* THAT REMAINED OUTSIDE OF OUR GRASP. YOUR CORPORATION IS FUNCTIONALLY *USELESS* TO US. TO BE PERFECTLY FRANK, I'LL BE GLAD TO AVOID ALL THE PAPERWORK.
NOW: REGARDING THE *DEMONSTRATION MODEL.*
90% OF THE CONSTRUCTION SUPPLIES AND SUPPORT PERSONNEL ARE ALREADY THERE. WE CAN START BUILDING THE DEMO ROUTE YOU'VE SPECIFIED AS SOON AS NECESSARY...
...200 KILOMETERS OF ULTRAMAGNETIC TRACK CUTTING ACROSS THE *K'UN-LUN MOUNTAINS.*
desert
Yellow Sea
Mt. Everest
CHINA
East China Sea
NOW-- BEFORE YOU GO-- *PLEASE--* CAN I SPEAK TO HER?
"CAN I SPEAK TO HER" *WHAT?*
CAN I SPEAK TO HER... *SIR?*
NO, YOU MAY NOT.

RRRRRRRUUMMMBLEEE

THIS ISN'T RIGHT.

THERE SHOULDN'T BE ANY TRAINS RUNNING UP THERE.

ORSON, IT'S THE MTA. THEY CAN'T EVEN KEEP THE TRAINS RUNNING TO *BROOKLYN* ON THE WEEKENDS.

THIS *ISN'T RIGHT*. WE'RE BEI INVADED. GET READY.

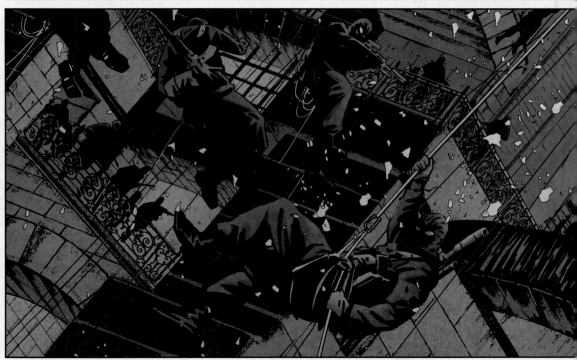

SO THEN I GUESS IT'S TIME TO SEE YOUR MIGHTY *GUN FU*.

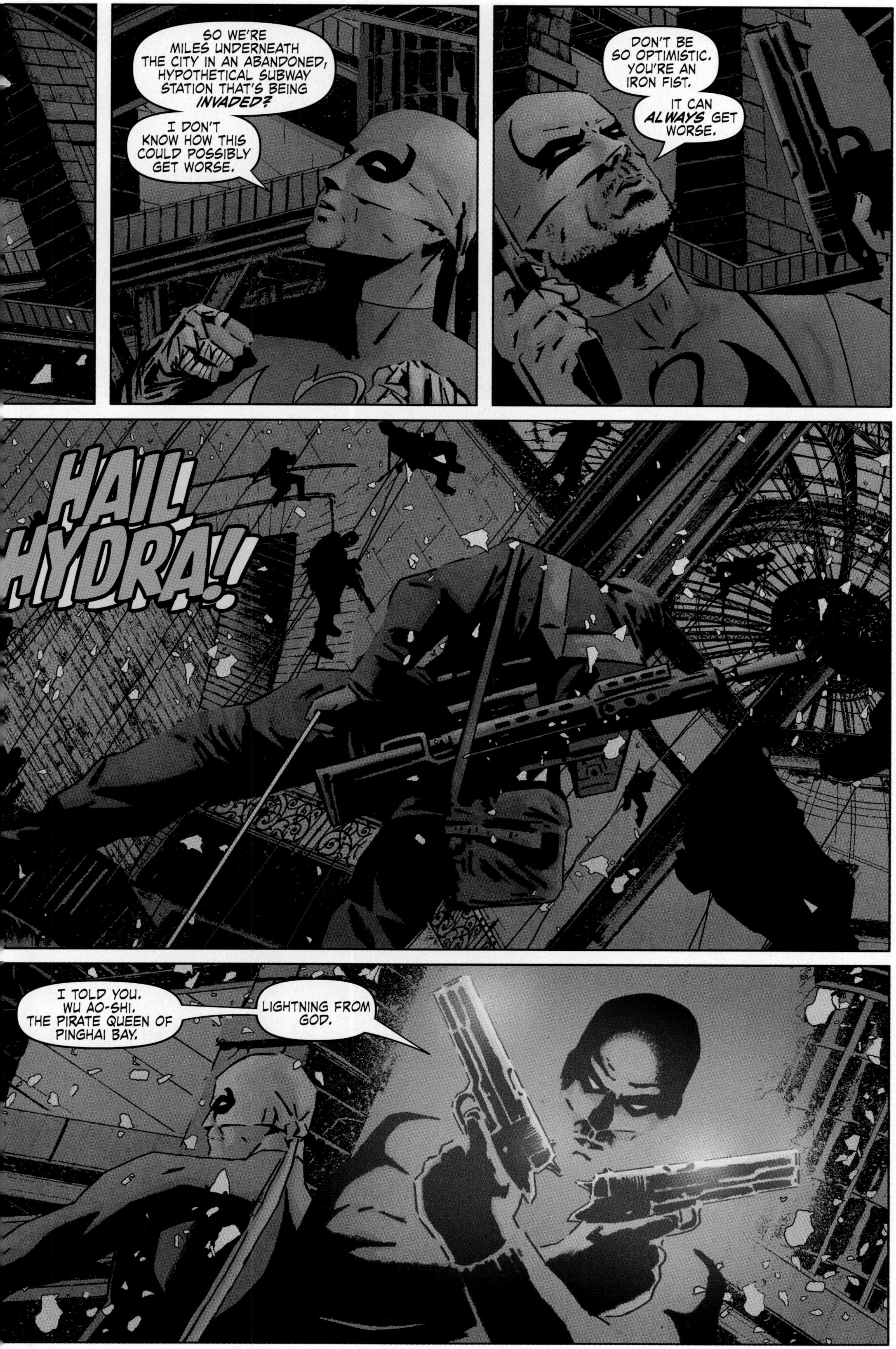
SO WE'RE MILES UNDERNEATH THE CITY IN AN ABANDONED, HYPOTHETICAL SUBWAY STATION THAT'S BEING *INVADED?*
I DON'T KNOW HOW THIS COULD POSSIBLY GET WORSE.
DON'T BE SO OPTIMISTIC. YOU'RE AN IRON FIST.
IT CAN *ALWAYS* GET WORSE.
HAIL HYDRA!!
I TOLD YOU. WU AO-SHI. THE PIRATE QUEEN OF PINGHAI BAY.
LIGHTNING FROM GOD.

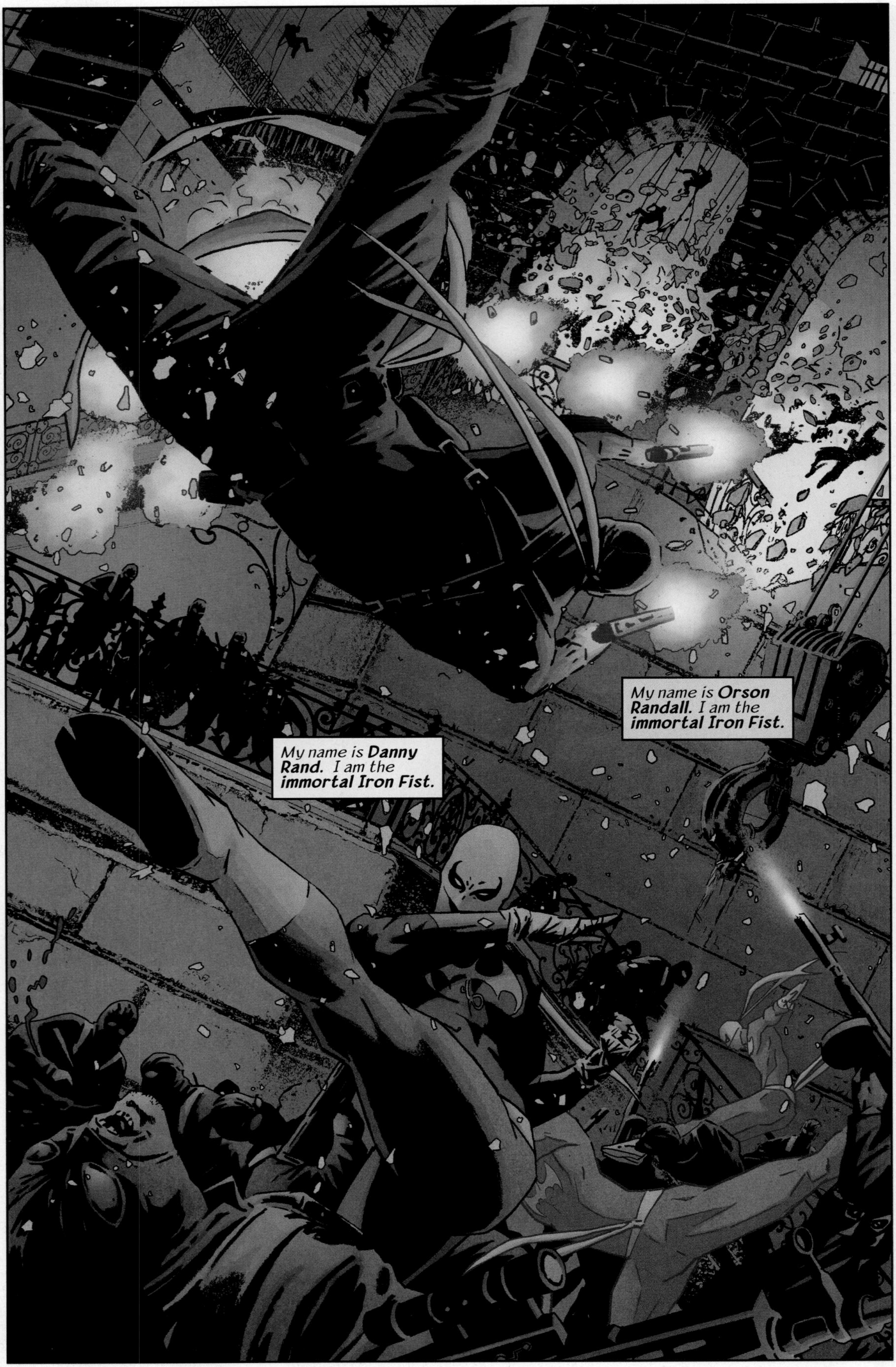
My name is **Danny Rand.** I am the **immortal Iron Fist.**
My name is **Orson Randall.** I am the **immortal Iron Fist.**

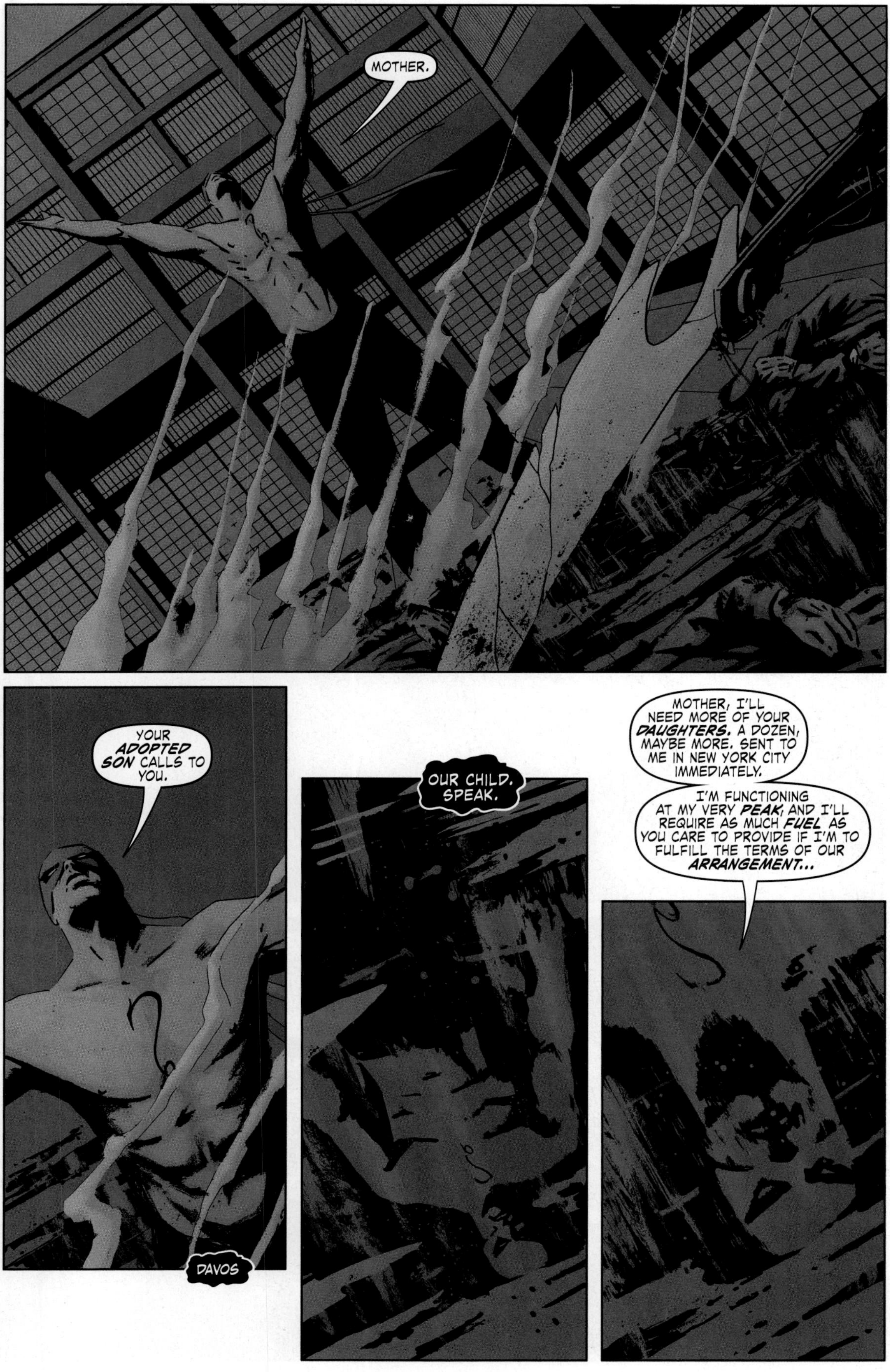
MOTHER.
YOUR ADOPTED SON CALLS TO YOU.
DAVOS
OUR CHILD. SPEAK.
MOTHER, I'LL NEED MORE OF YOUR DAUGHTERS. A DOZEN, MAYBE MORE. SENT TO ME IN NEW YORK CITY IMMEDIATELY.
I'M FUNCTIONING AT MY VERY PEAK, AND I'LL REQUIRE AS MUCH FUEL AS YOU CARE TO PROVIDE IF I'M TO FULFILL THE TERMS OF OUR ARRANGEMENT...

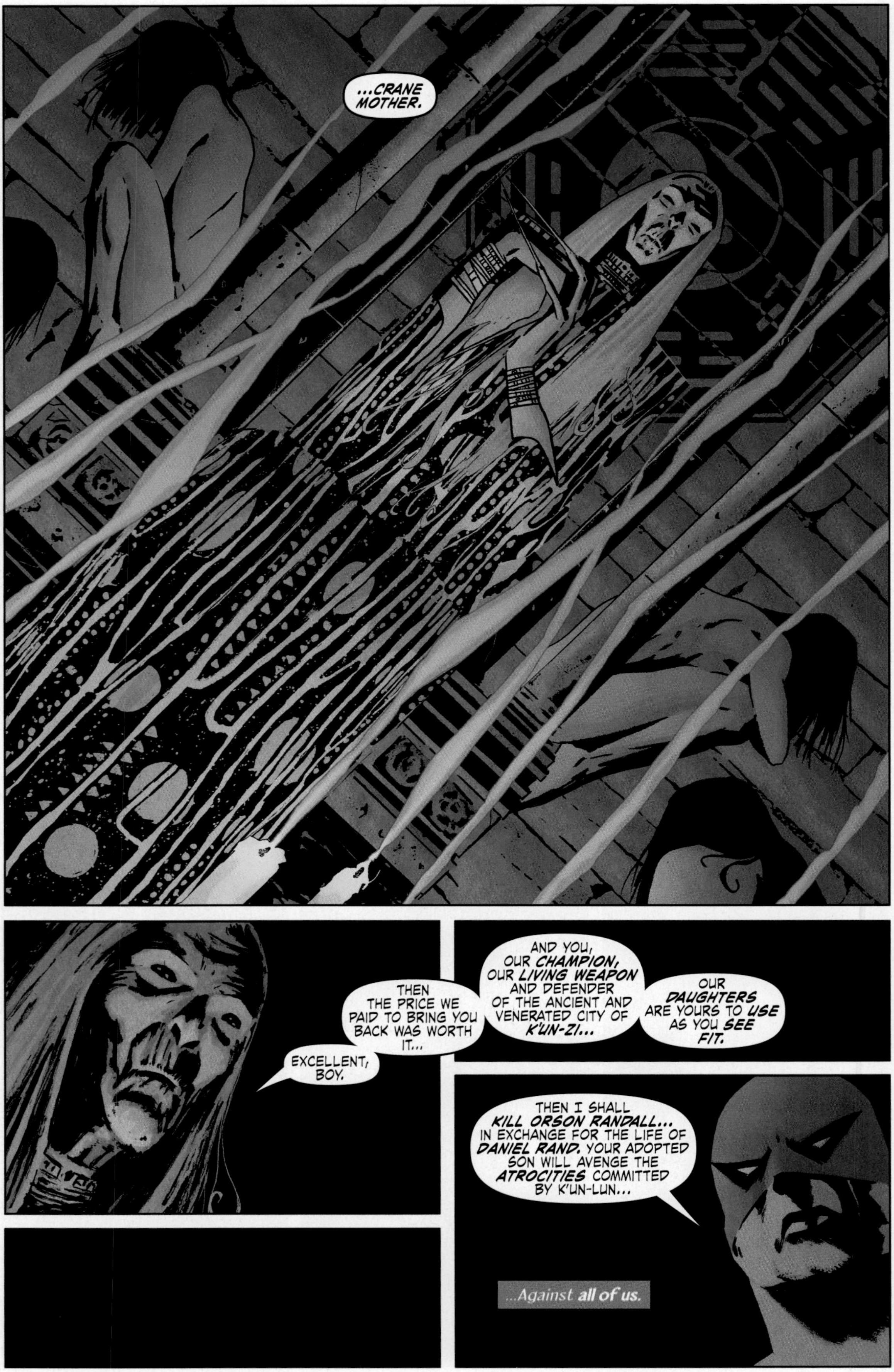
...CRANE MOTHER.
EXCELLENT, BOY.
THEN THE PRICE WE PAID TO BRING YOU BACK WAS WORTH IT...
AND YOU, OUR CHAMPION, OUR LIVING WEAPON AND DEFENDER OF THE ANCIENT AND VENERATED CITY OF K'UN-ZI...
OUR DAUGHTERS ARE YOURS TO USE AS YOU SEE FIT.
THEN I SHALL KILL ORSON RANDALL... IN EXCHANGE FOR THE LIFE OF DANIEL RAND. YOUR ADOPTED SON WILL AVENGE THE ATROCITIES COMMITTED BY K'UN-LUN...
...Against all of us.

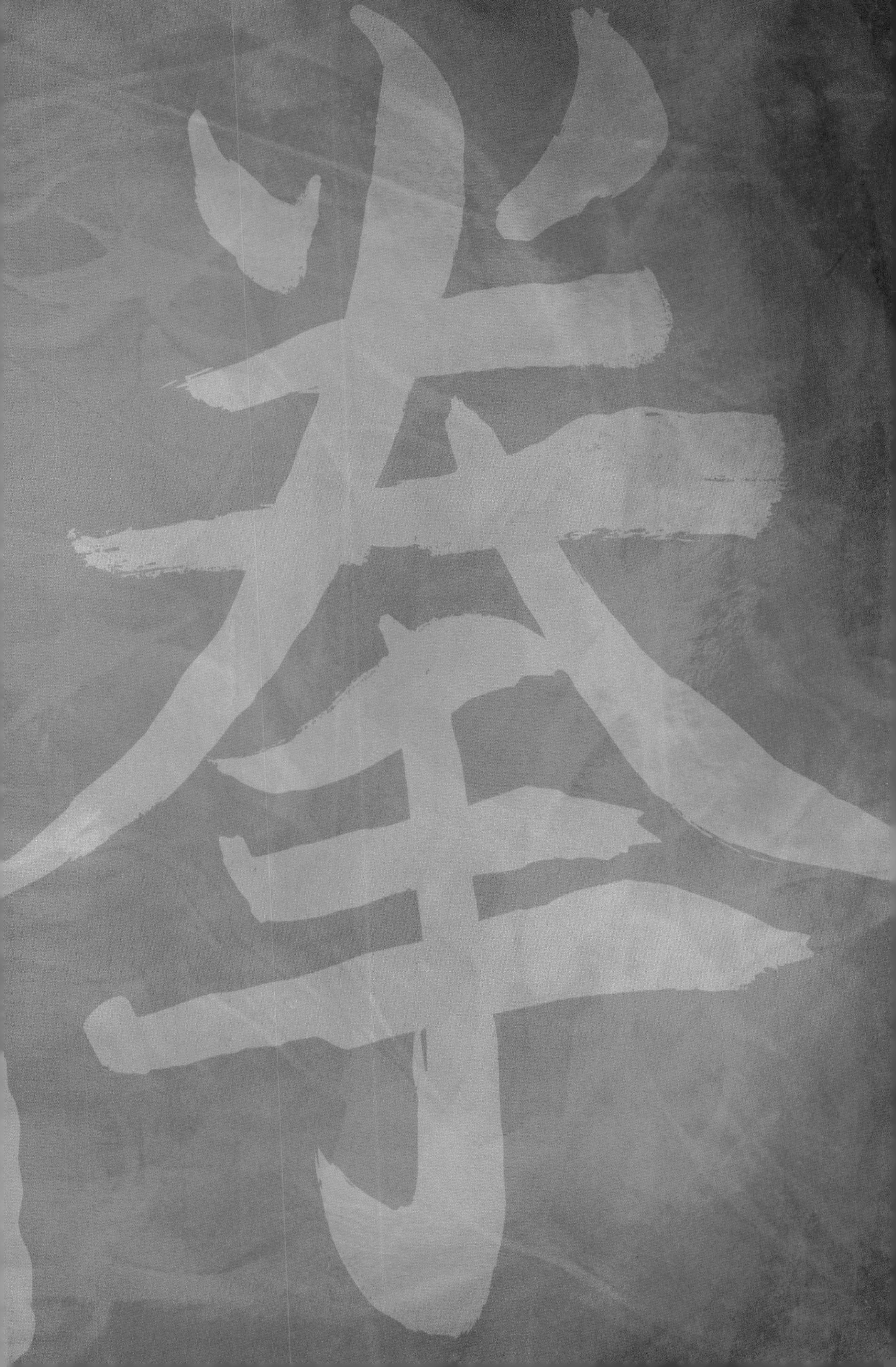
拳

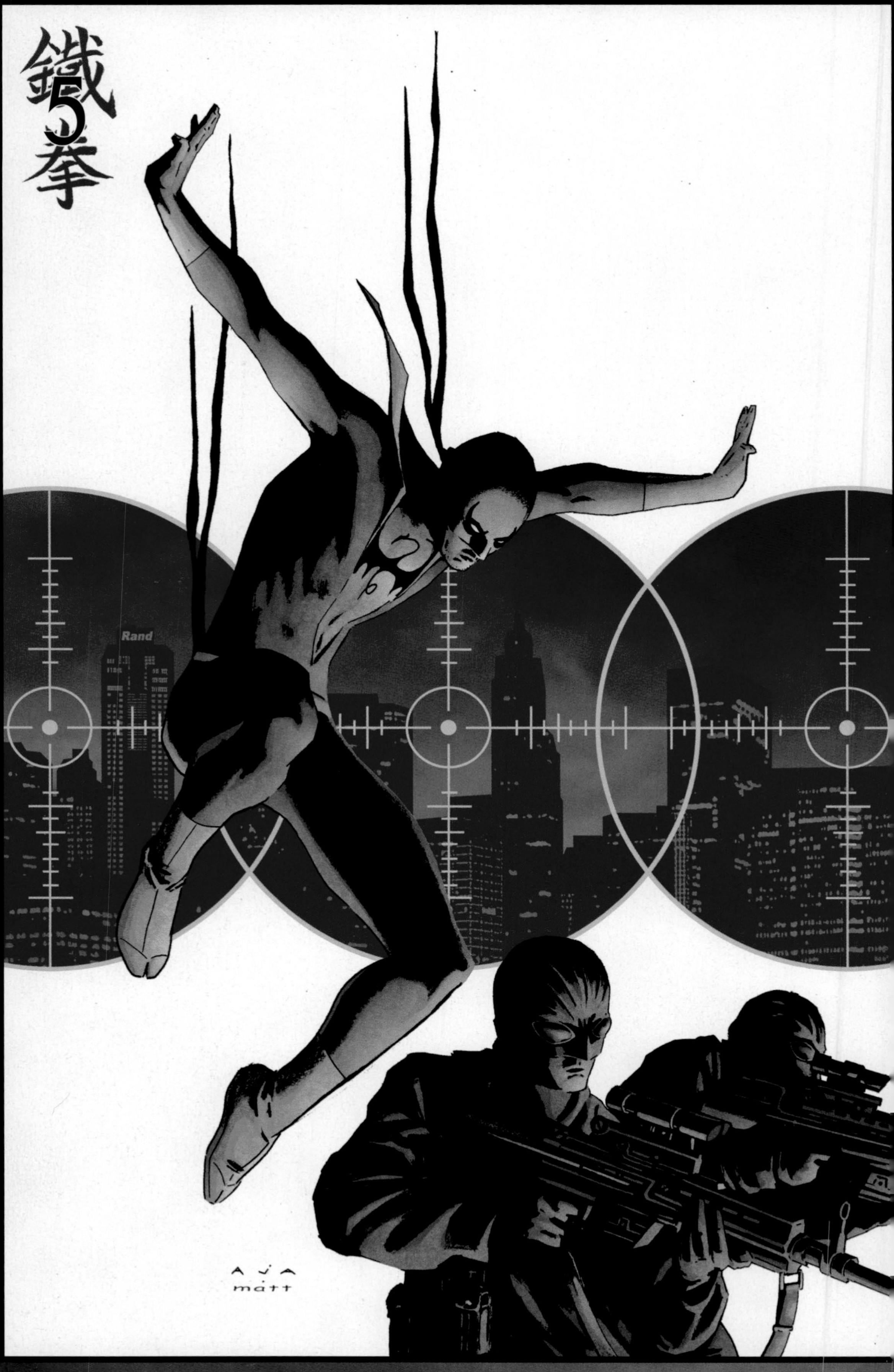
鐵
5
拳
Rand
AJA
matt

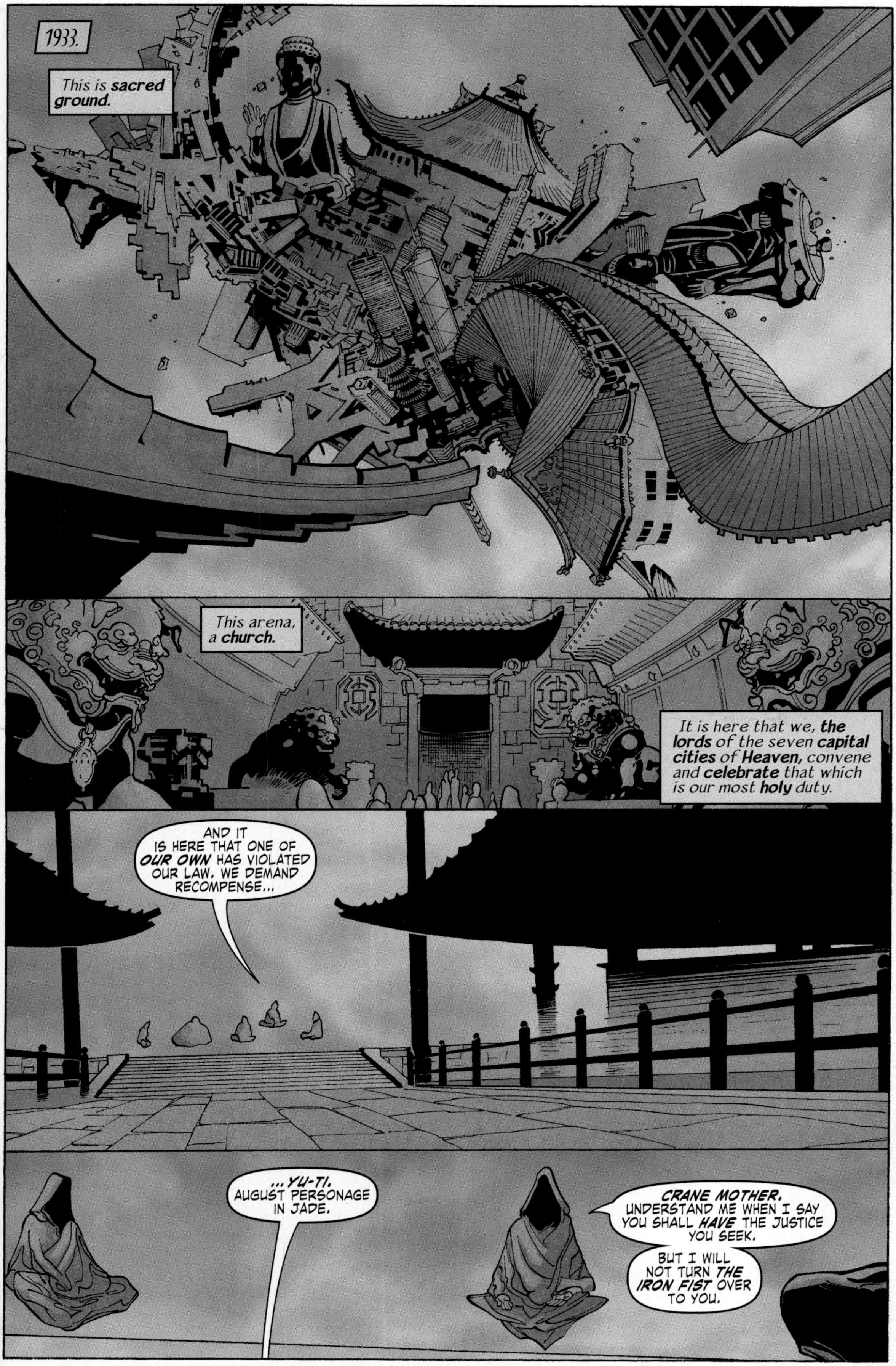
1933.
This is **sacred ground.**
This arena, a **church.**
It is here that we, **the lords** of the seven **capital cities** of **Heaven,** convene and **celebrate** that which is our most **holy** duty.
AND IT IS HERE THAT ONE OF ***OUR OWN*** HAS VIOLATED OUR LAW. WE DEMAND RECOMPENSE...
...*YU-TI.* AUGUST PERSONAGE IN JADE.
CRANE MOTHER. UNDERSTAND ME WHEN I SAY YOU SHALL ***HAVE*** THE JUSTICE YOU SEEK.
BUT I WILL NOT TURN ***THE IRON FIST*** OVER TO YOU.

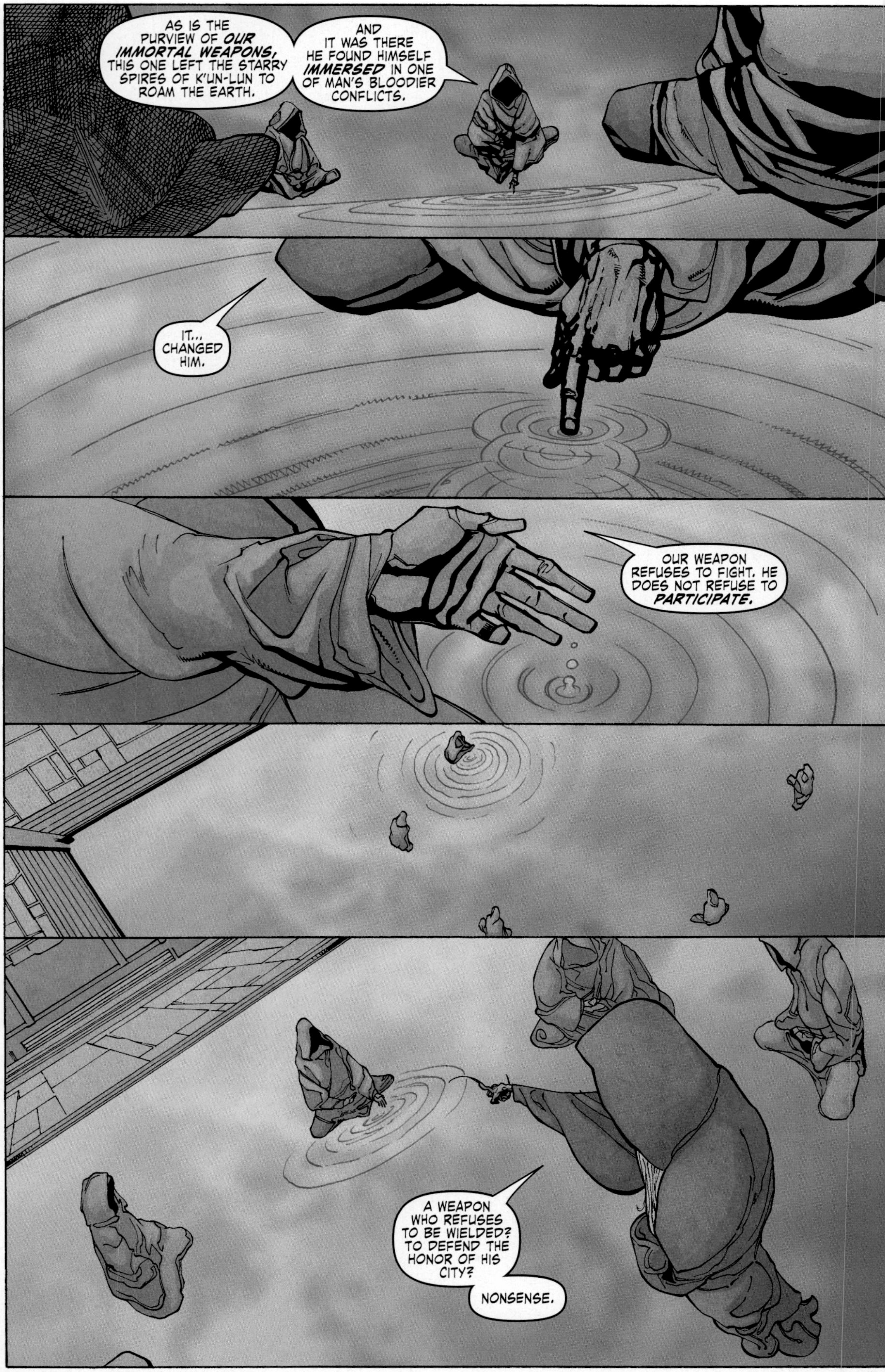
AS IS THE PURVIEW OF OUR IMMORTAL WEAPONS, THIS ONE LEFT THE STARRY SPIRES OF K'UN-LUN TO ROAM THE EARTH.
AND IT WAS THERE HE FOUND HIMSELF IMMERSED IN ONE OF MAN'S BLOODIER CONFLICTS.
IT... CHANGED HIM.
OUR WEAPON REFUSES TO FIGHT. HE DOES NOT REFUSE TO PARTICIPATE.
A WEAPON WHO REFUSES TO BE WIELDED? TO DEFEND THE HONOR OF HIS CITY?
NONSENSE.

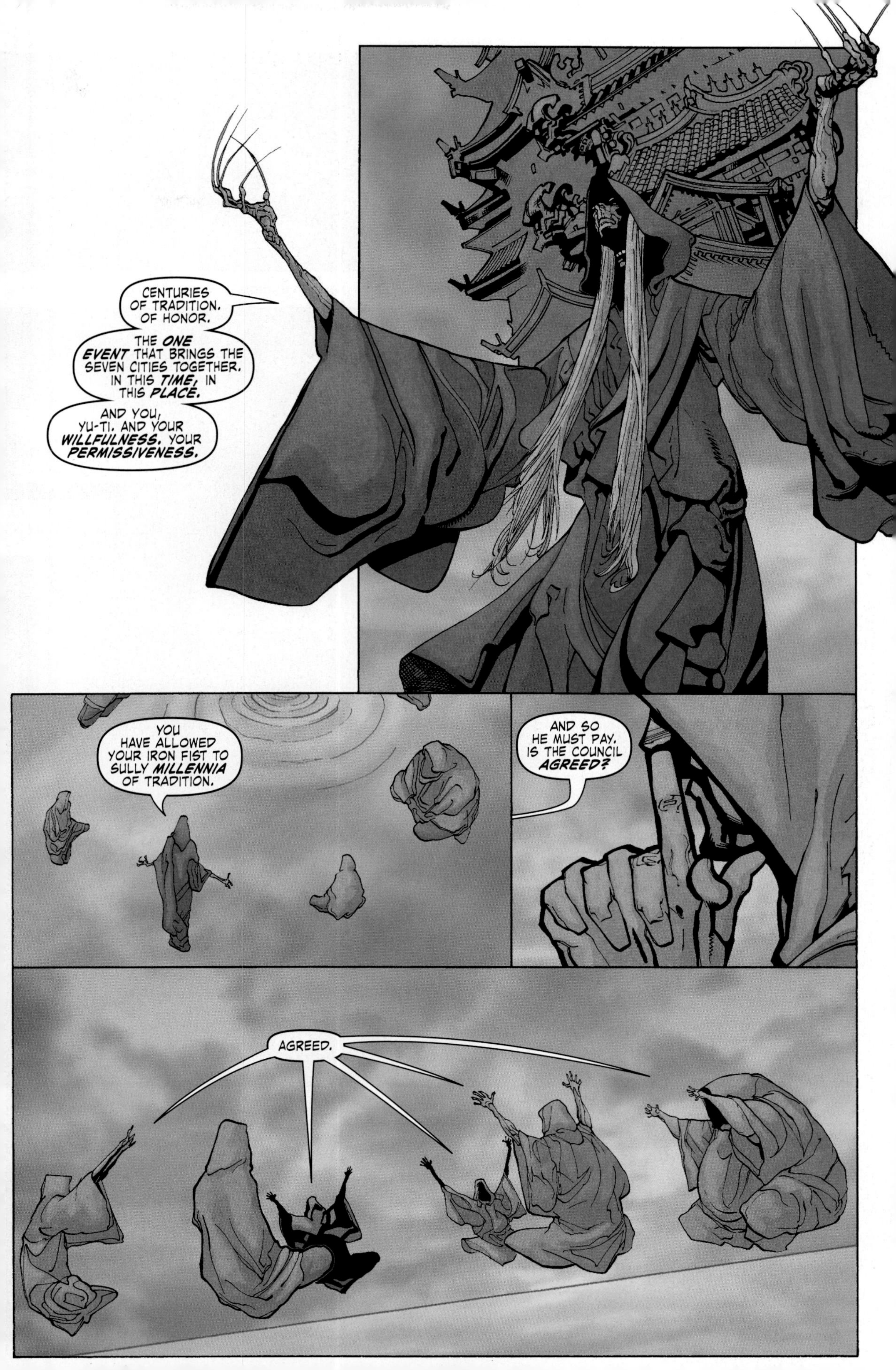
CENTURIES OF TRADITION. OF HONOR.
THE *ONE EVENT* THAT BRINGS THE SEVEN CITIES TOGETHER. IN THIS *TIME,* IN THIS *PLACE.*
AND YOU, YU-TI. AND YOUR *WILLFULNESS.* YOUR *PERMISSIVENESS.*
YOU HAVE ALLOWED YOUR IRON FIST TO SULLY *MILLENNIA* OF TRADITION.
AND SO HE MUST PAY. IS THE COUNCIL *AGREED?*
AGREED.

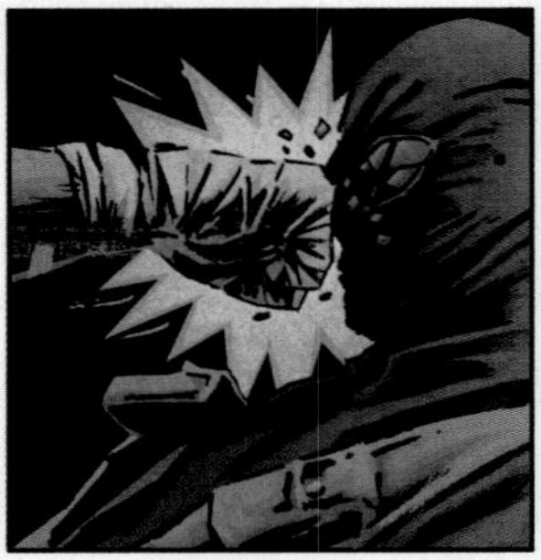

Golden star gouge.

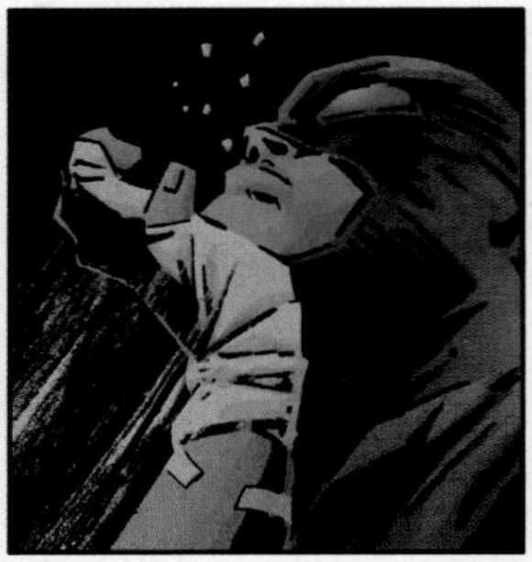

Strike of the silkworm's tooth.

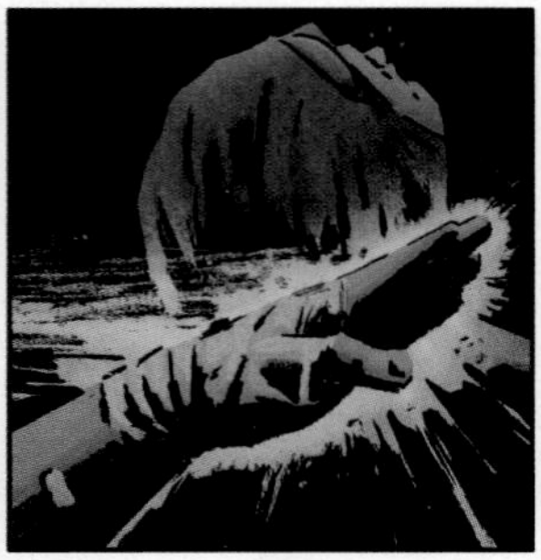

Burning dove chop.

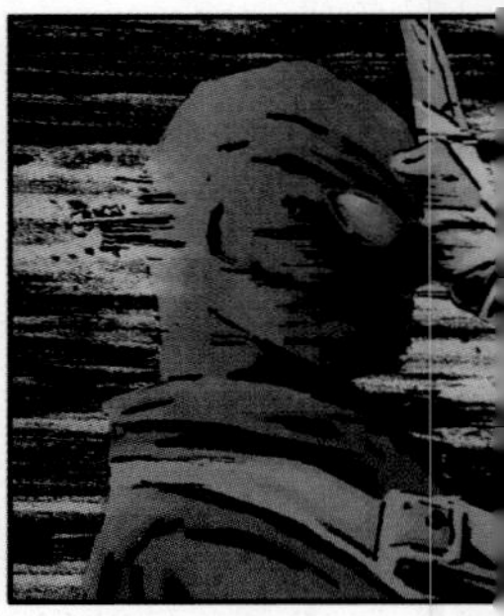

Palm of forty sorrows.

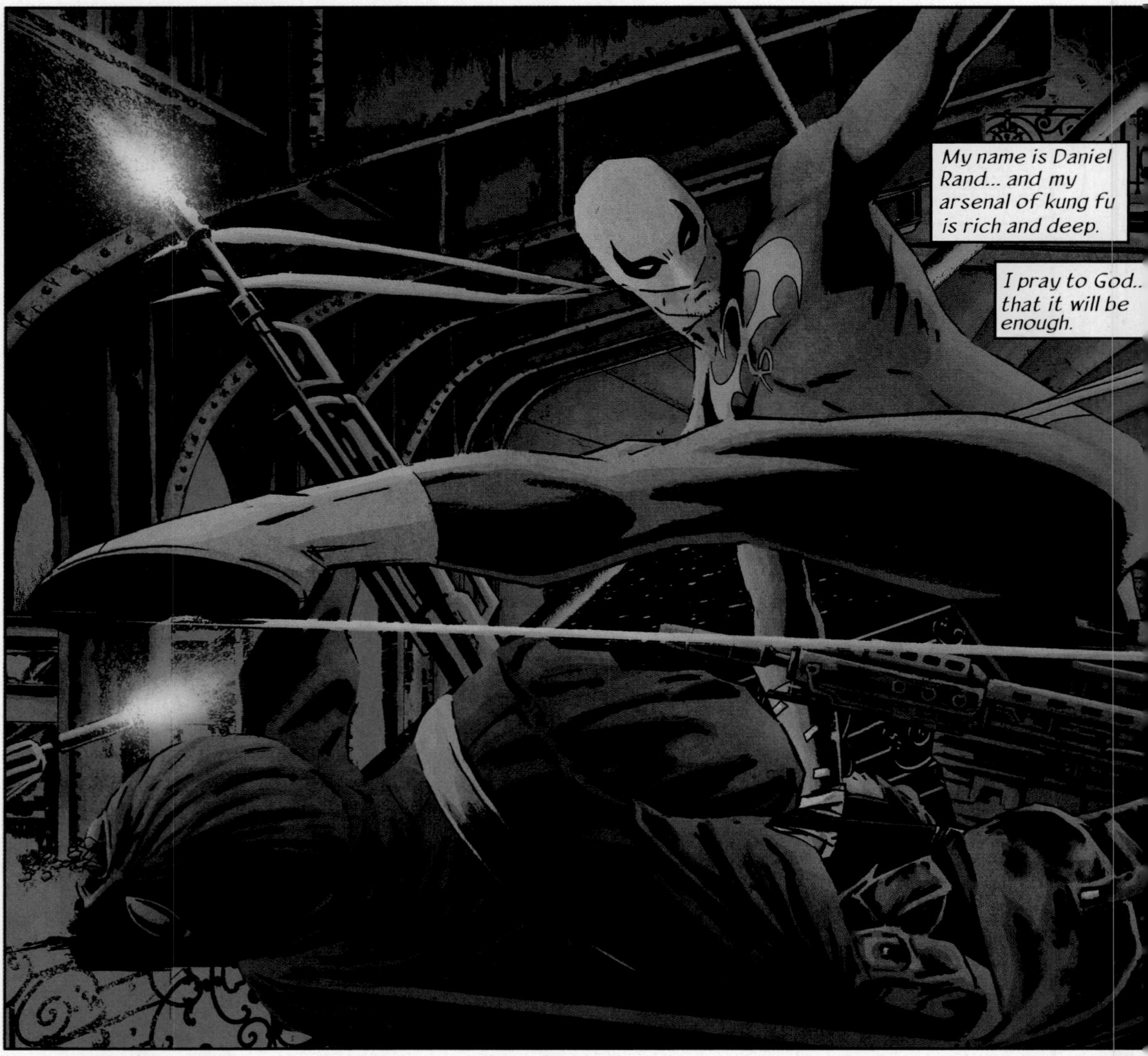
My name is Daniel Rand... and my arsenal of kung fu is rich and deep.
I pray to God.. that it will be enough.

For Tony.

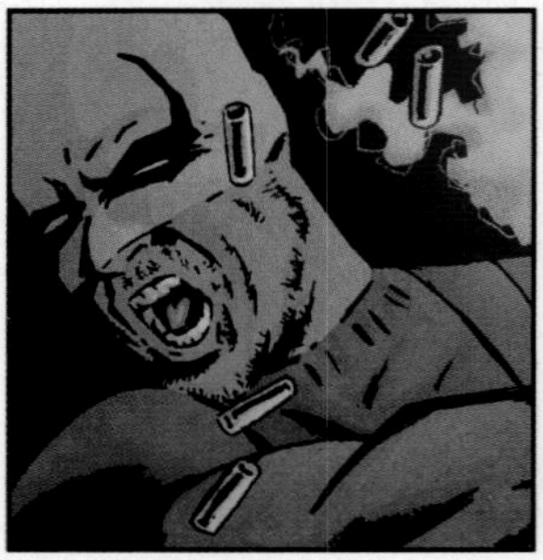

For Jean-Claude.

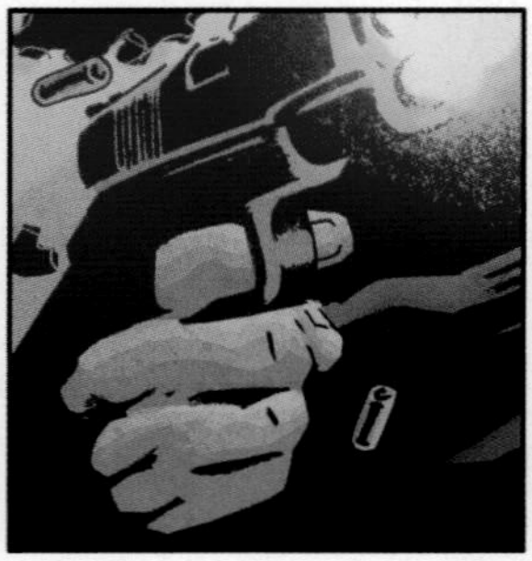

For Marie.

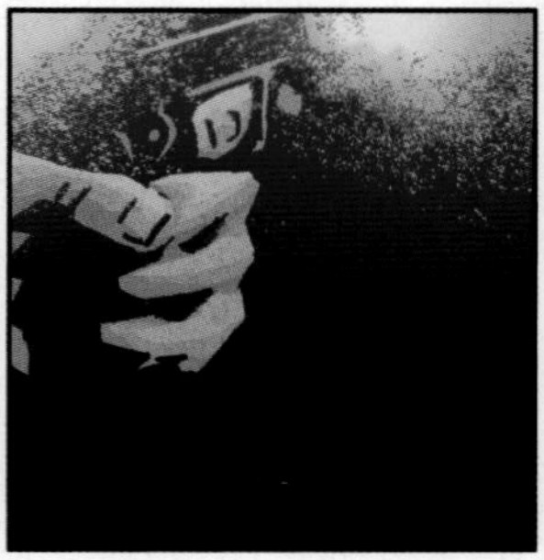

For Milo the cigarette do

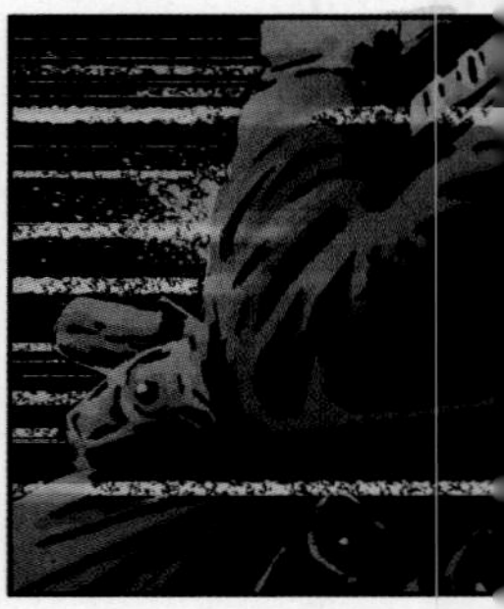

...ger scratch (2nd stance).   Drunken wasp sting.   Good fortune thunder kick.   Brooklyn headbutt.

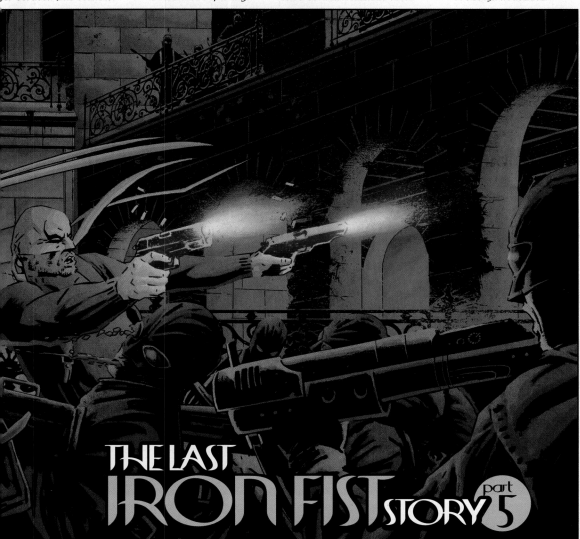

THE LAST
IRON FIST STORY part 5

...d Raymond and Peter.   And that kid from Iowa.   What was that kid's name?   Damn it, I can't remember his name anymore.

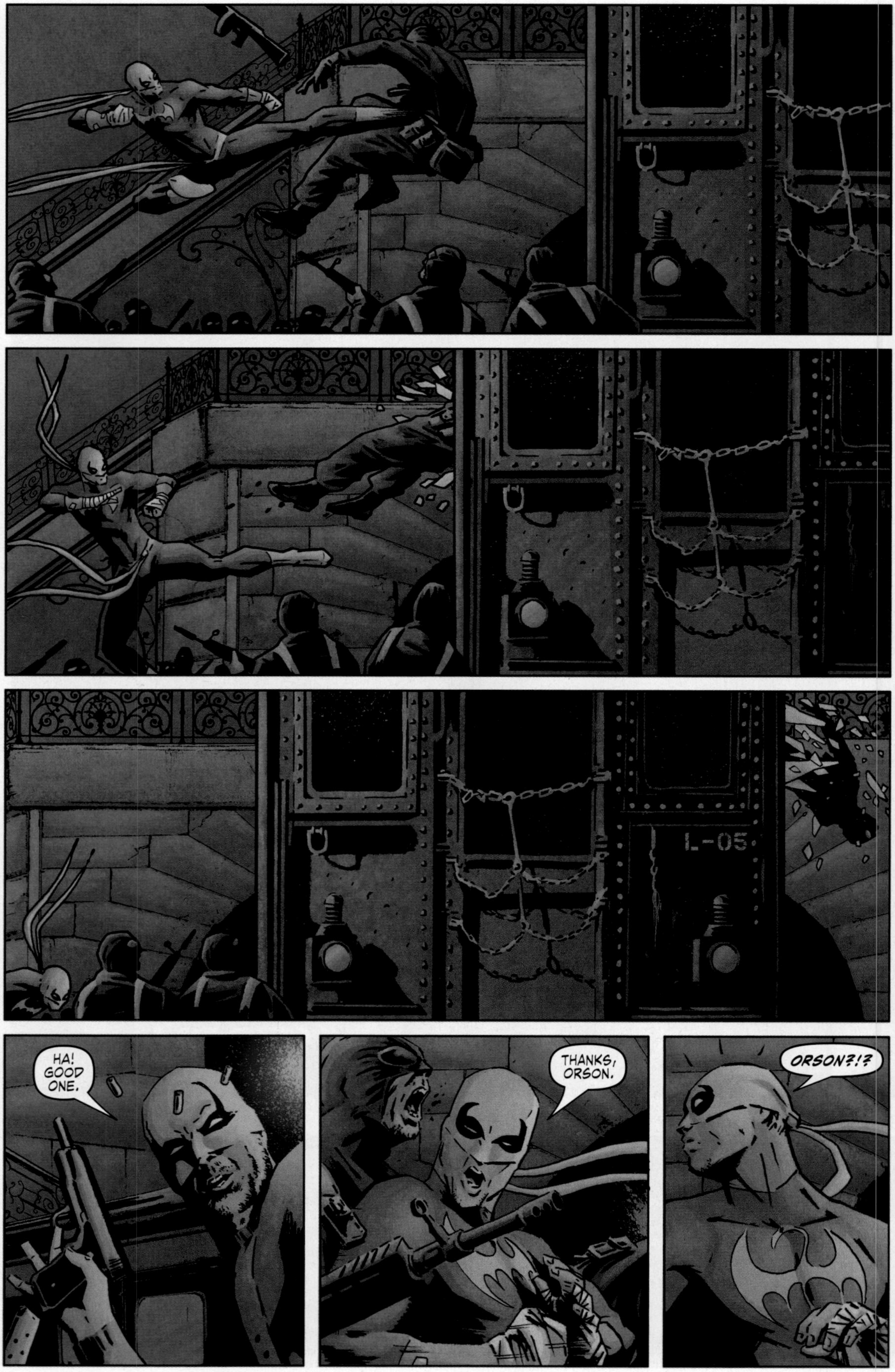
HA! GOOD ONE.
THANKS, ORSON.
ORSON?!?
L-05

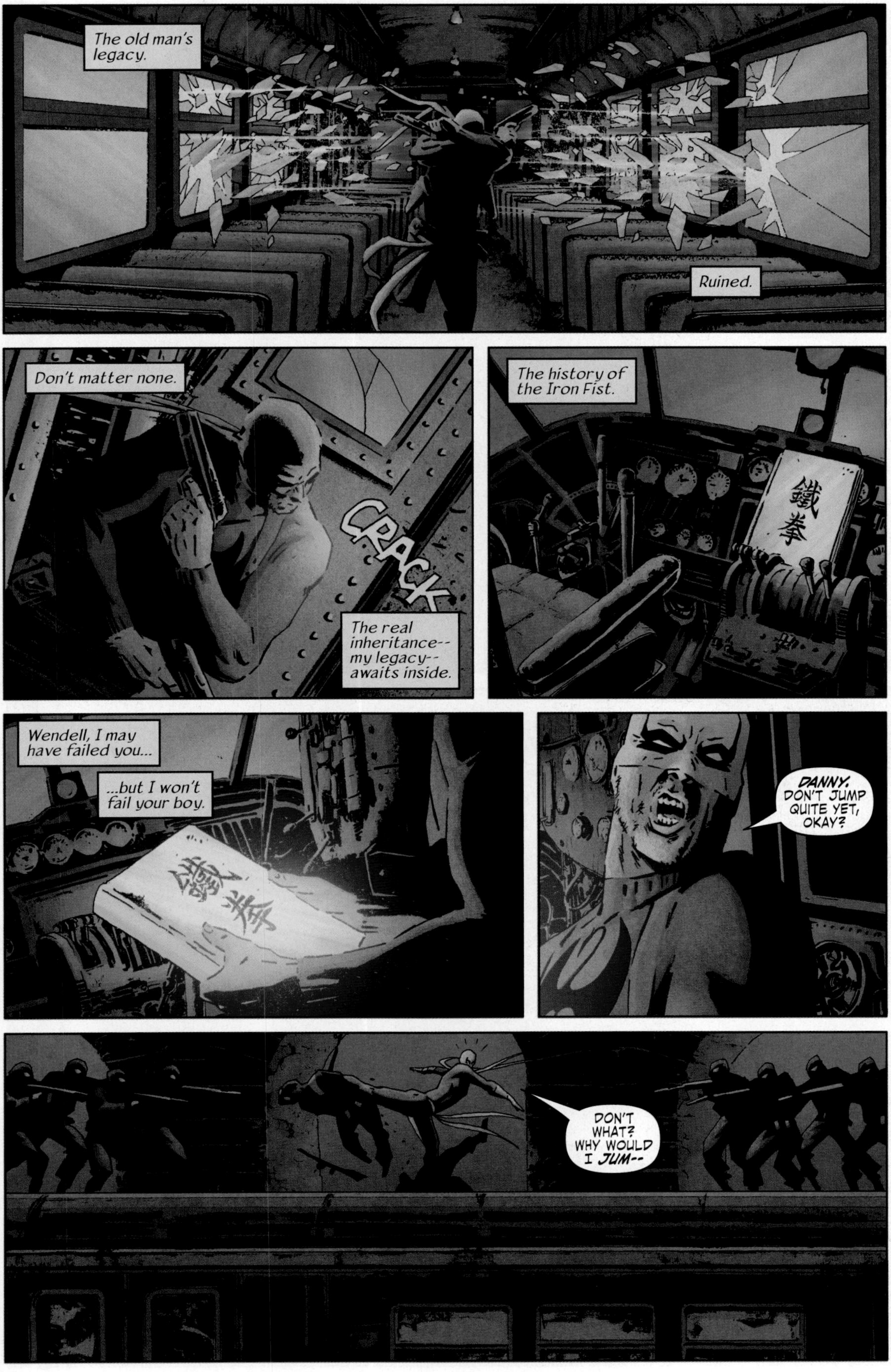
The old man's legacy.
Ruined.
Don't matter none.
CRACK
The real inheritance--my legacy--awaits inside.
The history of the Iron Fist.
鐵拳
Wendell, I may have failed you...
...but I won't fail your boy.
鐵拳
DANNY. DON'T JUMP QUITE YET, OKAY?
DON'T WHAT? WHY WOULD I JUM--

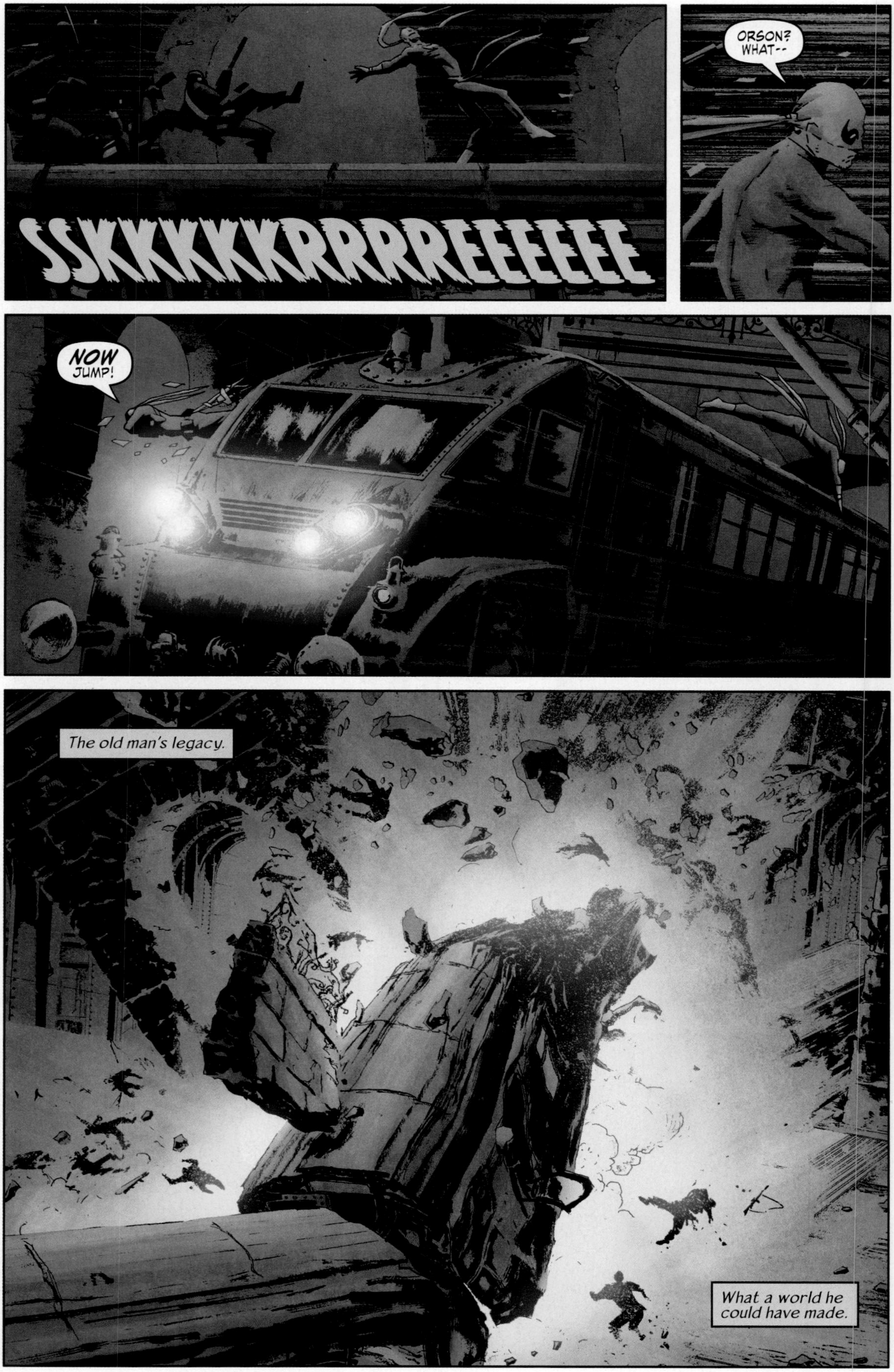
SSKKKKKRRRRREEEEEE
ORSON? WHAT--
NOW JUMP!
The old man's legacy.
What a world he could have made.

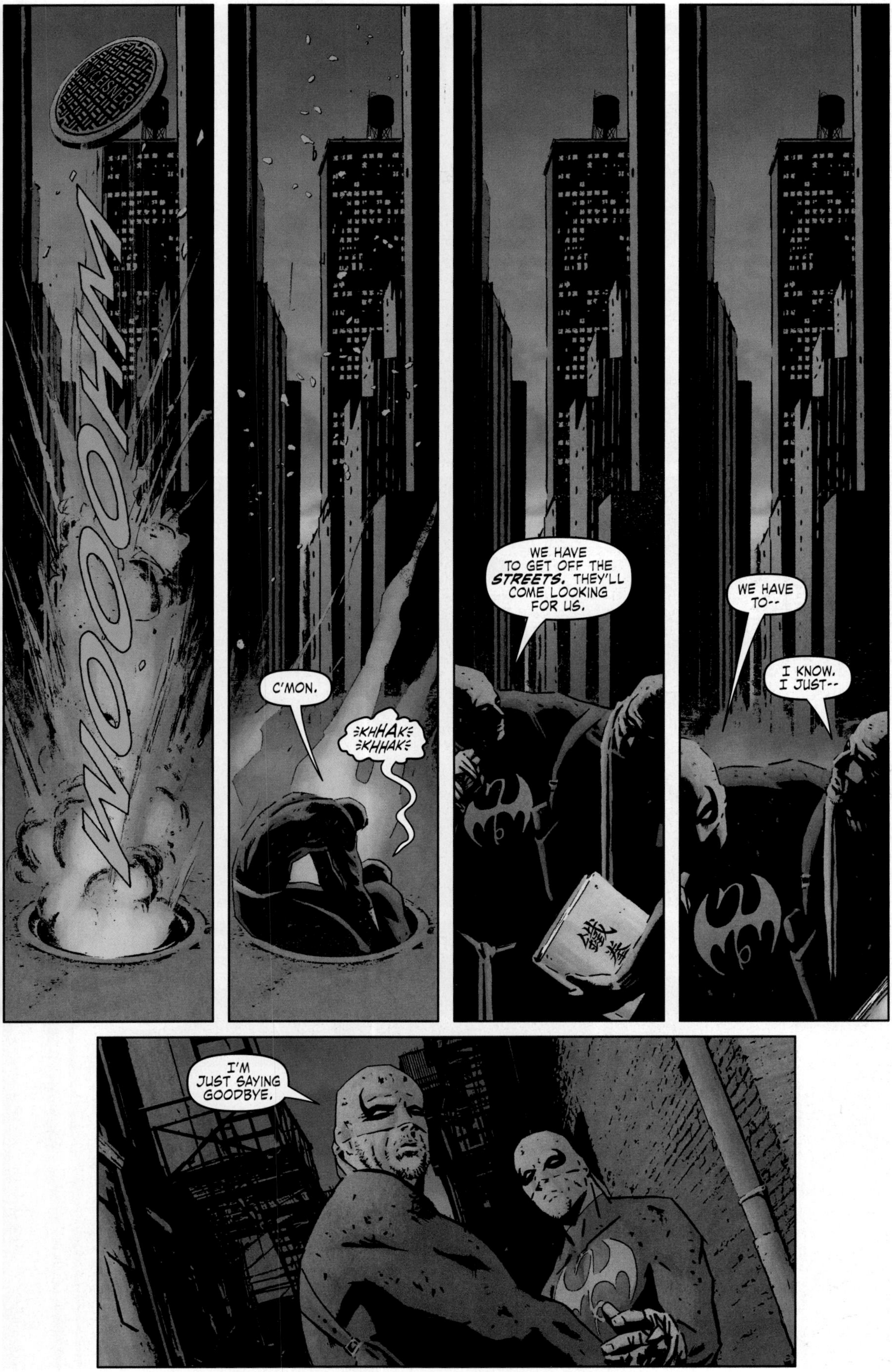
WHOOOOM
C'MON.
KHHAK KHHAK
WE HAVE TO GET OFF THE STREETS. THEY'LL COME LOOKING FOR US.
WE HAVE TO--
I KNOW. I JUST--
I'M JUST SAYING GOODBYE.

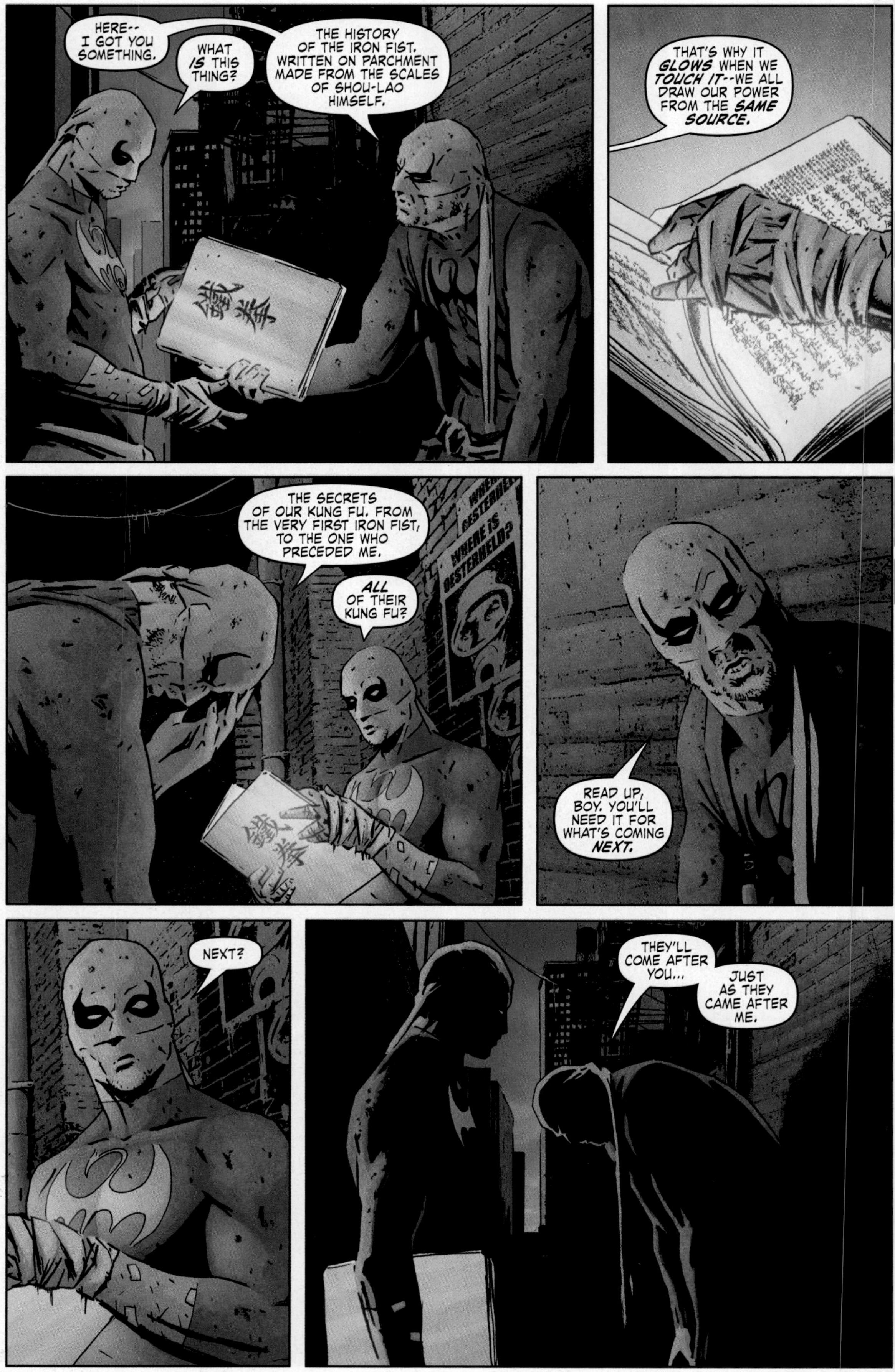
HERE-- I GOT YOU SOMETHING.
WHAT IS THIS THING?
THE HISTORY OF THE IRON FIST. WRITTEN ON PARCHMENT MADE FROM THE SCALES OF SHOU-LAO HIMSELF.
THAT'S WHY IT GLOWS WHEN WE TOUCH IT--WE ALL DRAW OUR POWER FROM THE SAME SOURCE.
THE SECRETS OF OUR KUNG FU. FROM THE VERY FIRST IRON FIST, TO THE ONE WHO PRECEDED ME.
ALL OF THEIR KUNG FU?
WHERE IS OESTERHELD?
READ UP, BOY. YOU'LL NEED IT FOR WHAT'S COMING NEXT.
NEXT?
THEY'LL COME AFTER YOU...
JUST AS THEY CAME AFTER ME.

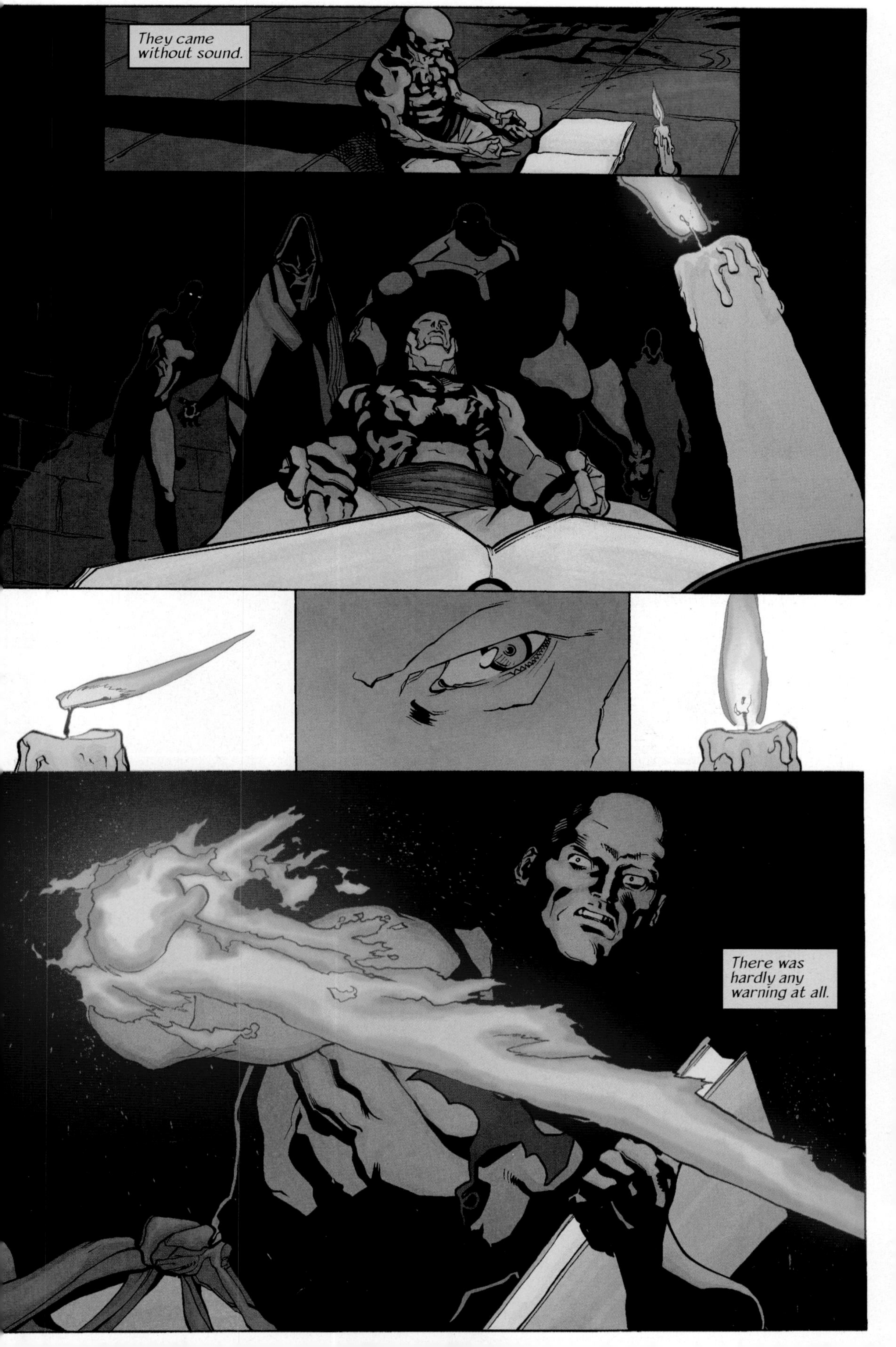
They came without sound.
There was hardly any warning at all.

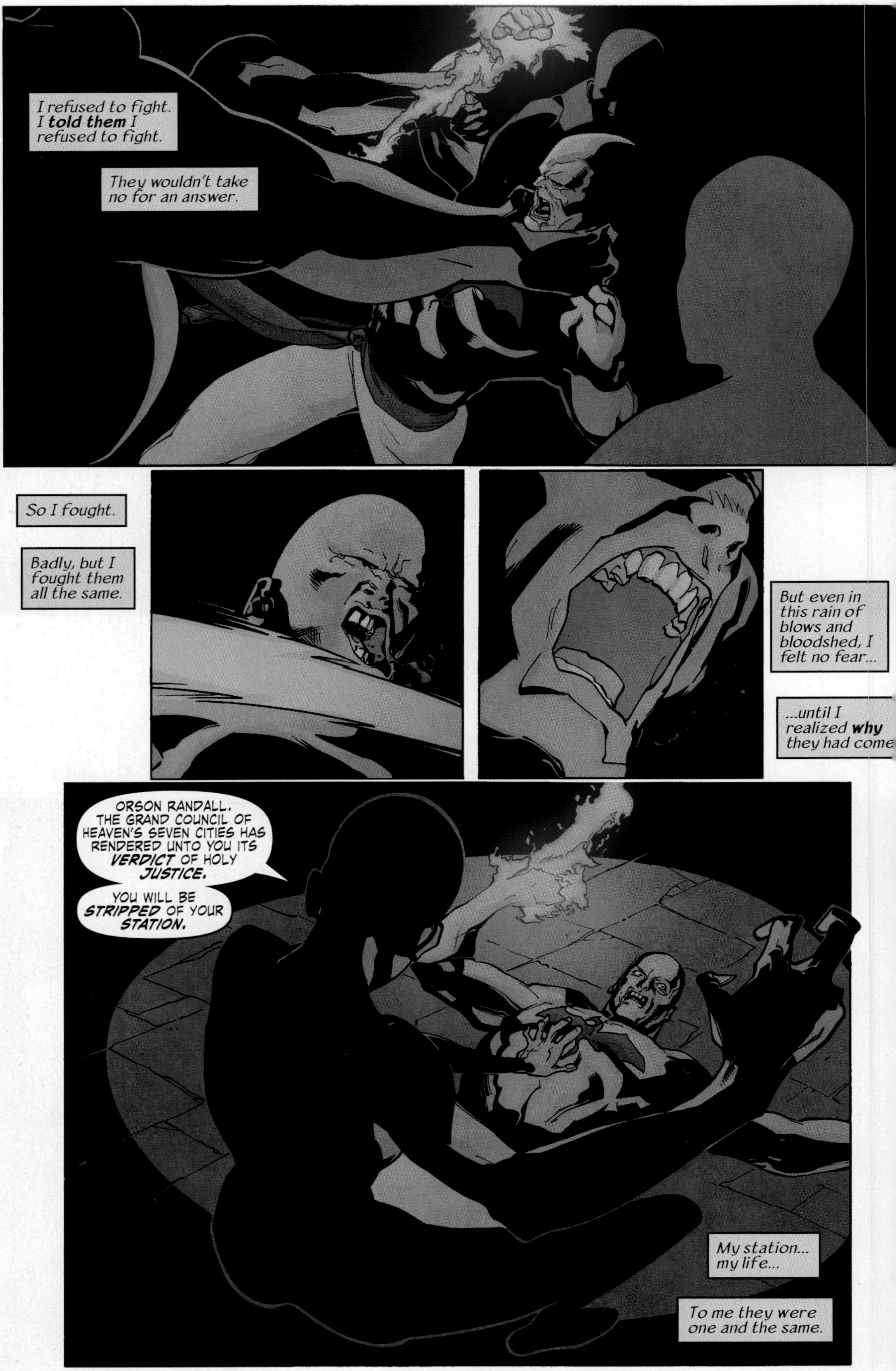
I refused to fight. I **told them** I refused to fight.
They wouldn't take no for an answer.
So I fought.
Badly, but I fought them all the same.
But even in this rain of blows and bloodshed, I felt no fear...
...until I realized **why** they had come
ORSON RANDALL. THE GRAND COUNCIL OF HEAVEN'S SEVEN CITIES HAS RENDERED UNTO YOU ITS ***VERDICT*** OF HOLY ***JUSTICE.***
YOU WILL BE ***STRIPPED*** OF YOUR ***STATION.***
My station... my life...
To me they were one and the same.

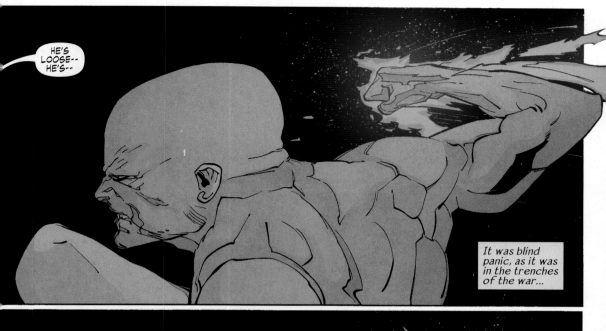

HE'S LOOSE-- HE'S--

It was blind panic, as it was in the trenches of the war...

KKRRRAAKKK

《HE'S KILLED HER.》

Then I did what any sane man would do...

I ran.

I ran from K'un-Lun...

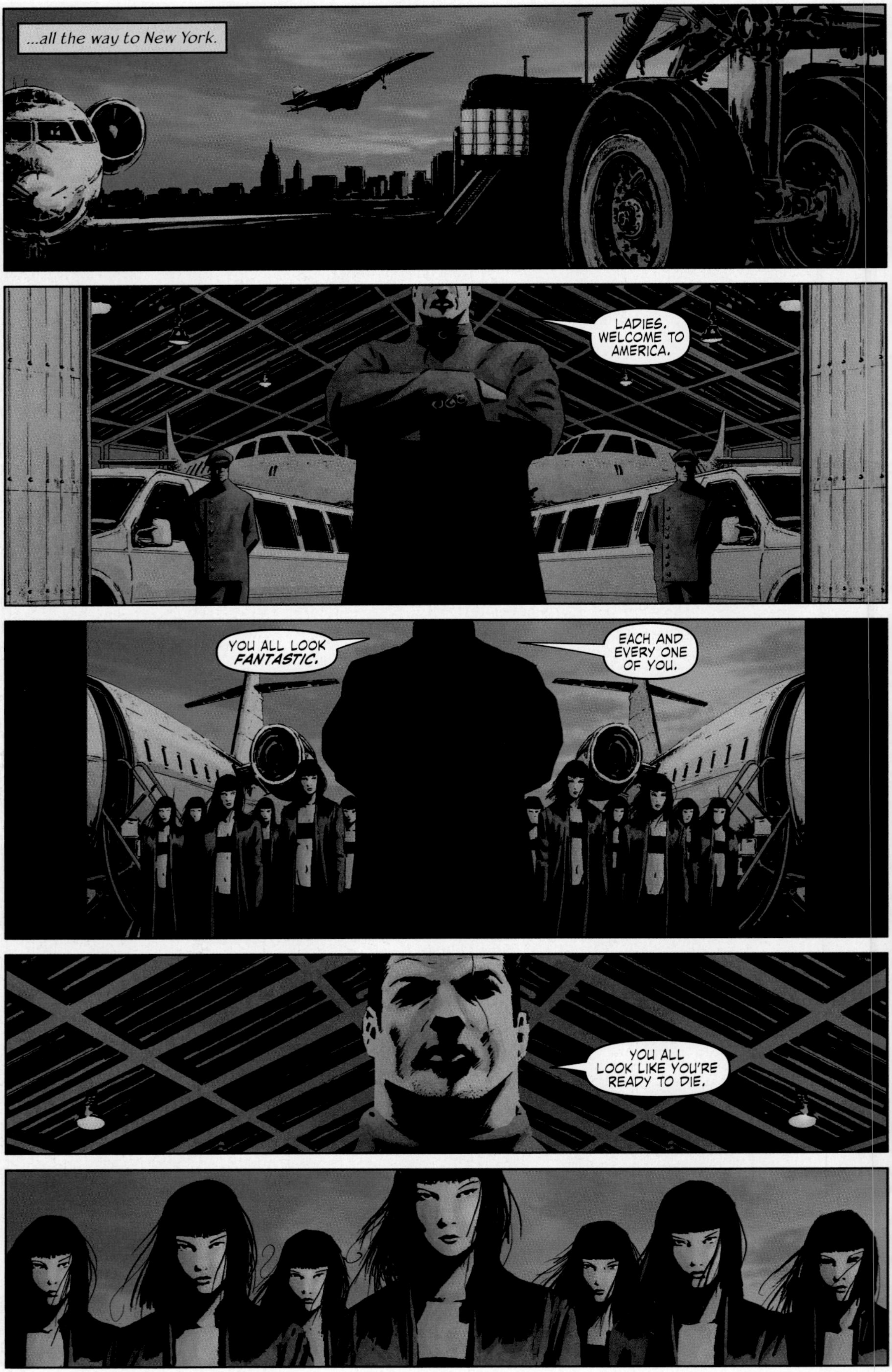
...all the way to New York.
LADIES. WELCOME TO AMERICA.
YOU ALL LOOK *FANTASTIC.*
EACH AND EVERY ONE OF YOU.
YOU ALL LOOK LIKE YOU'RE READY TO DIE.

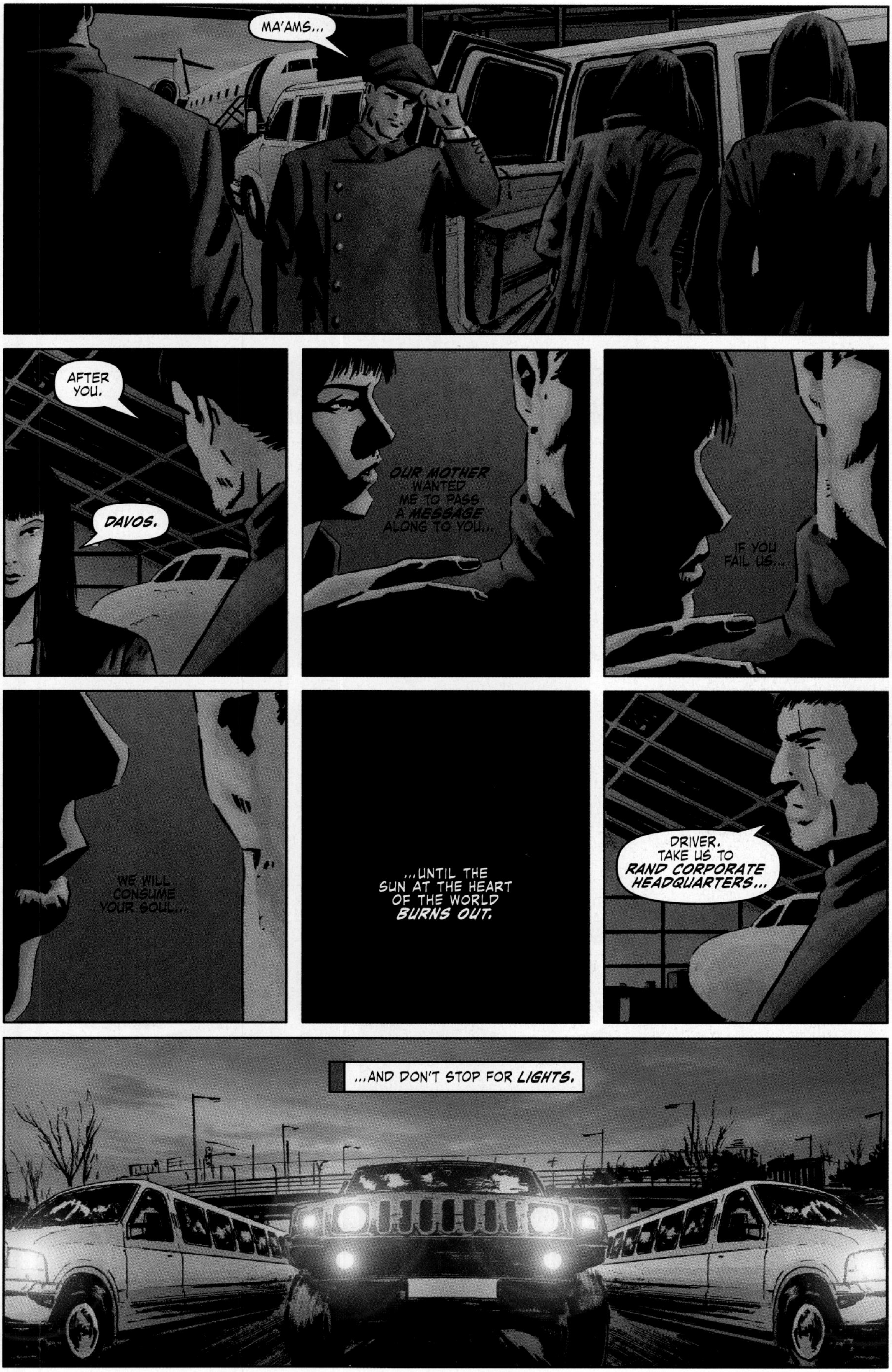
MA'AMS...
AFTER YOU.
DAVOS.
OUR MOTHER WANTED ME TO PASS A MESSAGE ALONG TO YOU...
IF YOU FAIL US...
WE WILL CONSUME YOUR SOUL...
...UNTIL THE SUN AT THE HEART OF THE WORLD BURNS OUT.
DRIVER. TAKE US TO RAND CORPORATE HEADQUARTERS...
...AND DON'T STOP FOR LIGHTS.

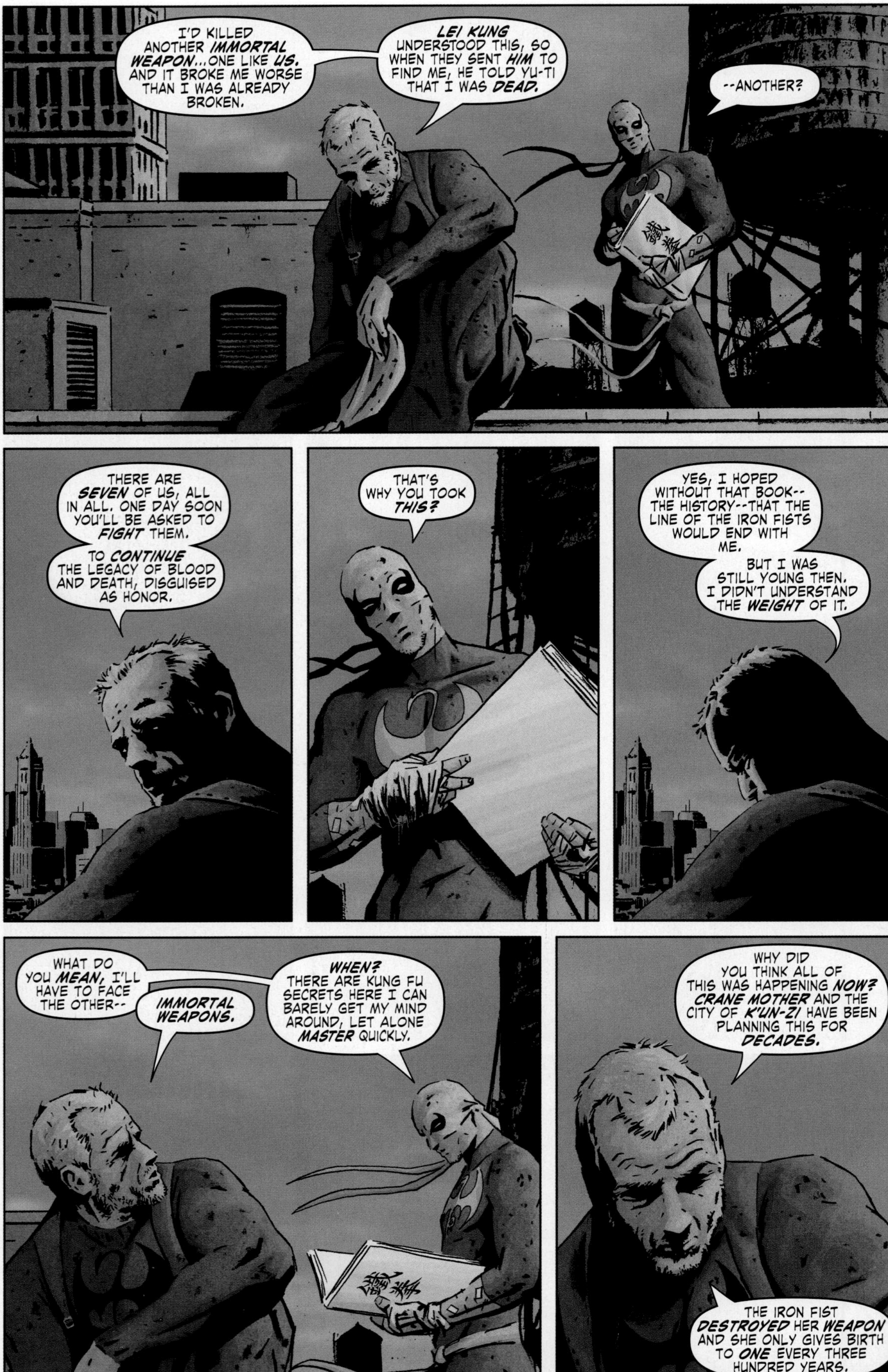
I'D KILLED ANOTHER IMMORTAL WEAPON...ONE LIKE US. AND IT BROKE ME WORSE THAN I WAS ALREADY BROKEN.
LEI KUNG UNDERSTOOD THIS, SO WHEN THEY SENT HIM TO FIND ME, HE TOLD YU-TI THAT I WAS DEAD.
--ANOTHER?
THERE ARE SEVEN OF US, ALL IN ALL. ONE DAY SOON YOU'LL BE ASKED TO FIGHT THEM.
TO CONTINUE THE LEGACY OF BLOOD AND DEATH, DISGUISED AS HONOR.
THAT'S WHY YOU TOOK THIS?
YES, I HOPED WITHOUT THAT BOOK--THE HISTORY--THAT THE LINE OF THE IRON FISTS WOULD END WITH ME.
BUT I WAS STILL YOUNG THEN. I DIDN'T UNDERSTAND THE WEIGHT OF IT.
WHAT DO YOU MEAN, I'LL HAVE TO FACE THE OTHER--
IMMORTAL WEAPONS.
WHEN? THERE ARE KUNG FU SECRETS HERE I CAN BARELY GET MY MIND AROUND, LET ALONE MASTER QUICKLY.
WHY DID YOU THINK ALL OF THIS WAS HAPPENING NOW? CRANE MOTHER AND THE CITY OF K'UN-ZI HAVE BEEN PLANNING THIS FOR DECADES.
THE IRON FIST DESTROYED HER WEAPON AND SHE ONLY GIVES BIRTH TO ONE EVERY THREE HUNDRED YEARS.

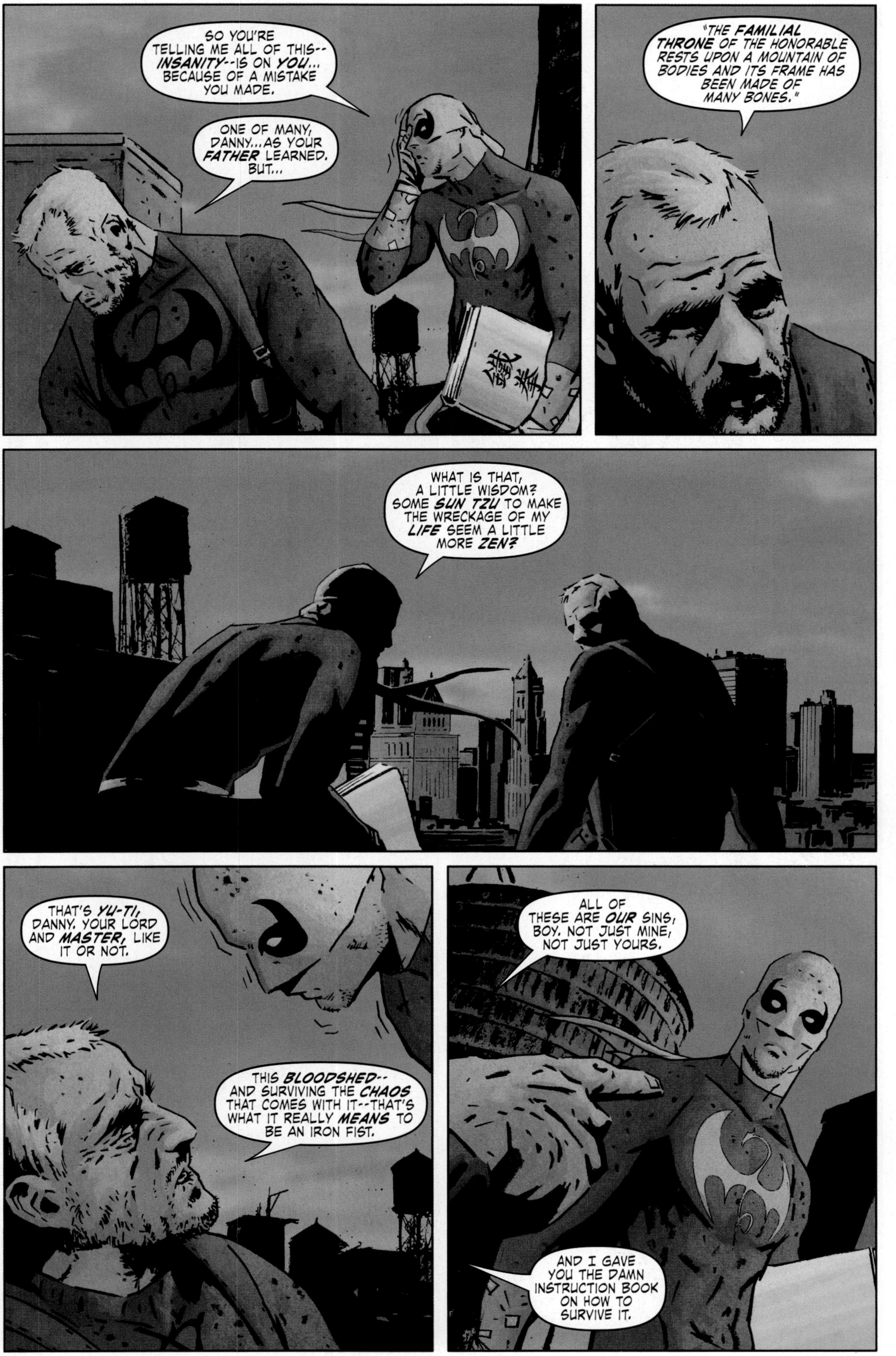
SO YOU'RE TELLING ME ALL OF THIS--INSANITY--IS ON YOU... BECAUSE OF A MISTAKE YOU MADE.
ONE OF MANY, DANNY...AS YOUR FATHER LEARNED. BUT...
"THE FAMILIAL THRONE OF THE HONORABLE RESTS UPON A MOUNTAIN OF BODIES AND ITS FRAME HAS BEEN MADE OF MANY BONES."
WHAT IS THAT, A LITTLE WISDOM? SOME SUN TZU TO MAKE THE WRECKAGE OF MY LIFE SEEM A LITTLE MORE ZEN?
THAT'S YU-TI, DANNY. YOUR LORD AND MASTER, LIKE IT OR NOT.
THIS BLOODSHED--AND SURVIVING THE CHAOS THAT COMES WITH IT--THAT'S WHAT IT REALLY MEANS TO BE AN IRON FIST.
ALL OF THESE ARE OUR SINS, BOY. NOT JUST MINE, NOT JUST YOURS.
AND I GAVE YOU THE DAMN INSTRUCTION BOOK ON HOW TO SURVIVE IT.

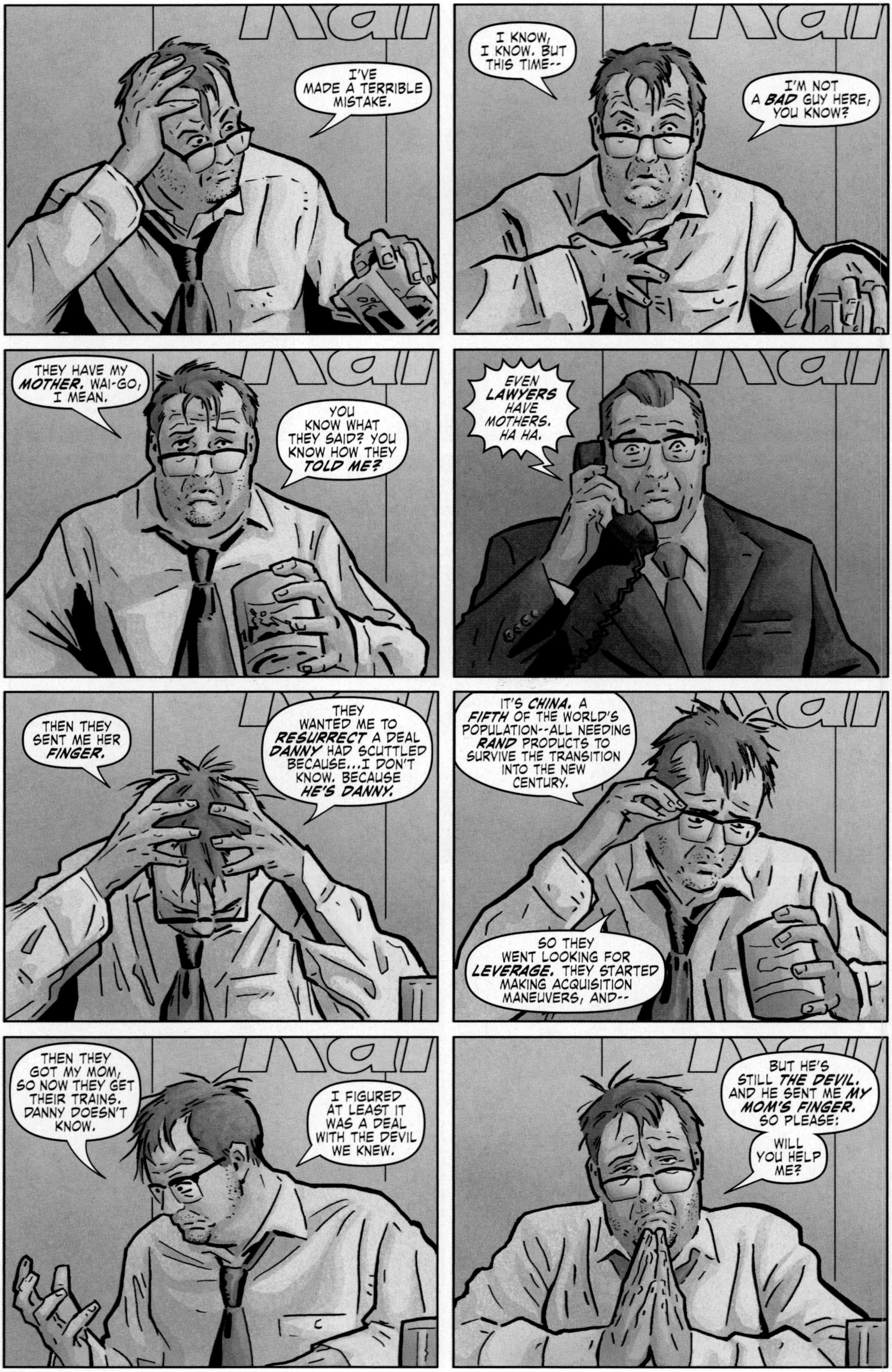
I'VE MADE A TERRIBLE MISTAKE.
I KNOW, I KNOW. BUT THIS TIME--
I'M NOT A BAD GUY HERE, YOU KNOW?
THEY HAVE MY MOTHER. WAI-GO, I MEAN.
YOU KNOW WHAT THEY SAID? YOU KNOW HOW THEY TOLD ME?
EVEN LAWYERS HAVE MOTHERS. HA HA.
THEN THEY SENT ME HER FINGER.
THEY WANTED ME TO RESURRECT A DEAL DANNY HAD SCUTTLED BECAUSE...I DON'T KNOW. BECAUSE HE'S DANNY.
IT'S CHINA. A FIFTH OF THE WORLD'S POPULATION--ALL NEEDING RAND PRODUCTS TO SURVIVE THE TRANSITION INTO THE NEW CENTURY.
SO THEY WENT LOOKING FOR LEVERAGE. THEY STARTED MAKING ACQUISITION MANEUVERS, AND--
THEN THEY GOT MY MOM, SO NOW THEY GET THEIR TRAINS. DANNY DOESN'T KNOW.
I FIGURED AT LEAST IT WAS A DEAL WITH THE DEVIL WE KNEW.
BUT HE'S STILL THE DEVIL. AND HE SENT ME MY MOM'S FINGER. SO PLEASE:
WILL YOU HELP ME?

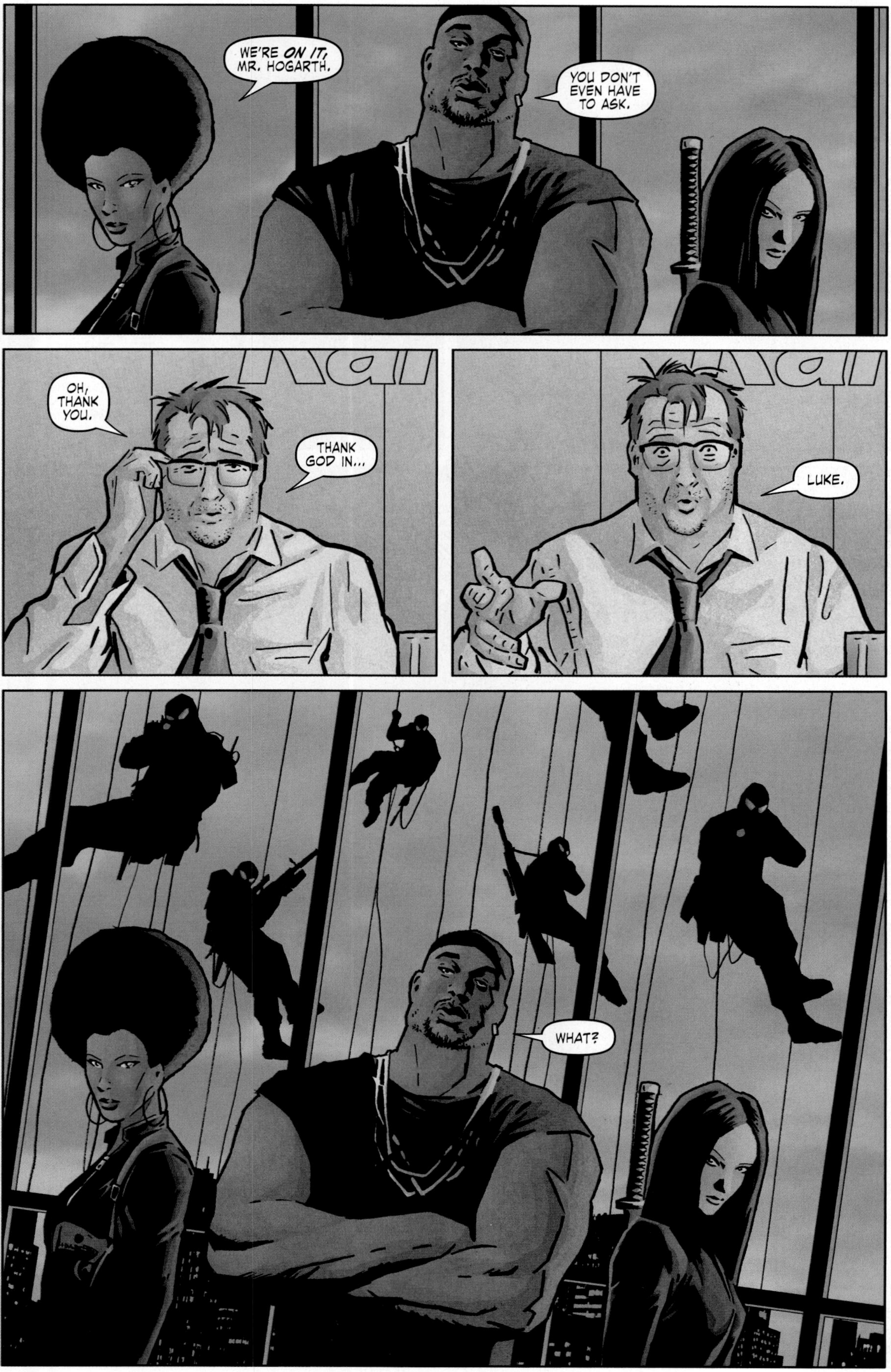
WE'RE *ON IT,* MR. HOGARTH.
YOU DON'T EVEN HAVE TO ASK.
OH, THANK YOU.
THANK GOD IN...
LUKE.
WHAT?

THERE'S A REASON I SPEND A LOT OF TIME JUMPING FROM ROOF TO ROOF.

OH YEAH?

SURE. I *OWN* A LOT OF 'EM.

ME, OR RAND CORP., OR SOME HOLDING COMPANY-- OWN MORE BUILDINGS IN MANHATTAN THAN ANYBODY ELSE IN THE *WORLD.*

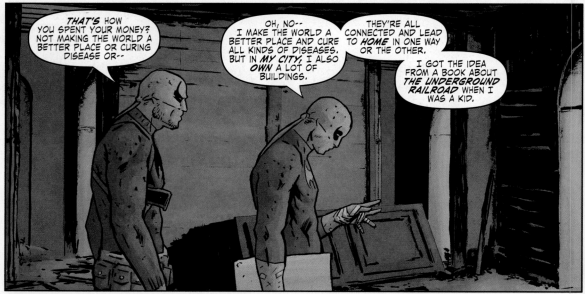

THAT'S HOW YOU SPENT YOUR MONEY? NOT MAKING THE WORLD A BETTER PLACE OR CURING DISEASE OR--

OH, NO-- I MAKE THE WORLD A BETTER PLACE AND CURE ALL KINDS OF DISEASES, BUT IN *MY CITY,* I ALSO *OWN* A LOT OF BUILDINGS.

THEY'RE ALL CONNECTED AND LEAD TO *HOME* IN ONE WAY OR THE OTHER.

I GOT THE IDEA FROM A BOOK ABOUT *THE UNDERGROUND RAILROAD* WHEN I WAS A KID.

GOING UP?

ARE YOU KIDDING ME?

I'M A *SUPER HERO,* ORSON. I HAVE TO GET FROM POINT A TO POINT B FAST AND I CAN'T *FLY.* SO I HAVE REAL ESTATE.

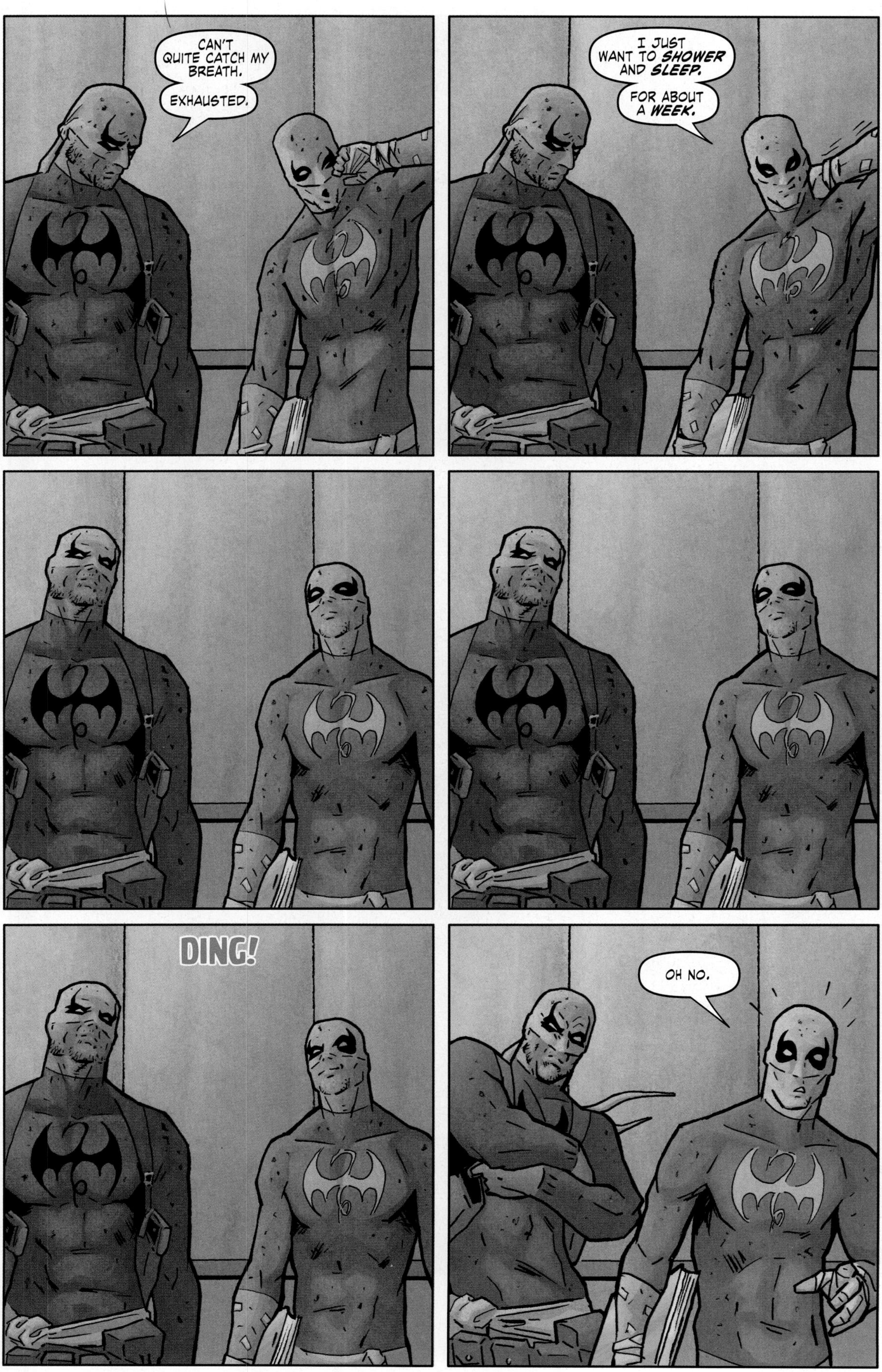
CAN'T QUITE CATCH MY BREATH.
EXHAUSTED.
I JUST WANT TO SHOWER AND SLEEP.
FOR ABOUT A WEEK.
DING!
OH NO.

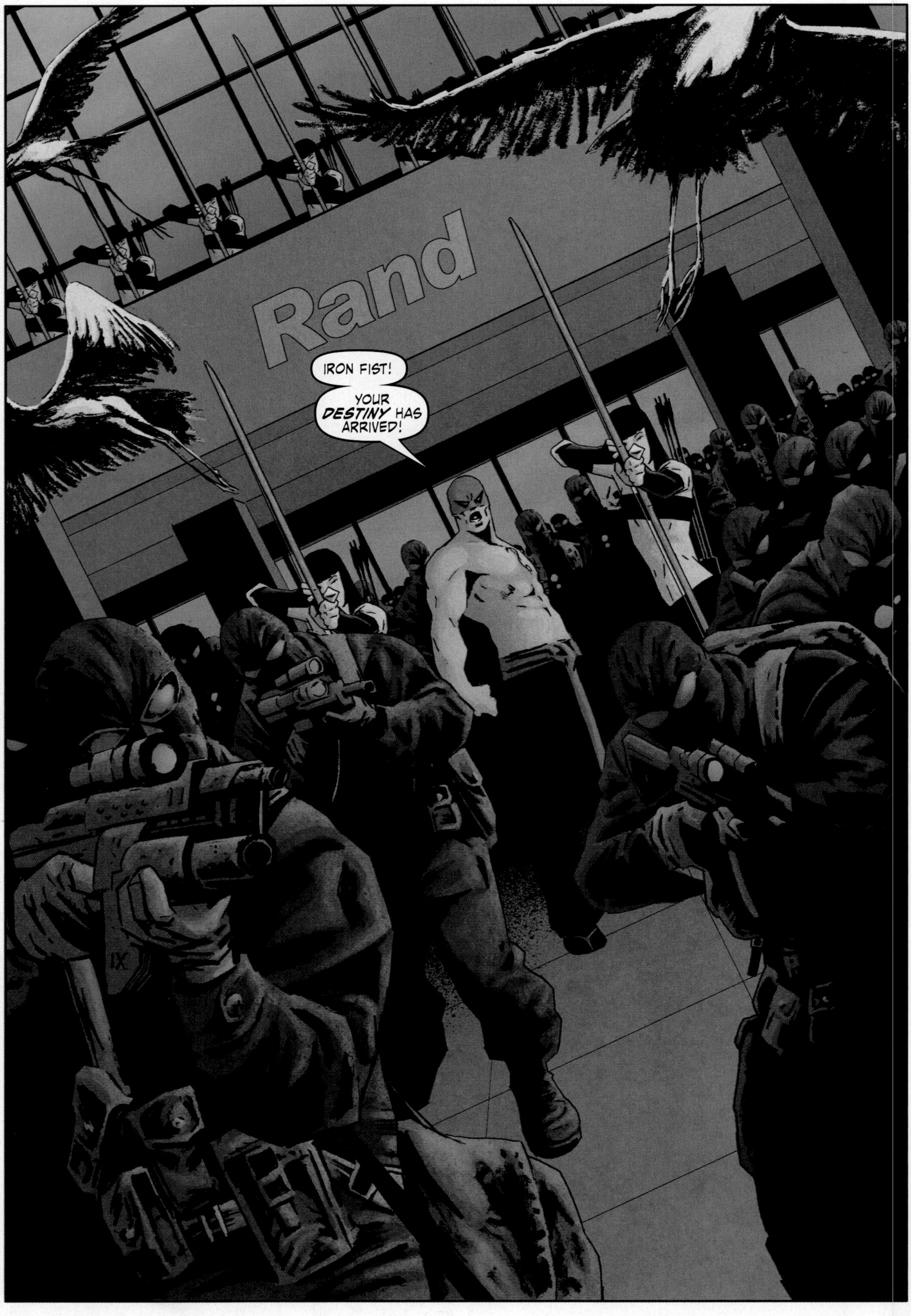

Rand
IRON FIST!
YOUR *DESTINY* HAS ARRIVED!

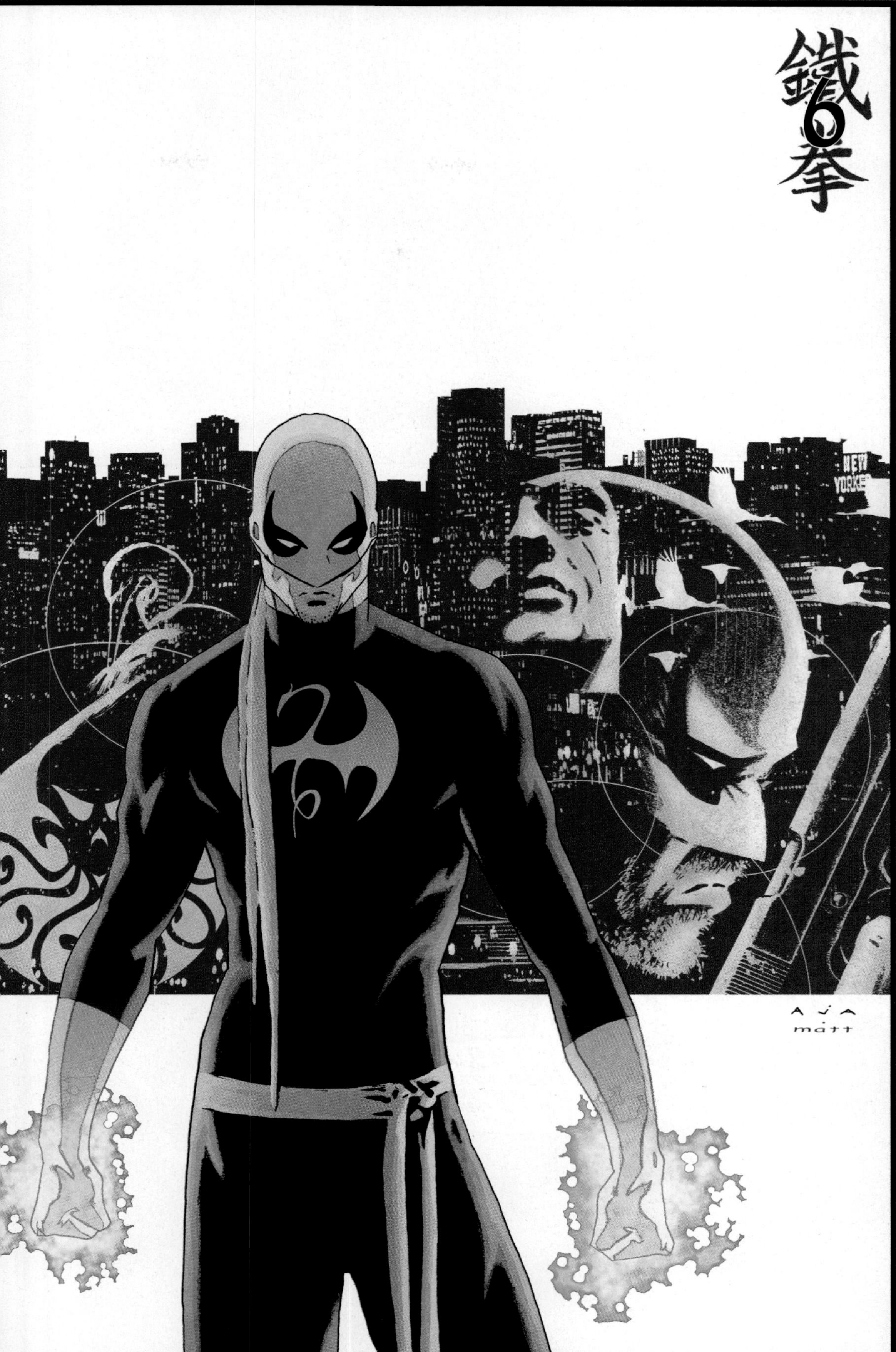
鐵
6
拳
NEW YORKER
AJA
matt

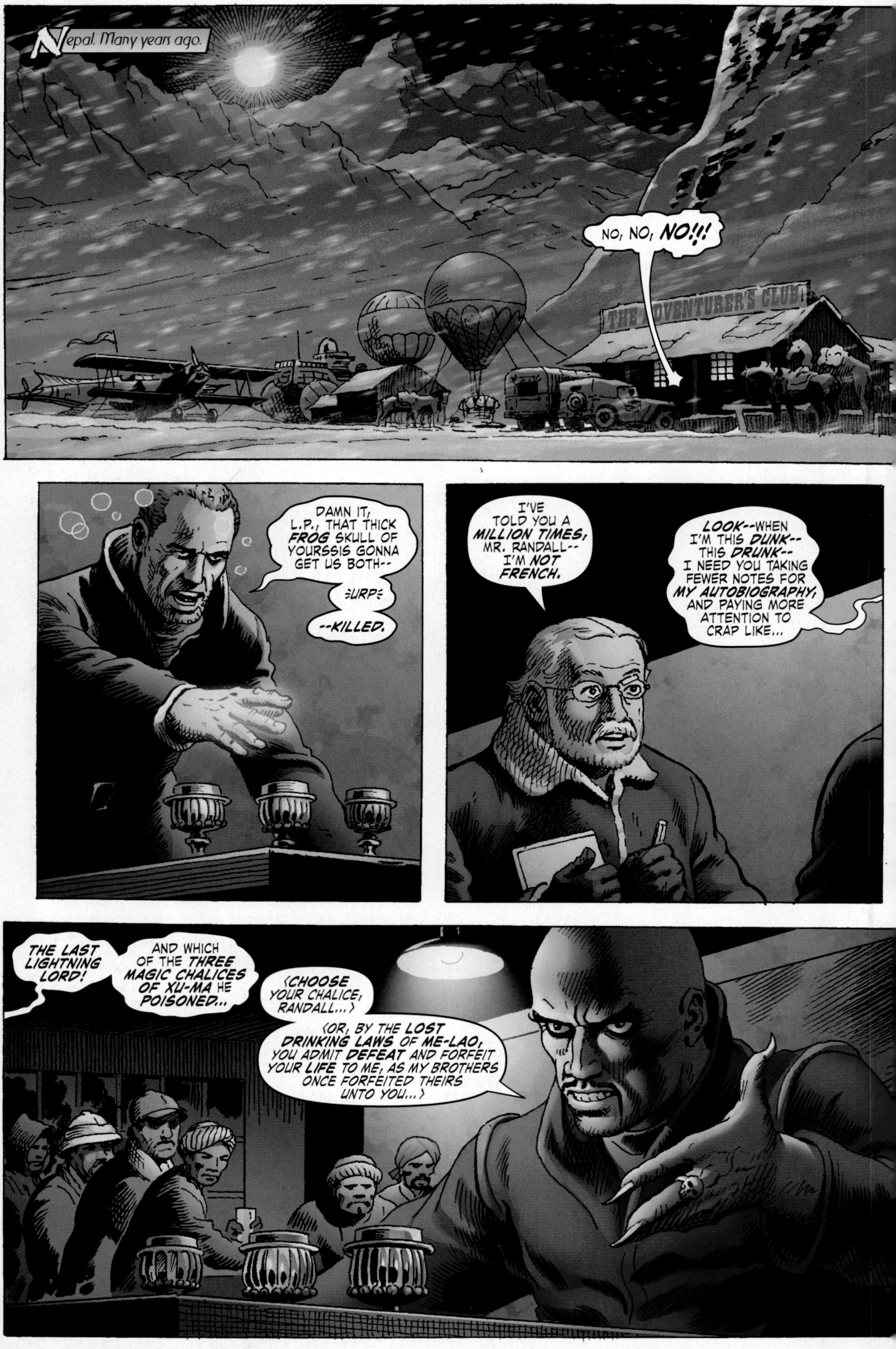
Nepal. Many years ago.
NO, NO, NO!!!
THE ADVENTURER'S CLUB
DAMN IT, L.P., THAT THICK FROG SKULL OF YOURSSIS GONNA GET US BOTH--
=URP=
--KILLED.
I'VE TOLD YOU A MILLION TIMES, MR. RANDALL-- I'M NOT FRENCH.
LOOK--WHEN I'M THIS DUNK-- THIS DRUNK-- I NEED YOU TAKING FEWER NOTES FOR MY AUTOBIOGRAPHY, AND PAYING MORE ATTENTION TO CRAP LIKE...
THE LAST LIGHTNING LORD!
AND WHICH OF THE THREE MAGIC CHALICES OF XU-MA HE POISONED...
<CHOOSE YOUR CHALICE, RANDALL...>
<OR, BY THE LOST DRINKING LAWS OF ME-LAO, YOU ADMIT DEFEAT AND FORFEIT YOUR LIFE TO ME, AS MY BROTHERS ONCE FORFEITED THEIRS UNTO YOU...>

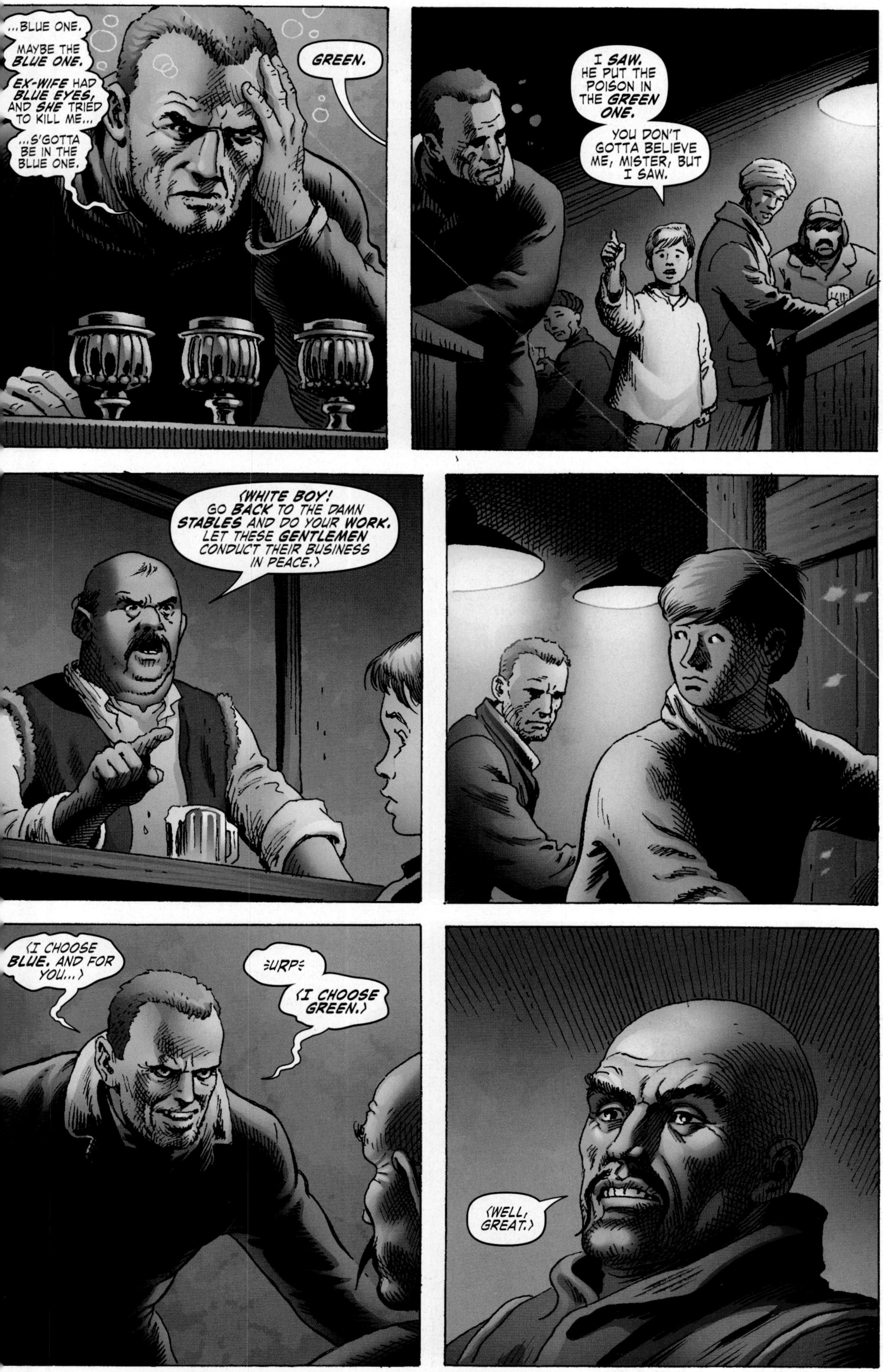
...BLUE ONE.
MAYBE THE BLUE ONE.
EX-WIFE HAD BLUE EYES, AND SHE TRIED TO KILL ME...
...S'GOTTA BE IN THE BLUE ONE.
GREEN.
I SAW. HE PUT THE POISON IN THE GREEN ONE.
YOU DON'T GOTTA BELIEVE ME, MISTER, BUT I SAW.
<WHITE BOY! GO BACK TO THE DAMN STABLES AND DO YOUR WORK. LET THESE GENTLEMEN CONDUCT THEIR BUSINESS IN PEACE.>
<I CHOOSE BLUE. AND FOR YOU...>
URP
<I CHOOSE GREEN.>
<WELL, GREAT.>

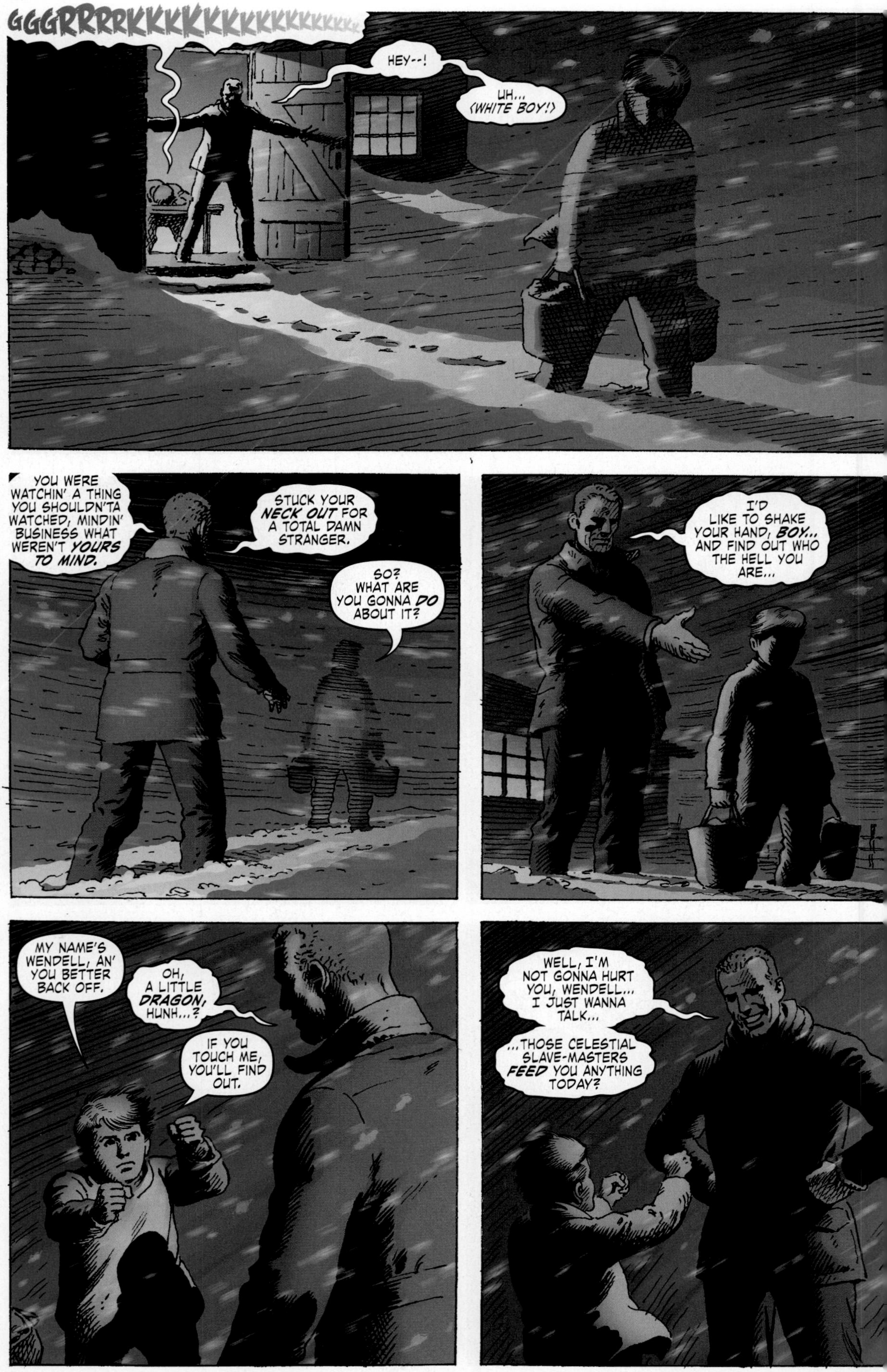
GGGRRRRKKKKKKKKKKKKKK
HEY--!
UH... <WHITE BOY!>
YOU WERE WATCHIN' A THING YOU SHOULDN'TA WATCHED, MINDIN' BUSINESS WHAT WEREN'T YOURS TO MIND.
STUCK YOUR NECK OUT FOR A TOTAL DAMN STRANGER.
SO? WHAT ARE YOU GONNA DO ABOUT IT?
I'D LIKE TO SHAKE YOUR HAND, BOY... AND FIND OUT WHO THE HELL YOU ARE...
MY NAME'S WENDELL, AN' YOU BETTER BACK OFF.
OH, A LITTLE DRAGON, HUNH...?
IF YOU TOUCH ME, YOU'LL FIND OUT.
WELL, I'M NOT GONNA HURT YOU, WENDELL... I JUST WANNA TALK...
...THOSE CELESTIAL SLAVE-MASTERS FEED YOU ANYTHING TODAY?

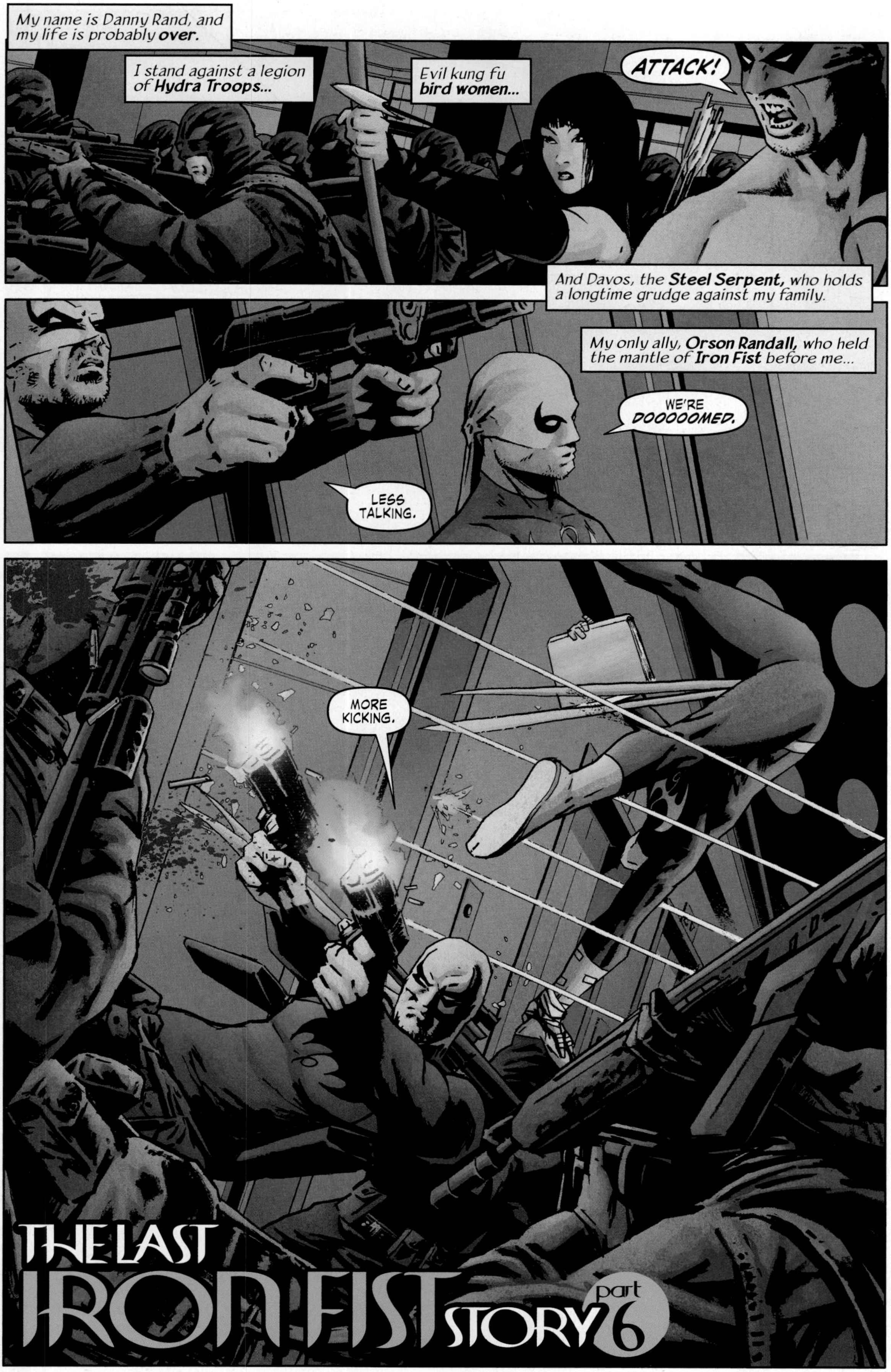
My name is Danny Rand, and my life is probably **over.**
I stand against a legion of **Hydra Troops...**
Evil kung fu **bird women...**
ATTACK!
And Davos, the **Steel Serpent,** who holds a longtime grudge against my family.
My only ally, **Orson Randall,** who held the mantle of **Iron Fist** before me...
WE'RE DOOOOOMED.
LESS TALKING.
MORE KICKING.
THE LAST IRON FIST STORY part 6

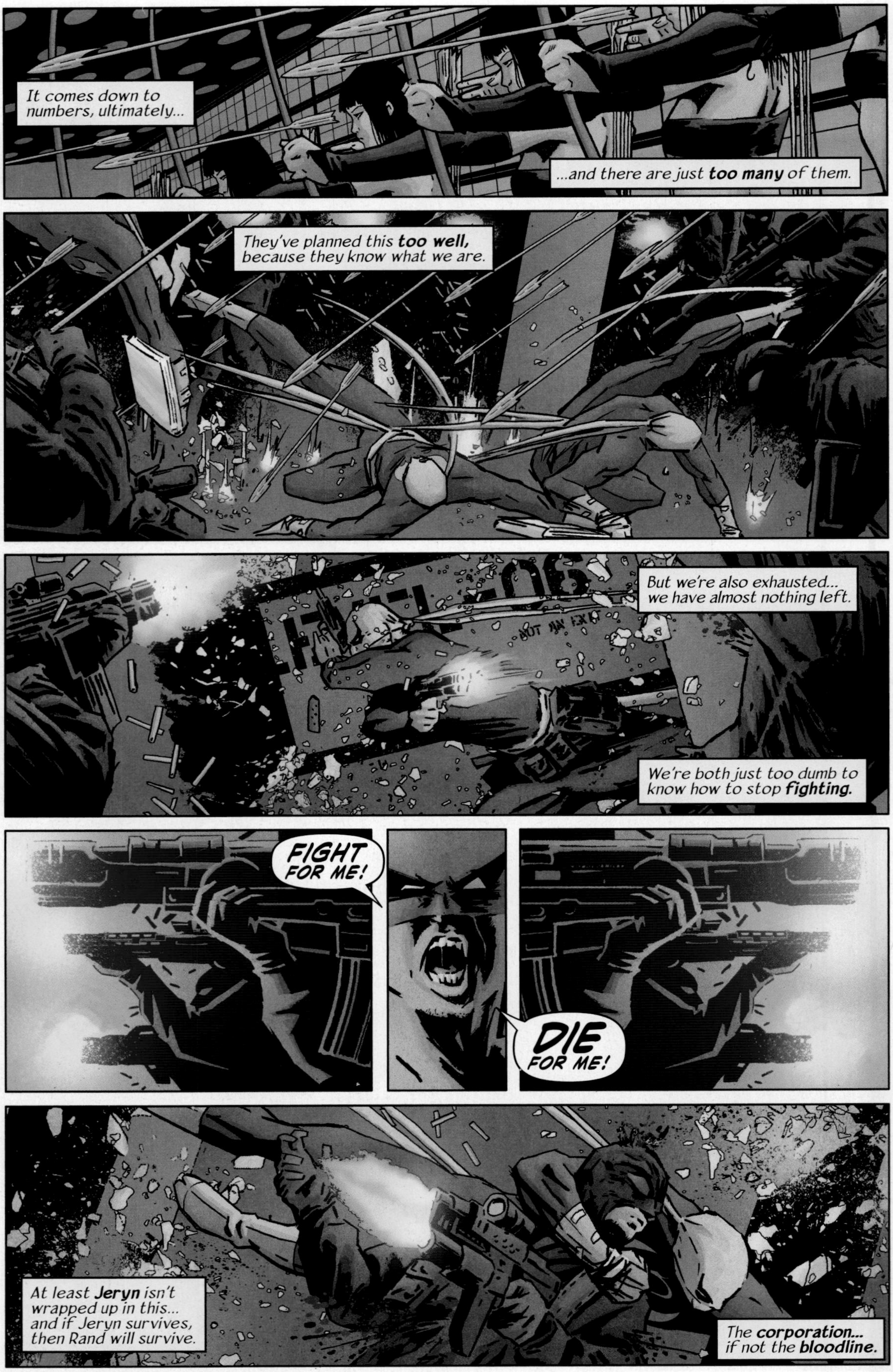

It comes down to numbers, ultimately...
...and there are just **too many** of them.
They've planned this **too well,** because they know what we are.
But we're also exhausted... we have almost nothing left.
We're both just too dumb to know how to stop **fighting.**
FIGHT FOR ME!
DIE FOR ME!
At least **Jeryn** isn't wrapped up in this... and if Jeryn survives, then Rand will survive.
The **corporation...** if not the **bloodline.**

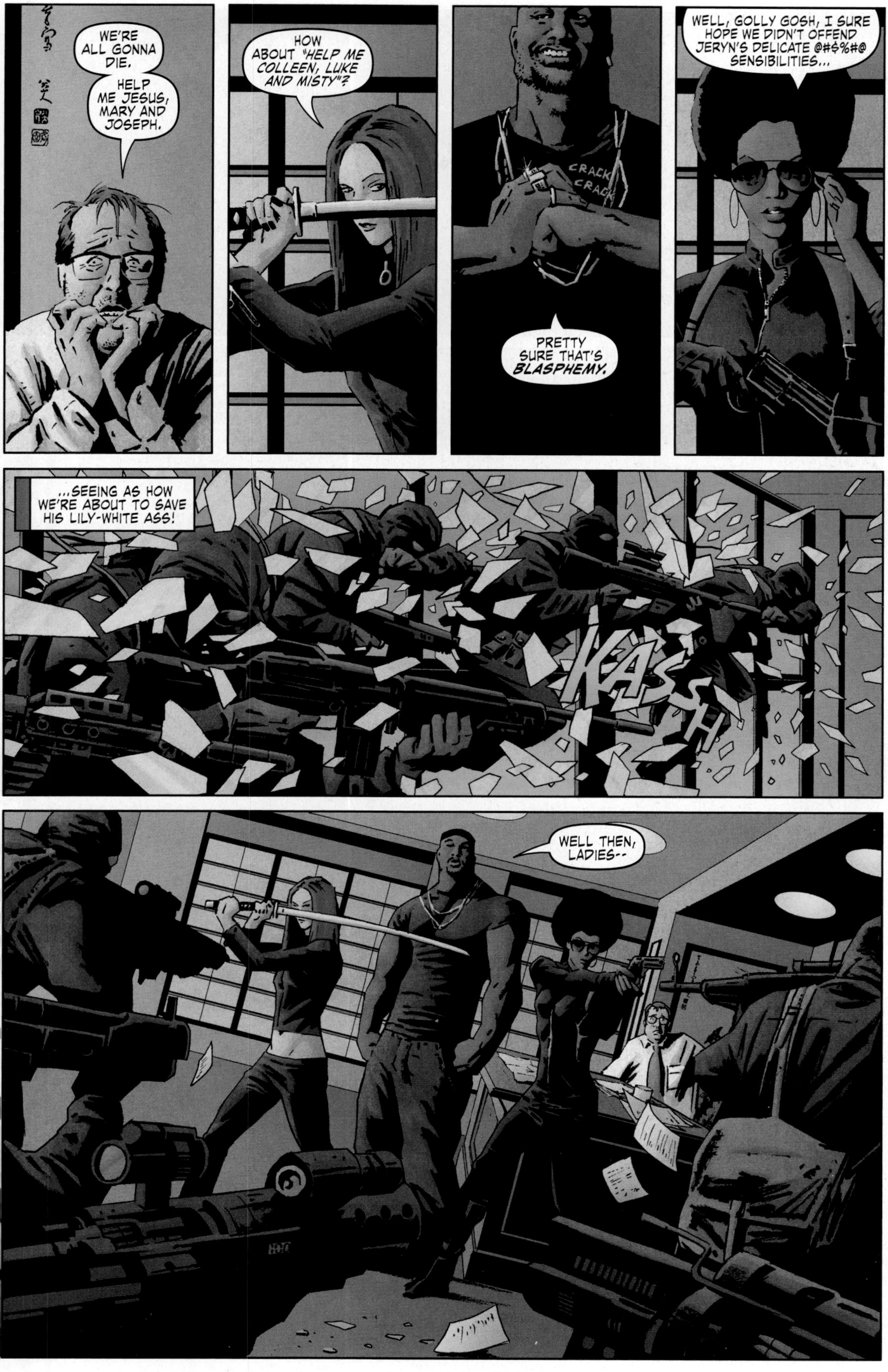

WE'RE ALL GONNA DIE.
HELP ME JESUS, MARY AND JOSEPH.
HOW ABOUT "HELP ME COLLEEN, LUKE AND MISTY"?
CRACK CRACK
PRETTY SURE THAT'S BLASPHEMY.
WELL, GOLLY GOSH, I SURE HOPE WE DIDN'T OFFEND JERYN'S DELICATE @#$%#@ SENSIBILITIES...
...SEEING AS HOW WE'RE ABOUT TO SAVE HIS LILY-WHITE ASS!
KASSH
WELL THEN, LADIES--

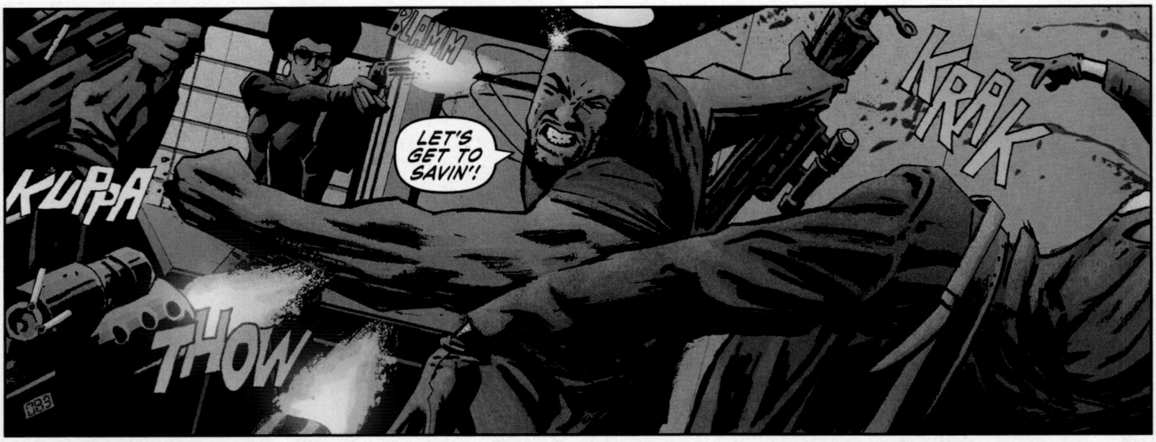
BLAMM
LET'S GET TO SAVIN'!
KRAK
KUPPA
THOW

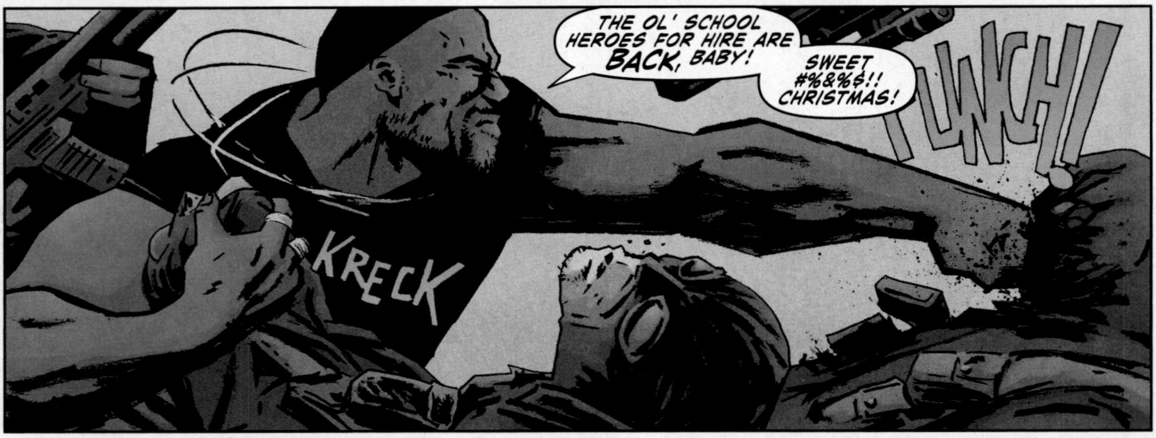
THE OL' SCHOOL HEROES FOR HIRE ARE BACK, BABY!
SWEET #%&%$!! CHRISTMAS!
KRECK

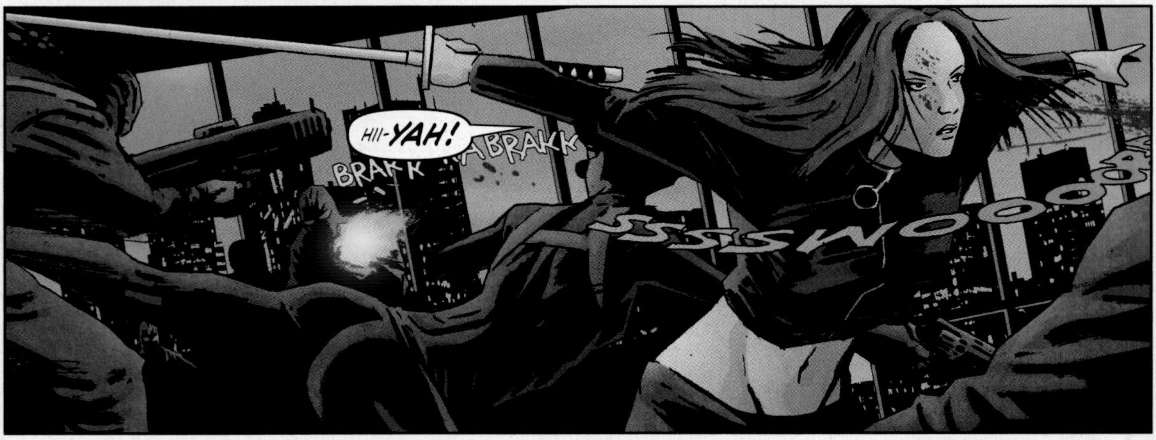
HII-YAH!
BRAKK

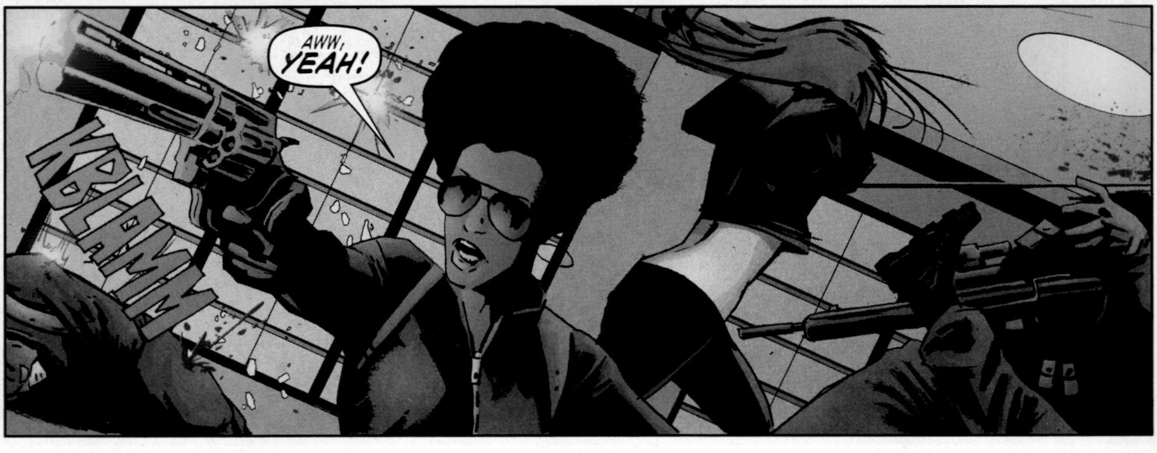
AWW, YEAH!
KBLAMM

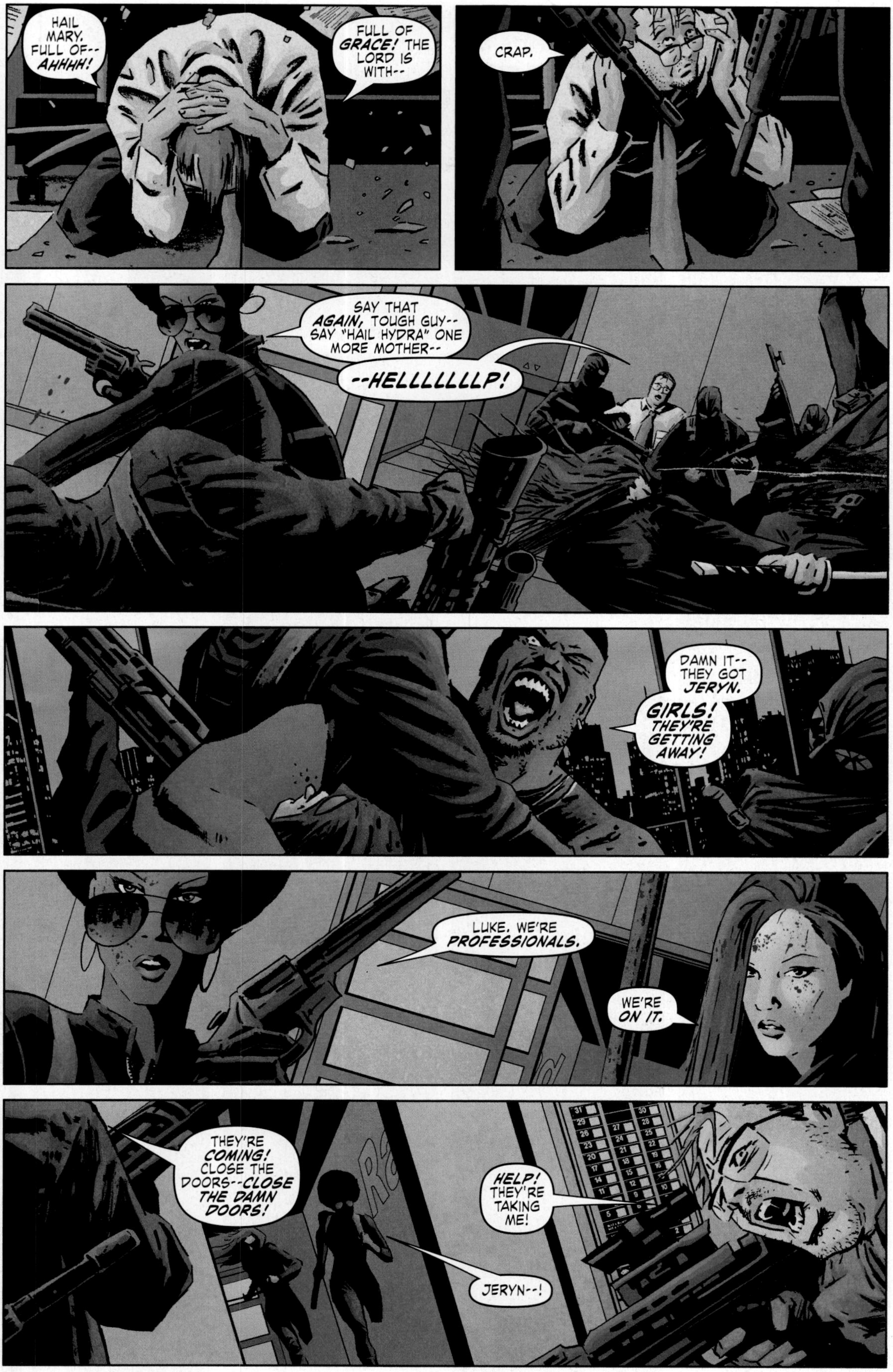
HAIL MARY. FULL OF-- AHHHH!
FULL OF GRACE! THE LORD IS WITH--
CRAP.
SAY THAT AGAIN, TOUGH GUY-- SAY "HAIL HYDRA" ONE MORE MOTHER--
--HELLLLLLLLP!
DAMN IT-- THEY GOT JERYN.
GIRLS! THEY'RE GETTING AWAY!
LUKE. WE'RE PROFESSIONALS.
WE'RE ON IT.
THEY'RE COMING! CLOSE THE DOORS--CLOSE THE DAMN DOORS!
HELP! THEY'RE TAKING ME!
JERYN--!

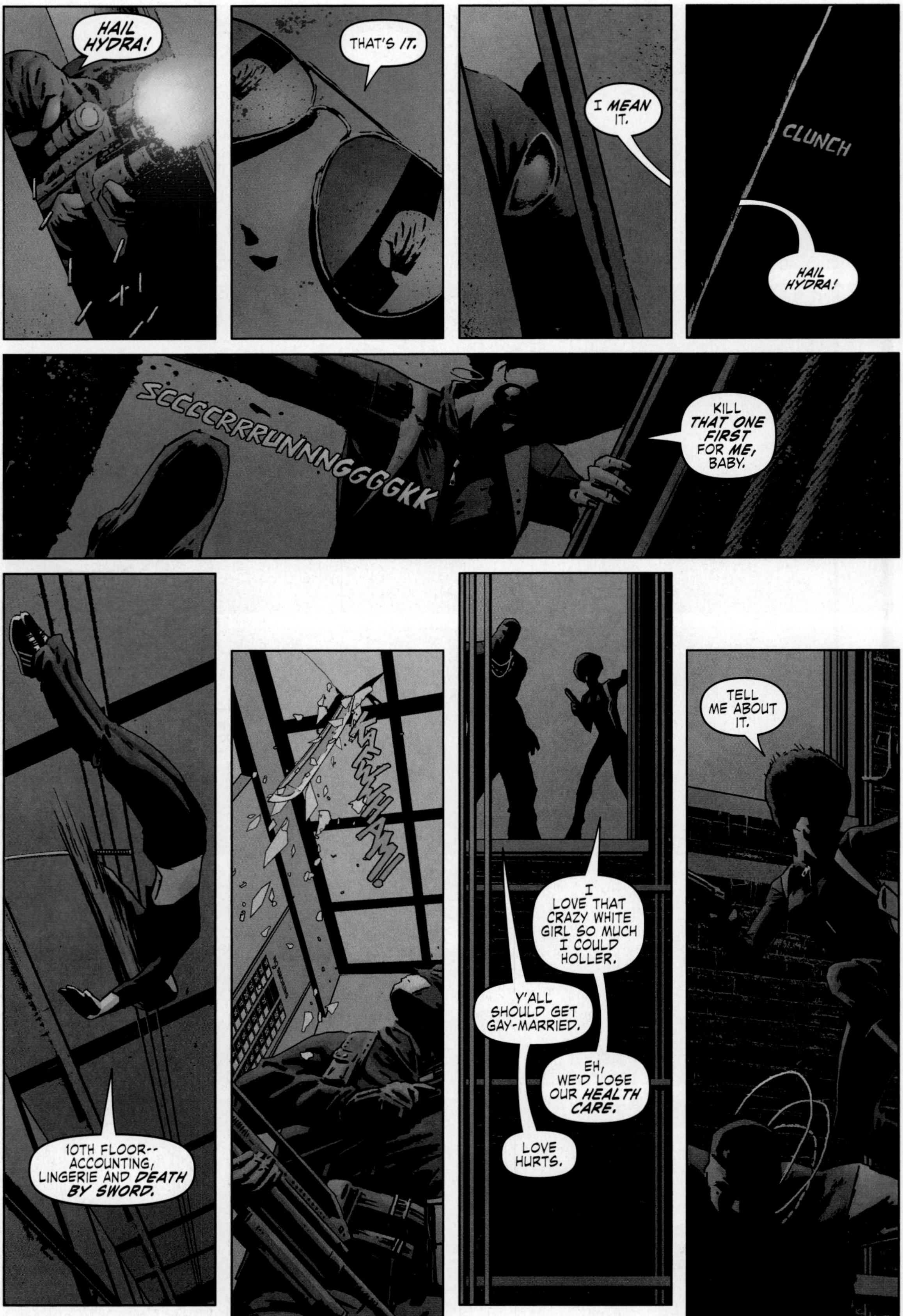
HAIL HYDRA!
THAT'S *IT.*
I *MEAN* IT.
CLUNCH
HAIL HYDRA!
SCCCCRRRRUNNNNGGGGKK
KILL *THAT ONE FIRST* FOR *ME,* BABY.
10TH FLOOR-- ACCOUNTING, LINGERIE AND *DEATH BY SWORD.*
KEWHAM!!
I LOVE THAT CRAZY WHITE GIRL SO MUCH I COULD HOLLER.
Y'ALL SHOULD GET GAY-MARRIED.
EH, WE'D LOSE OUR *HEALTH CARE.*
LOVE HURTS.
TELL ME ABOUT IT.

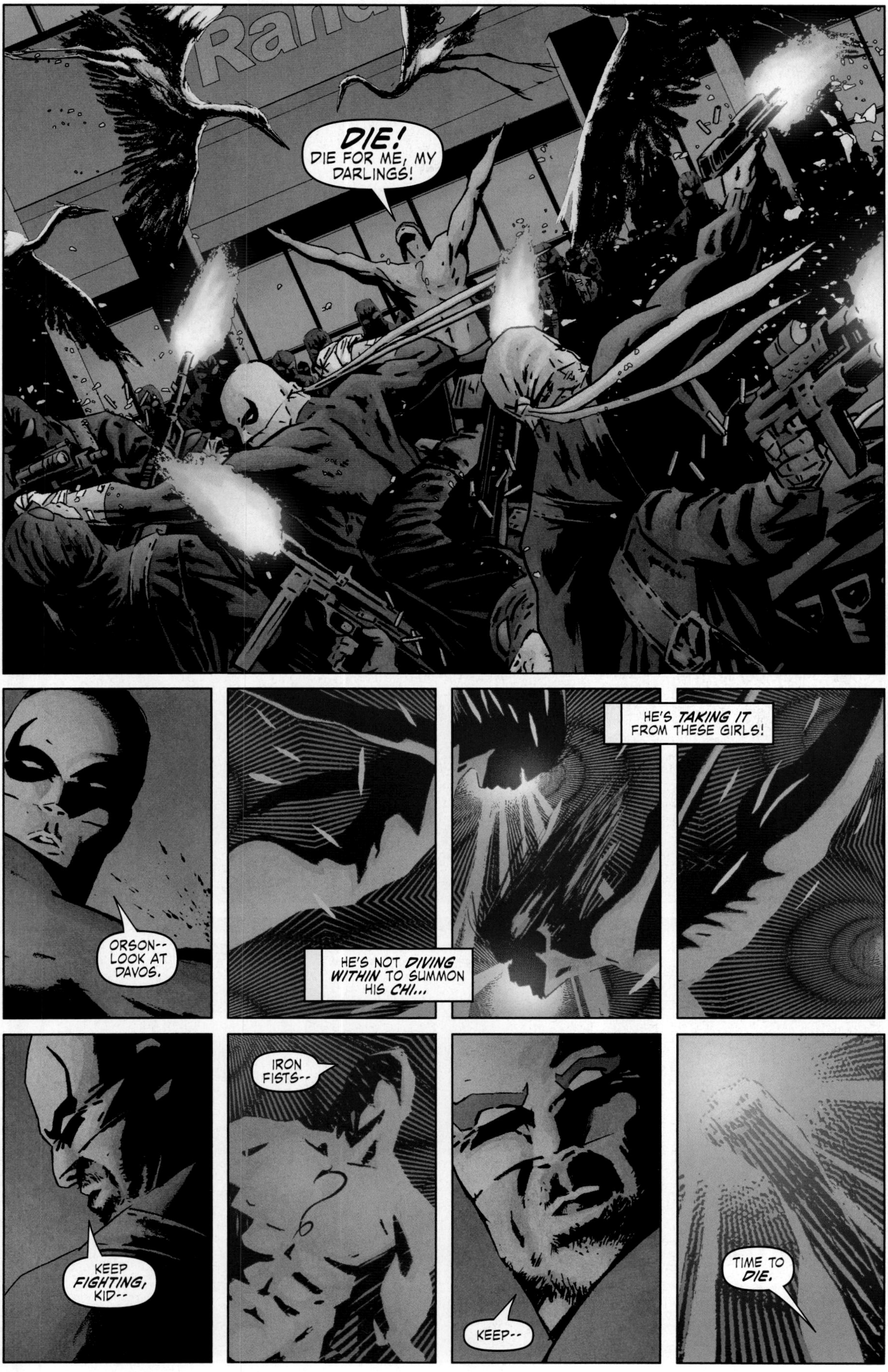

DIE! DIE FOR ME, MY DARLINGS!
ORSON-- LOOK AT DAVOS.
HE'S NOT *DIVING WITHIN* TO SUMMON HIS *CHI*...
HE'S *TAKING IT* FROM THESE GIRLS!
KEEP *FIGHTING,* KID--
IRON FISTS--
KEEP--
TIME TO *DIE.*

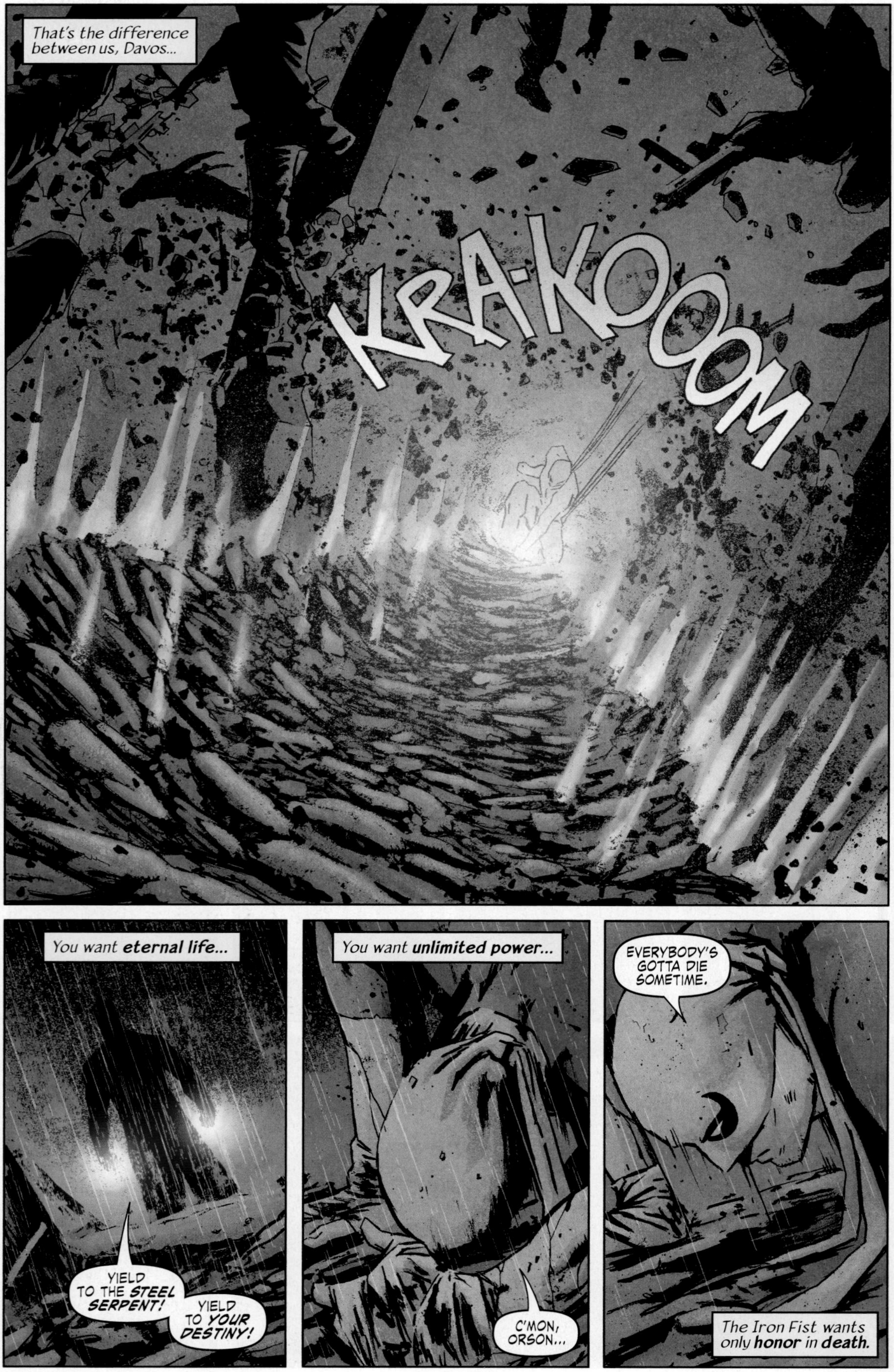
That's the difference between us, Davos...
KRA-KOOOM
You want *eternal life...*
YIELD TO THE ***STEEL SERPENT!***
YIELD TO ***YOUR DESTINY!***
You want *unlimited power...*
C'MON, ORSON...
EVERYBODY'S GOTTA DIE SOMETIME.
The Iron Fist wants only ***honor*** in ***death.***

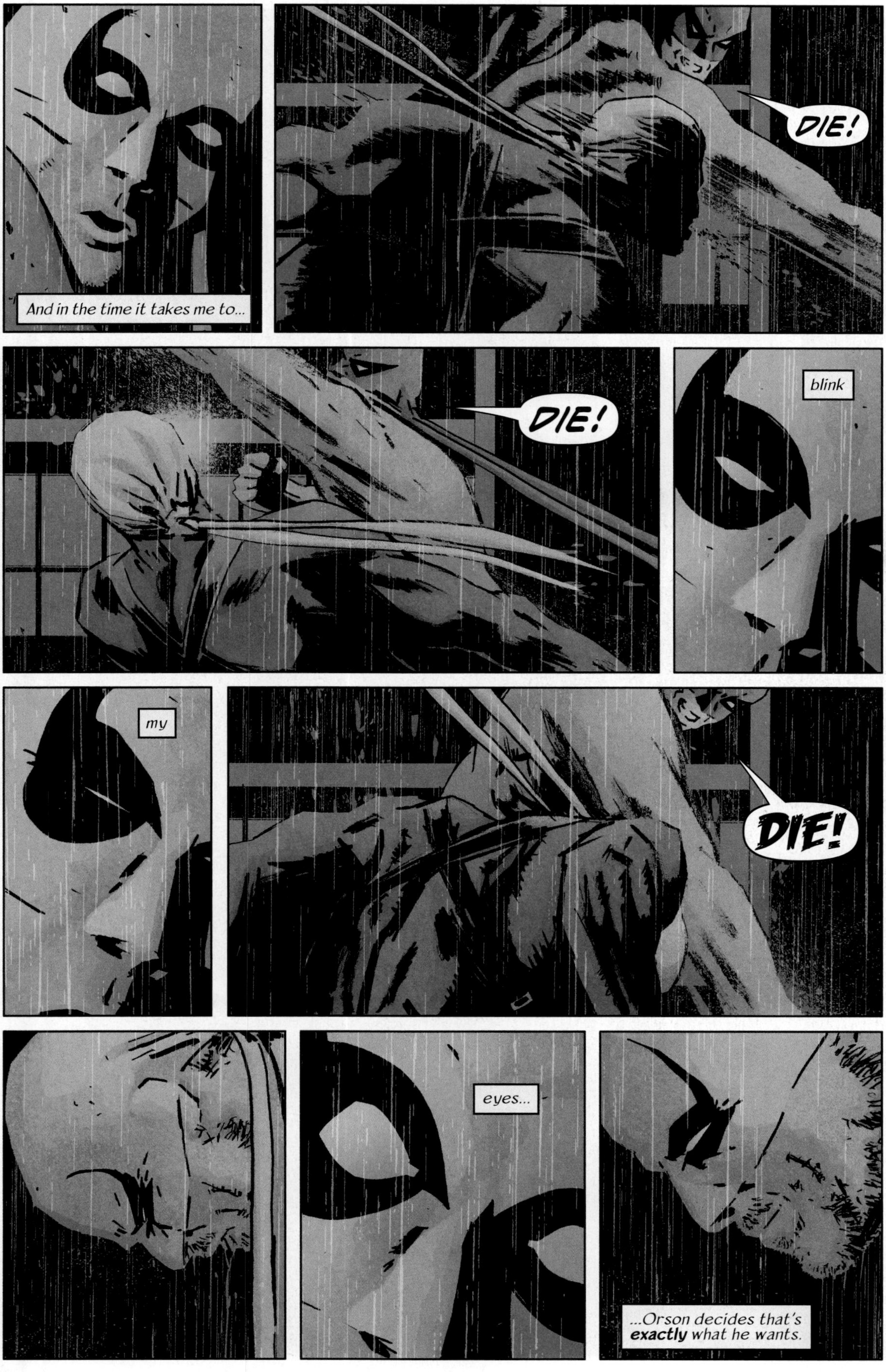
And in the time it takes me to...
DIE!
DIE!
blink
my
DIE!
eyes...
...Orson decides that's
exactly what he wants.

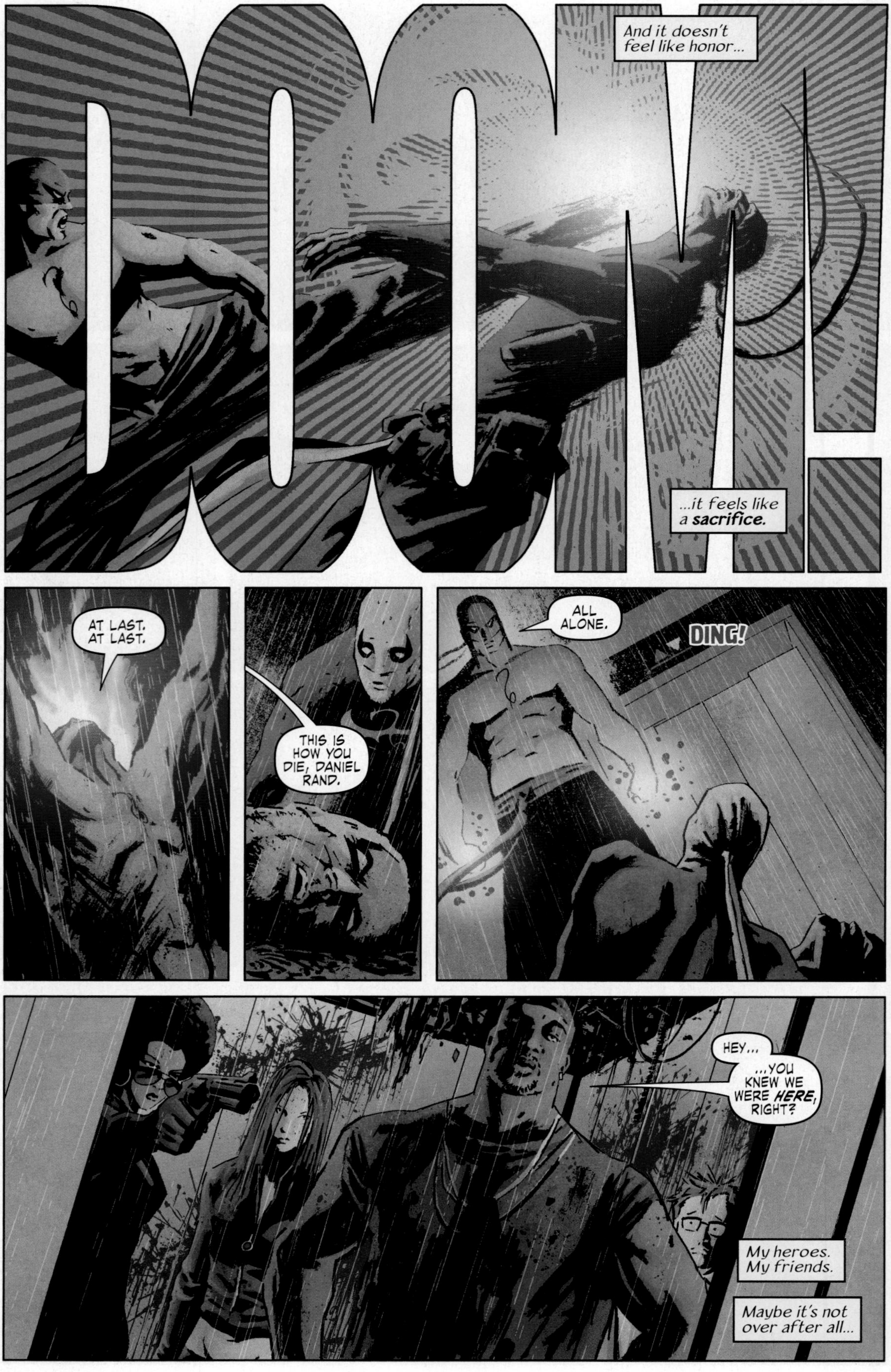
DOOM!
And it doesn't feel like honor...
...it feels like a **sacrifice.**
AT LAST. AT LAST.
THIS IS HOW YOU DIE, DANIEL RAND.
ALL ALONE.
DING!
HEY...
...YOU KNEW WE WERE *HERE*, RIGHT?
My heroes. My friends.
Maybe it's not over after all...

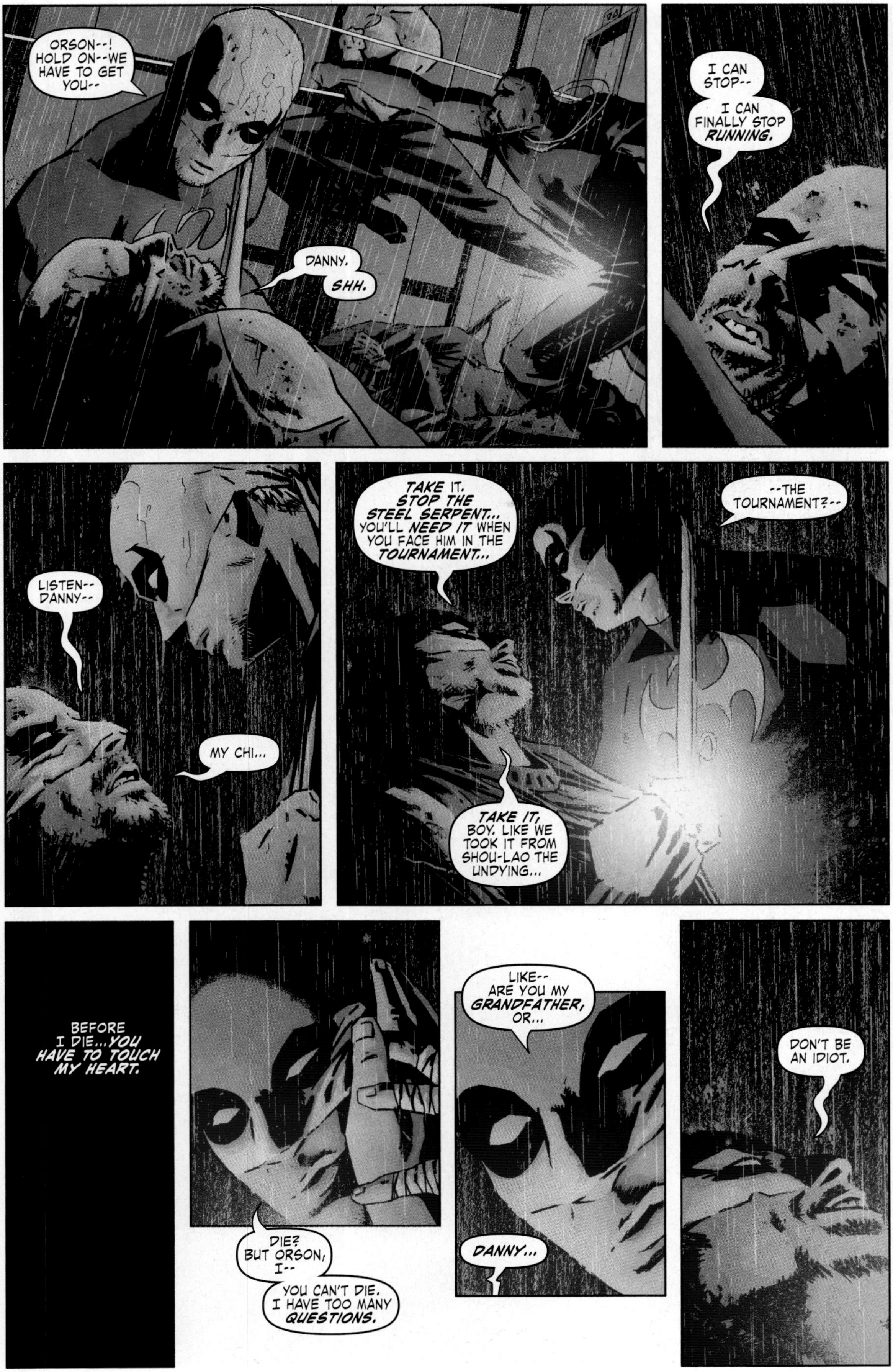
ORSON--! HOLD ON--WE HAVE TO GET YOU--
DANNY. SHH.
I CAN STOP--
I CAN FINALLY STOP RUNNING.
LISTEN-- DANNY--
MY CHI...
TAKE IT. STOP THE STEEL SERPENT... YOU'LL NEED IT WHEN YOU FACE HIM IN THE TOURNAMENT...
--THE TOURNAMENT?--
TAKE IT, BOY. LIKE WE TOOK IT FROM SHOU-LAO THE UNDYING...
BEFORE I DIE...YOU HAVE TO TOUCH MY HEART.
DIE? BUT ORSON, I--
YOU CAN'T DIE. I HAVE TOO MANY QUESTIONS.
LIKE-- ARE YOU MY GRANDFATHER, OR...
DANNY...
DON'T BE AN IDIOT.

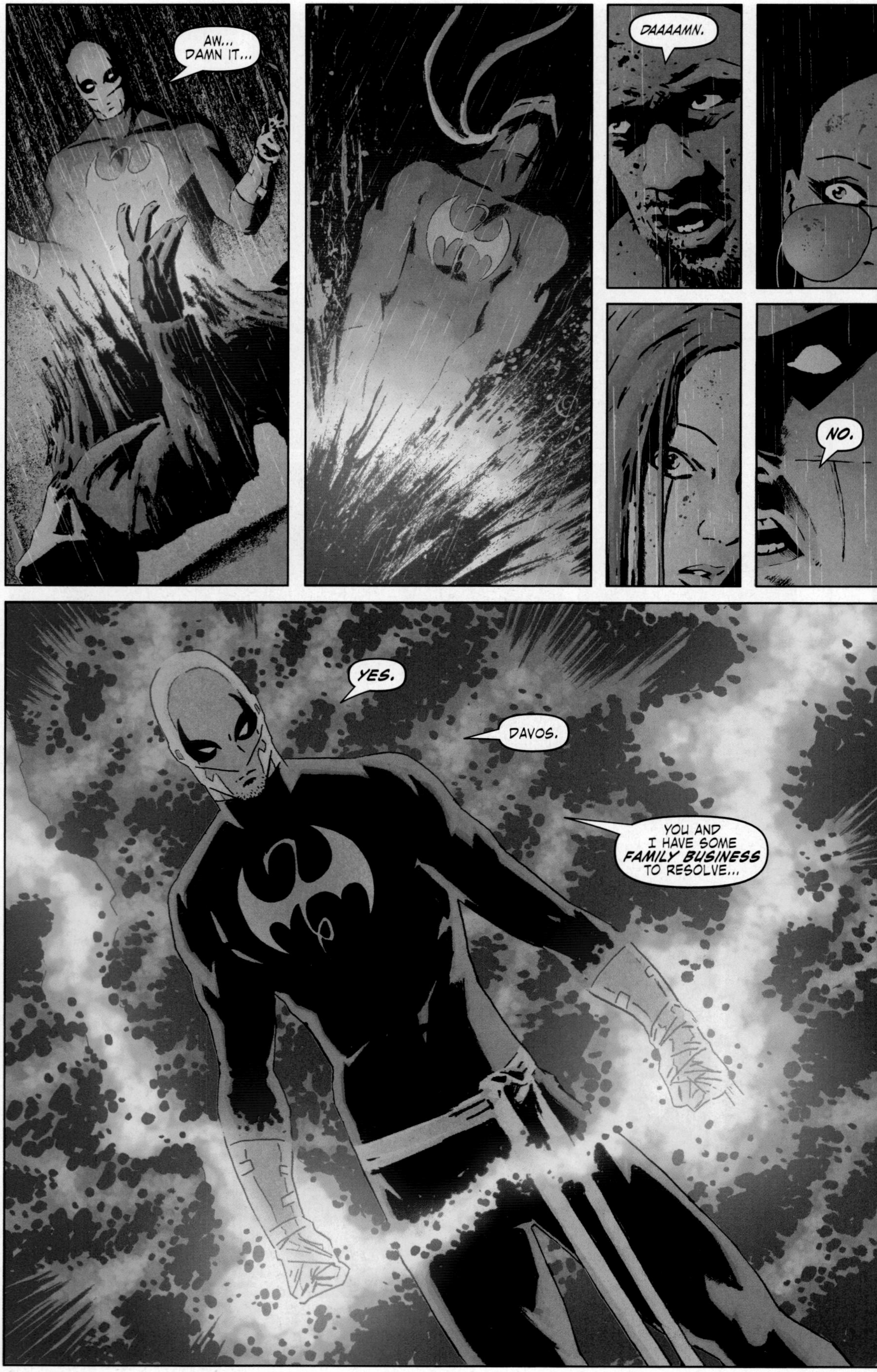
AW... DAMN IT...
DAAAAMN.
NO.
YES.
DAVOS.
YOU AND I HAVE SOME *FAMILY BUSINESS* TO RESOLVE...

YOU'RE NOT *MY FATHER*, ORSON. I'M GOING TO *FIND* K'UN-LUN AND YOU CAN'T STOP ME.

I'M GOING TO FIND K'UN-LUN AND *I'LL* BECOME THE *IRON FIST.*

YOU'LL SEE, *I KNOW* I CAN DO IT.

PFFF. K'UN-LUN.

WHADD*YOU* KNOW ABOUT K'UN-LUN? YOU DONNNN'T KNOW... ANNNNYTHING. AN' I KNOW *EVERYTHING...* STUPID KID...

YOU *DON'T* KNOW EVERYTHING, ORSON! YOU'RE JUST A BURNED-OUT OLD *DRAGON-CHASER.*

I'M THROUGH WITH YOUR *PROPHECIES* AND *PREDICTIONS.*

YOU SAID IT'S A CITY OF *GOLD, PARADISE ON EARTH!* AND *YOU* TAUGHT ME HOW TO FIGHT! YOU *KNOW* I CAN HANDLE MYSELF!

DAMN IT, ORSON, IF YOUR CALCULATIONS ARE RIGHT, THEN IT'LL BE APPEARING SOON...ALL I HAVE TO DO IS--

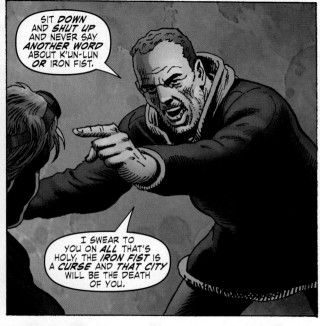

SIT *DOWN* AND *SHUT UP* AND NEVER SAY *ANOTHER WORD* ABOUT K'UN-LUN OR IRON FIST.

I SWEAR TO YOU ON *ALL* THAT'S HOLY, THE *IRON FIST* IS A *CURSE* AND *THAT CITY* WILL BE THE DEATH OF YOU.

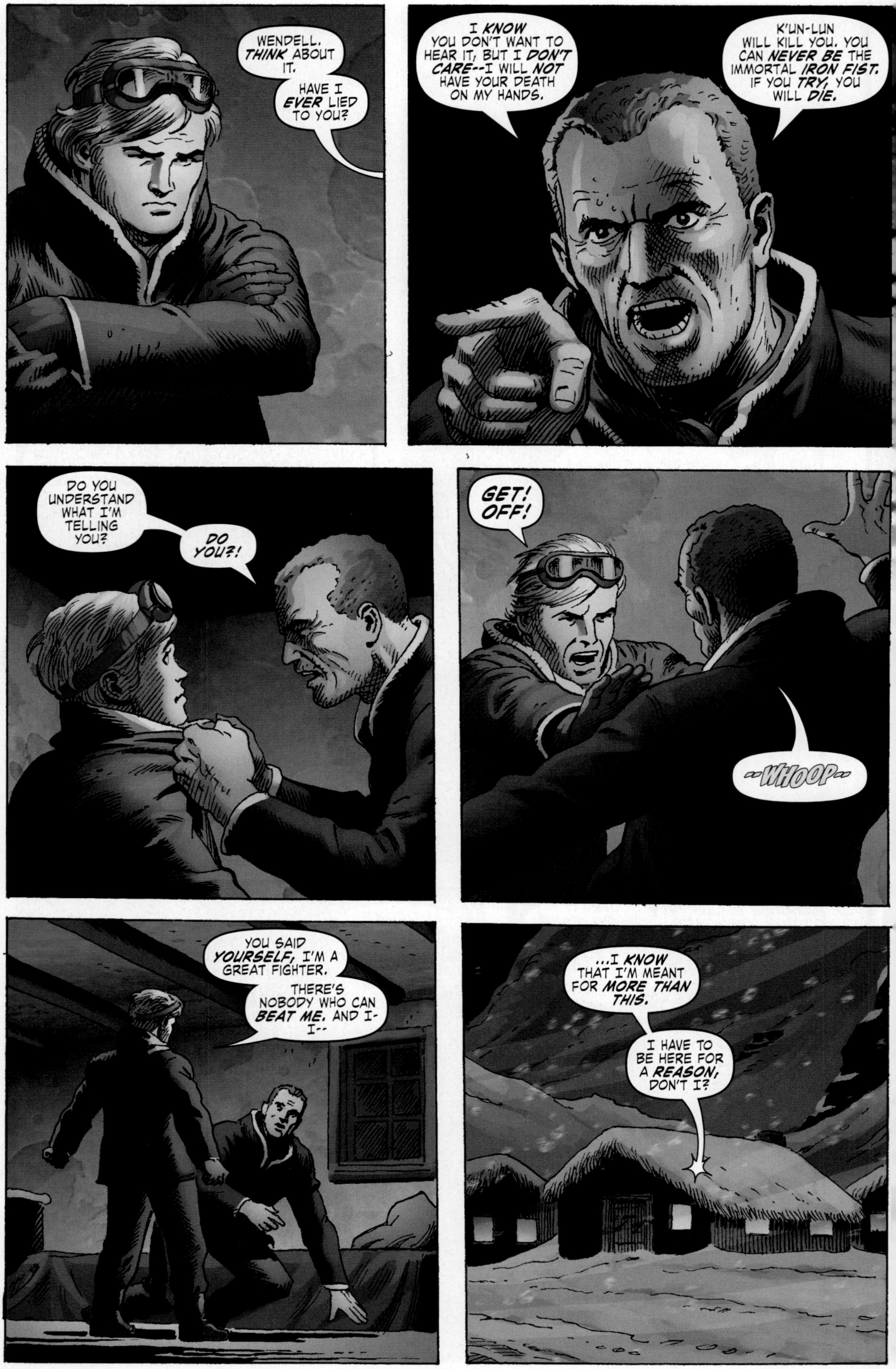
WENDELL. THINK ABOUT IT.
HAVE I EVER LIED TO YOU?
I KNOW YOU DON'T WANT TO HEAR IT, BUT I DON'T CARE--I WILL NOT HAVE YOUR DEATH ON MY HANDS.
K'UN-LUN WILL KILL YOU. YOU CAN NEVER BE THE IMMORTAL IRON FIST. IF YOU TRY, YOU WILL DIE.
DO YOU UNDERSTAND WHAT I'M TELLING YOU?
DO YOU?!
GET! OFF!
--WHOOP--
YOU SAID YOURSELF, I'M A GREAT FIGHTER.
THERE'S NOBODY WHO CAN BEAT ME. AND I- I--
...I KNOW THAT I'M MEANT FOR MORE THAN THIS.
I HAVE TO BE HERE FOR A REASON, DON'T I?

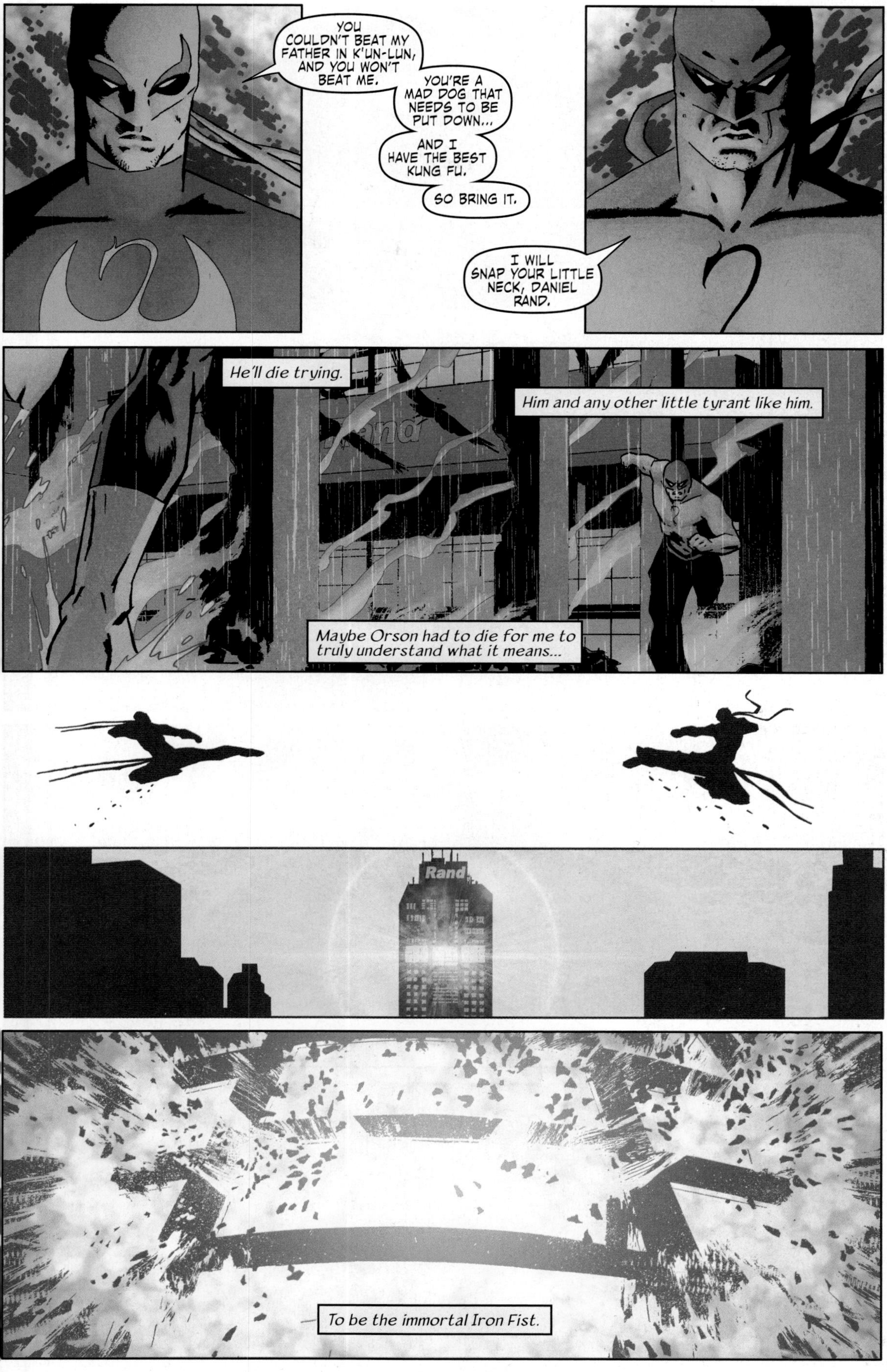
YOU COULDN'T BEAT MY FATHER IN K'UN-LUN, AND YOU WON'T BEAT ME.
YOU'RE A MAD DOG THAT NEEDS TO BE PUT DOWN...
AND I HAVE THE BEST KUNG FU.
SO BRING IT.
I WILL SNAP YOUR LITTLE NECK, DANIEL RAND.
He'll die trying.
Him and any other little tyrant like him.
Maybe Orson had to die for me to truly understand what it means...
Rand
To be the immortal Iron Fist.

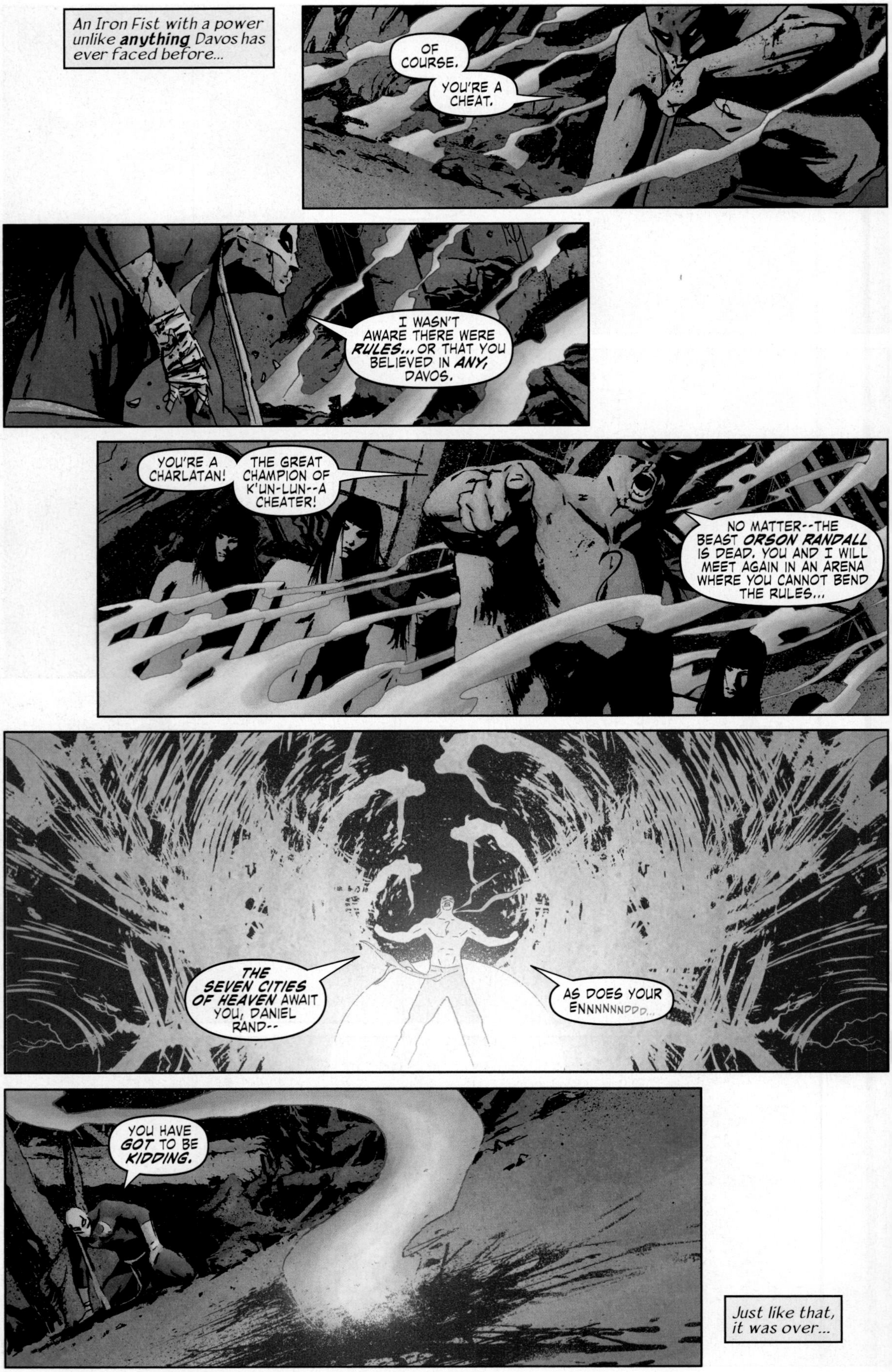

An Iron Fist with a power unlike **anything** Davos has ever faced before...
OF COURSE.
YOU'RE A CHEAT.
I WASN'T AWARE THERE WERE ***RULES...*** OR THAT YOU BELIEVED IN ***ANY,*** DAVOS.
YOU'RE A CHARLATAN!
THE GREAT CHAMPION OF K'UN-LUN--A CHEATER!
NO MATTER--THE BEAST ***ORSON RANDALL*** IS DEAD. YOU AND I WILL MEET AGAIN IN AN ARENA WHERE YOU CANNOT BEND THE RULES...
THE SEVEN CITIES OF HEAVEN AWAIT YOU, DANIEL RAND--
AS DOES YOUR ENNNNNNDDD...
YOU HAVE ***GOT*** TO BE ***KIDDING.***
Just like that, it was over...

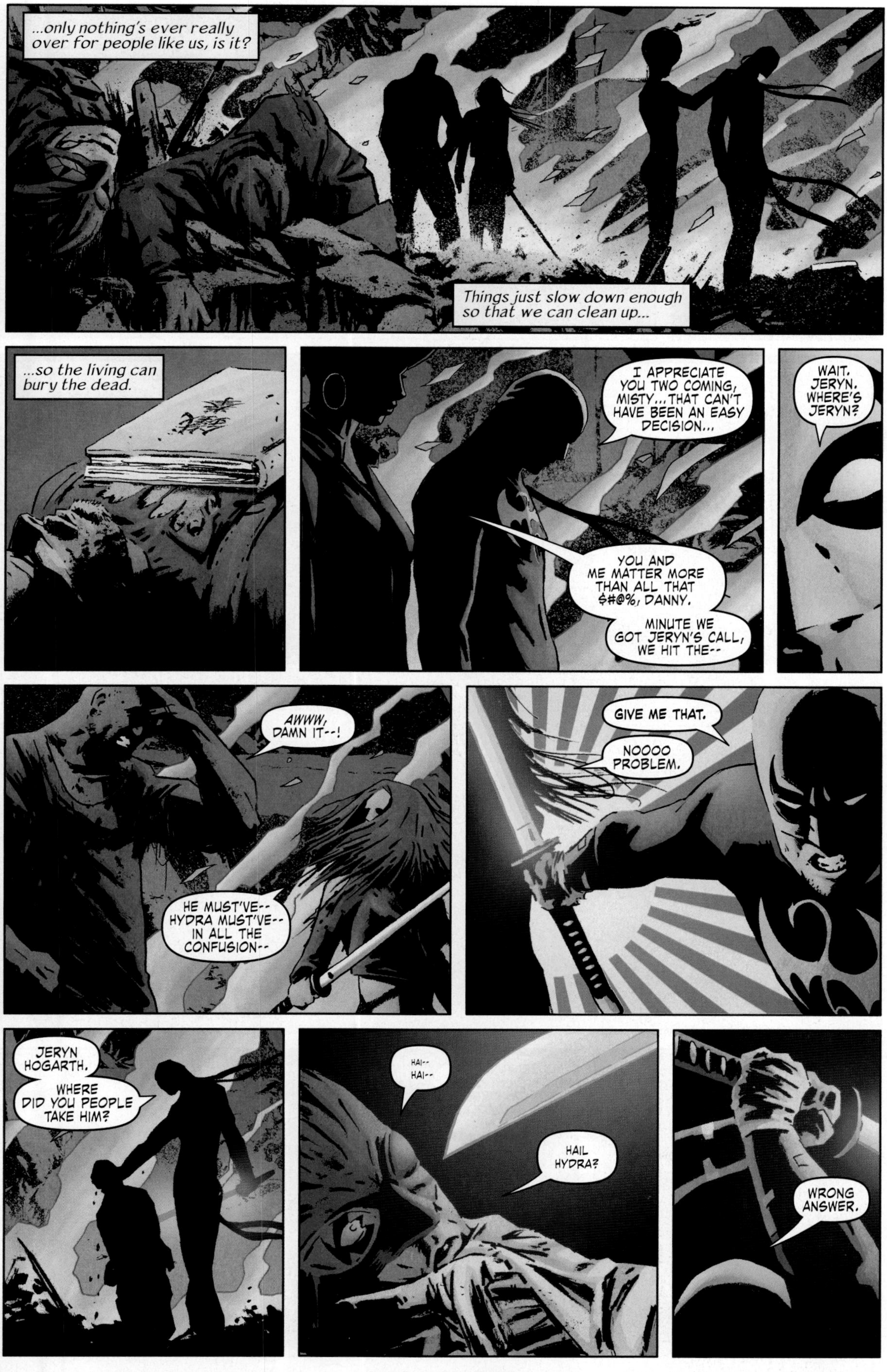

...only nothing's ever really over for people like us, is it?
Things just slow down enough so that we can clean up...
...so the living can bury the dead.
I APPRECIATE YOU TWO COMING, MISTY...THAT CAN'T HAVE BEEN AN EASY DECISION...
YOU AND ME MATTER MORE THAN ALL THAT $#@%, DANNY.
MINUTE WE GOT JERYN'S CALL, WE HIT THE--
WAIT. JERYN. WHERE'S JERYN?
AWWW, DAMN IT--!
HE MUST'VE-- HYDRA MUST'VE-- IN ALL THE CONFUSION--
GIVE ME THAT.
NOOOO PROBLEM.
JERYN HOGARTH.
WHERE DID YOU PEOPLE TAKE HIM?
HAI-- HAI--
HAIL HYDRA?
WRONG ANSWER.

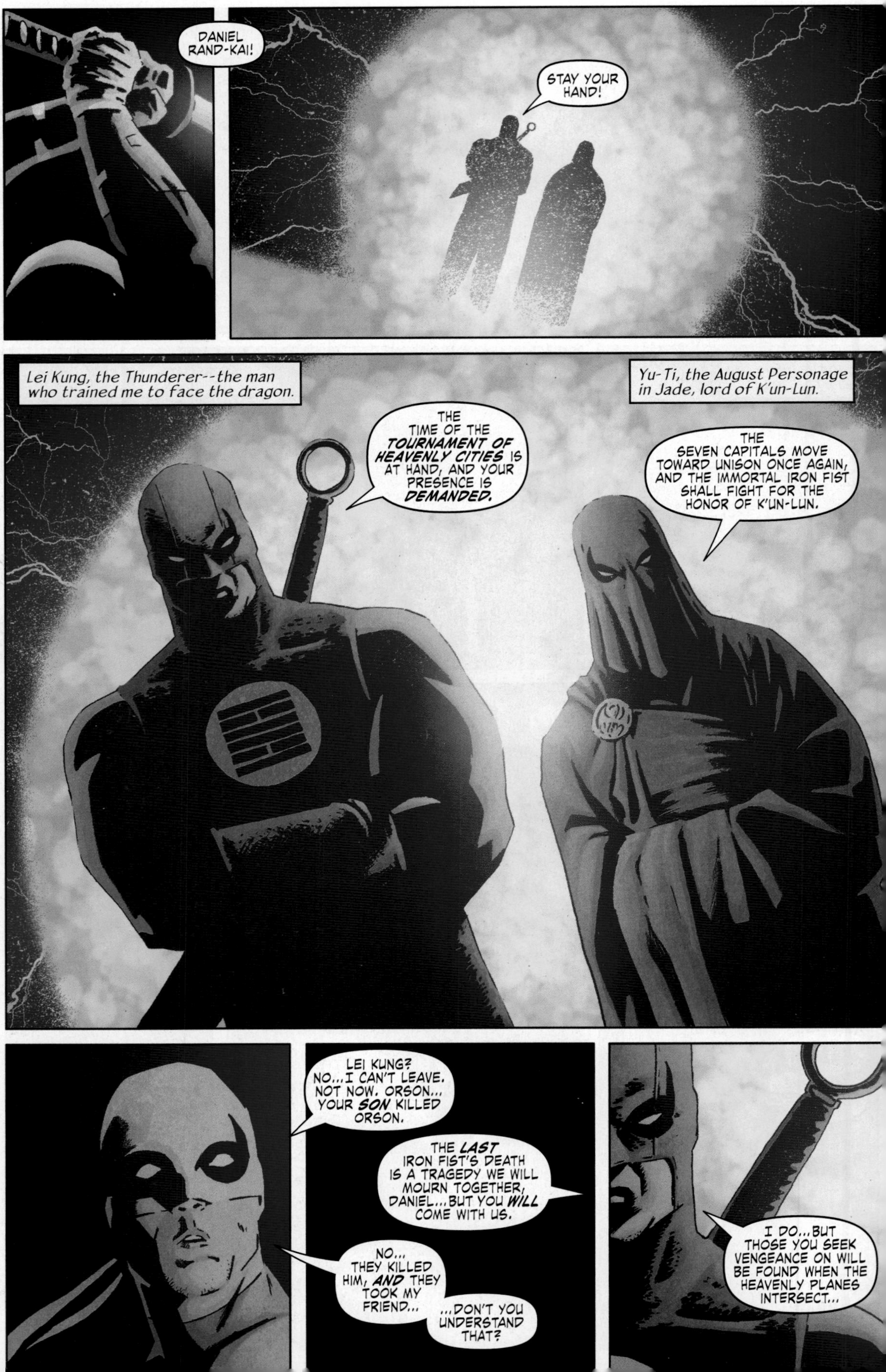

DANIEL RAND-KAI!
STAY YOUR HAND!
Lei Kung, the Thunderer--the man who trained me to face the dragon.
Yu-Ti, the August Personage in Jade, lord of K'un-Lun.
THE TIME OF THE **TOURNAMENT OF HEAVENLY CITIES** IS AT HAND, AND YOUR PRESENCE IS **DEMANDED.**
THE SEVEN CAPITALS MOVE TOWARD UNISON ONCE AGAIN, AND THE IMMORTAL IRON FIST SHALL FIGHT FOR THE HONOR OF K'UN-LUN.
LEI KUNG? NO...I CAN'T LEAVE. NOT NOW. ORSON... YOUR **SON** KILLED ORSON.
NO... THEY KILLED HIM, **AND** THEY TOOK MY FRIEND...
...DON'T YOU UNDERSTAND THAT?
THE **LAST** IRON FIST'S DEATH IS A TRAGEDY WE WILL MOURN TOGETHER, DANIEL...BUT YOU **WILL** COME WITH US.
I DO...BUT THOSE YOU SEEK VENGEANCE ON WILL BE FOUND WHEN THE HEAVENLY PLANES INTERSECT...

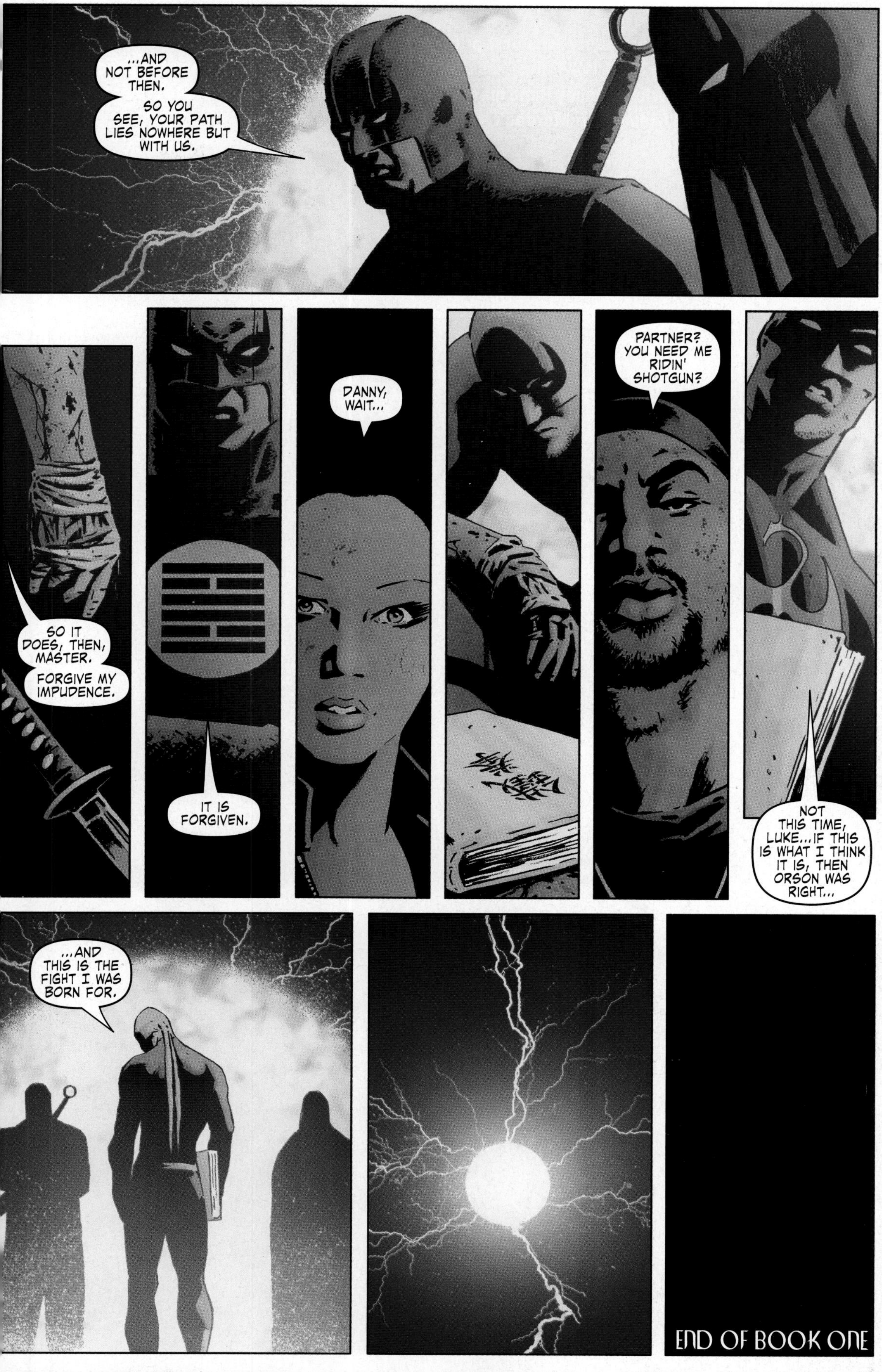
...AND NOT BEFORE THEN.
SO YOU SEE, YOUR PATH LIES NOWHERE BUT WITH US.
SO IT DOES, THEN, MASTER.
FORGIVE MY IMPUDENCE.
IT IS FORGIVEN.
DANNY, WAIT...
PARTNER? YOU NEED ME RIDIN' SHOTGUN?
NOT THIS TIME, LUKE...IF THIS IS WHAT I THINK IT IS, THEN ORSON WAS RIGHT...
...AND THIS IS THE FIGHT I WAS BORN FOR.
END OF BOOK ONE

The following 8-page story was first printed in the one-shot *CIVIL WAR: CHOOSING SIDES*. Tying into *CIVIL WAR,* this "issue #0" story bridges the gap between the pages of Daredevil — where Danny Rand masqueraded as the Man without Fear to cover for his imprisoned friend Matt Murdock — and *IRON FIST #1.*

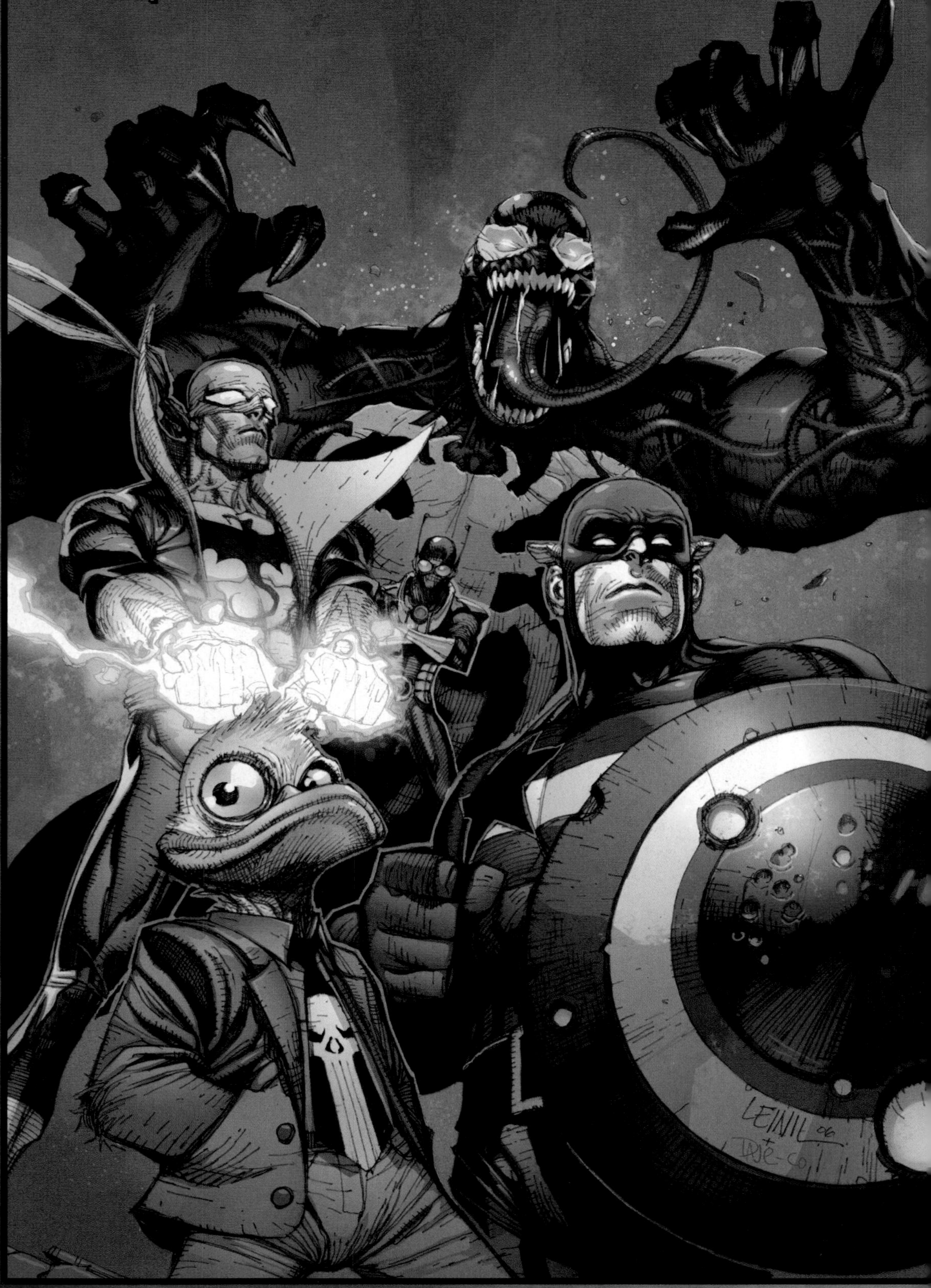

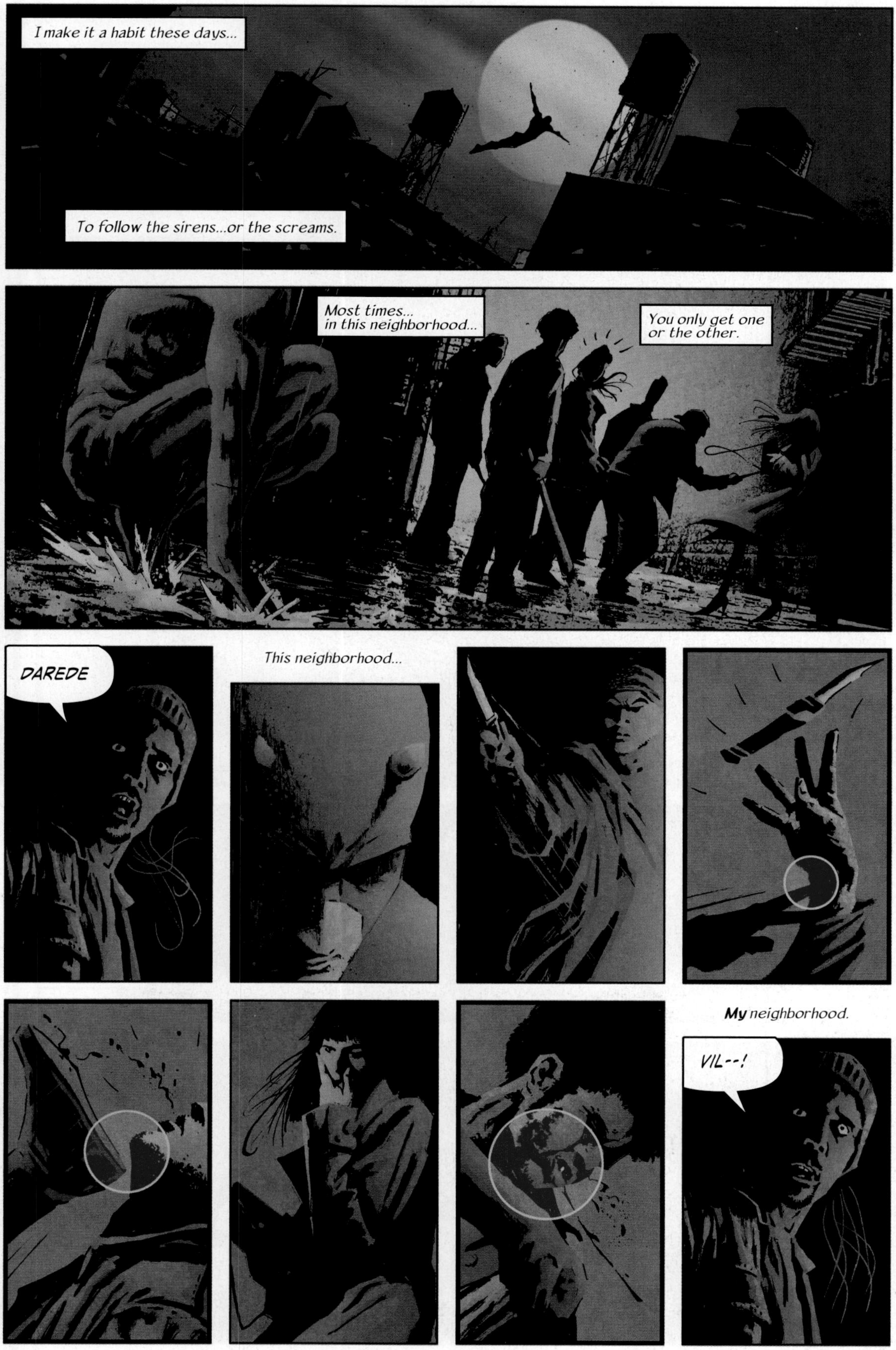
I make it a habit these days...
To follow the sirens...or the screams.
Most times... in this neighborhood...
You only get one or the other.
DAREDE
This neighborhood...
My neighborhood.
VIL--!

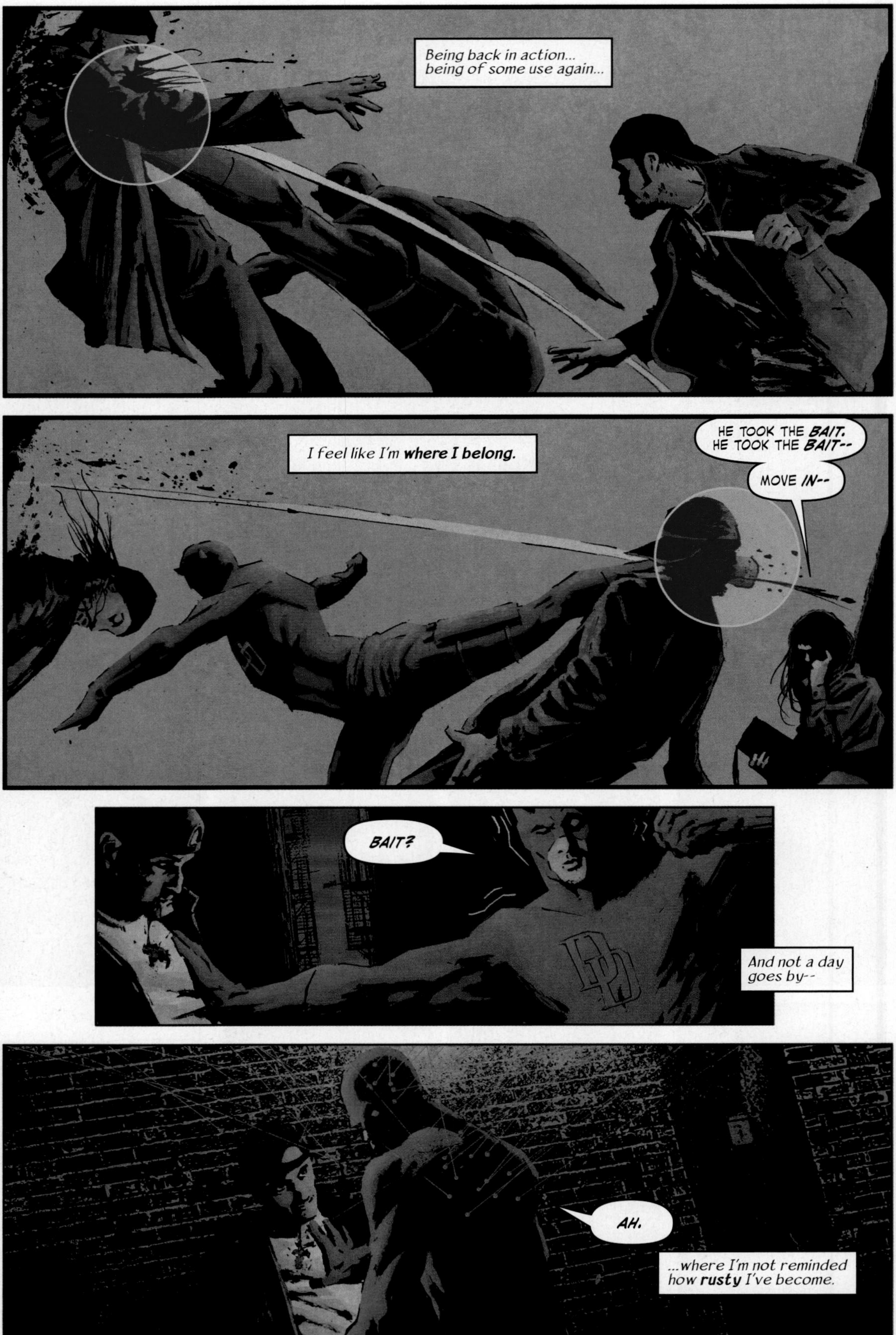
Being back in action... being of some use again...
I feel like I'm **where I belong.**
HE TOOK THE *BAIT.* HE TOOK THE *BAIT--*
MOVE *IN--*
BAIT?
And not a day goes by--
AH.
...where I'm not reminded how **rusty** I've become.

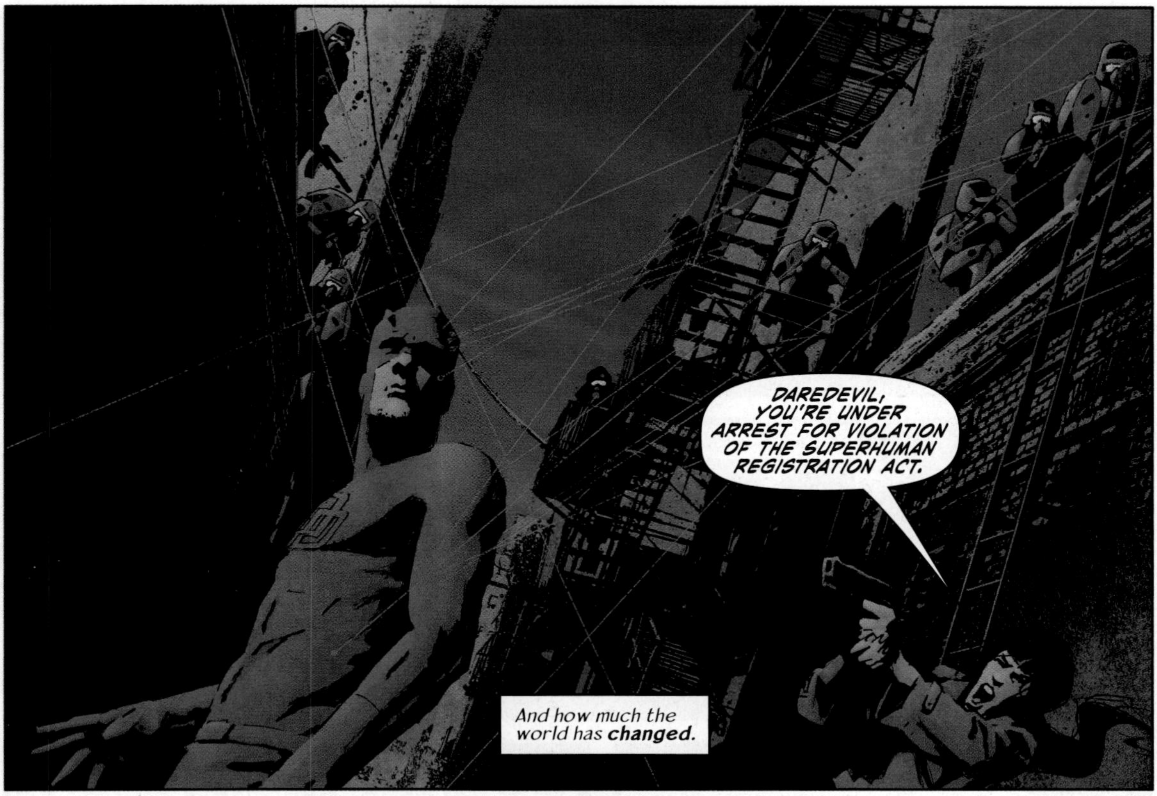

DAREDEVIL, YOU'RE UNDER ARREST FOR VIOLATION OF THE SUPERHUMAN REGISTRATION ACT.
And how much the world has **changed.**

THE IMMORTAL IRON FIST
"CHOOSING SIDES"

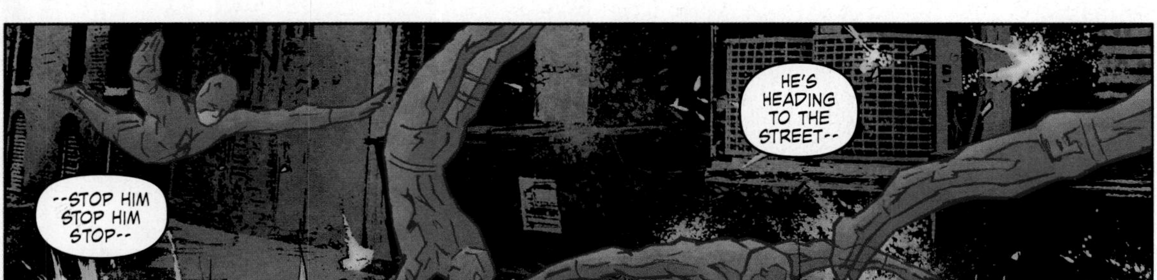

HE'S HEADING TO THE STREET--
--STOP HIM STOP HIM STOP--

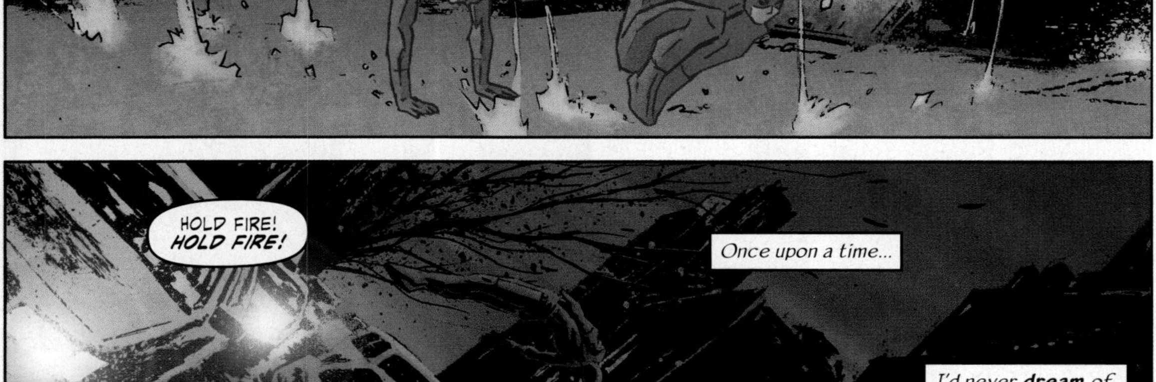

HOLD FIRE! ***HOLD FIRE!***
Once upon a time...
I'd never **dream** of using the civilian populace as **cover...**

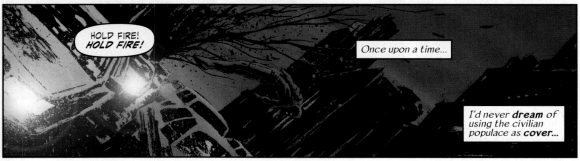

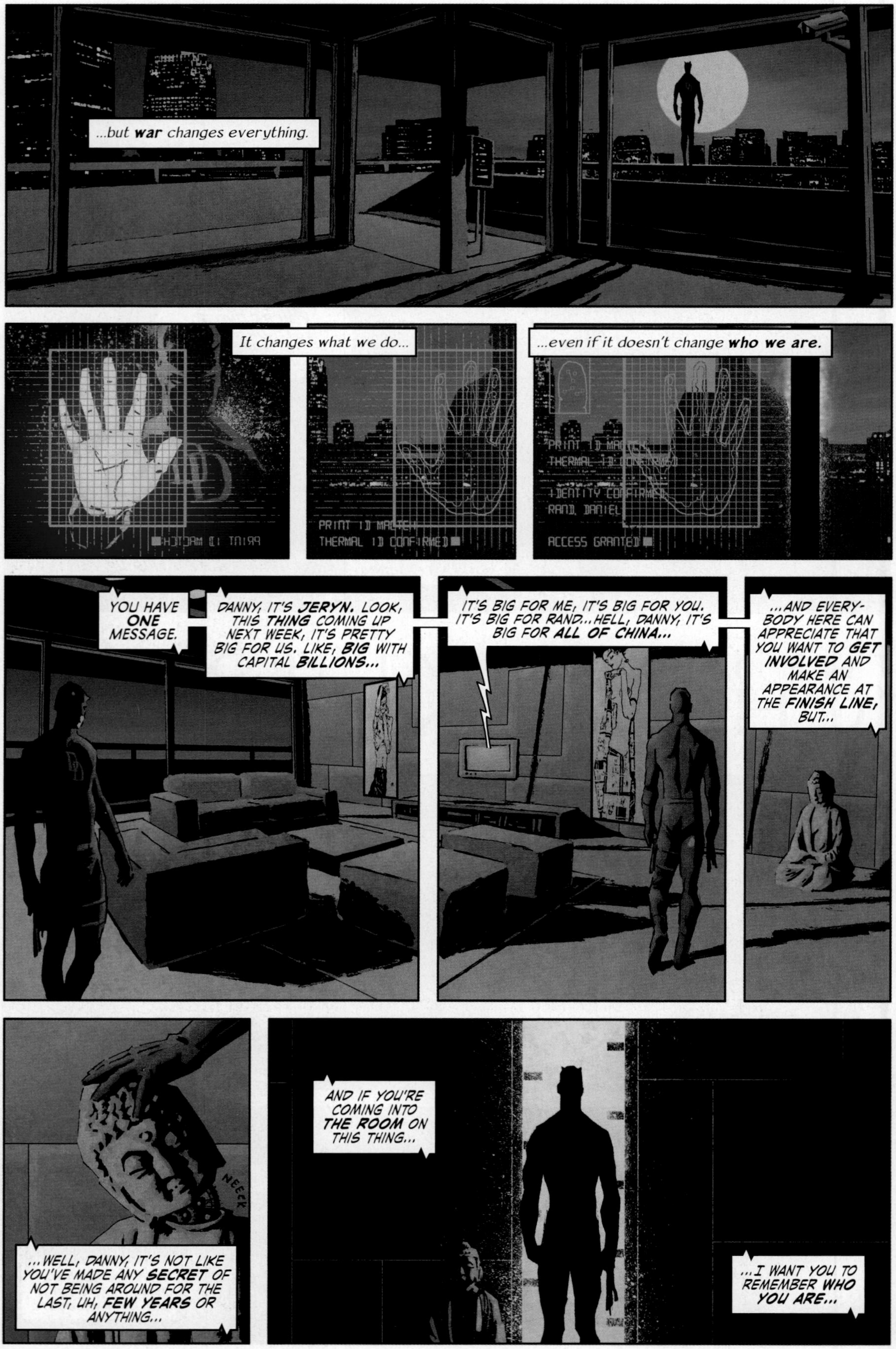
...but war changes everything.
It changes what we do...
PRINT ID MATCH
THERMAL ID CONFIRMED
...even if it doesn't change who we are.
PRINT ID MATCH
THERMAL ID CONFIRMED
IDENTITY CONFIRMED
RAND, DANIEL
ACCESS GRANTED
YOU HAVE ONE MESSAGE.
DANNY, IT'S JERYN. LOOK, THIS THING COMING UP NEXT WEEK, IT'S PRETTY BIG FOR US. LIKE, BIG WITH CAPITAL BILLIONS...
IT'S BIG FOR ME, IT'S BIG FOR YOU. IT'S BIG FOR RAND...HELL, DANNY, IT'S BIG FOR ALL OF CHINA...
...AND EVERYBODY HERE CAN APPRECIATE THAT YOU WANT TO GET INVOLVED AND MAKE AN APPEARANCE AT THE FINISH LINE, BUT...
NEECK
...WELL, DANNY, IT'S NOT LIKE YOU'VE MADE ANY SECRET OF NOT BEING AROUND FOR THE LAST, UH, FEW YEARS OR ANYTHING...
AND IF YOU'RE COMING INTO THE ROOM ON THIS THING...
...I WANT YOU TO REMEMBER WHO YOU ARE...

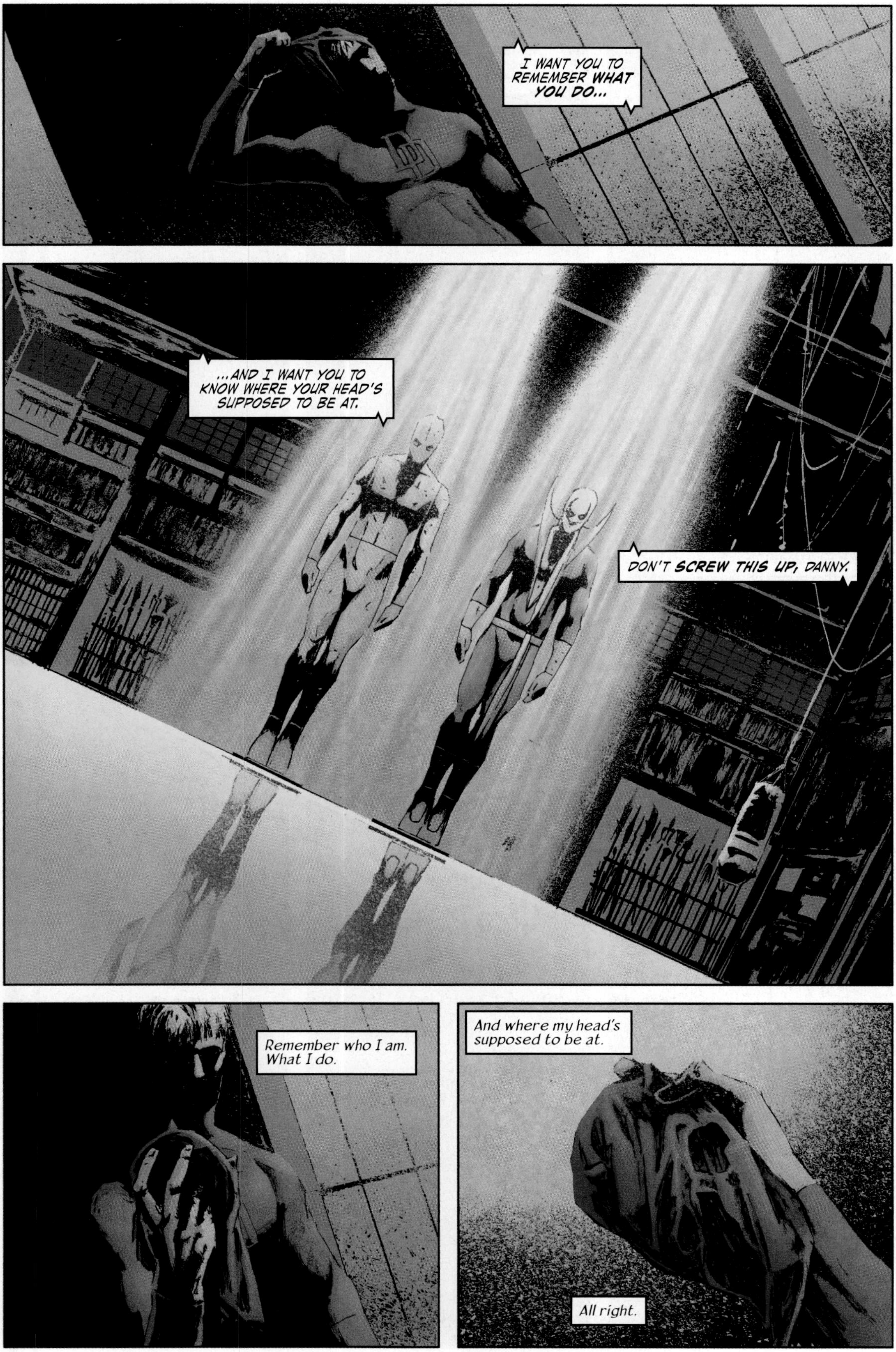
I WANT YOU TO REMEMBER WHAT YOU DO...
...AND I WANT YOU TO KNOW WHERE YOUR HEAD'S SUPPOSED TO BE AT.
DON'T SCREW THIS UP, DANNY.
Remember who I am. What I do.
And where my head's supposed to be at.
All right.

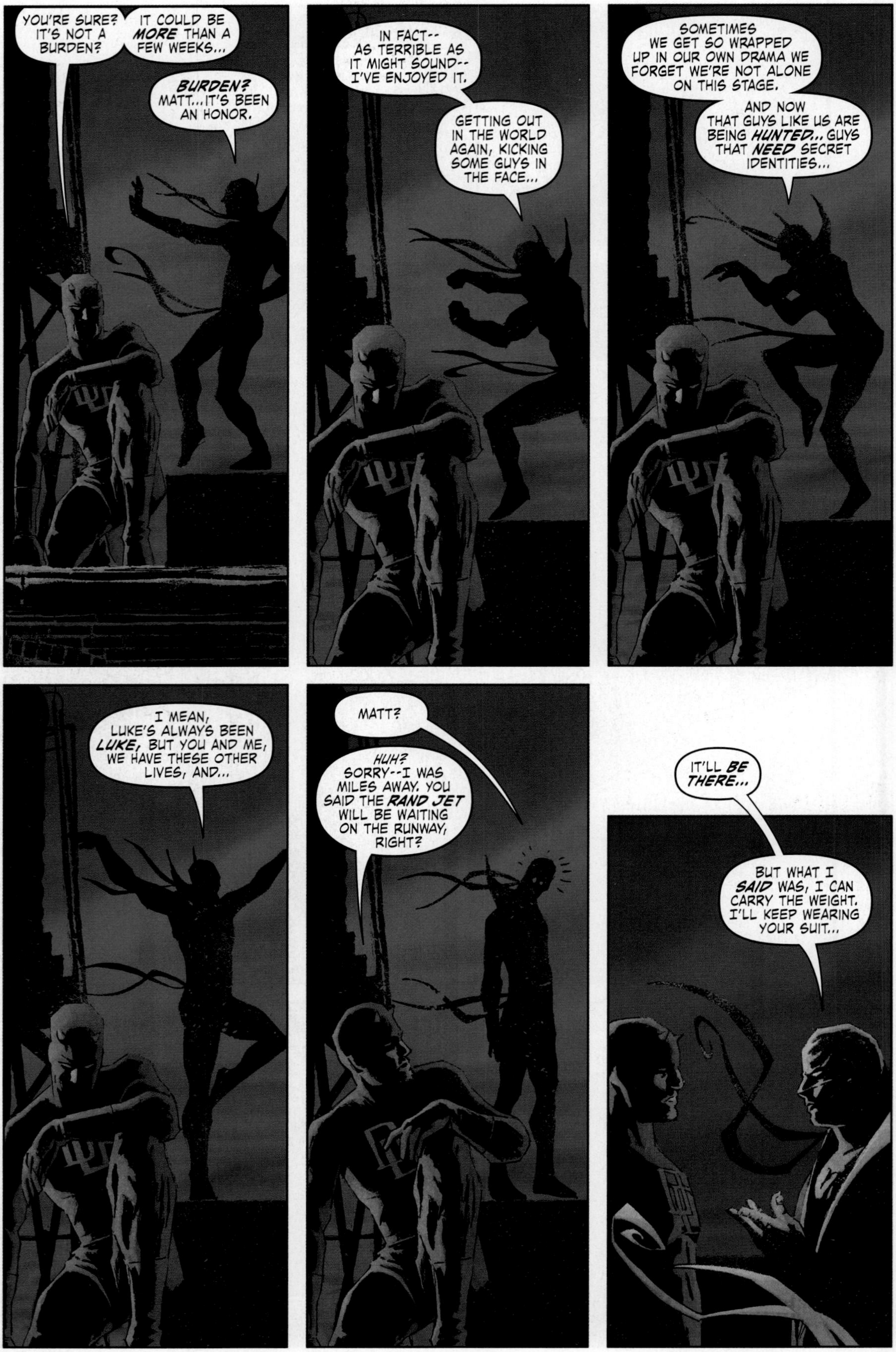
YOU'RE SURE? IT'S NOT A BURDEN?
IT COULD BE *MORE* THAN A FEW WEEKS...
BURDEN? MATT...IT'S BEEN AN HONOR.
IN FACT-- AS TERRIBLE AS IT MIGHT SOUND-- I'VE ENJOYED IT.
GETTING OUT IN THE WORLD AGAIN, KICKING SOME GUYS IN THE FACE...
SOMETIMES WE GET SO WRAPPED UP IN OUR OWN DRAMA WE FORGET WE'RE NOT ALONE ON THIS STAGE.
AND NOW THAT GUYS LIKE US ARE BEING *HUNTED...* GUYS THAT *NEED* SECRET IDENTITIES...
I MEAN, LUKE'S ALWAYS BEEN *LUKE,* BUT YOU AND ME, WE HAVE THESE OTHER LIVES, AND...
MATT?
HUH? SORRY--I WAS MILES AWAY. YOU SAID THE *RAND JET* WILL BE WAITING ON THE RUNWAY, RIGHT?
IT'LL *BE THERE...*
BUT WHAT I *SAID* WAS, I CAN CARRY THE WEIGHT. I'LL KEEP WEARING YOUR SUIT...

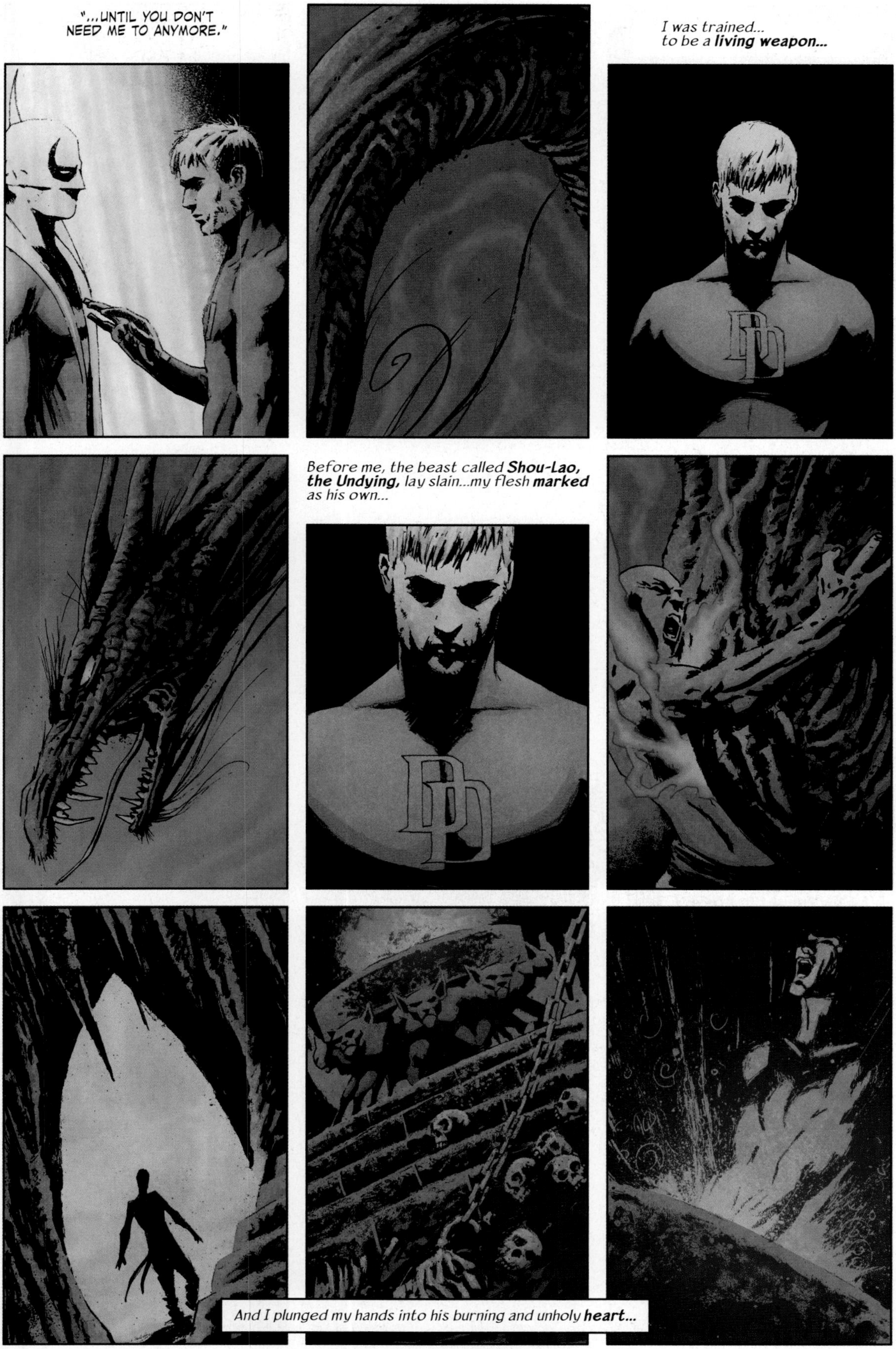
"...UNTIL YOU DON'T NEED ME TO ANYMORE."
I was trained... to be a **living weapon...**
Before me, the beast called **Shou-Lao, the Undying,** lay slain...my flesh **marked** as his own...
And I plunged my hands into his burning and unholy **heart...**

And my fist became like unto...

..a thing of **iron**.

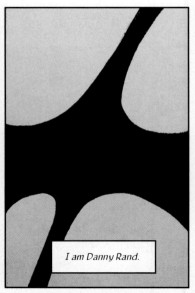

I am Danny Rand.

The Immortal Iron Fist.

I made a promise to Matt Murdock to wear his mask...I've fought this war in his place... And I'll continue to.

But I haven't **forgotten** who I am...

...and soon it will be time to carry my **own** burdens again.

END

CHARACTER DESIGNS
with commentary by artist David Aja

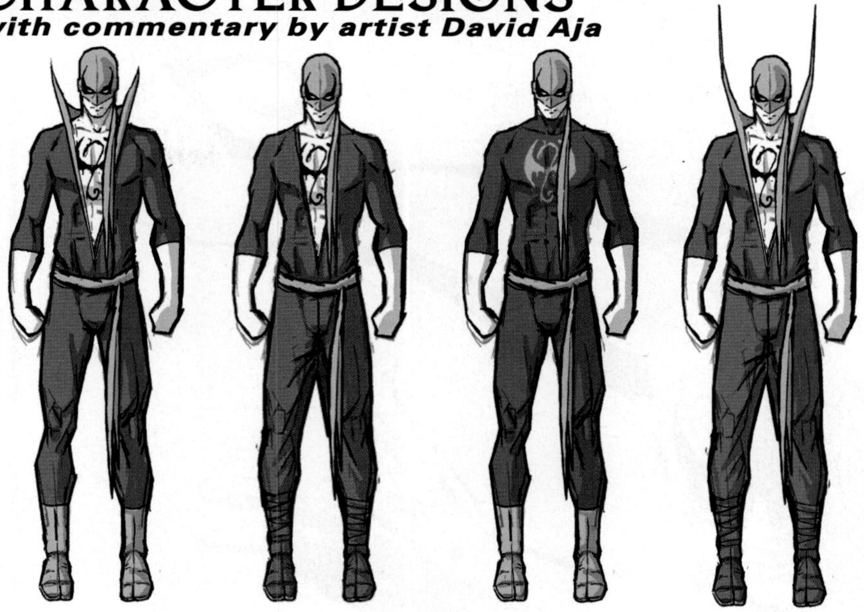

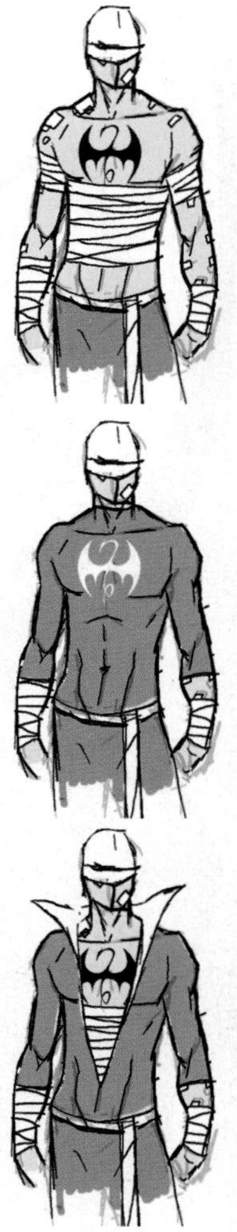

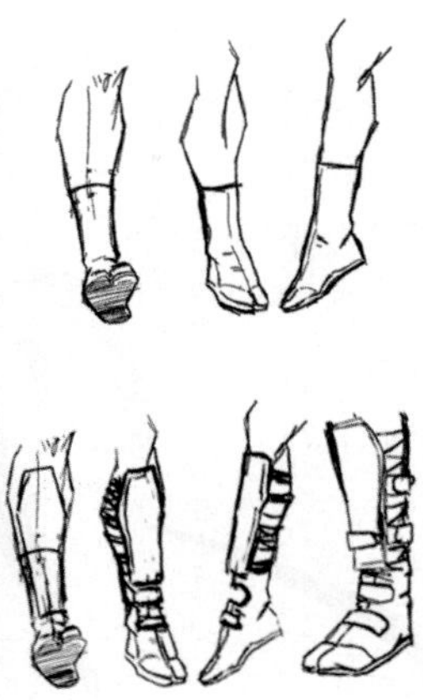

We all agreed the costume needed a minor update, and the first thing Ed suggested was changing his ankle slippers for 'ninja'-type boots. After that, we started working out the details: wide pants, cinched pants; collar, no collar; combinations of colors...but always keeping the spirit of the original costume.

Changing the suit was always part of my plan. I think the collar takes away some of the dynamic impact, and the open chest could work in the '70s...but today, not really. I intended to visualize the new costume design [at right] side by side with the current Luke Cage and still have them match. So when I saw that the Mechagorgon destroyed Danny's original costume, I thought, 'This is my chance!' It also looked better with Danny's bandages than the open chest would have.

Matt suggested we do a costume sort of like Bruce Lee's yellow track suit in 'Game of Death,' and I came up with these just to show him how crappy it would look. It's horrible.

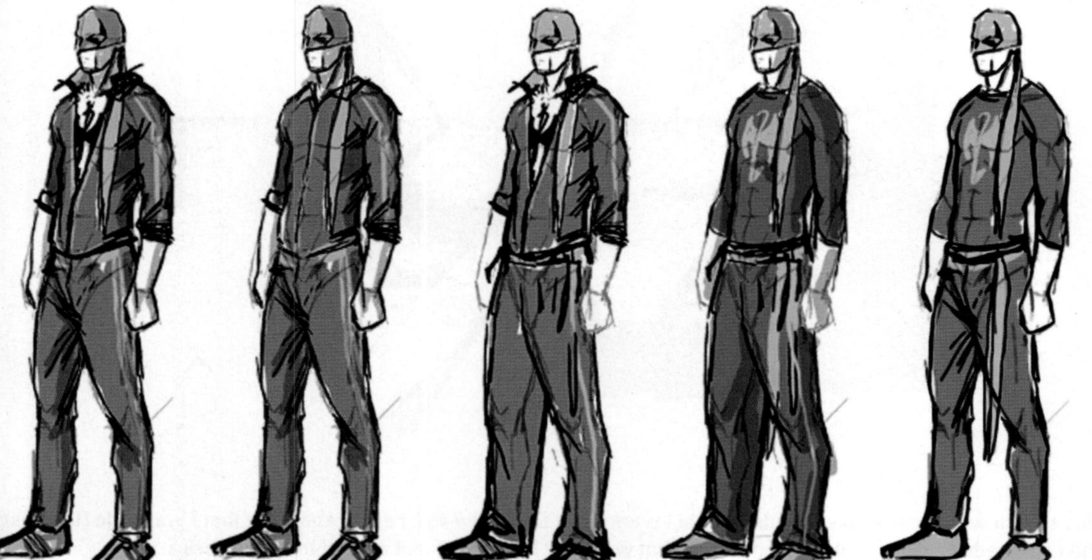

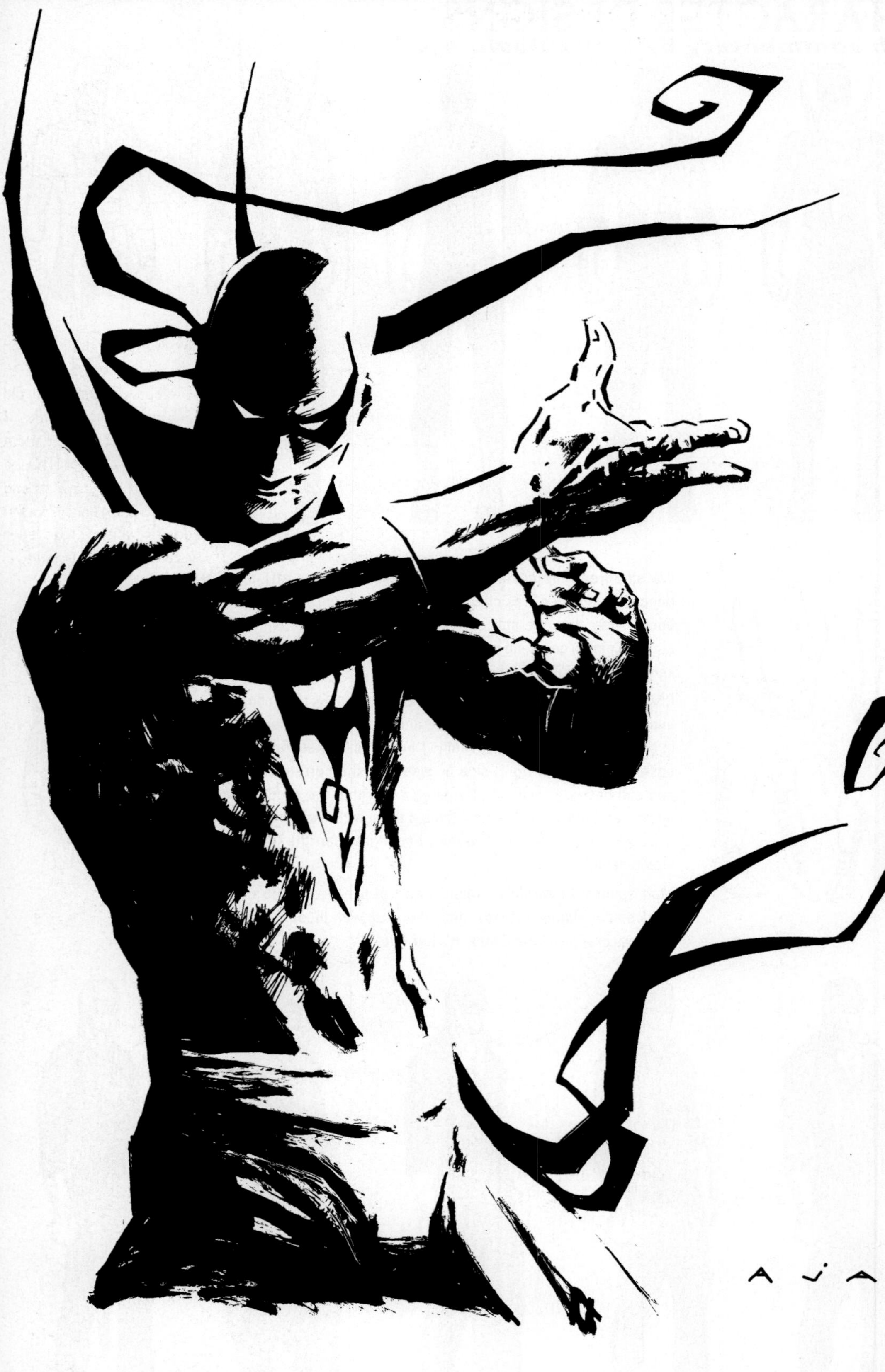
AJA

This sketch was created one morning while I worked on *Daredevil #88*. I didn't know yet that I would do [Iron Fist] and I still hadn't started to design anything. That was how I found out and agreed to do the series.

This was one of the many small ideas I had during the sketching process. In case Danny became a Hero for Hire again, this was for him to greet his clients in a more elegant costume.

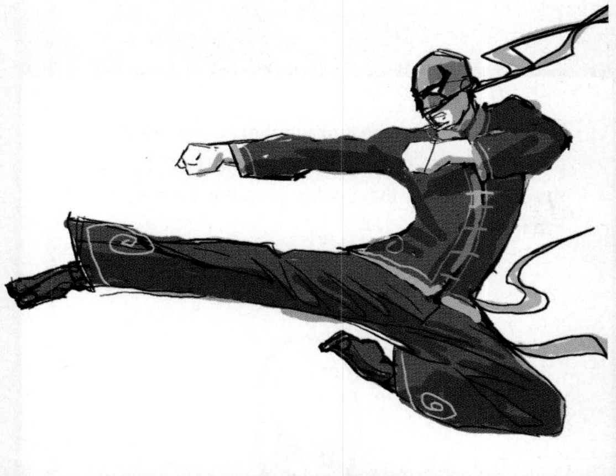

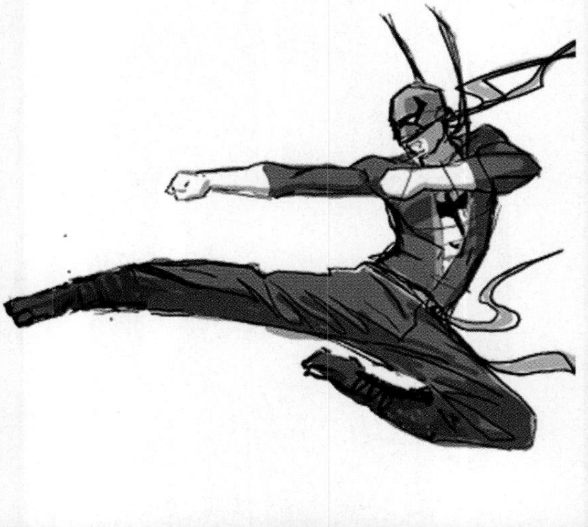

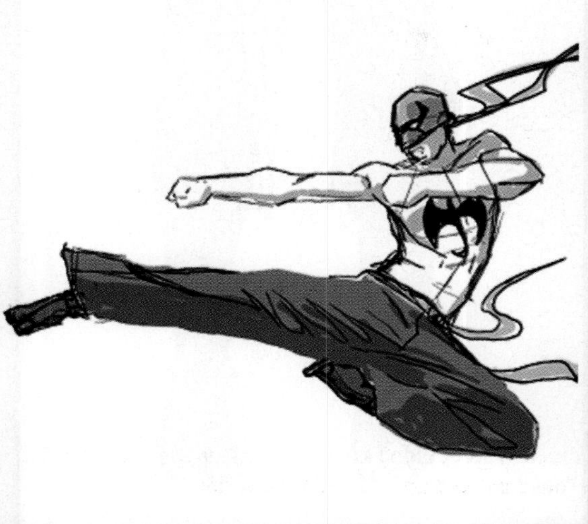

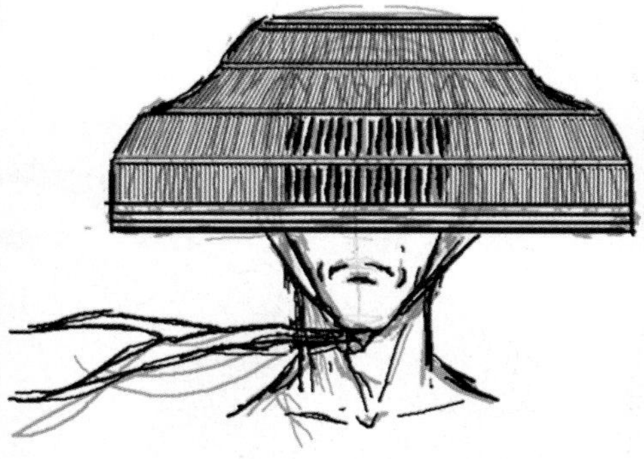

The first thing I was clear on [when designing the past Iron Fists] was that there couldn't be spandex before the 20th century, and from there on it was research, looking at old paintings and woodcuts, Hong Kong period movies, etc...I also wanted to evolve the characters' attire as a precedent to Danny's current costume. For Bei Ming-Tian, I based myself on the classic vestments of Shaolin monks. Matt and Ed wanted to add a 'ronin'-style hat, so, basing myself on the styles of Chinese straw hats, I added a mesh for his eyes more in the Japanese style. I also added a scar on his eye, possibly from his encounter with Shou-Lao.

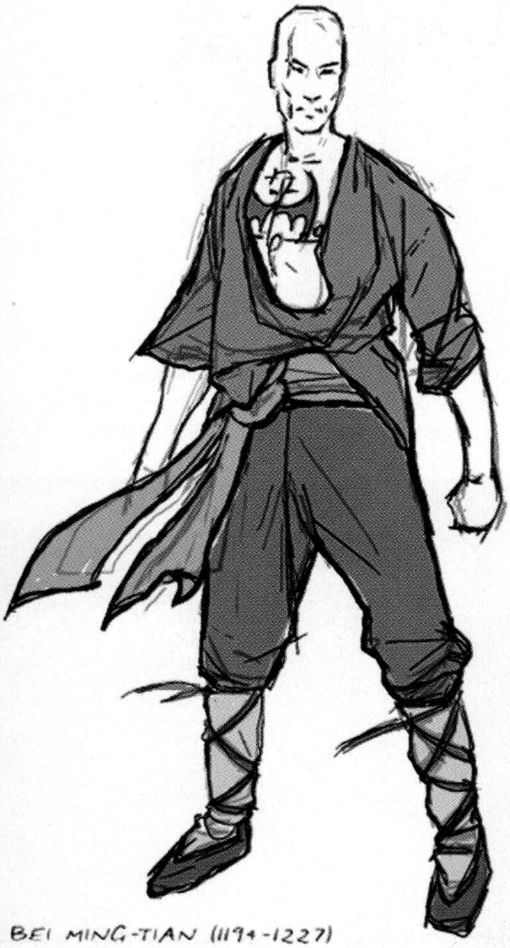

BEI MING-TIAN (1194-1227)

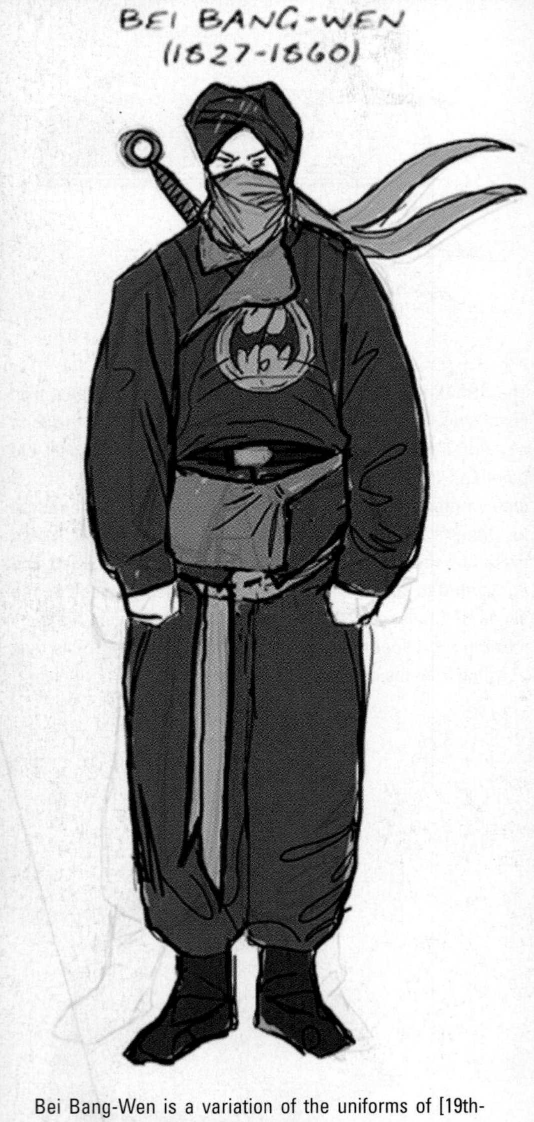
BEI BANG-WEN
(1827-1860)

Bei Bang-Wen is a variation of the uniforms of [19th-century Chinese revolutionaries] the Boxers. I wanted to create the feeling of a pretty "informal" costume.

For Orson Randall, the look was very clear: a little bit of [classic pulp heroes] the Phantom, Doc Savage, the Shadow and the Spider, plus the current Iron Fist mask.

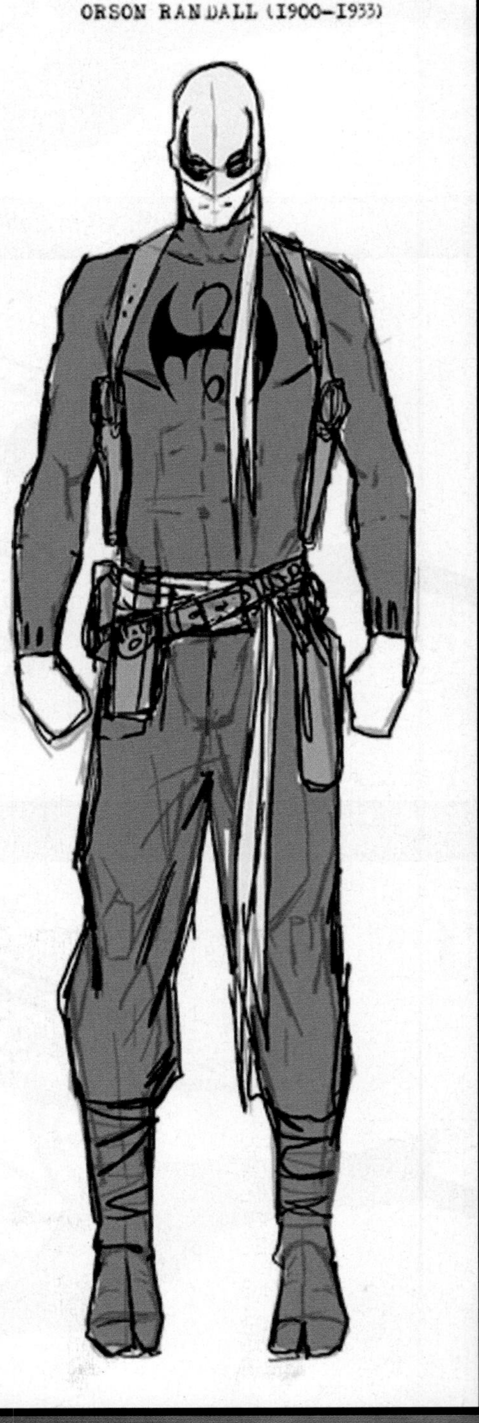
ORSON RANDALL (1900–1933)

Wu Ao-Shi would have her eyes painted in honor of Bei's scar, which would later become the typical feature of the eyes of the Iron Fist mask.

WU AO-SHI (1517-1550)

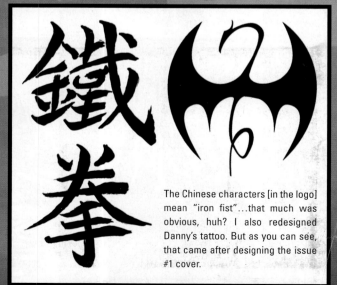

The Chinese characters [in the logo] mean "iron fist"...that much was obvious, huh? I also redesigned Danny's tattoo. But as you can see, that came after designing the issue #1 cover.

THE IMMORTAL IRON FIST #1

COVER PROCESS

The idea with the cover design was to create a unifying look for the entire mini-series, which later became just the first story arc. I also tried to make the title treatment and logo another essential part of the cover, to play an important part in the design. I veered off into big, white areas mainly because it's not something you tend to see on super hero books, and would call attention to the book on the stands. Also, anybody would be able to see from far away that a new issue had come out.

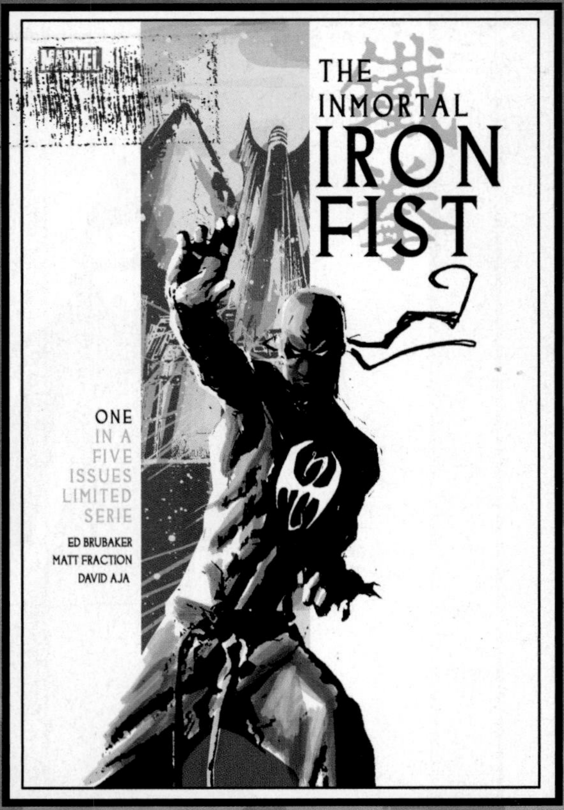
MARVEL
THE
INMORTAL
IRON
FIST
ONE
IN A
FIVE
ISSUES
LIMITED
SERIE
ED BRUBAKER
MATT FRACTION
DAVID AJA

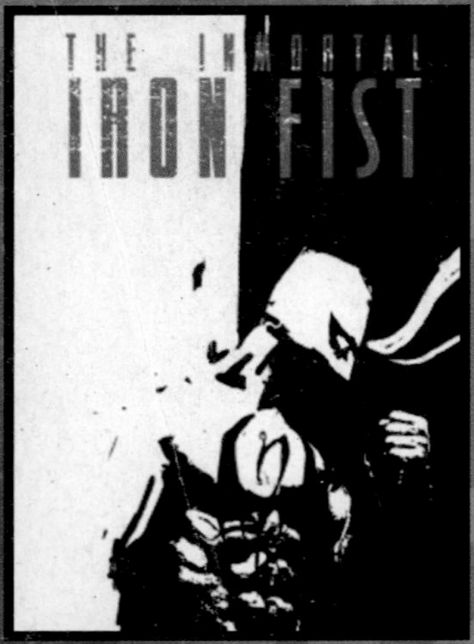
THE IMMORTAL
IRON FIST

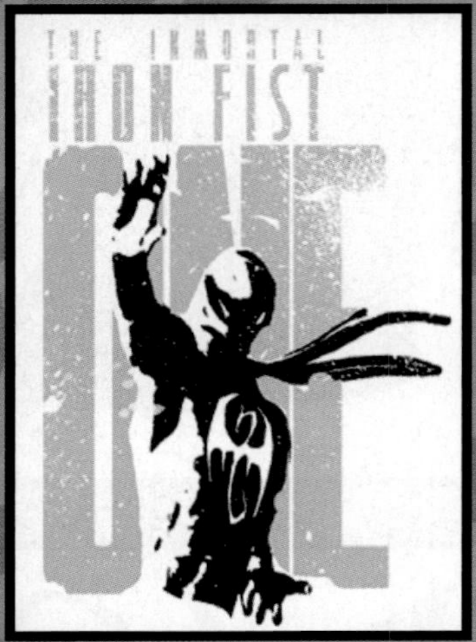
THE IMMORTAL
IRON FIST
ONE

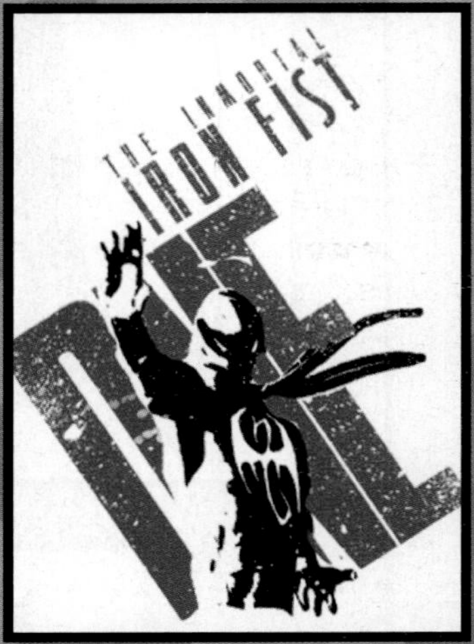
THE IMMORTAL
IRON FIST
ONE

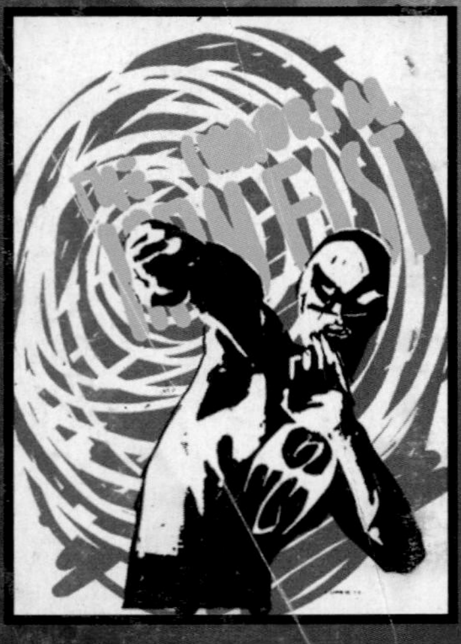

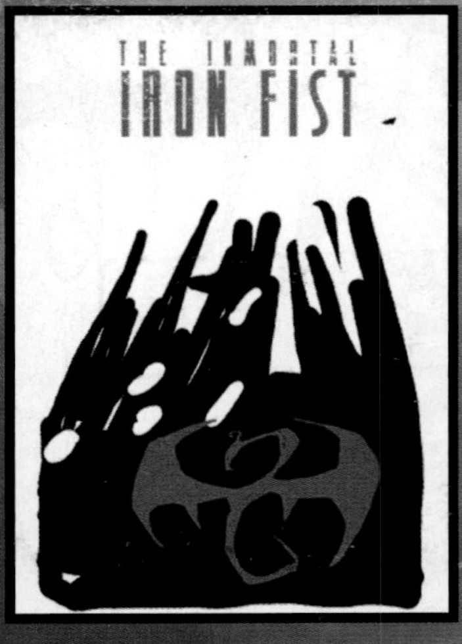
THE IMMORTAL
IRON FIST

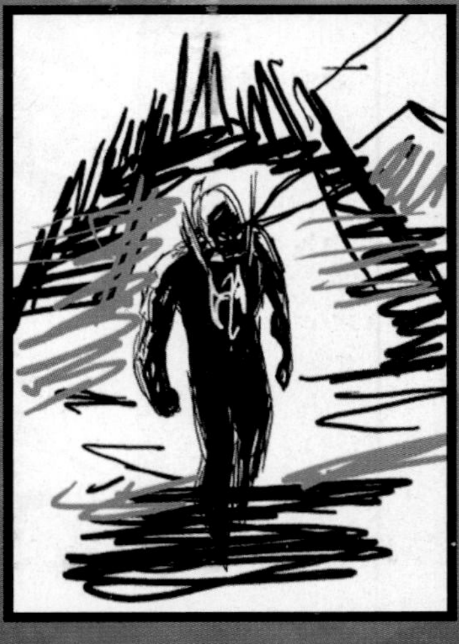